TRAVELER

barcelona

NATIONAL
GEOGRAPHIC

TRAVELER

barcelona

by Damien Simonis

National Geographic
Washington, D.C.

CONTENTS

914.672
NAT

TRAVELING WITH EYES OPEN 6

CHARTING YOUR TRIP 8

History & Culture 13
Barcelona Today 14   History of Barcelona 20   The Arts 36
Feature: Festes de la Mercè & Other Barcelona Festivals 42   Food & Wine 54

Barri Gòtic 57
Introduction & Map 58   Roman Barcelona Walk 66
Feature: Barcelona's Jewish Quarter 74   Feature: Towers of Strength 82

La Rambla & El Raval 85
Introduction & Map 86   Walk: Rambling Along La Rambla 88
Feature: From Xino to Boho 94

The Waterfront 99
Introduction & Map 100   Feature: When Columbus Sailed
the Ocean Blue 110   Feature: Life's a Beach 114

La Ribera 117
Introduction & Map 118   Feature: Young Picasso 122
Feature: To Market, to Market 136

Passeig de Gràcia 139
Introduction & Map 140   More Modernisme Walk 146

La Sagrada Família to Park Güell 155
Introduction & Map 156   Feature: Gaudí & Güell 164
Feature: Breaking New Ground 168

Northern Barcelona 171
Introduction & Map 172   Feature: F.C. Barça—More Than a Club 179

Montjuïc 183
Introduction & Map 184

Excursions 203
Introduction & Map 204   Wine & Monasteries Drive 210
Feature: Delirium Dalí 228   Drive Along the Costa Brava 234

TRAVELWISE 239
Hotels & Restaurants 247   Shopping 258
Entertainment & Activities 261

INDEX 265   CREDITS 270

Pages 2–3: Montjuïc's Magic Fountain offers a sociable spectacle and great nocturnal vistas.
Left: Joan Miró pavement mosaic, La Rambla

TRAVELING WITH EYES OPEN

Alert travelers go with a purpose and leave with a benefit. If you travel responsibly, you can help support wildlife conservation, historic preservation, and cultural enrichment in the places you visit. You can enrich your own travel experience as well.

To be a geo-savvy traveler:

- Recognize that your presence has an impact on the places you visit.

- Spend your time and money in ways that sustain local character. (Besides, it's more interesting that way.)

- Value the destination's natural and cultural heritage.

- Respect the local customs and traditions.

- Express appreciation to local people about things you find interesting and unique to the place: its nature and scenery, music and food, historic villages and buildings.

- Vote with your wallet: Support the people who support the place, patronizing businesses that make an effort to celebrate and protect what's special there. Seek out local shops, restaurants, and inns. Use tour operators who love their home—who love taking care of it and showing it off. Avoid businesses that detract from the character of the place.

- Enrich yourself, taking home memories and stories to tell, knowing that you have contributed to the preservation and enhancement of the destination.

That is the type of travel now called geotourism, defined as "tourism that sustains or enhances the geographical character of a place—its environment, culture, aesthetics, heritage, and the well-being of its residents." To learn more, visit National Geographic's Center for Sustainable Destinations at *nationalgeographic.com/travel/sustainable*.

TRAVELER

barcelona

ABOUT THE AUTHOR

Damien Simonis, born and raised in Sydney, Australia, has had a little trouble settling down since he took a one-way flight to Cairo in 1989. In his baggage was a B.A. in modern languages from Melbourne University (itchy feet had led him away from Sydney years earlier) and seven years' experience as a reporter and copy editor on some of Australia's leading dailies, including the *Australian,* the *Age,* and the *West Australian.*

Since landing in the Egyptian capital, Simonis has lived, studied, and worked all over Europe and the Middle East. In 1992 he started writing guidebooks and travel articles for publications in Australia, the U.K., and North America. He hasn't stopped since. His wanderings have taken him from Ukraine to Sudan, from Syria to Morocco, from the Alps to the Strait of Gibraltar. On his two greatest passions, Spain and Italy, he has written extensively. A fluent speaker of Spanish, Italian, French, Catalan, and German (and a stutterer of Arabic), Simonis divides his time between London, Barcelona, and the road. The feet remain as itchy as ever, and Simonis continues to write and shoot photographs wherever the assignment (or whim) takes him.

Charting Your Trip

With over 2,000 years of history and a glittering present, Barcelona is an intense urban ride that has long appealed to travelers. At the heart of this compact, maritime city is Ciutat Vella, the Old Town; its narrow lanes and squares are peppered with fine monuments and grand houses, many dating from the Middle Ages yet built on Roman remains.

Expansion of the city beyond its medieval walls in the 19th century led to a building boom at a time of great industrial and creative activity giving rise to the Eixample district, virtually an open-air museum of modernista (the Catalan art nouveau architecture led by the genius Gaudí and his contemporaries). This *eixample* (extension) linked the Old Town to outlying villages, such as Gràcia and Sarrià, pleasant enclaves well worth exploring today.

How to Visit: If You Have One Week

Most visitors arrive with a mission to see two of the city's most famous landmarks, Gaudí's unfinished La Sagrada Família church and the world-famous boulevard La Rambla. The latter is a good starting point for **Day 1.** Head to Plaça de Catalunya, and, after a coffee in Café Zurich, go with the flow down the three-quarter-mile (1.2 km) La Rambla, which ends by the port. Enjoy distractions like La Boqueria market, flower stalls, and the opera house. Drop into handsome Plaça Reial for a terrace lunch, or Palau Güell, an early but extraordinary Gaudí town house. When you reach the port, take the elevator to the top of the Columbus statue for a panoramic view of the city or sit back in a Golondrina pleasure boat to take in the skyline from the sea.

On **Day 2** immerse yourself in history in the Barri Gòtic, off La Rambla, exploring its labyrinth of medieval streets and peaceful squares like Plaça del Pi, popping into the cathedral and its geese-filled cloisters. Trace the remains of the walls of the Roman city and get a slice of Roman life from the ruins within the Museu d'Història (MUHBA) in timeless Plaça del Rei.

The statue of Ramon Berenguer III, Count of Barcelona, in the Old Town

Visitor Information

The main office of the tourist board, **Turisme de Barcelona,** *(tel 93 285 3834, barcelonaturisme.com)* is located in the central square, Plaça de Catalunya, close to the airport bus terminal. It is packed with information and offers services such as last-minute hotel reservations, walking tours, travel cards and mobile apps for do-it-yourself tours on specific themes. It also has an excellent website, via which you can plan your trip and book visits or tours before arriving. The Turisme de Barcelona also has branches in the airport, main railway stations, and Plaça Sant Jaume, as well as booths in key points of the city (La Sagrada Família, La Rambla,

etc.). The city website *(bcn.cat)* has a guide to the city plus news of fiestas and other activities, while **La Virreina** *(La Rambla 99)* is the place to go for cultural information, including a ticket service for events.

Monthly local English freebie **Metropolitan** *(barcelona-metropolitan.com)* brims with news of what's on and restaurant recommendations. It is available in central restaurants, bookshops, and pubs.

Pick up leaflets and maps on the rest of Catalonia, as well as details of festivals and day trips in the **Palau Robert** *(Passeig de Gràcia 107, catalunya.com)*. Watch, too, for interesting exhibitions frequently held in its charming, peaceful garden.

Use **Day 3** to complete the Old Town, starting with El Raval to the right of La Rambla as you come down from Plaça de Catalunya, with its dazzling new cultural centers, the MACBA and the CCCB. Contrast these wide-open spaces, part of the city's urban regeneration scheme, with the enclosed, peaceful complex of the medieval Antic Hospital de la Santa Creu, pausing for a drink in its garden café. Catch the multicultural buzz of Carrer Hospital, do some vintage shopping, and enjoy lunch in the brand new Rambla del Raval before making your way over to La Ribera and El Born. This medieval commercial area has star pieces like the Museu Picasso and the soaring Gothic church of Santa Maria del Mar. The cobbled streets off the Passeig del Born are crammed with stylish, indie boutiques, bars, and restaurants. New jewel in the crown of Catalonia is the Born CC, a former market building where one of Europe's largest archaeological

NOT TO BE MISSED:

A wander down La Rambla **88–91**

L'Aquàrium, home to a dozen circling sharks **106–109**

A day at the beach and cocktails at a *chiringuito* **114–115**

A concert in the Església de Santa Maria del Mar **131–132**

La Boqueria, one of Europe's great markets **136–137**

La Pedrera, an eccentric Gaudí apartment block **145, 149–151**

La Sagrada Família, Gaudí's unfinished church **158–162**

A soccer match at F.C. Barcelona's Camp Nou stadium **179**

Romanesque art in the Museu Nacional d'Art de Catalunya **186–190**

sites has been uncovered, highly symbolic in Catalonia's history. If you can, take in a concert at the wildly modernista Palau de la Música. By **Day 4** take time off from monuments to wander along the waterfront, starting with the Museu Marítim's historic nautical collection and the old quays of the Port Vell marina, keeping kids happy in L'Aquàrium, and ending with relaxation on the beaches that lead to Diagonal Mar. Seek out old bars for seafood tapas in the backstreets of Barceloneta.

Now you should be ready for *modernisme,* Catalonia's take on art nouveau and a prized feature of the city, so use **Day 5** to walk up Passeig de Gràcia and its side streets in the Eixample area, with eyes wide open for the riot of details of this extravagant decorative art. Peep into doorways, look up at balconies, check out the hexagonal paving (designed by Gaudí) and don't miss the streetlights, ceramic tiles, brass doorknobs, elevator doors, and stained glass windows. Amid the high-end shops and chic hotels of this elegant avenue stands the so-called Block of Discord, a showpiece of contrasting styles of the main architects of the time including Gaudí's Casa Batlló. Farther up is his astounding apartment block La Pedrera. Round off the day going up to the charming former village of Gràcia, where you can eat alfresco.

Use **Day 6** to take all the time you need for La Sagrada Família, probably the world's most famous work in progress. Book ahead online to avoid lines. Afterward follow pedestrian Avinguda Gaudí to another magnificent UNESCO World Heritage site, the modernista Sant Pau complex, designed by Domènech i Montaner as a hospital and open to the public after major refurbishment. Complete the modernista experience in the Park Güell up the hill, a Gaudí gem with views.

Luckily, you have all of **Day 7** to explore Montjuïc, but be selective as it offers a huge range of entertainment, from the vast Museu Nacional d'Art de Catalunya to the minimalist Mies van der Rohe pavilion, the exciting CaixaForum to the fine Joan Miró museum and acres of gardens for walking.

Sights Open on Mondays

Monday is a rest day for many sights in Barcelona, but fear not! Plenty of places make an exception to this rule, so all that's needed is a little planning. Among the sights that do open on Mondays are: CaixaForum; Casa-Museu Gaudí (Park Güell); Gran Teatre del Liceu; Jardí Botànic; La Catedral; La Pedrera; La Sagrada Família; Monument a Colom; Museu de Cera; Museu d'Art Contemporani de Barcelona; Museu de la Xocolata; Museu del Futbol Club Barcelona; Museu Marítim; Museu Olímpic i de l'Esport; Palau de la Música Catalana; the Pavelló Mies van der Rohe; and Poble Espanyol.

If You Have More Time

You will still find plenty to do, firstly returning to Montjuïc to reach the Castell on its summit offering panoramic views. Or you may prefer to delve further into the hidden corners or museums of the endlessly fascinating Old Town.

For more panoramic views, another day could be spent on Tibidabo, the hill which forms a backdrop to the city but is an easy excursion from Plaça de Catalunya. On the way down drop into the brilliant CosmoCaixa, the interactive science museum; from here

Montjuïc Children's Dance Group at Poble Espanyol

you can walk through the lofty residential areas to get to Torre Bellesguard, a private family house designed by Gaudí that has recently opened to the public.

Soccer fans will want to take the full tour of Camp Nou, home to world-famous Barça (F.C. Barcelona) and with luck get to a match. While in upper Avinguda Diagonal take a stroll through the Jardins del Palau de Pedralbes and check out another Gaudí curio, the Pabellons of the Finca Güell. For an antidote to the urban din, seek out the eminently peaceful cloisters of the Monestir de Pedralbes, another easy FGC train ride from Plaça de Catalunya, with a detour to the quiet Sarrià neighborhood. ∎

Getting Around

The walkability of Barcelona, combined with its efficient public transportation system, means a lot can be achieved in a day (including a compulsory stop for lunch like the locals). The economical T10 travel cards can be used on bus, metro, FGC suburban trains, and RENFE regional trains just beyond the city limits (see Travelwise p. 242). Cycling is an increasingly good option with well-located rental companies and miles of bike lanes, though pay due caution to the crazy traffic. Plaça de Catalunya is a central square located where the Old Town meets the Eixample. Acting as a transportation hub to most parts of the city and beyond, the terminus of the airport bus and the official Bus Turístic is a strategic spot to start many excursions. If all else fails, you can hail a black and yellow taxi on any corner for a reasonable rate.

History & Culture

Barcelona Today   14–19

Experience: Watch Barcelona's Match of the Day   18

History of Barcelona   20–35

Experience: Take Shelter from an Air Raid!   34

The Arts   36–53

Feature: Festes de la Mercè & Other Barcelona Festivals   42–45

Experience: Rock in Barcelona   43

Experience: See Barcelona in the Movies   50

Food & Wine   54–56

Local Catalans support their soccer team—Fútbol Club Barcelona. Opposite: Huge pillars soar into the vaulted ceiling of the Catedral.

Barcelona Today

Sometimes there is something to the clichés. As the aircraft loses altitude for its final approach along the Barcelona waterfront toward the airport, the panorama is stunning. Even in winter, while other cities in less fortunate climes shiver under mantles of snow, Barcelona lies resplendent in precocious spring sunshine, its beaches lapped by the scintillating Mediterranean.

The mildness of the climate is just one of the arrows in this ancient but rapidly changing city's quiver. Modern art, manic architecture, fine food, seething nightlife, and a certain metropolitan dynamism are only some of Barcelona's trump cards.

One of the most densely populated (about 1.6 million inhabitants) and noisiest cities in Europe, it was long the undisputed economic powerhouse of Spain. Since the 1990s, as much local industry has crumbled in the face of global competition, the city has also ceded economic ground to archrival Madrid. The latter, as the country's national capital, attracts a growing number of multinationals and direct foreign investment.

Although traditionally given to a degree of self-indulgent complaining in the face of what many Catalans see as discrimination from Madrid, Barcelonans have not exactly sat around lamenting their destiny. Since the late 1980s, the city has been engaged in a profound remake of itself, inviting squadrons of local and international architects to participate in the process. It is determined to become a center of hi-tech excellence, setting aside a generous chunk of a former industrial zone to attract cutting-edge companies in computer science, multimedia, and related sectors. At the same time, it aims to become an international focal point of biomedical research. The MareNostrum supercomputer, in action in Barcelona since 2004, is one of the most powerful in the world.

....

French novelist Prosper Mérimée said: "If you're interested in talking to intelligent people, ask for Barcelona."

....

All this might pass unobserved by casual visitors—and there is no shortage of them! Since the 1992 Olympic Games, Barcelona has shot from relative unknown to one of Europe's top city break holiday destinations, with an estimated 7.5 million visitors in 2013.

As many businesspeople as tourists are attracted by the city's sunny disposition, but in spite of the benign weather, the "sunny Spain" image of sea, sangria, and siesta seems wholly inadequate for such a dynamic and complex place.

Northern Europeans traveling to Spain in the 19th century, imbibing the self-indulgent ideas of the Romantics, seemed determined to find in this long-neglected land a heady, exotic cocktail of dark flamenco sensuality and an almost Oriental mysteriousness. Much of this was little more than a product of a collective, fevered imagination.

In Barcelona, midway down the Catalan coast in northeastern Spain, it was harder still to confirm such fantasies. Comparing Barcelona with other parts of Spain, French novelist Prosper Mérimée said: "If you're interested in talking to intelligent people, ask for Barcelona." However, he also said: "The Catalans seem to me a poor version of the

Busy virtually around the clock, La Rambla de Canaletes is the first stage of Barcelona's best known boulevard.

Catching the rays on the serpentine public benches of Gaudí's Park Güell; the ceramic design is the work of Josep Maria Jujol.

French, a little coarse and with a great desire to make money." Not at all the hot-blooded gypsy atmosphere he had perhaps expected.

From such remarks other observers frequently go one further. That Barcelona is the "most European" of Spanish cities has become a household maxim. "European" means many things to many people. To some disapproving Madrileños, the term implies a workaday conformity with an increasingly homogeneous standard that the people of the capital profess to disdain heartily. For them, the "real Spain" is another beast altogether—nocturnal and wild at heart on the one hand, tough and weather-beaten on the other. For others, Barcelona is in the vanguard of the arts in Spain, closely linked with France and hence the rest of "cultured" Europe to the north. It signals efficiency and industriousness and frequently attracts comparisons with Milan or Brussels.

You might, however, be astonished to see how much serious partying this city does. From Thursday night onward in particular, the city's restaurants, bars, and discos are full to bursting. La Rambla seems as busy with traffic and pedestrians at 5 a.m. on a Saturday as at 5 p.m. on a Friday. The clubs thump on until 6 a.m. and a handful of places well beyond dawn. It may not be quite as frenetically hedonistic as Madrid but most other European cities look anemic beside the Catalan capital.

Always the Bridesmaid

For all its evident dynamism and strong identity, it is difficult to escape the impression that Barcelona has an inferiority complex. You may not feel it in the air but you certainly read it in the press. Like a jealous older sibling, Barcelona seems unable to avoid bickering with Madrid, trying to score points and feeling hurt at what it sees as haughty and discriminatory treatment from Spain's capital. There is a long history to this, and it is currently reaching fever pitch.

In Roman times, Barcelona was a self-contented but not terribly important provincial town that cowered in the shadow of Tarraco, today's Tarragona, the capital of a Roman province encompassing more than half of present-day Spain. In the Middle Ages it was, until the 12th century, at the head of a small principality that gradually carved out for itself a political and cultural reality—Catalonia. Yet Catalonia never became a nation.

Even after the Catalan counties were joined with Aragón to create the Crown of Aragón, the count-kings that ruled it were kings of Aragón but counts of Barcelona. The 13th and 14th centuries were the glory days of a city that headed up a considerable merchant empire.

The absorption of the Crown of Aragón into a united Spain under the Catholic Monarchs (Ferdinand and Isabella) in the 15th century tied the fate of Barcelona ineluctably to that of a central state that, in subsequent years, came to be regarded as an oppressor. Until the late 18th century, Madrid barred Barcelona from the lucrative transatlantic trade with the American colonies.

The presence of the fortress on Montjuïc and, until the mid-19th century, the enormous citadel, symbolized Barcelona's submission to an essentially foreign power. Most Barcelonans shrugged their shoulders and set about turning their city into the country's powerhouse. The political muscle might well reside in Madrid but, by the end of the 19th century, it was clear which of the two was in better economic shape.

As if profoundly depressed at having to drag along the dead weight of bureaucratic Madrid, Barcelona looked north to the rest of Europe for inspiration. The city's artists went to Paris, and the art nouveau style that would become *modernisme* in Barcelona filtered down across the Pyrenees. With its universal exhibitions of 1888 and 1929, Barcelona was bent on getting the rest of the world to sit up and take notice.

The chaos of the 1930s and the civil war of 1936–1939 were heady, if tragic, moments. For the first time in centuries, Catalonia gained real autonomy. The city, whose workers had, since the late 19th century, imparted a strong leftist tendency to its politics, was for a while converted into an anarchist "paradise." The end of the war and General Francisco Franco's (1892–1975) victory again brought repression.

What's in a Euro?

The currency of Spain and 17 other European Union member countries is the euro (€). Euros come in coins of 1, 2, 5, 10, 20, and 50 cents and 1 and 2 euros. Bills are 5, 10, 20, 50, 100, 200, and 500 euros. Since it went into circulation in 2002, the euro has established itself as one of the world's major currencies. The bills are the same all over the EU, but each country produces its own coins with national symbols. Spain has for years been awash in €500 bills, a sign that police claims of major money-laundering operations in the country probably have something to them! Barcelona is teeming with banks and ATMs *(caixer automàtic/cajero automático)* for cash withdrawals.

The return of democracy and the devolution of many powers to the regions in the late 1970s returned Barcelona to a position of control over its own destiny that it had not enjoyed since 1714. Since then, a duel with Madrid has continued unabated. For 23 years under the Catalan nationalist Jordi Pujol, his Catalan Socialist successors and currently a nationalist coalition led by Artur Mas, Barcelona has waged a steady campaign of attrition to win a greater share of political and fiscal power from the central state.

EXPERIENCE: Watch Barcelona's Match of the Day

Fútbol Club (F.C.) Barcelona (see p. 179) is one of the world's great *fútbol* (soccer) teams, and for many sports fans a pilgrimage to the Camp Nou stadium is near to a religious duty. Therefore, managing to be in town for a game borders on ecstasy for many soccer fans.

With 170,000 members, who are also shareholders, Barcelona is one of the biggest soccer clubs in Europe. Obtaining tickets for Spain's grudge game known as "El Clásico" against arch-rivals Real Madrid is virtually impossible, but getting a spot for other matches is usually not too hard (after all, the stadium holds 100,000 spectators). There are several ways of doing this. You can call *(tel 902 189900 from within Spain or tel 34 93 496 36 00 from overseas)*, purchase them online

(fcbarcelona.com), or buy them at the stadium itself *(10 a.m.–6:30 p.m. Mon.–Sat., 10 a.m.–2:15 p.m. Sun.)*. You can also buy through Ticketmaster *(ticketmaster.es)* or in one of the official FCB shops in town, e.g. Ronda Universitat. On match day (or night) you can get tickets at the stadium, too. You'll also find lots of scalpers hawking tickets, often for considerably less, around the ticket windows. However, this does have a small amount of risk attached.

F.C. Barcelona's supporters tend to be vocal but hardly rowdy (with the exception of a small group of hooligans known as the Boixos Nois, now banned from the stadium). The atmosphere at a major game, when the stadium is close to full, is undeniably electric, and ranks as one of those "once-in-a-lifetime" experiences.

The issues are complex. Devolution has meant the transfer of control in areas such as health, education, police, and much more from the center to the regions. Where Catalans champ at the bit is on the subject of taxes and distribution of wealth. Although concessions have been made to the regions, the bulk of tax is raised by the state, or funneled from the regions to the state and then redistributed to the regions according to broad principles of equity. Increasingly, Catalonia and other richer regions complain that they contribute far too much and receive far too little.

In the same way, long after Franco's demise, the debate on regional identity is kept on the boil. Nowhere is this more evident than in the language issue. The Generalitat (regional government) has engaged in an unwavering policy of raising the status of Catalan. The language was largely suppressed during the Franco years. Officially, Catalan and Castilian (Spanish) now have equal standing, but, in practice, Catalan is often favored. Public servants are obliged to speak Catalan and Castilian, and the bulk of primary and secondary education is carried out in Catalan. Although little statistical proof indicates it, some fear that, in the long term, Castilian will be reduced to an imperfectly mastered foreign language in Catalonia. In 2014, the central government tried to impose the teachings of some subjects in Castilian, a plan that prompted huge protests in Catalonia.

In more practical terms, Barcelonans claim that Catalan infrastructure has been allowed to rot while money is poured into Madrid. On the surface of it, the Catalans may have a point. Since the mid-1990s, Madrid has modernized its Metro system at breakneck speed, doubled its airport capacity, added ring roads around the rapidly growing city, and come close to being selected to host the Olympic Games.

In Barcelona, extension of the Metro (including a line to the airport) proceeds at a snail's pace. The high-speed AVE train link with Madrid was completed only in 2008, years behind schedule. The much vaunted high-speed link with France, originally due by

2009, did not become a reality until 2013. Investment in highways and port development has been tardy and much needed expansion of Barcelona's airport delayed. The suburban rail network, run by the national Renfe rail company, has seen little investment while those in Madrid and other major cities have been noticeably improved.

Looking Ahead

The glass is either half full or half empty. Visitors from Madrid frequently express admiration for the urban projects under way in Barcelona. Schemes such as the building of university faculties, several new hotels, and a national film theater in what was once regarded as the red-light district, El Raval, or the enterprising 22@ new business district in a neglected, former industrial zone near Plaça de les Glòries, are sure signs of vitality and Catalan determination to attract foreign investment.

It is not only the physical appearance of the city that is changing. Until the early 1990s, Barcelona was a fairly homogeneous city, made up in equal measures of Catalans and Spanish "immigrants" from the 1950s and 1960s. The influx of Europeans, South Americans, North Africans, and Asians has brought Barcelona a multicultural dimension that before 1990 would have been unimaginable. They have brought with them not only new cultural ways but new customs and cuisines.

The boom in tourism that has escalated since Barcelona put itself firmly on the map with the 1992 Olympics has led to seemingly unstoppable hotel building. Add to this the fact it has been named Mobile World Capital from 2012–2018, and there are endless reasons to believe in the future of this Mediterranean metropolis. Whatever the outcome of the current wrangling over independence from the rest of Spain, the canny Catalans will ensure the continual growth of their capital city. ■

The rides of Tibidabo's Parc d'Atraccions, watched over by the Temple del Sagrat Cor

History of Barcelona

Evidence of 2,000 years of history can still be witnessed in Barcelona. Roman Barcino was a small town, but in the Middle Ages the city reached its apogee as head of a vigorous Mediterranean merchant empire. Things began to go downhill after Spanish unification under the Crown of Castile. By the 19th century Barcelona had again picked up steam as Spain's leading industrial and business city, a position it has managed to occupy ever since.

This 13th-century depiction of St. Ursula and the virgins traveling to Rome shows Catalan confidence in crossing the Mediterranean in the wake of Jaume I's conquest of Mallorca.

Antiquity

Archaeologists have revealed that Stone Age tribes were wandering about the Pyrenees as many as 70,000 years ago. As the millennia swept by and the tribes became more sophisticated and less fearful, they began to move into the more exposed plains to the south.

These Iberian tribes were joined from about the seventh century B.C. by fresh blood—Celts migrating across Europe from the east. How they rubbed along is difficult to tell. To outsiders such as the Greeks, who landed in Catalonia about a century later, they already seemed well integrated. The mix resulted in what historians now refer to as the Celt-Iberians.

It appears at least one of these Celt-Iberian tribes, the Laietani, lived in the area around present-day Barcelona for several centuries, but no one knows if they actually

settled. Given the Celt-Iberian penchant for creating settlements on defensible hilltops, the most likely location for any such village would have been Montjuïc.

The arrival of Phoenician and Greek traders along the Spanish coast had a telling effect on the Celt-Iberians. Exchange with the Greeks was especially important, and in Catalonia they set up trading depots at Rodes (near modern Roses) and Emporion (Empúries). You can still see vestiges of the latter today (see p. 237). The use of coinage and a great deal of Celt-Iberian art (particularly in ceramics) were clearly inspired by contact with the Greeks.

It is said that the great Carthaginian general and father of the legendary Hannibal (247–181 B.C.), Hamilcar Barca (died 228 B.C.), established the first settlement on the site of Barcelona, but no evidence of this has come down to us. Even less likely is the claim that the mythical Hercules himself founded the city!

What is sure is that the sworn enemy of the Carthaginians, Rome, landed troops in Spain in 218 B.C. in an attack on Hannibal's rear. Hannibal had invaded Italy from the north that same year in the opening stages of the Second Punic War, and in the first years of this conflict, he marched from victory to victory. But reinforcements from Carthaginian Spain, cut off by the Roman armies that had marched south from Emporion, could not reach him. The war in Spain was over by 206 B.C., and the peninsula's destiny forever changed as it was then slowly absorbed into the burgeoning Roman Empire.

It is not entirely clear just when Barcino

was formed, but there is little doubt it began life as a garrison, as did many other Roman towns. It was planned around the standard north–south axis (decumanus) and crossroad (cardo), with the forum and temple near the intersection. Peace had long reigned in the area when Caesar Augustus (63 B.C.–A.D. 14) arrived around 15 B.C. He must have liked his reception in the prosperous provincial center because he bestowed it with the rather magnificent sounding title of Colonia Julia Augusta Faventia Pia. Four hefty columns of the temple raised to worship the emperor still stand today (see p. 67).

Dark Times

The first walls were raised around Barcino as early as the first century A.D.—probably no more than a perfunctory measure, as the Pax Romana rendered warfare or invasion unlikely. By the fourth century storm clouds were gathering across the length and breadth of the increasingly troubled empire. Stouter walls were raised, and it was as though the citizens of Barcino, among them a growing Christian minority, could do little more than prepare themselves and await the onslaught.

And come it did. Like locusts, waves of barbarian marauders swarmed into Spain from the north, bringing death and destruction and then moving on. The Christianized Visigoths, who first arrived in 415 and made Barcelona their temporary capital, were intent on staying. They spread their control across Spain, but their hold on power was always tenuous. Small in numbers and prone to violent internecine squabbling, the Visigoths brought little stability to the former Roman provinces.

The marked Visigothic tendency toward assassination and treachery was of no help when a Muslim army landed at Gibraltar in 711. Inspired by their faith and the prospect of endless loot, the mixed Berber and Arab army swept across the entire Iberian Peninsula, encountering little effective resistance. The people of Barcelona mounted the ramparts of the city, but their stand was futile. Barcelona succumbed as easily as the rest and the Muslim advance was only finally checked by the Franks at Poitiers in France 21 years later.

Counts of Barcelona

The Franks repelled the Muslims back across the Pyrenees, and in 801 Louis the Pious (778–840) liberated Barcelona. From then on, a rough line from Barcelona to the northwest marked the divide between Muslim-occupied land to the south and Christian counties to the north. Together, the northern lands came to be known as the Spanish March, a Frankish buffer zone designed to keep the Muslims at arm's length.

These were momentous times in Europe, for the Frankish king (and father of Louis the Pious), Charlemagne (742–814), had been proclaimed Holy Roman Emperor in 800.

Catalan Flag History

The Senyera, Catalan for "flag," came about in some form during the early Middle Ages. The four red stripes on the golden field are taken from the shield of the Crown of Aragón. The four red swaths each represent a territory under Aragonese control, and the golden field represented submission to the pope. But an apocryphal legend has it that during the siege of Barcelona in 897, Guifré el Pelós was mortally wounded. King Charles the Bald dipped his hand into his compatriot's wound and dragged his bloody fingers down the count's golden shield, leaving the red stripes. The Estelada is the independence supporters' variant with a white star on a blue triangle. These days you can't miss them flying from rooftops and draped over balconies manifesting support for the growing movement to separate from Spain.

The counts who dominated the Spanish March were either direct imperial appointees or at least required the emperor's blessing to rule. Although theoretically agents of the imperial Crown, they had a large degree of autonomy and cheerfully engaged in local spats. By the middle of the ninth century, the struggle for supremacy south of the Pyrenees was a two-horse race, represented by Sunifred (died 848), the Count of Urgell, and Bernat, head of the Septimania dynasty. The latter's allies controlled many of the counties of what would one day come to be known as Catalonia.

Bernat's death in 844 created a power vacuum into which Sunifred's son, Guifré el Pelós (Wilfred the Hairy, circa 840–897), stepped some 20 years later. Between 870 and 878 he and his brothers took control of almost all the counties south of the Pyrenees, including Barcelona.

In subsequent centuries, Guifré came to be venerated as the father of the Catalan "nation" as medieval propagandists sought to create a suitably heroic history for the principality. No doubt an able warrior and astute politician, he was no Catalan nationalist. Indeed, the earliest surviving documented references to "Catalonia" date only from the 12th century, and Guifré actively sought imperial blessing for his conquests. He knew how to win good publicity, though, and was particularly assiduous in founding religious institutions across Catalonia. Some of these grand churches and monasteries, such as Santa Maria de Ripoll and Sant Joan de les Abadesses, remain standing to this day. In return, the only class in society with serious education, the clergy, spared no effort in eulogizing their hirsute benefactor. To this busy frontier warlord who founded the Casal de Barcelona (House of Barcelona) and conquered much of what would later be called Catalunya Vella (Old Catalonia) was thus attributed the birth of Catalonia, a nation that would never truly be.

After repeated campaigns, Count Ramon Berenguer I (R. 1035–1076) bought the French lands of Carcassonne and Béziers.

Under Guifré's successors, the Comtes de Barcelona (Counts of Barcelona), the city slowly expanded and became their preferred residence. Devastation came in 985 when the Muslims, under the great general Al-Mansur (938–1002), mounted their last successful raid on the city. Calls for aid to the Franks, still theoretically suzerains of the Spanish March, went unheeded and so, understandably, the counts felt themselves released from even nominal bonds of allegiance. By the end of the 11th century, the Counts of Barcelona were firmly in control of a solid chunk of territory encompassing Old Catalonia and French land extending as far as Carcassonne and Béziers. Farther to the south, Tarragona was wrested from the Muslims in a campaign that led to the fall of Tortosa and Lleida.

Finally, in 1153, the white flag went up over the last Muslim stronghold, Siurana de Prades,

Ramon Berenguer IV was betrothed to the infant heiress Petronilla of Aragón in 1137.

and the reconquest of Catalonia Nova (New Catalonia) was complete. Early in the 13th century, a diplomatic campaign saw the Catalans take control of vast areas of Occitania in southern France, and their influence extended well into what is now the region of Provence.

Crown of Aragón

A turning point came in 1137 when Count Ramon Berenguer IV (1113–1162) was betrothed to the one-year-old heiress to the throne of neighboring Aragón. It is odd that until this time the rulers of the House of Barcelona had not thought to proclaim themselves kings of Catalonia. For almost three centuries Catalan rulers, or *comtes-reis* (count-kings), would continue foremost as kings of Aragón and secondly as Counts of Barcelona. Catalonia quite clearly existed, but it was as though someone had forgotten to label it properly.

Under the terms of the union, each party retained a high degree of independence, preserving many of their own laws and customs. The deal suited the more populous and prosperous Catalonia, allowing it to pursue the expansion of its nascent commercial empire while the Aragonese formed a bulwark against the Castilian kingdom that dominated central Spain. Aragonese nobles soon came to resent the Catalans and centuries later would burst Barcelona's bubble by engineering a union with Castile. For now, though, the Catalans were embarking on their Golden Age.

Imperial Adventure: It might seem odd that the most spectacular expansion of Catalan territory and trade should come in the wake of a sinister defeat. After a long and complex series of events, and against his will, Pere I (1174–1213) found himself at the head of a Catalan army facing off against the French in the Battle of Muret in 1213. The result was an unmitigated disaster as, against all expectations, the Catalans were trounced, and Pere died in combat. In one fell swoop all the careful work of the previous century was undone. The French took control of much of Occitania, leaving the Catalans with Roussillon, Cerdanya, and part of Provence (including the city of Montpellier).

The day Pere died, his young son Jaume was captured by the French. Pope Innocent III interceded on his behalf and the five-year-old was returned to Catalonia, where he was proclaimed king. Jaume I (1208–1276) finally took power in 1225. Young Jaume gave no thought to avenging his father, because he had more ambitious plans. The path before him was clear, for although Barcelona lacked a decent port, it was already an important trading center with a growing merchant marine and navy. The city's single greatest handicap, however, lay in the Balearic Islands, whose North African masters used them as an extortionate customs post and pirate base. As long as this obstacle remained in place, Catalan merchants could never hope to compete with the Genovese and Venetians for a piece of the lucrative eastern Mediterranean trade.

> In 1229, Jaume el Conqueridor set out with a fleet of 150 vessels and 2,000 men to take Mallorca.

In 1229, Jaume el Conqueridor set out with a fleet of 150 vessels and 2,000 men to take Mallorca. The campaign was an unqualified success, and the merchants of Barcelona immediately began to cash in. Ibiza fell six years later, but the easternmost of the islands, Menorca, held out until 1287. The conquest of that island proved a bloody, ignoble, and largely futile chapter in what may fairly be termed Catalan imperial history.

The Aragonese had remained aloof from Jaume's island campaign but had their eyes on another objective, the Muslim fiefdom of Valencia. Jaume embarked with equal vigor on the conquest of this fertile coastal strip, which he completed by 1245. However, he enraged the Aragonese, who wanted the conquered territory placed under their laws, by creating a kingdom of Valencia with its own statutes, similar to those of New Catalonia.

From Jaume I's death until the early years of the following century, the Crown of Aragón's overseas possessions grew—in fits and starts and often against the will of the Aragonese. The wars, revolts, and intrigues that at one stage saw a French army invading Aragón and the count-king Jaume II fighting his brother Frederic for the possession of Sicily make for confusing reading.

After much bloodshed and with the royal coffers suffering, the Crown of Aragón ended up at the head of a confederation that was to all intents and purposes a major mercantile empire. On the mainland her territories included Catalonia, Aragón, Valencia, Murcia, Roussillon, and Montpellier. Beyond, the largely Catalan offensive effort had netted the Balearic Islands, Sicily, and Sardinia (invaded in 1323). For a brief moment Catalan duchies also controlled Athens, Malta, and Gozo.

Historians remain divided as to the utility of the effort. There is no doubt that Catalan trade profited; Barcelona's merchants by now ranged across the entire Mediterranean. They dominated the western half and established trading posts in North Africa and as far off as the Middle East. However, the purchase price had been high and the maintenance was still more prohibitive. Revolts were the order of the day in Sardinia and, to a lesser extent, from Sicily to Valencia. Attempts to take Corsica and penetrate Muslim Andalucía ended in costly failure.

....

In 1249, the first city assembly was authorized, and by 1274 it had taken shape. Five *consellers* (ministers) ran the city's affairs.

....

Home Front: Whatever the pros and cons of royal empire-building, Barcelona was a prime beneficiary. From the time of Jaume I's "great deed"—the invasion of Mallorca—the city had become a boomtown. The count-king's need for money and men to realize his conquests put the wealthy merchants of the city in a strong bargaining position. Jaume's decision to gradually shift municipal control of the city into the hands of its citizens must inevitably be seen in that light. In 1249, the first city assembly was authorized, and by 1274 it had taken shape. Five *consellers* (ministers) ran the city's affairs. These were elected for a year from a representative assembly. They formed a tightly knit oligarchic group acting in the interests of the premier merchant class. In one form or another, the Consell de Cent (Council of One Hundred), as the assembly came to be known, ran city hall until 1714.

In 1283 another key institution sat for the first time: the Corts Catalanes, a kind of regional parliament. It was matched by similar institutions in the other constituent parts of the Crown of Aragón, including Aragón and Valencia. Members of the Corts came from three social classes: nobles, clerics, and high-ranking citizens. Initially, the Corts were called into session yearly (later every three years), generally by the count-king, to consider his proposals and, more often than not in the early days, to rubber-stamp them. The Corts also passed laws and the budget, and increasingly the count-kings turned to them for funding, in return for which the Corts extracted a greater say in lawmaking and other privileges. It could hardly be described as democracy at its best.

As the Corts sat so infrequently, an executive council in permanent session emerged. Made up of a dozen *diputats* (deputies), its principle roles were to collect taxes

Palma de Mallorca was already an impressive city when Jaume I's war vessels convened outside its walls to invade.

(or *generalitats*) and keep the royal finances oiled. Over the centuries this Diputació de la Generalitat, later simply called the Generalitat, took on greater political responsibilities and eventually made its seat the Palau de la Generalitat (see pp. 77–78), where the Catalan regional government still sits today.

By the middle of the 14th century, Barcelona was a major city with a population of 50,000. Jaume I had extended the city walls as far southwest as La Rambla—in those days a sewage-clogged stream. This wall became the city's main defensive bulwark. At the same time, the economic nerve center of the city had shifted beyond the cramped city to the area

By the Middle Ages, Barcelona had become one of the Mediterranean's leading ports. Its shipyards, the Drassanes, were probably second only to the great Arsenale of Venice.

now known as La Ribera. Pere III (1319–1387) again extended the walls to take in La Ribera and, southwest of La Rambla, the higgledy-piggledy suburban sprawl known as El Raval. Those walls were eventually knocked down in the 19th century, but the layout can still be identified today: To see it, start in the south where Avinguda del Paral-lel heads west from the waterfront and follow Ronda de Sant Pau, Ronda de Sant Antoni, Ronda de l'Universitat, Ronda de Sant Pere, and, finally, the boundary formed by Parc de la Ciutadella.

At either end of this medieval city grew the two great arms of Catalan mercantile wealth. The traders, grown rich on the back of military expansion, congregated around Carrer de Montcada, which to this day is lined with Gothic and Renaissance mansions that once were home to the most powerful families of the city. The street was laid out to connect the main road northeast out of Barcelona with what was then the waterfront. By contrast, the long, broad Passeig del Born was a hive of commercial activity. Catalan mariners used to say: "*Roda el mon i torna al Born*—Go around the world and come back to the Born." For centuries this space was the center of much of the city's grand theater. From early medieval jousts to the grim autos-da-fé (burning of heretics by the Inquisition) that began late in the 15th century, the Born was certainly never dull.

On the other side of town, one of the great monuments of Gothic architecture was raised—the Drassanes, or shipyards. Modified in the 16th and 17th centuries, this Gothic-style building now houses the fascinating Museu Marítim (see pp. 102–104). These ship-yards were among the greatest in Europe and furnished not only vessels for the merchant fleet but a good number of the Crown of Aragón's warships. They would continue to play a key role long after the Crown of Aragón had thrown in its lot with that of Castile to create a united Spain.

Prosperous Times

So, by the time Pere III built the new city walls, Barcelona had become a rich and prosperous city, with its own civil administration and seat of the regional parliament. Not everyone fared equally well, however. The townsfolk were divided roughly into three groups: the so-called *ciutadans honrats* (honorable citizens), a moneyed, aris-tocratic elite; a middle class made up of traders, professionals, shipbuilders, lawyers, and others; and finally the lower classes, *menestrals,* made up of artisans and laborers. These people formed the bulk of the city's population and did most of the work.

While the artisans and skilled workers were afforded some protection and representa-tion in their trade guilds—a medieval combination of trade union and mutual support society—unskilled laborers had precious little. Riots broke out frequently, with the biggest disturbances in 1285, 1334, 1348, and 1391. That the people had any energy at all to riot in 1348 (the year the bubonic plague decimated Europe) is a source of considerable surprise. What lay behind the riots is not clear. The 1391 pogrom was as savage as it was inexplicable. There is, however, little doubt that the distribution of wealth was uneven.

The latter half of the 14th century was a strange time in Barcelona. The Black Death of 1348 had decimated the city's population and foreign wars continued to drain the coffers, yet it was now that much of the Gothic city you see today was built. Somehow, Pere III and his immediate successors found the funds to initiate ambitious new building programs and con-tinue older ones.

The city was getting prettier, but this was not mirrored in its murky politics. The Consell de Cent, whose members decided on their own replacements from one year to the next, remained an old-money club to which not even wealthy Johnnies-come-lately had access. Thus, two factions emerged, the Biga and the Busca. The latter was made up of frustrated aspirants to power who wanted not so much to shake the establishment Biga as simply be a part of it. Cor-ruption was rife and several count-kings meddled in the city's affairs, pitting factions against one another and even fomenting riots in the name of reform. No doubt royal backing for the Busca came attached to a price that the latter was more than happy to pay.

When the Busca finally grabbed control of the Consell de Cent in the mid-15th century, the group enacted important fiscal reforms, but they did not last. In any case, events were fast overtaking them.

Black Death

As a major port, Barcelona was right in the bubonic plagues's path as it swept across Europe; in March 1348, a ship coming from the port of Rous-sillon brought the disease to town. Within weeks, the panic-stricken city was organizing mass religious proces-sions to ward off the pestilence. As the months went on, the magnitude of death became so absurd that gravediggers would often play guitar and tambourines to lighten the mood while they carted the dead away. After all, who wants to live in a world without music?

The Calamity of 1714

Catalonia's decline had begun even before the union of the Crowns of Aragón and Castile in 1479 (signaling the end of Catalonia as a fully independent entity). This union was engineered by the Aragonese against the will of the Catalans. That it retained wide autonomy and commanded respect is reflected in the stately receptions frequently accorded Barcelona's emissaries to the Castilian court now and in later centuries.

However, where it counted, Castile gradually assumed control, especially under the rule of Charles I and Philip II, who presided over the zenith of Spanish glory, that brief moment when continental domination and American gold combined to make Spain the greatest power on Earth. The introduction of the Inquisition in Barcelona and laws that excluded direct trade between Catalonia and the Americas made it perfectly clear who was master.

> **Exhausted by continuing war and negligent economic policy, Spain quickly slipped from its exalted position after the death of Philip II.**

Exhausted by continuing war and negligent economic policy, Spain quickly slipped from its exalted position after the death of Philip II. And struggle as it might against the tendency, Catalonia inexorably slipped with it. Wars and revolution, including the popular peasant rising, or the Guerra dels Segadors (Reapers War) of 1640–1652, only served to devastate the Catalan countryside. On this occasion royal troops reduced Barcelona during a siege in what must have been seen in hindsight as a dry run for the disaster still to come.

The death in 1700 of Charles II left Spain without an heir. Like vultures, all of Europe came to the table to play, and thus ensued the War of the Spanish Succession (1702–1714), in which Catalonia threw in its lot with an anti-French coalition. The French prevailed and a Bourbon king, Philip V, ascended the throne. The allies left Catalonia to its fate, which took the form of a merciless siege and bombardment of Barcelona in 1714. On September 11, the city surrendered and Philip V abolished every trace of Catalan autonomy. An absolutist in the mold of Louis XIV, Philip set about creating a fully centralized state. Catalonia lost its privileges, overseas possessions, and even its language, the use of which was prohibited.

Reawakening

The shock had been considerable, but the city slowly became accustomed to the new situation. From the late 18th century, when finally the ban on direct trade between the Latin American colonies and Catalonia was lifted, until 1898, when Spain lost the last of those colonies—Cuba, Puerto Rico, and the Philippines—in a humiliating defeat by the U.S. Navy, Barcelona recovered to the point of becoming Spain's leading city. It had been a bumpy ride.

interest in the Catalan tongue and literature. At the same time, modernisme (the local version of art nouveau) exploded onto the Barcelona art scene. This movement was regarded by many as further evidence of Catalan renewal. Modernisme's great exponents, especially in architecture, tended to be Catalan nationalists. In 1892 a loose political movement promulgated the Bases de Manresa, the blueprint for a Catalan government and self-rule.

War & Peace

Barcelona was bubbling by the beginning of the 20th century. Indeed, all of Spain was in ferment. A century of political uncertainty, coup and countercoup, and economic mismanagement had left the country increasingly ripe for conflict.

Barcelona could hardly remain aloof, and events seemed to be spinning beyond control. The city's population doubled to one million between 1900 and 1930, and the restless and growing industrial working class turned increasingly to the radical left, especially the anarchists. In July 1909, a call-up of reservists to boost beleaguered Spanish forces in their ill-organized campaign in northern Morocco sparked a week of violence in Barcelona, the Setmana Tràgica (Tragic Week), in which anticlericalism was especially vented with the torching of churches across the city. Violence both on the right and the left was becoming the norm, not only in Barcelona but also elsewhere in the country. In Barcelona, calls for self-rule in Catalonia grew louder by the day.

Fears of a general workers' revolt led General Miguel Primo de Rivera to stage a coup in 1923. His dictatorship lasted until 1930 but achieved little more than to stall the inevitable. Catalan nationalists saw their opportunity with the 1931 election victory in Madrid of a leftist coalition. Under Francesc Macià and Lluís Companys, the Esquerra Republicana de Catalonia party (ERC, Republican Left of Catalonia) proclaimed a republic within the newly declared Spanish republic. Madrid quashed this but within a year had granted limited self-rule. The struggle between right and left intensified. In February 1936, when the leftist Popular Front coalition won the national elections, Companys again proclaimed the Catalan republic. It was all in vain. In July of the same year General Franco launched an army rebellion in Spain's North African enclaves. His aim was to topple the left-wing republican government in Madrid and install a Nationalist government in its stead. The Spanish Civil War had begun.

> The Renaixença began as a cultural movement in which a minority of intellectuals fomented interest in the Catalan tongue and literature. At the same time, modernisme exploded onto the Barcelona art scene.

Years of Agony: For the next three years Spain went through the agony of civil war. In Barcelona the army attempted to rise up in support of Franco, but it was quickly defeated by the police, who were loyal to the government, and bands of armed anarchists.

Thus began a surreal period. Lluís Companys, nominal head of the recently resurrected Generalitat, was powerless to prevent a coalition of anarchists and Trotskyist militia—the Partido Obrero de Unificación Marxista (POUM), or Workers Party of Marxist Unification—from taking control of the city. The former in particular, with their red-and-black flags, were dominant. Factories, public transportation, and social services all ended up in anarchist hands. Revolution hung in the air as the anarchists and POUM were as much interested in creating a new social order right away as defeating a common enemy.

By May 1937, it was clear that the war was not going particularly well for the Republicans. In Barcelona, a burgeoning Communist party and its militia gained the upper hand and, with Companys's blessing, openly began an assault on the anarchists and POUM. After three days and the loss of 1,500 lives, the latter two groups surrendered and were disarmed. Several months onward the central Republican government set up shop in Barcelona.

At this point the writing was on the wall, however. The last great clash of the war, the Battle of the Ebro, which was fought out along that river in southwestern Catalonia in the summer of 1938, brought yet another defeat for the Republicans, who were now virtually incapable of defending the city of Barcelona. The Nationalist troops, watched in silence by those people in Barcelona who had opted not to flee into exile in France, marched into the city in January 1939. Two months later the civil war came to an end.

For the next 36 years Spain was to live in the vice-like grip of General Franco. A great believer in central government, Franco abolished all the usual things: the Generalitat, the use of Catalan, the right to hold demonstrations, and so on. The repression was at its bloodiest during the 1940s—Companys was executed in 1940 in Montjuïc castle. Opposition was never completely silenced, however. Strikes and protests began to occur as early as the 1950s and continued through the 1960s. At the same time, Franco was encouraging the massive migration of people from the poorer regions of Spain, such as Andalucía and Extremadura, to Barcelona. About three-quarters of a million swelled the population of Barcelona and its satellites during the 1960s alone.

Rebirth: The death of Franco in 1975 sparked a remarkable process that brought Spain in from the cold and returned to Catalonia a degree of self-rule not seen since before 1714. In 1978 a system of devolution of power to the regions was agreed upon. The following year, a specific Autonomy Statute for Catalonia was given royal

---

EXPERIENCE: Take Shelter from an Air Raid!

Until the horrors of World War II, Barcelona was the city that had been most heavily bombed from the air. During the Spanish Civil War (1936–1939), Italian bombers based in Mallorca regularly raided the city, launching an especially fierce assault over three days in March 1938. By the end of the war, some 3,000 Barcelonans had been killed and 7,000 wounded. More than 1,300 air-raid shelters were created in the course of the war. A guided visit to one of them, the **Refugi 307** (*Carrer Nou de la Rambla 169, tel 93 256 21 22, tours in Catalan 10:30 a.m.,*

12:30 p.m., in Spanish 11:30 a.m., Sun., $), provides insight into a momentous chapter in the city's history. Carved into a fold of the Montjuïc mountain in Poble Sec, its very existence is a testimony to the grit of the city's people. Local citizens began digging the tunnels in March 1937 with pick and shovel. As the war progressed, so did the web of tunnels in this shelter. Theoretically, the tunnels could hold up to 2,000 people by war's end. Like other shelters, it was simply abandoned after the war. For tours in English or French you must book ahead.

Artur Mas, president of the Catalan Generalitat since 2010

assent by King Juan Carlos I, the constitutional monarch at the head of the Spanish state after Franco's death. In 1980 the first regional elections were held and Jordi Pujol, at the head of a right-of-center Catalan nationalist coalition, became president of Catalonia. He astutely ruled until 2003, when former mayor, Catalan Socialist leader Pasqual Maragall, won elections at the head of a three-party coalition.

Pujol's Convergència i Unió party returned to power in 2010 under Artur Mas, and also took the city council from PSC, the Socialist party, for the first time since the advent of democracy. Against the backdrop of recession, growing disenchantment with cutbacks to health and education, unemployment rising to more than 25 percent, and a refusal by the ruling right-wing PP (Partido Popular) in Madrid to negotiate a better economic deal for Catalonia, a massive march took place in Barcelona on September 11, 2012. On this day, Diada, Catalonia's national day, the crowd clamored for independence. Emboldened by the force of this movement, Mas has made a dramatic turn toward separatism, in league with ERC, the left-wing *independentistas,* and ICV (Initiative for Catalonia and Green party). Their mission is to hold a referendum to measure Catalans' views on separating from Spain, despite the claim by Madrid that such a poll would not be constitutional. The Catalans are also willing to turn a deaf ear to the European Union's threat of not recognizing a newly declared state of Catalonia. Interesting times lie ahead for Barcelona. ■

The Arts

An overwhelming sense of confidence about the city's prospects has on two occasions spurred a building and design frenzy in Barcelona. The activity unleashed has left us with two remarkably rich and distinct artistic legacies: the Gothic of the old center and the sometimes delirious modernista whims of the late 19th and early 20th centuries.

The city is also home to a rich collection of paintings from the early medieval Romanesque period. In the 20th century the city was awash with genius—Pablo Picasso and Joan Miró laid the foundations of their careers here, and Salvador Dalí remained true to his Catalan roots throughout his life.

Architecture

As if caught in a time warp, central Barcelona embraced Gothic styles of building long after they had been abandoned elsewhere. This legacy and the wonderful outpouring of imagination that came with *modernisme* (the Catalan take on Art Nouveau) are the main sources of visual feasting in the streets of the Catalan capital.

> In the 20th century the city was awash with genius—Pablo Picasso and Joan Miró laid the foundations of their careers here, and Salvador Dalí remained true to his Catalan roots throughout his life.

Roman Barcelona: Barcino, the town known to us today as Barcelona, was a standard example of Roman garrison town planning. Rectangular and crisscrossed by a north–south axis (the *decumanus*) and an east–west thoroughfare (the *cardo*), the city center was made up of a forum (roughly where Plaça de Sant Jaume is today) and a temple, of which several columns remain standing. Aside from lower levels of sections of the city wall and towers, and a small cemetery, the best view of excavated ancient Barcino is in the basement of the Museu d'Història de Barcelona, or MUHBA (see pp. 68–71).

Visigoths and, for a short time, Muslim invaders followed the Romans' time in charge of Barcelona, but virtually nothing remains to testify to their presence.

Romanesque: It was in the early Middle Ages that a new and vigorous building style known as Romanesque swept across Christian Europe. Lombard artisans from northern Italy began transmitting it across Catalonia and to the city of Barcelona from about the 11th century.

Romanesque is appealingly simple and forceful, and survives today almost exclusively in churches—generally consisting of a simple rectangular plan with no transept—and some elements of monasteries. Characterized by the use of stone to create angular and largely unadorned buildings, the softening touch comes with the semicircle—arches, vaults, doorways, and windows all take this shape. A tall, square-based bell tower flanks

The towering columns of the temple dedicated to Caesar Augustus are among the few reminders of Roman presence.

Napoleon's occupation and the Peninsular War (1808–1814) had been disastrous for the entire country, and the faltering industrialization (textiles, shipbuilding, iron, the first Spanish railway, cork and wine production) had brought wealth to some and slum misery to most.

Nevertheless, in the final 20 years, the city's fathers were in an ebullient mood. Having knocked down the city walls, they embarked on an ambitious urban development plan, creating the elegant grid-plan district between Barcelona and the then separate town of Gràcia. L'Eixample (the Extension), as the new area is still known, fueled a building and property boom. In 1888 the city hosted a Universal Exhibition.

The euphoria of those heady days was accompanied by political renewal. The Renaixença (Renaissance) began as a cultural movement in which a minority of intellectuals fomented

Besieged Barcelona had no hope of holding out against Madrid's forces at the tail end of the War of the Spanish Succession in 1714.

"Anarchist Books Are Arms in the Fight Against Fascism," proclaims the propaganda poster.

Architecture

Casa Batlló (p147)

Barcelona's architectural gift to the world was Modernisme, a flamboyant Catalan creation that erupted in the late 19th century. Barcelona's other great architectural epoch was during the Middle Ages, when mercantile wealth fuelled the creation of magnificent Gothic buildings. More recently, the city has continued to host cutting-edge designs and dramatic urban renewal projects that all began in the makeover before and after the 1992 Olympics.

Catalan Gothic

Barcelona's first great moment of creative electricity came when the city, grown rich on its Mediterranean trade and empire-building, transformed what is now the old city centre into the pageant of Gothic building that has survived in great part to this day.

Historically, Gothic sits between the Romanesque and Renaissance periods of medieval construction. It was an architectural style that emerged in France in the 1100s, but gradually spread throughout Europe, spawning numerous regional variations. The overlying themes, best exemplified in the ecclesial buildings of the day, were humungous scale (Gothic churches were the skyscrapers of their era), well-lit interiors, large windows, pointed arches, lofty pinnacles and spires, and majestic decoration.

The Best...
Gothic Masterpieces

1 La Catedral (p56)

2 Basílica de Santa Maria del Mar (p99)

3 Museu Marítim (p114)

4 Museu d'Història de Barcelona (p67)

Most of these themes were employed in medieval Barcelona in a raft of buildings that spanned the whole era and later inspired a small neo-Gothic revival in the mid-19th century. The Basílica de Santa Maria del Mar is a fairly unembellished example of Levantino (14th-century) Gothic style at its height and is usually considered the city's greatest Gothic achievement. The more decorative Catedral is the synthesis of a Levantino Gothic base overlaid with a neo-Gothic facade.

The Modernistas

The second wave of Catalan creativity, also carried on the wind of boom times, came around the turn of the 20th century. The urban expansion program known as L'Eixample (the Extension), designed to free the choking population from the city's bursting medieval confines, coincided with a blossoming of unfettered thinking in architecture that arrived in the back-draft of the 1888 International Exposition of Barcelona.

The vitality and rebelliousness of the Modernistas is best summed up in the epithets modern, new, liberty, youth and secession. A key uniting element was the sensuous curve, implying movement, lightness and vitality. But the movement never stood still. Gaudí, in particular, repeatedly forged his own path. As he became more adventurous he appeared a lone wolf. With age he became almost exclusively motivated by stark religious conviction and devoted much of the latter part of his life to what remains Barcelona's call sign – the unfinished La Sagrada Família.

Paradoxically, Modernista architects often looked to the past for inspiration. Gothic, Islamic and Renaissance design all had something to offer. At its most playful, Modernisme was able to intelligently flout the rule books of these styles and create exciting new cocktails.

Antoni Gaudí

Leading the way was Antoni Gaudí. Born in Reus to a long line of coppersmiths, Gaudí was initially trained in metalwork. In childhood he suffered from poor health, including rheumatism, and became an early adopter of a vegetarian diet. He was not a promising student. In 1878, when he obtained his architecture degree the school's headmaster is reputed to have said: 'Who knows if we have given a diploma to a nutcase or a genius. Time will tell.'

As a young man, what most delighted Gaudí was being outdoors, and he became fascinated by the plants, animals and geology beyond his door. This deep admiration for the natural world would heavily influence his designs. 'This tree is my teacher,' he once said. 'Everything comes from the book of nature.' Throughout his work, he sought to emulate the harmony he observed in the natural world, eschewing the straight line and favouring curvaceous forms and more organic shapes.

The spiral of a nautilus shell can be seen in staircases and ceiling details, tight buds of flowers in chimney pots and roof ornamentation. Meanwhile undulating arches evoke a cavern, overlapping roof tiles mimic the scales of an armadillo and flowing walls resemble waves on the sea. Tree branches, spider webs, stalactites, honeycombs, starfish, mushrooms, shimmering beetle wings and many other elements fror nature – all were part of the Gaudían vernacular.

IN FOCUS ARCHITECTURE

Gaudí was a devout Catholic and a Catalan nationalist. In addition to nature, he drew inspiration from Catalonia's great medieval churches and took pride in utilising the building materials of the countryside: clay, stone and timber. In contrast to his architecture, Gaudí lived a simple life, and was not averse to knocking on doors, literally begging for money to help fund construction on the cathedral.

His masterpiece was La Sagrada Família (begun in 1882), and in it you can see the culminating vision of many ideas developed over the years. Its massive scale evokes the grandeur of Catalonia's Gothic cathedrals, while organic elements foreground its harmony with nature. As Gaudí became more adventurous he appeared as a lone wolf. With age he became almost exclusively motivated by stark religious conviction and devoted much of the latter part of his life to what remains Barcelona's call sign – the unfinished La Sagrada Família. He died in 1926, struck down by a streetcar while taking his daily walk to the Sant Felip Neri church. Wearing ragged clothes with empty pockets – save for an orange peel – Gaudí was initially taken for a beggar and taken to a nearby hospital where he was left in a pauper's ward. He died two days later. Thousands attended his funeral, in a half-mile procession to Sagrada Família where he was buried in the crypt.

Domènech i Montaner

Although overshadowed by Gaudí, Domènech i Montaner (1849–1923) was one of the great masters of Modernisme. He was a widely travelled man of prodigious intellect, with knowledge in everything from mineralogy to medieval heraldry, and he was an architectural professor, a prolific writer and a nationalist politician. The question of Catalan identity and how to create a national architecture consumed Domènech i Montaner, who designed over a dozen large-scale works in his lifetime.

The exuberant, steel-framed Palau de la Música Catalana is one of his masterpieces. Adorning the facade are elaborate Gothic-style windows, floral designs (Domènech i Montaner also studied botany) and sculptures depicting characters from Catalan folklore and the music world as well as everyday citizens of Barcelona. Inside, the hall leaves visitors dazzled with delicate floral-covered colonnades, radiant stained-glass walls and ceiling and a rolling, sculpture-packed proscenium referencing the epics of musical lore.

Puig i Cadafalch

Like Domènech, Puig i Cadafalch (1867–1956) was a polymath; he was an archaeologist, an expert in Romanesque art and one of Catalonia's most prolific architects. As a politician – and later president of the Mancomunitat de Catalunya (Commonwealth of Catalonia) – he was instrumental in shaping the Catalan nationalist movement.

One of his many Modernista gems is the Casa Amatller, a rather dramatic contrast to Gaudí's Casa Batlló next door. Here the straight line is very much in evidence, as is the foreign influence (the gables are borrowed from the Dutch). Puig i Cadafalch has designed a house of startling beauty and invention blended with playful Gothic-style sculpture.

Trencadís

The Arabs invented the ancient technique of *trencadís*, but Gaudí was the first architect to revive it. The procedure involves taking ceramic tiles or fragments of broken pottery or glass and creating a mosaic-like sheath on roofs, ceilings, chimneys, benches, sculptures or any other surface. Noted art critic Robert Hughes even suggested that Gaudí's *trencadís* was undoubtedly influential on the development of Picasso's fragmented forms in his Cubist period.

The Best...
Modernista Creations

1 La Sagrada Família (p130)

....

2 Palau de la Música Catalana (p102)

....

3 Park Güell (p178)

....

4 Casa Batlló (p147)

....

5 Recinte Modernista de Sant Pau (p139)

....

6 La Pedrera (p142)

....

Other important works by Puig i Cadafalch include the Casa Martí (better known as Els Quatre Gats), which was one of Barcelona's first Modernista-style buildings (from 1896), with Gothic window details and whimsical wrought-iron sculpture.

Barcelona Since the Olympic Games

Barcelona's latest architectural revolution began in the 1980s, when in the run up to the 1992 Olympics the city set about its biggest phase of renewal since the heady days of L'Eixample.

The Olympic makeover included the transformation of the Port Vell waterfront, the long road to resurrecting the 1929 International Exhibition sites in Montjuïc (including the refurbishment of the Olympic stadium) and the creation of landmarks such as Santiago Calatrava's (b 1951) Torre Calatrava.

Post-1992, landmark buildings still went up in strategic spots, usually with the ulterior motive of trying to pull the surrounding area up by its bootstraps.

One of the most emblematic of these projects was the gleaming white Museu d'Art Contemporani de Barcelona (MACBA), opened in 1995. The museum was designed by Richard Meier and incorporates the characteristic elements for which the American architect is so well known – the geometric minimalism, the pervasive use of all-white with glass and steel – and remains much debated in architectural circles.

Another big recent project (mostly completed in 2004) is Diagonal Mar, a whole district built in the northeast coastal corner of the city where before there was a void. Striking additions include high-rise apartments, waterfront office towers and a gigantic photovoltaic panel that provides some of the area's electricity.

The most visible addition to the skyline came in 2005. The shimmering, cucumber-shaped Torre Agbar is emblematic of the city's desire to make the developing hi-tech zone of 22@ (*vint-i-dos arroba*; www.22barcelona.com) a reality. The centerpiece is the new Disseny Hub (design museum), a building completed in 2013 that incorporates sustainable features in its cantilevered, metal-sheathed building. Vaguely futuristic (though some say it looks like a stapler), it has a rather imposing, anvil-shaped presence over the neighbourhood.

Nearby, stands the Els Encants Vells ('the Old Charms' flea market), which was given a dramatic new look by local architecture firm b720 Fermín Vázquez Arquitectos. Traders now sell their wares beneath a giant, mirrored canopy, arrayed a geometric angles and held aloft with long, slender poles. It opened to much acclaim in 2013.

In a rather thoughtful bit of recycling, British architect Lord Richard Rogers transformed the former Les Arenes bullring on Plaça d'Espanya into a singular, circular leisure complex, with shops, cinemas and more, which opened in 2011. He did so while still maintaining its red-brick, 19th-century Moorish-looking facade. Perhaps its best feature is the rooftop with 360-degree views from the open-air promenade and cafes and restaurants.

In the *ciutata vela* (old city), El Raval continues to be the focal point for urban renewal. The Filmoteca de Catalunya is a hulking rather brutalist building of concrete and glass, with sharp angles. It was designed by Catalan architect Josep Lluís Mateo and completed in 2011. It sits near the Richard Meier-designed MACBA, which opened in 1995.

Modern Art

Fundació Antoni Tàpies (p135)

Barcelona is to modern art what Greece is to ruined temples. Three of the figures at the vanguard of 20th-century avant-gardism – Picasso, Miró and Dalí – were either born or spent their formative years here. Their powerful legacy is stamped all over Barcelona in museums and public installations. In the contemporary art world, Catalonia continues to be an incubator for innovative works, with instrumental figures like Antoni Tàpies leading the way.

The Crucial Three

Spain has been a giant in world art ever since Velázquez etched his haunting *Las Meninas* and ushered in the glittery Siglo de Oro (c 1492–1680), though Catalonia was a little late to the ball.

Picasso

It wasn't until the late 19th century that truly great artists began to emerge in Barcelona and its hinterland, led by dandy portraitist Ramón Casas (1866–1932). Casas, an early Modernista, founded a Barcelona bar known as Els Quatre Gats, which became the nucleus for the city's growing art movement, holding numerous shows and expositions. An early host was a young then unknown Malagueño named Pablo Picasso (1881–1973).

Picasso lived sporadically in Barcelona between the innocence-losing ages of 16 and 24, and the city heavily influenced his early painting. This was the period in which he amassed the raw materials for his Blue Period. In 1904 the then-mature Picasso moved to Paris where he found fame, fortune and Cubism, and went on to become one of the greatest artists of the 20th century.

Miró

Continuing the burst of brilliance was the Barcelona-born experimentalist Joan Miró (1893–1983), best remembered for his use of symbolic figures in primary colours. Declaring he was going to 'assassinate art', Miró wanted nothing to do with the constricting labels of the era, although he has often been called a pioneering surrealist, Dadaist and automatist.

Dalí

Rising on Miró's coattails was the extravagant Catalan surrealist and showman, Salvador Dalí (1904–89), from nearby Figueres, who mixed imaginative painting with posing, attention-seeking and shameless self-promotion. Dalí is hard to avoid anywhere in the world, especially Barcelona.

Public Art

The streets, squares and parks of Barcelona are littered with the signatures of artists past and present, famous and unknown. They range from Modernista sculptors, such as Josep Llimona, to international star sculptors, such as Roy Lichtenstein and Fernando Botero. Picasso and Joan Miró both left lasting reminders in the city.

Since the return of democracy in the late 1970s, the town hall has not been shy about encouraging the placement of sometimes grandiose and often incomprehensible contemporary works in the city's public spaces. Reactions range from admiration to perplexity.

Justly proud of its rich street-art heritage, the council has created an extensive archive of it all on the internet at www.bcn.cat (click on Art Públic). The site is rich in description of hundreds of items scattered across the city, and includes commentary on the history of the city through its street art. You can search particular items by district, period and key word.

The best thing about art in the streets is that it is open to all comers.

Art goes Informal

Picasso, Miró and Dalí were hard acts to follow. Few envied the task of Catalan Antoni Tàpies in reviving the red hot Modernista flame. An early admirer of Miró, Tàpies soon began pursuing his own esoteric path embracing 'art informal' (a Jackson Pollack–like use of spontaneity) and inventing painting that utilised clay, string and even bits of rubbish. In April 2010 King Juan Carlos I elevated Tàpies to the Spanish nobility for his contribution to postwar art with the hereditary title the 1st Marquess of Tàpies. He was arguably Spain's greatest living painter during his lifetime.

Contemporary Art

In the wake of the big three, Barcelona has been a minor cauldron of activity, dominated by the figure of Antoni Tàpies (1923–2012). Early in his career (from the mid-1940s onwards) he seemed keen on self-portraits, but also experimented collage using all sorts of material wood to rice.

A poet, artist and man Joan Brossa (1921–98 beacon in Barcelona.

lithographs and other artworks in which letters generally figure, along with all sorts of objects, make his world accessible to those who can't read his Catalan poetry.

Joan Hernández Pijuan (1931–2005), one of Barcelona's most important 20th-century abstract painters, produced work concentrating on natural shapes and figures, often using neutral colours on different surfaces.

Jaume Plensa (b 1955) is possibly Spain's best contemporary sculptor. His work ranges from sketches, through sculpture, to video and other installations that have been shown around the world.

Susana Solano (b 1946), one of Barcelona's best painters and sculptors, also works with video installations, collages and jewellery.

The Best...
Places to See Modern Art

1 Museu Picasso (p92)

2 Fundació Joan Miró (p167)

3 Fundació Antoni Tàpies (p135)

4 MACBA (p81)

An FC Barcelona fan

JEAN-PIERRE LESCOURRET/GETTY IMAGES

To understand a country – any country – you must first decipher its sporting rituals. In Barcelona that means football. Challenging the cathedral as the city's primary place of worship is Camp Nou, home of FC Barcelona – football club, international brand and fervent bastion of Catalan identity. Its blue-and-red stripes can be seen on everyone from football-mad Thai schoolkids to goat herders in the African bush.

A Cultural Force

The story starts on 29 November 1899, when Swiss Hans Gamper founded FC Barcelona, four years after English residents had first played the game here. His choice of club colours – the blue and maroon of his home town Winterthur – has stuck. By 1910 FC Barcelona was the premier club in a rapidly growing league and had picked up its first Spanish Cup. When Spain's La Liga was founded in 1929, Barcelona ran away with the first title, though its playing record became patchier as the decades wore on and the Franco regime suppressed all manifestations of Catalan-ness.

FC Barça's reemergence as a footbal and cultural force coincided with th of Franco and an influx of foreigr starting with Dutch midfield ? Cruyff in 1973. More legen

many a Catalan Romanesque church and, again, the semicircle tops all its openings. At the back of the church was added a semicylindrical apse. With time, builders became more ambitious and raised grander buildings; some churches were blessed with triple and even quintuple apses. Doorways might be adorned with a series of arches within arches, and the occasional item of stone and wooden statuary was added to enliven things.

Monastery cloisters were often of great elegance. Double sets of columns seem to parade around the perimeter of the courtyards, topped by capitals with increasingly rich adornment representative of biblical stories or other religious imagery.

The comparative lack of sculptural ornament on the walls and ceiling also needs to be understood in light of the fact that church interiors were frequently covered in brightly colored frescoes, while the altars might be surrounded by wood panels, also richly painted with images of Christ, the Apostles, and religious episodes. Most of that has disappeared, but a visit to Barcelona's Museu Nacional d'Art de Catalunya (see pp. 186–190) is a polychromatic eye-opener.

In Barcelona, examples of the Romanesque style are few (seek out in particular Església de Sant Pau del Camp; see p. 98). Those with a hunger for it can sate themselves in northern Catalonia, notably in the Pyrenees—although largely beyond the scope of this book, you'll find mention of one worthy exception, Cardona (see p. 238).

Close to the hearts of Barcelonans, Santa Maria del Mar in La Ribera is also one of the finest examples of austere Catalan Gothic.

Gothic Heights: The building of a Mediterranean trading empire brought enormous wealth to Barcelona in the 13th and 14th centuries, although the latter was marked also by several serious reverses, not the least of them being repeated waves of the bubonic plague. It was, however, a boom time, reflected in an explosion of new and ambitious building. Increasingly sophisticated techniques gave rise to what is now termed Gothic construction.

These methods were first developed in France and then spread to the rest of Europe. Medieval engineers perfected load-bearing and weight-distribution techniques, and the greater use of pillars and arches and buttresses and ribbed vaulting in the ceiling resulted in far loftier buildings than ever before.

In religious construction engineers aimed high and churches seemed to soar heavenward. They were designed to leave their visitors awestruck; even today one's eyes are inevitably drawn upward. Huge rose windows of stained glass, assisted by ranks of narrow windows with pointed arches along the aisles, filled the immense spaces with filtered daylight. There was a marked tendency to overwhelm with ornament. Inside and out, churches were covered with sculptural whimsy. In the great cathedrals the volume of adornment matched their dizzying height.

> Medieval engineers perfected load-bearing and weight-distribution techniques, and the greater use of pillars and arches and buttresses and ribbed vaulting in the ceiling resulted in far loftier buildings than ever before.

In Barcelona, Catalans applied their own spin to Gothic. Although there are exceptions, Catalan Gothic is characterized by breadth and sobriety. The extraordinary Església de Santa Maria del Mar is virtually as wide as it is high, creating a generous sense of volume that is often lacking in the classic Gothic churches farther north. And, like most other Gothic buildings in Barcelona, it is only sparingly decorated; bare surfaces predominate inside and out. Studying its western entrance is one way of comprehending what sets apart the Catalan version of Gothic. Aside from the entrance, the facade is virtually bereft of decoration, and instead of a forest of densely decorated pinnacles, all that rises above it are two austere, octagonal bell towers. Another fine example is the mass of Santa Maria del Pi, its facade broken only by its enormous rose window. In Barcelona, the main cathedral does not follow the local norm, but its facade was added in the 19th century. The great Cistercian monasteries outside Barcelona (see pp. 210–215) were also more inspired by French models and contrast greatly with their Catalan Gothic counterparts.

One key characteristic to emerge from the importance attached by Catalan builders to breadth is the development of the wide, flat arch, a common feature of many Gothic structures in Barcelona. Where designers opted for rounder arches, they still seem to have been determined to stretch them to the limit—the 48-foot-wide (15 m) arches in the Saló del Tinell, for instance, are among the largest ever built without reinforcement. Gothic private mansions, albeit often with baroque modifications, still grace the old city, too, particularly along Carrer de Montcada in La Ribera (see p. 129).

The city's energetic spurt of monumental building was largely over by the end of the 14th century, although the Palau de la Generalitat was a later addition, built under the guidance of Marc Safont (active in the 15th century).

The scaly, fishlike appearance of Gaudí's Casa Batlló (finished 1906) is perhaps the most eccentric product of this modernista genius.

Baroque: The Renaissance made little impact on Barcelona's architecture, which remained rooted in Gothic tradition long after it had been consigned to the past in other parts of Europe. The arrival of the more boisterous baroque period in the latter stages of the 17th century had more of an effect. A handful of churches (such as Església de la Mercè and Església de Sant Felip Neri) were built in a comparatively sober version of the style, which had sprung out of the Renaissance in Italy. Several other buildings, including some of the Gothic mansions on Carrer de Montcada, were the subject of baroque modifications. Apart from its clear roots in classicism, the style is dominated by use of curves; round, porthole-style windows are one easily noticeable element.

Modernisme (Art Nouveau): Barcelona's next moment of architectural greatness came toward the end of the 19th century. The city's population was exploding, the property market was booming, and the wealthy business class was flush.

In this optimistic climate, the local version of art nouveau flourished from the 1880s until about 1910, then tapered off into the 1920s. In part influenced by Japanese painting, art nouveau sought to emulate nature in architecture, painting, and the decorative arts, insomuch as it represented a rejection of straitlaced and straight-lined building—especially the imitation of classical models. In Barcelona, the movement came to be called modernisme, and its protagonists were a broad mix of designers with a still wider spectrum of interpretations of what this new "freedom" meant.

> **Barcelona's modernista architects helped revive the nearly extinct figure of the artisan.**

While the inspiration in nature and its harmonious forms remained a constant, modernisme's leading exponents also sought their muses in the past—not in the classical lines of Greece or Rome, but in the rich heritage of Spain and its Gothic and Islamic building cultures. Drinking at the fount of this knowledge, modernista architects felt no compunction about adapting what they learned.

They never slavishly aped any one style or period but rather sought to create new expression through a dynamic mix of old and new, using raw materials until then largely disdained, such as unclad brick and wrought iron. Barcelona's modernista architects helped revive the nearly extinct figure of the artisan. This is especially apparent in the "handmade" decoration, and sometimes construction, of their buildings. The relatively new building materials of steel and iron were exploited to the full: as frames on which to hang walls and in decoration. Glass and ceramic tiles also played a key role, both used in ways that reflected past glories but in abruptly novel styles. Architects fostered the old skills of the craftsmen, whose knowledge had been handed down from generation to generation, starting with the medieval guilds. Of all these tradesmen, sculptor Eusebi Arnau (1864–1934) was one of the most outstanding. He left his mark in the Hospital de la Santa Creu i Sant Pau (see p. 163), the Palau de la Música Catalana (see pp. 120–121), and many others.

The modernistas got an enthusiastic response from Barcelona's moneyed families, and many splendid results, although not to everyone's taste then or now, can still be seen dotted about the city. These buildings are especially prominent in L'Eixample (the Extension), the new grid-plan part of town developed outside the former city walls in the second half of the 19th century.

(continued on p. 46)

Festes de la Mercè & Other Barcelona Festivals

Crowds jostle in front of the cathedral waiting, as it were, for all hell to break loose. Around 9 p.m., a pyromaniac's dream evening begins as towering, fire-spitting dragons, squat and equally scintillating monsters, and band after band of demons armed to the teeth with high-caliber fireworks launch themselves onto the onlookers in an unnerving spectacle of hellfire and noise.

During Barcelona's biggest festival, the Festes de la Mercè, wild characters throw themselves into the pyrotechnic madness of the *correfoc*, or fire-running.

The braver (or more foolhardy) tempt fate, challenging the bursts of flame in what is known as the ***correfoc,*** fire-running. The parade makes its way through the Gates of Hell on Via Laietana and then heads to the waterfront, where it reaches its culmination.

The correfoc, a distinctly Catalan festive activity, is one of the climactic points in Barcelona's biggest yearly festival, the September **Festes de la Mercè,** a four-day feast of fun to see off the summer.

Held in honor of one of the city's co-patrons, Nostra Senyora de la Mercè (Our Lady of Mercy), this is a perfect opportunity to see some of the classic elements of a Catalan *festa major,* which just about every town celebrates once a year. Among the more colorful sets of characters are the *gegants* (giants) and *capgrossos* (big heads). On one afternoon of the festivities a grand parade of gegants, striding by in stately pairs, such as a Moorish prince and Christian princess, takes place along La Rambla. They are accompanied by a merry band of impish capgrossos, marching bands, traditional dance groups, horsemen, and many others. The Festes de la Mercè also provides a fine opportunity to see *castellers*, human castle-builders, in action (see pp. 82–83). All over the city you can see musical performances, from folk to rock, classical to electronic. The floodlit cathedral makes for a dramatic stage backdrop. And most of it is free. Many museums hold "Open Doors," and fireworks illuminate the night skies.

More Festivals

The Mercè is the biggest of Barcelona's bashes, but the calendar is full of festive opportunities. What Christmas Day is to children in northern European countries and elsewhere, **El Dia dels Reis** (Three Kings' Day, or Epiphany) is to Catalan children, when they receive gifts and have inordinate amounts of attention lavished on them. On January 5, the eve of the holiday, Barcelona's kids are treated to the **Cavalcada dels Reis** (Kings Parade). The Three Kings (aka the Three Wise Men) land at Moll de la Fusta in Port Vell (see pp. 105–109) and parade around the center of town, much to the delight of young onlookers, especially if they manage to catch some of the candy hurled into the crowd.

A couple of weeks later, the feast day of St. Anthony, patron saint of domestic animals, is marked by the **Festes dels Tres Tombs** (Festival of the Three Circuits). Horseback riders and mule-driven carriages meander around a circuit in the Raval area, including Ronda de Sant Antoni, named after the saint.

Barcelona's other patron, Santa Eulàlia, gets her turn for several days around February 12 in a mini-version of the Mercè. **Carnestoltes** (Carnival) is a fun-filled week of parades,

EXPERIENCE: Rock in Barcelona

Music fans and lovers of mega-concerts regularly descend on Barcelona for one of a growing number of music events. Locals and visitors are thrown together in a joyous, musical mix for these events, which generally last two to four days.

The season kicks off in a big way with **Primavera Sound** (*primaverasound.com*), a three-day festival featuring everything from rock bands to DJ stars. The list of performers can be overwhelming, and the crowds in waterside Parc del Fòrum are equally impressive.

For more than twenty years, Barcelona has hosted one of Europe's biggest electronic music get-togethers. **Sónar** (*sonar.es*) is held over three days during mid-June, in the Gran Via fairgrounds on the road between the airport and central Barcelona. This huge celebration sees acts from around the world converging on the city to showcase their creativity. Among the hits of 2014 were Yelle, Massive Attack, and Ben Frost.

A relatively new festival in the lineup is **Cruïlla Barcelona** (*cruillabarcelona .com*), held over two days in July in Parc del Fòrum. In the past it has attracted a broad range of artists from Snoop Dogg to Rufus Wainwright and Morcheeba. The next major event is **BAM** (Barcelona Acció Musical; *bcn.cat/bam*), a series of concerts, mostly free and occasionally including big-name international artists, held around town during the city's Festes de la Mercè in September.

During the Festa Major de Gràcia, neighborhoods compete for the best-dressed street.

music, and parties, marking the end of winter but also the onset of Lent, traditionally a period of fasting and sobriety in the run-up to Easter.

If the innocent fun of Barcelona's Carnival is too slow for your liking, head down to Sitges (see pp. 216–218) for what is basically a wild street party.

Easter itself is not celebrated with the same passion as in some other parts of Spain. If you do want to see a traditional Spanish Easter procession, with heavy floats bearing images of the Virgin Mary; solemn members of religious confraternities dressed in flowing *sotanas* and *capirotes* (those long pointy hats) and bearing staffs; and penitent barefoot

Festival Practicalities

First of all, be sure to have ample amounts of *cava* on hand. Cava is a Catalonian sparkling white wine, and it might as well be on tap during the festivals, considering how many people are drinking it and the vast quantities consumed.

For this and other reasons, the worst decision you could make is to try to drive while festival-going. Even if the masses of revelers don't deter you, just remember the *correfoc* (fire-running). And while it sounds odd, try to wear closed-toe shoes. When you see the sparkling fields of broken bottles, you'll understand.

Plan to stop by the tourist information office below Plaça de Catalunya, or the Palau de la Virreina information center (*La Rambla 99*), where you can pick up festival schedules and literature so you don't miss a beat.

---

women dressed in black and dragging crosses and chains wrapped around their ankles, head for Església de Sant Agustí in El Raval on Good Friday afternoon.

Sant Jordi (St. George) the dragon-slayer is Catalonia's patron saint, and his feast day is celebrated on April 23 in very gentle style. Men traditionally give women a red rose while women present men with books. Book and flower stalls pop up all over the city, and Catalan publishers profit from the occasion to launch new titles.

Another big festival with fire in its blood belongs to yet another saint, **Sant Joan** (St. John the Baptist). His feast day, June 24, is a public holiday that most locals use to sleep off the night before, marked by bonfires and fireworks all over town (beware of children throwing firecrackers about the place!). Locals munch on *coca de Sant Joan,* a sweetish pastry, drink, and generally make merry on a night that is also commonly known as La Nit de Foc (Fire Night).

As the full heat of summer breaks over the city, some of its *barris* (quarters) put on their party clothes. By far the busiest shindig is the **Festa Major de Gràcia.** Around August 15 the locals literally dress up a dozen or so of its narrow streets to different themes—the best-dressed street gets a big municipal pat on the back. Meantime, people set up trestle tables in the streets and load them up to groaning point with food and drink. Every night the area heaves to the joyous din of competing bands of various descriptions.

No sooner has Gràcia packed everything away and cleaned up the streets than another district takes up the baton. The **Festa Major de Sants,** which kicks off around August 24, depending when the weekend falls, is not as big an event as its Gràcia counterpart but gets busy enough. Then follows the **Festa Major de la Barceloneta** in early October and the **Festa Major de les Corts** shortly after.

The Festes de la Mercè's *capgrossos* (big heads)

The top names in modernista architecture were to some extent Catalan nationalists. Riding on a wave of renewed popular interest and sentiment in all things Catalan, the Renaixença, the modernista architects frequently saw their projects as a means of giving vital expression to a renewed Catalan identity.

Towering above them all was the (some would claim divinely) inspired Antoni Gaudí (1852–1926), the figure who has come to symbolize modernisme. More than any of his peers, this eccentric figure went out on a limb in the pursuit of the style's ideals. If you had to summarize his credo, it would be "There are no straight lines in nature." None of Gaudí's rivals displayed his technical daring. He alone created pillars that lean with the sinewy power of ancient tree trunks, undulating floors, ceramic ceilings, serpentine benches, and chimney pots that look like *Star Wars* characters on acid.

Although he had projects beyond Barcelona and even a handful outside Catalonia, the bulk of Gaudí's handiwork is on display in this city. Important examples include the Palau Güell (see pp. 92–93), La Pedrera (see pp. 145–151), Casa Batlló (see pp. 142–143), Park Güell (see pp. 166–167), and Barcelona's claim to fame, the incomplete Sagrada Família church (see pp. 158–162). Palau Güell was one of his earliest commissions and is a fine introduction. Although in many respects a solemn edifice, it is nevertheless loaded with innovation. The gentle parabolic arch is a key Gaudí item, and he is faithful to modernisme in his expansive use of bare brick and wrought iron. The former has its roots in Islamic Spain. The Muslims built mostly in brick, and as the Christians reconquered the peninsula, Mudéjar (Muslims living in Christian territory) tradesmen passed on this tradition.

La Pedrera, Casa Batlló, and Park Güell are all marvelously playful gems, executed for three different masters. The fantastical rooftop of La Pedrera has to be seen to be believed, and each of the apartments below is a singular dream home. Living in Casa Batlló wouldn't be too bad either, but the exterior, which has the appearance of a scaly dragon, is so bizarre that even after years of living in Barcelona one cannot help but regard it with admiring bemusement. Park Güell, one of Gaudí's last commissions, was supposed to be a select little suburb for the well-to-do, but funding and interest ran out. Its ceramic-lined stairways, decorated with strange beasts, lead you into a fairy-tale world of design fantasy.

That tale ends with the Temple Expiatori de la Sagrada Família (Expiatory Temple of the Holy Family). Conceived originally as a pseudo-Gothic offering from Barcelona's pious citizens to a God thought to be increasingly displeased with the not-so-faithful, it soon turned into the century's most ambitious art-architecture project. Gaudí took over the job two years after it was launched in 1882.

He stuck with the Gothic theme insofar as he sought inspiration for the church in the grandeur of the past. Not content merely to create a neo-Gothic church, he applied

Discount Cards

ArTicket *(articketbcn.org)* **gives you admission to six important art centers for €30 and is valid for three months. The galleries are the Museu Picasso, Museu Nacional d'Art de Catalunya (MNAC), Museu d'Art Contemporani de Barcelona (MACBA), Fundació Antoni Tàpies, Centre de Cultura Contemporània de Barcelona (CCCB), and Fundació Joan Miró. The Arqueo-Ticket** *(€13)* **gives entry to the Museu Marítim, Museu d'Història de la Ciutat, Museu d'Arqueologia de Catalunya, Museu Egipci, and the Born Centre Cultural. You can get both at tourist offices and at some of the museums.**

The sleek white lines of the MACBA modern art museum helped breathe new life into the traditionally neglected district of El Raval.

his belief that architecture should follow nature's lines and designed a structure of extraordinary harmony and lightness. When he was run over by a tram in 1926, he was barely a quarter of the way through. Amid much controversy, work continued slowly, but the end is now in sight.

But Gaudí was not alone. What is perhaps most striking is that modernisme was so densely rich with genius. At least two of Gaudí's contemporaries require mention: Lluís Domènech i Montaner (1850–1923) and Josep Puig i Cadafalch (1867–1956).

The most cursory examination of a few key creations by these two and Gaudí reveals just how broadly were interpreted the "rules" of modernisme. A visit to Domènech i Montaner's Hospital de la Santa Creu i Sant Pau (see p. 163) and Puig i Cadafalch's Casa Amatller (see p. 143) is instructive. The former combines a microcosm of urban planning and joyous decoration (in ceramic tiles) with Gothic nostalgia. The latter is a rectilinear curve ball—straight off an Amsterdam canal with its squared-off gables, and just as full of colorful fantasy as its more outlandish neighbor, Casa Batlló. Domènech i Montaner's Palau de la Música Catalana (see pp. 120–121) is a must-see landmark, a lavish celebration of the decorative arts in a way Gaudí buildings never could be.

To the Present: After the exuberance of modernisme, anything else was bound to seem a little staid. The uncertain years between the World Wars and the long night of the Franco years put the brakes on inventive building. With the advent of democracy and the hosting of the 1992 Olympics, a new creative wave began. Via an ambitious urban renovation program, leading international and local architects have changed the face of the city. The Museu d'Art Contemporani de Barcelona, designed by Richard Meier, and the Teatre Nacional de Catalunya (see p. 170), by local architect Ricard Bofill, are two striking examples, along with the work of Sir Norman Foster (Torre de Collserola; see p. 182) and Arata Isozaki (Palau Sant Jordi; see p. 195). Since the 1990s the momentum has continued with Jean Nouvel's cucumber-shaped Torre Agbar (see p. 169) and Herzog & de Meuron's triangular Edifici Fòrum (see p. 116), which in theory, finance willing, will be joined by a Frank Gehry complex for the future high-speed train station in La Sagrera District. Gehry had already contributed his waterfront "Peix" (see p. 116).

On the road between the airport and downtown, Toyo Ito has built the Porta Fira towers at the city's new trade fairgrounds, and Richard Rogers has reinvigorated the former bullring, Las Arenas, now a shopping mall. Bofill's sail-shaped hotel tower has

"I Am the Light of the World," proclaims Christ in this fine Romanesque fresco in the Museu Nacional d'Art de Catalunya.

transformed the waterfront, while local star Enric Miralles (1955–2000) created the dazzling Mercat de Santa Caterina (see p. 136). The latest showcase for star architects is the 22@ business district in the former industrial Poble Nou area (see pp. 168–169).

Painting & Sculpture

It is probably fair to say that, while much art of high quality was produced in Barcelona through the centuries, greatness has only been associated with the city in modern times. Three very different figures with some connection to Barcelona (although only one born and bred) are the 20th-century stars that shine over an otherwise unexceptional panorama.

> **Romanesque painting nearly always dealt with religious subjects and always in a seemingly childlike fashion.**

Middle Ages: The Romanesque churches littering the northern Catalan countryside once boasted brightly colored frescoes that have now largely disappeared. Some of the most remarkable survivors are on display in Barcelona's Museu Nacional d'Art de Catalunya (see pp. 186–190).

Romanesque painting nearly always dealt with religious subjects and always in a seemingly childlike fashion. To understand the predilection for such a naïve style, one has to travel into the early medieval European mind. Mostly illiterate, brutish, and short-lived, the God-fearing Europeans got their religious education through pictures; the medium was less important than the message.

Imagery of Christianity's key figures (Christ, the Virgin, the Evangelists, the Apostles, and the saints) were repeated over and over, accompanied by biblical episodes (mostly from the New Testament). Their unreal two-dimensionality served to underline the idea that such divine beings were on a level far removed from that of common mortals.

The counterpoints to the murals were wooden sculptures, most often of the Crucifixion of Christ or the Virgin Mary with the Christ Child on her lap. Although you can rarely see it now, they were brightly painted. In stone, the most exquisite work was done on the sarcophaguses of eminent corpses. Some remarkable works, especially later in the Gothic period, were produced in other materials such as alabaster.

Initially artists (regarded as skilled tradesmen) remained anonymous, although certain works are now associated with particular workshops. As Romanesque gave way to Gothic in the 13th and 14th centuries, these artisans began to sign their works.

The passage from Romanesque is sometimes barely perceptible to the untrained eye: The key is the growing humanity and thematic suppleness of Gothic works. More lifelike figures with human expression and movement appear, and an increasing variety of themes, many secular in nature (like the conquests of Jaume I), are illustrated. What's more, frescoes began to give way to wooden panels and other longer-lasting bases.

Among the most important Catalan artists of the Gothic period were Ferrer Bassa (circa 1290–1348), Bernat Martorell (died 1452), and Jaume Huguet (1415–1492). A few of their works can be seen in city collections, notably the prized Bassa murals in the Monestir de Santa Maria de Pedralbes (see pp. 174–176).

Lackluster Centuries: Largely due to Barcelona's marginalization, little of greatness was achieved between the 15th and early 20th centuries. By the middle of the 19th, realism was all the rage but produced pedestrian work. Modernisme closed the century with a dreamy, whimsical movement from which little more than talented dilettantes emerged, among them Ramón Casas (1866–1932) and Santiago Rusiñol (1861–1931). At the forefront of the bohemian scene in early 1900s Barcelona, neither was destined for immortality. A new movement, *noucentisme*, came as a conservative reaction to the perceived excesses of modernisme and preached a return to classic forms and subjects. It soon fragmented and some of its senior protagonists—Joaquim Sunyer (1874–1956) and Isidre Nonell (1876–1911)—set off in other directions and were influenced by France's Paul Cézanne.

EXPERIENCE: See Barcelona in the Movies

Lights! Camera! Barcelona! Since the mid-1990s, the city has emerged as an exciting new movie star in its own right. Woody Allen's decision to shoot a film here in 2007 was like manna from heaven for the Barcelona Film Commission (*bcncatfilm commission.com*).

Spain's quirky star director, Pedro Almodóvar, really opened the way by setting his 1999 Oscar-winning *Todo Sobre Mi Madre (All About My Mother)* here. In typically near-hysterical style, Almodóvar weaves a complex web of relations between several women (and a couple of transsexuals). Not all locations are easily recognizable (e.g., the area near Camp Nou where transsexual prostitutes operate), and often we see them at night (as with La Sagrada Família). Cédric Klapisch's *L'Auberge Espagnole (The Spanish Apartment)*, shot in 2001, depicts the life of international students, with scenes at La Rambla, La Sagrada Família, Park Güell, and more. Tom Tykwer's *Perfume: The Story of a Murderer* (2006), based on Patrick Süsskind's novel *Perfume* and starring Ben Wishaw as the psychopathic Jean-Baptiste Grenouille, is rich in scenes around the old town, Parc del Laberint d'Horta, and El Poble Espanyol, where crowd scenes were shot. Producers had to scour the city in suntanned midsummer in search of suitably pale extras!

Woody Allen left the city agog as he, Scarlett Johansson, Penelope Cruz, and Javier Bardem shot Allen's vision of Barcelona, *Vicky Cristina Barcelona* (2008), in 2007. Bardem came back again to shoot *The Gunman* (2014) with fellow Hollywood hunks Idris Elba and Sean Penn.

For plenty of location detail on these and other movies, check out *barcelona movie.com* and put together your own movie-set walking tours.

Picasso and pals hang out on Carrer de la Mercè, where the artist lived for a while.

Pablo Picasso: Lapping up the tavern lifestyle of the modernistas was young Pablo Ruiz Picasso (1881–1973). Born in Málaga, he spent his formative years in Barcelona before moving to Paris in his early 20s. He later settled there and last visited Barcelona in 1934 (see pp. 122–123).

"Guernica" portrays the 1937 German bombing of the Basque town Gernika . . . Today it hangs in Madrid's Museo Nacional Centro de Arte Reina Sofía.

By the time Picasso moved to France, he had begun a seemingly inexorable advance from one artistic phase to the next that would continue through to his final days. He started with his Blue and then Pink (or Rose) periods, in which those colors shaded and informed all his output. The former tended to the melancholy, while the Pink Period had a lighter air.

With "Les Demoiselles d'Avignon" (1907), inspired by the prostitutes of the street Avinyó in Barcelona, Picasso broke with tradition, introducing a deformed, even shattered perspective that would spill over into cubism. In the 1920s he flirted with surrealism. One of his best known works, "Guernica," portrays the 1937 German bombing of the Basque town Gernika during the Spanish Civil War. Today it hangs in Madrid's Museo Nacional Centro de Arte Reina Sofía.

In 1957 Picasso concentrated on a pair of projects. The more intriguing is his series of studies of "Las Meninas" by Diego Velázquez (1599–1660). The other is a more lighthearted series called "Pichones" (Pigeons). Both works can be seen in the Museu Picasso (see pp. 125–129). Also a gifted sculptor, ceramicist, and graphic designer, Picasso kept pumping out work until his death.

Joan Miró: Born and raised in central Barcelona, Joan Miró (1893–1983) was an altogether different character. Unsure about his talent, Miró got off to a slow start. Although he, too, spent time in Paris, he summered on the Catalan coast, turning out paintings that ranged from the seemingly realist to the naïve. Then, in the early 1930s, he proclaimed that "painting must be murdered" and turned to collage, lithography, and other media.

During World War II, Miró turned to the themes for which he is best known: women, birds (the link between earth and the heavens), and stars (imagination). His arrangement of distinct lines and shapes in primary colors depicts these and other figures in their essence. Miró was also a sculptor and ceramicist and left several public works scattered about Barcelona. For more, see pp. 196–198.

Salvador Dalí: Completing the grand trio is Salvador Dalí i Domènech (1904–1989), who was born and died in Figueres (see pp. 230–233) in northern Catalonia and barely deigned to visit Barcelona. This larger-than-life figure and self-promoting showman with the extravagant moustache was a rapid-fire genius, whipping off his works with disconcerting speed. His nightmare landscapes and hallucinatory scenes reveal, if nothing else, a tormented mind, although they form only a part of a greatly varied opus.

As obsessed with his lifelong companion, Gala, as he was with his art, Salvador Dalí sometimes managed to combine the two.

Contemporary Art: Until his death, Antoni Tàpies (1923–2012) was Spain's best known contemporary artist. The one constant feature in his work is the use of unlikely materials in three-dimensional collage effects. His grand works may be loaded with anything from wood and sand to rice, and he achieved a texture so heavy that the observer is tempted to reach out and touch his "canvases." His foundation (see p. 144) gives an insight into his work.

The best place to get your finger on the pulse of what is going on in the art scene today is to visit the MACBA contemporary art museum (see pp. 96–97). A short list of the more established local figures includes Susana Solano (1946–), Jaume Plensa (1955–), Perejuame (1957–), and Jordi Colomer (1962–). ■

Catalan native Joan Miró poses at one of his numerous one-man shows (1966).

Food & Wine

Led by that indefatigable kitchen wizard Ferran Adrià and a merry band of fearless culinary innovators (like Sergi Arola, Carles Abellán, and the Roca brothers), Catalonia has spearheaded a Spanish cooking revival that has taken the world by storm. Even the French have doffed their toques to the *nueva cocina española*.

Catalan cuisine has, however, a long tradition that warrants exploration. And an increasingly multicultural Barcelona is peppered with establishments offering everything from Nepalese to Japanese. As long ago as the 13th century, Catalans were writing recipe books, wine guides, and manuals on good table manners. The most venerated tome on the subject of fine eating was Robert de Nola's *Llibre del Coc* (15th century), much of which still holds good.

Barcelona's markets have long been awash with variety. The Greeks and Romans brought the fundamentals: wheat, olives (and hence the oil), wine, and salted fish. Muslims from North Africa introduced the eggplant, artichoke, red pepper, and various spices. It's conceivable that they introduced rice and pasta to the Iberian Peninsula, too. Extension of the Catalan merchant empire from the mid-13th century to the 15th century opened markets and palates to new taste sensations from around the Mediterranean, while discovery of the Americas added still more previously unknown basics such as potatoes, tomatoes, and corn. All of these elements have long been absorbed into Catalan traditions.

> **Catalan cooking is defined by geography—seafood along the coast, and meat dishes, stews, and broths in the Pyrenees.**

Catalan cooking is defined by geography—seafood along the coast, and meat dishes, stews, and broths in the Pyrenees. The staples (wheat, olives, and wine) remain inviolate, but apart from these, Catalan chefs have no trouble mixing and matching. One of the cornerstones of even the simplest Catalan cooking is *mar i muntanya* (surf and turf), in which meat and seafood are cheerfully thrown together—a common dish is the surprisingly good *mandonguilles amb sípia* (meatballs with cuttlefish). Catalans like to mix fruit and nuts with their fish and meat dishes, too. Fish is frequently prepared with almonds, and you may be offered chicken with pears or apricots, or duck with figs.

Sauces are an important part of many Catalan dishes. Standards include *allioli* (a pounded garlic and olive oil mix resembling mayonnaise), which frequently accompanies rice and noodle or meat dishes; *romesco* (almond, tomato, garlic, vinegar, and olive oil, also used as salad dressing); *sofregit* (a fried onion, tomato, and garlic mix); and *samfaina,* which is basically sofregit with eggplant and red pepper thrown in.

Other traditions run deep. Catalans love their sausages *(botifarra)* and mushrooms *(bolets).* In the autumn the tasty *rovellons* are particularly sought after. The night before All Saints' Day (November 1) is Halloween to some, but in Barcelona it is the

Hanging hams and casks of aging wines are age-old traditions in Catalonia; tapas have now also become a joyous mainstay of many a Barcelona mealtime.

which houses the exquisite alabaster sarcophagus of Santa Eulàlia, co-patron saint of Barcelona. The grim story of her gruesome martyrdom, which supposedly took place in pre-Christian Barcelona in the early fourth century, is told in the panels of the sarcophagus. According to one study, a Pisan sculptor, Lupo di Francesco, did the work around 1327.

Above the crypt, the **altar** at the center of the presbytery rests on two sturdy Visigothic capitals preserved from the original church. Behind it is the 14th-century alabaster *catedra*, the seat that symbolizes the spiritual

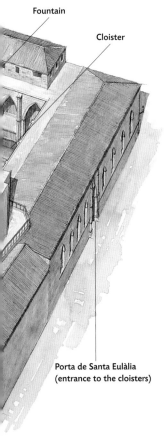

Fountain

Cloister

Porta de Santa Eulàlia (entrance to the cloisters)

The faithful keep candles burning in front of the Catedral's many chapels.

sovereignty of the bishop and the loyalty of the faithful to the successors of St. Peter. It is from this that the word *cathedral* derives.

Along with the presbytery, the **apse** is the oldest part of the church. Of its ten chapels, the most interesting is the one dedicated to San Benito (third around from the exit to the cloister). It contains the restored series of panels known as the **Transfiguració** (Transfiguration) by Bernat Martorell (died 1452), one of the most outstanding Catalan artists of his time. The panels depict various episodes in the life of Christ.

In the **Capella de les Animes del Purgatori** (Souls of Purgatory Chapel), in the northeast transept, an elevator takes you to the **roof** of the cathedral (purchase tickets by the northeast transept). Walkways allow you to wander across the top of the church and enjoy the splendid views over central Barcelona. Watch out for seagulls and remember to take an umbrella if it's raining. From here a claustrophobic stairwell climbs up inside the main tower.

Back down inside the church, go out to have a look at the **Porta de Sant Iu,** an early example of the *ogive* (pointed) arch in Catalan Gothic. Plaques in the wall confirm that construction of the Gothic cathedral began in 1298. Returning inside the church, cross the transept toward the cloister. Before heading out, look for the sarcophaguses of Count Ramon Berenguer I and his wife suspended from the wall to the left. Virtually next door is the entrance to the modest **sacristy.** Behind it is the church's treasury, which unfortunately is not open to the public.

The Cloister

The leafy cloister is a peaceful haven, entered via a doorway that came from the Romanesque cathedral (evident when viewed from the cloister). During the procession of Corpus Cristi (on the ninth Sunday after Easter Sunday), one of the cloister fountains is adorned with flowers, and an empty eggshell (supposedly representative of the holy host) is set to dance about on the jet of water. This *ou com balla* (dancing egg) has been a part of Barcelona's tradition since at least the 18th century. The 13 geese in residence represent (according to local lore) the age of the martyr Santa Eulàlia and act as cackling versions of watchdogs when all is shuttered at night.

Several chapels of interest line the cloister. The second on your left after you exit the cathedral is dedicated to the Verge de la Llum (Our Lady of Light), the patron of electricity and plumbing. Mass is held in the chapel on the first Saturday of the month. Directly ahead

Geese make fine watchdogs for the Catedral cloister.

of you in the western flank of the cloister is a chapel dedicated to the memory of 930 priests and other members of religious orders killed during the Spanish Civil War (1936–1939). On the northern side is the *sala capitular* (chapter house), which houses a shop and, in a hall next door, a modest art collection of mostly religious

the tranquility of its 15th-century courtyard. Inside the glass doors you can look at what remains of the fourth-century B.C. Roman wall against which the medieval building was constructed.

Palau Episcopal, on Carrer del Bisbe Irurita, also has a fine courtyard. You may be able to take a look inside if its great gates happen to be open.

Casa de l'Ardiaca
🕐 Closed from 1 p.m. Sat. & all day Sun

Museu Diocesà
🕐 Closed Sun p.m. & Mon.
💲 $

Top Ten Local Phrases

Si us plau/por favor	Please
Gràcies/gracias	Thank you
Quant és?/¿Cuánto vale?	How much is it?
Parla anglès?/¿Habla inglés?	Do you speak English?
No entenc/No entiendo	I don't understand
Si us plau, parli més a poc a poc/ Por favor, hable más despacio	Please speak more slowly
On és?/¿Dónde está?	Where is?
Em pot ajudar?/¿Me puede ayudar?	Can you help me?
Quina hora és?/¿Qué hora es?	What time is it?
On es troba el cibercafè més a prop?/ ¿Dónde está el cibercafé más cercano?	Where's the nearest Internet café?

paintings and altarpieces. The 11th-century baptismal font by the shop counter is a rare four-leaf-clover pre-Romanesque piece.

The Romanesque **Capella de Santa Llúcia** takes up the north-western corner of the cloister. If you step onto the street and look back, you will see clearly that this was a separate structure absorbed into the Gothic project. The giveaway signs are the simple, low facade and semicircular arches above the doorway and window.

Directly opposite the chapel is **Casa de l'Ardiaca,** or archdea-con's house, which is now used to store the city's historic archives and host occasional exhibitions. Enter and go up the stairs to savor

Across Plaça de la Seu stands **Casa de la Pia Almoina,** once an almshouse and now home of the **Museu Diocesà** (Diocesan Museum). Inside is a comparatively thin but well presented permanent collection of mainly Romanesque and Gothic religious artwork, including altar panels, wooden busts, and processional crosses. Of most interest are the restored murals dating from 1122 on the first floor and an altar panel by Bernat Martorell depicting John the Baptist (from 1420) on the second floor. The Pia Almoina was built within what remained of the old Roman walls and a tower, which the visitor can still appreciate today. ∎

Roman Barcelona Walk

A millennium after the demise of the Romans, the people of Barcelona were still living protected within the walls that testify to their robust imperial legacy. What the Romans called Barcino was a minor city, but enough has survived for us to take a measure of the place.

The Roman necropolis in Plaça Vila de Madrid was uncovered in the 1950s.

Start beyond what was the Roman perimeter at Plaça de la Vila de Madrid, site of a modest **Roman cemetery.** Carrer de la Canuda, which leads east onto Avinguda del Portal de l'Àngel and onto Plaça Nova, may follow the branch road that connected Barcino to the Via Augusta—the imperial road from Rome to Cádiz. Regardless, travelers from the north would have arrived before the city gate on **Plaça Nova ❶**. Not until the third century, though, would the walls have confronted them; previously the Pax Romana had rendered such defenses superfluous.

Two hefty **towers** flank the entrance to Barcino, their lower parts Roman, the upper levels

NOT TO BE MISSED:

Gate and walls on Plaça Nova • Pati Llimona • Temple Romà d'August • Museu d'Història de Barcelona

added and modified over the centuries. Jutting out from the left tower is an incipient arch—a reproduction of one of the two **aqueducts** that once helped slake Barcino's thirst. The most visible stretch of Roman **wall** fronts Plaça Nova; you can also get a close look at the inside when you visit **Casa de l'Ardiaca** (see p. 65).

To get some idea of the dimensions of the Roman town, follow the line of the wall around to the east. You will see the outside of **Casa de la Pia Almoina ❷** (see p. 65), built into the wall. Follow Carrer de la Tapineria southeast and pause in Plaça Ramon Berenguer to see how the medieval buildings of the Plaça del Rei were built on the Roman walls. Continue along Carrer del Sots-Tinent Navarro. To your right are more remains of the original Roman walls exposed recently with the demolition of 19th-century housing that had been built against them.

Duck into Carrer de la Poma d'Or and you emerge onto leafy little Plaça dels Traginers, dominated by the base of another defensive **Roman tower ❸**. Follow Carrer del Correu Vell to Carrer de Regomir and turn right to reach the square of the same name. Just before it is the civic center known as **Pati Llimona ❹** (closed Sun.), in which you can see preserved parts of the southernmost city gate, the Porta de Mar (Sea Gate), more of the wall and recently discovered thermal baths. If you wander up to Carrer del Call (the heart of the former medieval Jewish ghetto) and enter the jewelry shop at No. 5, you can see remnants of the **Western Wall ❺**.

From here turn east again, cross Plaça de Sant Jaume (the northern edge of which may overlap with the site of the ancient forum), and then dogleg your way around Carrer del Paradís. Inside No. 10 stand four proud fluted Corinthian columns of what was the **Temple Romà d'August ❻** (open 10 a.m.– 2 p.m. Mon., 10 a.m.–7 p.m. Tues.– Sun.), which was erected to worship Caesar Augustus.

To complete your Roman tour, visit the **Museu d'Història de**

Barcelona ❼ (see pp. 68–71). Continue north along Carrer del Paradís until you reach the cathedral. Turn right and go straight ahead to Plaça del Rei. Just off the square to the south is the museum entrance. Below ground is an impressive excavated section of the Roman city, including the ruins of houses, shops, wineries, and public baths.

⚞	See also area map p. 59
▶	Plaça de la Vila de Madrid
⬌	1 mile (1.6 km)
🕑	1.5 hours
▶	Museu d'Història de Barcelona

Plaça del Rei

The King's Square was, from the early Middle Ages, home to one of the main residences of the counts of Barcelona and rulers of the Crown of Aragón—the Palau Reial (Royal Palace). Built into the Roman walls, the early structure resembled a fortress, but as the centuries wore on, buildings were raised on all sides of the square.

For centuries the Plaça del Rei (King's Square) and its buildings formed the city residence of the counts of Barcelona.

The bulk of what we see today dates from the 14th and 15th centuries; along with the archaeological remains below the square, it constitutes the fascinating Museu d'Història de Barcelona— a voyage into the first 1,500 years of the city's life in one compact package.

Museu d'Història de Barcelona

Just off Plaça del Rei is the entrance to Casa Padellàs, a 15th-century noble mansion through which you access the Museu d'Història de Barcelona. The elegant courtyard and staircase are typical of high-class Gothic houses. When you explore the Barri Gòtic, peek through doors opening onto similar courtyards.

From the ticket office you pass into a display area dedicated to the ancient history of Barcelona and the surrounding area. A handful of Roman sculptures and household items are accompanied by explanatory plans, maps and an audiovisual presentation.

Excavations: The real fun begins after this point. From the display area, take the elevator down to the excavations: You don't get out at the basement but at "–12" (that's 12 B.C.). From here, an elevated walkway leads right through this underground archaeological treasure chest.

Initially you follow the *intervallum*, the Roman path that separated the wall from the first line of houses (parts of the wall still stand) and allows access to remnants of a fourth-century **tower.** You then enter a small museum space; the model of a patrician Roman house is based on archaeologists' finds showing that there were houses of this magnitude and luxury in the ancient city of Barcino.

Next, wind your way past the remains of laundries and dye shops and a cold-water pool of what was certainly a bigger public bath complex. You soon arrive at part of **Cardo Minor,** one of the city's main cross streets. It is fronted by *tabernae,* or stores, and alongside runs a sewage drain. Then comes a part of town that was dedicated to the production of salted fish and *garum,* a gastronomic delicacy made by pounding fish innards to create a tangy sauce. Prawns, oysters, and

other seafood were sometimes added to enhance the flavor. It sounds ghastly, but for centuries this was the Latin world's favorite sauce. It was stored in vats known as *dolia,* whose eggshell-shaped bases can be seen here.

The walk then takes you past remnants of the early church and contiguous religious buildings dating from the fourth to the seventh centuries. Some may find the area that is dedicated to wine production, with its fermentation vats and grape-crushing rooms, of greater interest.

The final part of the walk takes you along the walls of the seventh-century Visigothic bishop's palace and then up ramps into a pair of high vaulted halls in the Royal Palace containing displays on medieval Barcelona, including a display of 13th-century frescoes.

INSIDER TIP:

Barcelona's architecture takes on a new dimension when illuminated at night. Be sure to give buildings a second look on your way to dinner.

—GREGORY SUTORIUS
National Geographic contributor

You emerge in a hall between the Saló del Tinell and the Capella Reial de Santa Àgata. Head right for the **Saló del Tinell.** It is now occasionally used for temporary exhibitions, so you may be required to pay for a separate ticket. Inaugurated in

Museu d'Història de Barcelona

- Map p. 59
- Carrer del Veguer 2
- 93 256 21 00
- Closed Mon.
- $$
- Metro: Línia 4 (Jaume I)

museuhistoria .bcn.cat

One for the Kids

It is entirely conceivable that children's patience with Roman ruins and grand churches will be limited. One method for preventing implosion might be the promise of a trip to **Port Aventura** *(64 miles/103 km SW of Barcelona, near Tarragona, tel 902 20 22 20 or 977 77 90 90 from outside Spain, portaventura.es, closed Mon.–Fri. Nov.–Easter, $$$$$)*, the Catalan answer to Disneyland. This is one of Europe's biggest amusement park complexes. One of its latest thrills is Shambhala, the highest roller coaster in Europe, and soon it will boast Ferrari Land, the racing car company's first theme park in Europe. Kids will relish the chance to become pirates in Costa Caribe Aquatic Park, part of the same complex. Access is easy by car or train from Barcelona.

1370, the hall is a splendid example of Catalan Gothic. Bereft of the decorative frills so evident in the Catedral, it is a magnificently sober feat of engineering. Seven 48-foot (15 m) arches support the weight of the ceiling and gallery above, backed by buttresses. Those on Plaça del Rei are clearly visible.

The hall was used as a throne room and reception hall for the great and the good when Palau Reial was still a royal palace. After the Crown of Aragón was subsumed into a unified Spain under Ferdinand and Isabella, the hall and indeed the entire palace complex began to lose importance. It is said that the Catholic Monarchs received Columbus in the Saló del Tinell to hear tales of his New World discoveries. By the 16th century, it had been converted for use as a branch of the royal courts. In 1718 the hall and much of the rest of the palace complex was handed over to nuns of the order of Santa Clara. They turned the hall into a chapel and veiled its Gothic splendor in a layer of baroque ornamentation.

During the civil war the nuns were relocated for safety reasons and restorers subsequently removed the baroque overlay. They discovered a set of murals depicting King Jaume I's conquest of Mallorca (see pp. 25–26). Executed around the end of the 13th century, the murals represent a curious cross between Romanesque and Gothic art.

INSIDER TIP:

The best way to take in the majestic facades of the Plaça del Rei is to observe from the stairs of the Palau Reial Major while listening to strolling musicians.

—ANNA BORRÀS
Viajes National Geographic

From the Saló, return to the central hall, from where you enter the **Capella Reial de Santa Àgata.** This palace chapel was begun in 1302, replacing an earlier Romanesque version. It is a single-nave, Gothic construction, simple but impressive with ribbed vaulting and high windows. The impressive *retaule* (altarpiece) is the work of Jaume Huguet and dates from 1465. The central panel depicts the adoration of the child Jesus by the Three Kings while the one above shows the Crucifixion. To the sides, six panels illustrate various episodes in the life of Christ and his mother, Mary. Equally magnificent is the *techumbre* (timber ceiling).

Exit from the hall to Plaça del Rei. In the northwest corner of the square rises the multistory **Mirador del Rei Martí** (King Martin's Lookout), built in 1555— a century and a half after the said

in Barcelona by Madrid. The viceroys never lived here, but for years various police forces used the building as their headquarters. King Philip V later ceded part of the building to Benedictine monks, who were thrown out in 1838. The building then became the seat of the Arxiu de la Corona de Aragò (Archives of the Crown of Aragon) in 1853, restored in 2006 and home to priceless historical documents. Although tacked on to the Palau Reial halfway into the 16th

Palau del Lloctinent

- Map p. 59
- Carrer dels Comtes de Barcelona
- Open 10 a.m.– 7 p.m.
- Metro: Línia 4 (Jaume I)

The Catholic Monarchs supposedly heard Columbus report on his first voyage of discovery beneath the Gothic arches of the Saló del Tinell.

king's death. Martí was the last of the Catalan kings, and it is thought the tower was built partly to replace an older version and partly to commemorate the end of a dynasty.

Palau del Lloctinent

The Mirador (*closed to the public*) connects the Palau Reial to the Palau del Lloctinent, built in 1549 as a residence for the *lloctinents reials* (viceroys) installed

century, the Renaissance building's style reflects its Gothic surroundings. You can enter from Plaça del Rei and Carrer dels Comtes de Barcelona. Have a look upward from the staircase to the timber *artesonado,* a sculpted ceiling carried out in the 16th century by Antoni Carbonell. Exhibitions are often held on aspects of Catalan history through its documents. ∎

EXPERIENCE: Dance Flamenco & Rumba Catalana

Say "flamenco" and "Barcelona" in one breath and one of the first names to come to mind is Carmen Amaya (1913–1963). One of the greatest flamenco dancers ever, Amaya was born in Somorrostro, a shanty town in the area around Port Olímpic, then a tough, industrial area. In 2011, this part of the beach was named Somorrostro in memory of its former inhabitants.

Flamenco, a passionate mix of dance, music, and singing, has known plenty of ups and downs. Its origins are hotly debated, but by the 19th century it was well established in Andalucía's Gitano (Roma people) communities. *Cantaores* (flamenco singers),

Dancing flamenco

usually accompanied by a *tocaor* (guitar player) and others providing accompaniment with a *cajón* (a kind of sound box on which the player sits and beats out rhythms with his hands) and *palmas* (clapping), seem to pour out a world of emotion and passion. Pure flamenco

singing can be an acquired taste, but when a *bailaor* (dancer) dominates the stage, all can turn electric. Goose bumps are inevitable when the performances are good. There is much more to it than is readily apparent.

Barcelona is not known as a center of flamenco, but it has always had a strong Gitano community and the city has produced national stars. Apart from Amaya, great contemporary Catalan cantaores include Juan Cortés Duquende (1965–), Miguel Poveda (1973–), and *cantaora* (female) Mayte Martín (1965–).

Gitano flamenco purists sometimes affirm that only they possess *duende* (an indefinable spirit that renders flamenco so powerful). This doesn't stop *payos* (non-Gitanos) from trying their hand. Plenty of locals and foreigners forge a flamenco path in the city. For an initial approach, get fully equipped at **Flora Albaicín** (*Carrer Canuda, 3, tiendaflamenco.com*), a tiny shop just off La Rambla, owned by the daughter of the eponymous "bailaora."

Several dance schools are dotted about town. Handily located and good, but with crowded classes, is the **Escuela de Baile José de la Vega** (*Carrer d'Aribau 19, tel 93 454 31 14,*

josedelavega.com). Two other fine schools are less centrally located. Claiming to be the oldest flamenco school in the world and seriously professional is the **Instituto de Flamenco Flora Albaicín** (*Carrer de Vallirana 71–73, tel 93 418 23 09, www.flora-albaicin.com*). The **Escuela de Baile La Tani** (*Carrer d'Alella 27, tel 93 349 60 54, latani .com*) is also excellent.

Try heading for a local club, often in the outskirts of the city, where Gitanos might simply start impromptu performing—this can be the most genuine, heartfelt side of flamenco. For information, look at *deflamenco.com*.

Rumba Catalana

A strictly Barcelona sound, *rumba catalana* is a mix of flamenco with Latin American sounds that emerged in the 1950s, faded in the 1980s, and is making a comeback. It grew from the Catalan-speaking gypsy communities in Barcelona, and was led by Peret, a much loved legend (now in his late seventies). Today, it is undergoing a revival with a new generation, including groups like Ai Ai Ai and Sabor de Gracia. Pick up a rumba catalana concert in **Sala Apolo** (*Carrer Nou del Rambla 113, sala-apolo .com*) or **Bikini** (*Avinguda Diagonal 547, bikinibcn.com*).

Museu Frederic Marès

Housed in part of the former Palau Reial, this museum contains the extraordinary collection of Frederic Marès i Deulovol (1893–1991), sculptor, traveler, and eccentric. The building itself became home to the Spanish Inquisition when the Catholic Monarchs (Ferdinand and Isabella) ordered the Holy Office to set up a Barcelona branch in 1484.

Marès's former study, part of the museum, contains his papers and a collection of his own statues.

That move was made against the will of the locals, who rightly predicted a flight of Barcelona's Jews and their wealth, and saw in the Inquisition's arrival a move to tighten central control over Catalonia. The Inquisitors were finally ousted in 1834.

Access the museum from Plaça de Sant Iu via a shady courtyard that flourished during the 15th century is a luxuriant garden of fruit trees and rare birds.

Marès concentrated primarily on his collection of medieval wooden polychrome sculptures and busts, of which there are both Romanesque and Gothic examples. These occupy much of the first and second floors of the building—the two predominant figures are Christ on the Cross and the Virgin Mother and the Christ Child. Most of the items exhibited here are from Catalonia or other regions of Spain. In an underground hall of the museum stands a proud Romanesque portal taken from a 13th-century church in Aragón and reconstructed here.

The collection takes a leap into the 19th and 20th centuries on the top two floors. Here you will find enormous diversity, from toy soldiers and old playing cards through to a room, once Marès's study, that is dedicated to the collector's own sculpture. ∎

Museu Frederic Marès

- 🅰 Map p. 59
- ✉ Plaça Sant Iu 5–6
- ☎ 93 256 3500
- 🕐 Closed Mon.
- 💲 $ (free Sun. after 3 p.m.)
- 🚇 Metro: Línia 4 (Jaume I)

museumares.bcn.cat

Barcelona's Jewish Quarter

In the 600 years since Joan I abolished the city's old Jewish quarter, or Call, in 1401, virtually every sign of its once busy existence has disappeared. But armed with a little imagination (and aided by the information panels scattered about these streets) you can still wander its claustrophobic lanes today.

Curious little shops, such as the Sombrería Obach, fill the streets of the Call.

Documents referring to a street that led to the *callem judaicum* (street where Jews live) demonstrate the presence of a strong Jewish community here from at least the 11th century. For Catalans, the Latin word *Calle,* shortened to *Call,* came to mean Jewish quarter. The Lateran Council of 1179 promulgated severe restrictions on Jewish people in Europe, and the Barcelona Call, delimited by Carrer del Call, Carrer de Sant Honorat, Carrer de Sant Sever, the Baixada de Santa Eulàlia, and the Roman wall, was closed off. A second Call, Call Menor (lesser Call), was later founded around Carrers dels Tres Llits and de la Lleona.

The Call

The Jewish people were under the direct protection of the king within the Call. Beyond the Call, they had to submit to a series of regulations, including the display of a distinguishing sign. Not all of Barcelona's Jews lived in the Call: Many had houses elsewhere in the city, and some had small farms. Most of the men were either artisans (cobblers, jewelers, tailors, and so on) or professionals (doctors, lawyers, and translators). Within the two Calls four public synagogues (including one for women only and another for French Jewish migrants) and two small private ones served religious needs.

In the narrow Carrer de Sant Domènec del Call, drop into atmospheric La Vinateria del Call, an excellent spot for traditional Catalan specialties.

—ANNA BORRÀS
Viajes National Geographic

What some think to be the main synagogue *(Carrer de Marlet 5, calldebarcelona.org, closed from 2:30 p.m. Sun., $)* was discovered in the 1990s. Nearby, the Centre d'Interpretació del Call *(Placeta de Manuel Ribé s/n, museuhistoria .bcn.cat, closed Mon, Tues.–Fri. from 2 p.m., Sat.–Sun. from 7 p.m., & holidays)* offers further historical detail on the Call in a building with 13th-century origins.

In 1160 a certain Abraham Bonastruch struck a deal with Count Ramon Berenguer IV to construct a bathhouse much along the lines of the public baths common throughout much of the Arab world. Of these Banys Nous (New Baths)—the Banys Vells (Old Baths) were near Santa Maria del Mar church—nothing remains. The 18th-century house with sgraffito decoration marks their exact location on the corner of Carrer dels Banys Nous and Carrer de la Boqueria.

A rare reminder of the Jewish presence is a stone inscription in Hebrew on Carrer de Marlet. It reads: "The Pious Foundation of Samuel Ha-Sardí. His light burns permanently." Medieval foundations of this sort were generally hospices for the poor and ill.

Pogrom & Inquisition

In 1391 a pogrom broke out in Seville and spread across the Iberian Peninsula.

The Barcelona Call was sacked on August 5 and 7. Ten years later, Joan I ordered the abolition of the Call and allowed Jewish people (including *conversos,* those converted to Christianity) to live where they chose. The town fathers moved in to repair the damage, and soon Christians bought up many of the houses.

Toward the end of the 15th century, Ferdinand and Isabella installed the Inquisition in Barcelona, and the Holy Office was diligent in its search for enemies of the faith. As Jewish people had been ordered to convert or leave in 1492, most of those remaining in Barcelona were conversos and many of them wealthy contributors to Catalan public finances. The Inquisition doubted the sincerity of their conversion and made life intolerable for them. As the Catalans had feared, the Jews fled, taking their wealth and skills with them.

St. Jordi, patron saint of Catalonia in Carrer del Call

Plaça de Sant Jaume

Named after a church dedicated to St. James that stood here until 1824, this square has been at the center of the city's political life since the 14th century. Today it is a nerve center for city celebrations and political demonstrations. In Roman times the forum lay just to the north, but by the early Middle Ages the square was little more than a discreet widening in the streets.

Ajuntament
- 🗺 Map p. 59
- ✉ Plaça de Sant Jaume
- 🕐 Open for visits 10 a.m.–1 p.m. Sun.
- 🚇 Metro: Línia 4 (Jaume I)

bcn.cat

That all began to change when construction started on what is now the **Ajuntament** (City Hall) on the south side of the square, and the Generalitat opposite it in the following century. The square took on its present form only in 1823. Until then, much of what is now open space had been occupied by a church and cemetery.

In 1274 the Consell de Cent (Council of One Hundred) had been formed from leading citizens to run city affairs, all with the consent of the count-kings. Construction of the Gothic Casa de la Ciutat, as the Ajuntament is also known, began in the 14th century, but to look at it from the outside, you'd never know. Virtually nothing of the Gothic facade remains, only a small part in the street to the left, Ciutat.

The 19th-century edifice is a rather uninspiring, neoclassical effort, while the flank facing Plaça de Sant Miquel and the offices attached to the back are almost inconceivably ugly. Some of the architectural meddling was the result of damage caused by a bombardment during a popular uprising of 1842 that was, needless to say, put down with little ceremony.

Fortunately, inside the building a great deal of the original Gothic splendor remains intact, even if it has been tinkered with repeatedly over the centuries. As you enter the courtyard you will probably be directed to the right, where you proceed up the **Escala d'Honor.** This regal staircase leads up to the Gothic gallery, from which you enter the onetime meeting hall of the Council of One Hundred, **Saló de Cent.** For centuries thereafter the town council held its plenary session here. (A plaque on the left wall commemorates the first session held here in 1373.) The broad vaulting is pure Catalan Gothic, and the timber ceiling

Although sardana dancers usually gather in front of the Catedral, they sometimes turn up outside the Generalitat building on Plaça de Sant Jaume.

demonstrates fine work. Not all that you see is the real McCoy, however. The wooden seating was added at the beginning of the 20th century, as was the grand alabaster retable at the back.

The modern city council now sits in the rather more modest **Saló de la Reina Regent,** built in

Company in the East) was formed; one of its aims was to avenge Roger de Flor. In what became known as the Venjança Catalana (Catalan Revenge), troops torched and pillaged the area around Constantinople (although they failed to enter the city). They then established themselves in the new

Dancing the Sardana

If it can be said that the passion of flamenco rules the heart of southern Spain, then it is true to say that Catalans dance to the beat of a different drum. The unkind would remark that the *sardana* reflects a chilly sobriety for which Catalans are known elsewhere in Spain. Dancers hold hands in a circle and, accompanied by about ten musicians playing various kinds of flutes, bob about in rather controlled

fashion—a series of steps to the right, one back, and then the same to the left. When the dancers get carried away, they raise their arms in the air for a moment. Many Catalans find it boring, but others turn up for a twirl at 6 p.m. on Saturdays and noon on Sundays in front of the Catedral, one of the best chances you will have to see the dance, whose origins lie in old folk dances of northeastern Catalonia.

1860 to the right of the Saló de Cent in honor of the then regent of Spain, Maria Cristina.

To the left of the Saló de Cent is the **Saló de les Croniques.** Here the series of 20th-century murals brings to life episodes of Catalonia's colorful efforts to extend its mercantile empire into Greece and the Near East. Temporarily unemployed knight errant Roger de Flor and 8,000 of his merry men had set off on a quixotic mercenary mission to fight the Ottoman Turks in the service of the tottering Byzantine Empire. In spite of Roger's successes, the Byzantines didn't feel obliged to pay up and the ensuing disagreements led to the assassination of Roger in 1305.

Shortly thereafter the Companyia Catalana a l'Orient (Catalan

duchies of Athens, Thebes, and Neopatras. The first two lasted under the patronage of the Catalan rulers of Sicily until the 1380s, but Byzantium retook Neopatras in 1335. The adventure was immortalized in purplish prose by the chronicler and propagandist Ramon Muntaner (1265–1336), who took part in some of the episodes. Scenes depicted include the taking of the Acropolis in Athens.

From the Saló de les Croniques a staircase leads back down to the courtyard, where there is a series of statues of women. One of them, although you may have trouble making out the connection between art and reality, is by Joan Miró.

Facing the Ajuntament is the **Palau de la Generalitat,** medieval home to the Diputació de la

Palau de la Generalitat

⬛ Map p. 59

✉ Plaça de Sant Jaume

🕐 Open 10 a.m.–1 p.m. 2nd & 4th Sun. (except Aug. & Dec.) with prior online reservation and all day (no tours) April 23, Sept. 11, & Sept. 24

Ⓜ Metro: Línia 4 (Jaume I)

gencat.cat

Generalitat (or permanent council of the Corts Catalanes—Parliament—which first met in 1283) and today seat of the regional Catalan government.

The building has evolved strangely over the centuries. After the pogrom of 1391 and the decree scrapping the neighboring Jewish quarter in 1401, some members of the Diputació acquired houses in the area, particularly along Carrer de Sant Honorat, which before had marked the limit of the Jewish quarter. The bulging wall of the Generalitat on that street is a reminder of the building's origins. Several of these houses were then connected by a garden to Carrer del Bisbe Irurita. In the following years a more organized plan to house the Diputació evolved.

The facade on Carrer del Bisbe Irurita by Marc Safont, sporting sculpted episodes in the story of St. George and the dragon, is the finest. It was once the main entrance and was completed in 1425. Sant Jordi, as he is called in Catalan, is the region's patron saint. The covered walkway across Carrer del Bisbe Irurita looks genuinely Gothic but was actually built in 1926. Today the palace's ceremonial entrance is directly on the square, but the facade is a rather disappointing Renaissance-era makeover.

If you are in town when the Palau is open to the public, take advantage. You enter from the rear and pass through several rooms with low vaulted ceilings before emerging upstairs in the raised courtyard known as the **Pati dels Tarongers.** The 16th-century

Sala Daurada i de Sessions, leading off the courtyard, is a splendid meeting hall lit up by huge chandeliers. The most spectacular of the Palau's seemingly endless halls, though, is the Renaissance **Saló de Sant Jordi.** It is used to receive visiting dignitaries. Finally, you descend the staircase from the magnificent Gothic gallery that frames the **Pati Central,** the final courtyard from which you exit onto Carrer del Bisbe Irurita.

Back on Plaça de Sant Jaume, notice the distinguished financial institution, La Caixa, facing the Ajuntament across the square. Monetary transactions have been carried out on this site for at least 600 years, for on this spot was the **Taula del Canvi** (literally "change table"). Established in 1401, it was

INSIDER TIP:

To avoid the long lines for the double-decker tourist buses, cross the street, get on the bus going in the opposite direction, travel one or two stops, and get off where there's no line for the bus headed where you want to go.

—A. R. WILLIAMS
National Geographic *magazine writer*

one of Europe's earliest public banking institutions, where the city kept its funds and citizens deposited savings, paid taxes, and took out their loans. It remained active until the 18th century. ■

Església de Santa Maria del Pi to Plaça Reial

By the 11th century, Barcelona began to burst its Roman walls. It would be another two centuries before new walls were raised, so in the meantime *ravals*, or satellite hamlets, sprang up beyond the walls. One grew around the Romanesque predecessor of the grand Gothic Església de Santa Maria del Pi.

The huge rose window is about the only decorative concession in the otherwise austere Església de Santa Maria del Pi.

Founded in 1322 to replace a Romanesque church, the austere Gothic structure that dominates busy Plaça del Pi and Plaça de Sant Josep Oriol was dedicated to the Virgin Mary. Plaça del Pi got its name from a pine tree (*pi* in Catalan), a descendant of which still graces the square, and the church soon came to be known as Santa Maria del Pi (Holy Mary of the Pine Tree).

The facade is a forbidding

Església de Santa Maria del Pi

- Map p. 59
- Plaça del Pi
- Open for visit to museum, crypt, garden, & bell tower Mon.–Sat. 10 a.m.–6 p.m., Sun. 4 p.m.–7 p.m.

- $
- Metro: Línia 3 (Liceu)

wall of stone, broken only by the immense rose window and the grand entrance portal. It is typical of the most sober of Catalan Gothic, eschewing virtually all exterior ornament. Think back to the ornate Catedral; the difference is notable. Inside, a vast, broad nave opens up before you, almost 56 feet (17 m) wide. Flanking it to either side is a series of chapels ensconced between the buttresses that help keep the huge structure standing. High above soars the ribbed vaulting that holds together the ceiling. Look back to the entrance to admire the long flat arch supporting the choir—a feature of Catalan Gothic and no mean feat of engineering. The church was filled with artworks of enormous value, many of them dating from the 14th century, but most were lost in the early volatile days of the civil war in 1936, when leftists torched this and other churches across the city.

Several religious *confraries* (brotherhoods) have their headquarters in this church. Members of one of these brotherhoods, the Arxiconfraria de la Puríssima Sang (Archfraternity of the Most Pure Blood), dedicated themselves to the task of accompanying the condemned to their place of execution and lending them spiritual solace in their final moments.

Plaça del Pi & Beyond

Directly opposite the church on Plaça del Pi is an attractive 17th-century building with 18th-century sgraffiti. It once housed one of the city *gremis* (guilds). The square gets busy on many evenings with a market offering all sorts of enticing food products. Running north of the square is narrow **Carrer de Petritxol,** which has been home to chocolate and pastry shops since the 18th century.

Around the corner from Plaça del Pi is another pleasing square, **Plaça de Sant Josep Oriol;** the entire western flank is occupied by the side of the church. Several cafés set up tables outside and there is a weekend art market, in what is doubtless one of the prettiest little corners of the old city. Facing the right flank of the

We Want to Sleep!

The squares of the central Barri Gòtic burst with history, stores, and tempting cafés. Some are also full of an endless din, and Plaça Reial and the surrounding streets were a nocturnal no-go zone until well into the 1980s. Although things have improved here and elsewhere in what was a decidedly unsavory part of town, the racket from revelers until the small hours sometimes drives the local residents to despair. Combined with all-night street musicians (especially the bongo brigade), the decibel count in a city already known as one of the noisiest in the world must be impressive. Local police are trying harder to impose order on the noise and the petty crime that also afflicts the area, but the long-suffering citizens frequently vent their frustration by hanging out plaintive placards of protest on their balconies. Be considerate here, and do watch your pockets.

Gaudí first set to work in Barcelona with a commission to create Plaça Reial's lampposts.

church across the square at No. 4 is a smart 16th-century mansion, **Palau de Fiveller,** built in 1571 for the influential aristocratic Fiveller family. The facade was reworked in the 18th century so horses and carriages could drive right inside.

Following the line of the church south through Plaça de Sant Josep Oriol you turn onto the less inviting Placeta del Pi, behind the church's apse, and then proceed down Carrer d'En Rauric to reach the unusually rectilinear **Carrer de Ferran.** This is no medieval thoroughfare, but was sliced through here in 1823 and named after Spain's anachronistically absolutist king, Fernando VII (Ferran to the Catalans). Along it is the facade of the **Església de Sant Jaume,** which started life as a synagogue and was later turned into a church and convent by Jewish converts. Joan Miró, one of Spain's great 20th-century artists, was born in 1893 in an apartment in Passatge del Crèdit, a covered arcade that runs south of Carrer de Ferran close to Plaça de Sant Jaume.

A brief stroll away you enter another world. Plaça Reial, laid out on the site of a former Capuchin convent, is now a focal point of nocturnal entertainment, an elegant space that received an early touch of Gaudí magic.

For those not expecting it, stumbling onto **Plaça Reial** (Royal Square), with its solid porticoes and slender palm trees, comes as quite a surprise. Nineteenth-century neoclassical facades mask grand rambling apartments and a boutique hotel. French and Castilian models inspired the design of the square, and it is hard to picture the convent that stood here previously. Look for the lampposts nearest the central fountain; they are the earliest known commission undertaken by Antoni Gaudí. The square and its southern backstreets contain some of Barcelona's classic restaurants and bars, while a muddle of lanes runs down to the busy Passeig de Colom and the waterfront (see pp. 99–116). ■

Towers of Strength

Catalans specialize in one highly bizarre sector of the construction industry—human castles, or *castells*. Castellers have been raising these "edifices" to new heights for 200 years in the southwest of Catalonia, particularly around Tarragona and the Penedès region. This folkloric activity—made an Intangible Cultural Heritage by UNESCO in 2010—may have its roots in medieval siege tactics, but is now a serious amateur sport.

Recipe for a *castell* (human castle): strong arms, steady legs—and bare feet

The first golden age came in the 1880s, when *colles* (teams) of several hundred people would form complex castells of varying dimensions as high as ten stories. The second golden age came in the 1990s, when the activity seemed suddenly to grab the attention of Catalans across the region. At the last count there were nearly 80 colles.

Several teams are active in and around Barcelona. They and other teams across the region (the best are from Valls and Vilafranca del Penedès) compete in town fiestas and on

holidays from about February through October. Every two years (in even years) a championship competition is held at the Tarragona bullring. During the Festes de la Mercè in September you can see local and outside teams competing in Barcelona's Plaça de Sant Jaume.

The Goal

Castellers attempt to build human layers as high as possible and then to dismantle the lot without collapsing in an undignified heap. The "basement" of the *tronc* (trunk) is a broad concentric scrum known as a *pinya* and upon this the castellers build their castle, which can be of many different types. About the best ever achieved is a *tres de deu*, or three by ten—that means ten levels of people standing on each other's shoulders. Other difficult formations include the *quatre de nou* (four by nine) and *cinc de vuit* (five by eight). Often the pinya does not provide sufficient support, and so the second level will be buttressed by castellers forming the *folre* (lining). *Manilles* (literally "handcuffs," but here it means another layer of people) are occasionally added at the third level. Where neither manilles nor folre is employed (which is harder), the castell is *net* (clean).

The successful *quatre de nou amb folre* will require a good 500 participants and look like this: at the base a populous pinya pushing into the center and on their shoulders the smaller folre. Above are four stories each of four people with their arms locked around each other's shoulders. The seventh level consists of two people, above whom one person crouches to form the penultimate story. The *agulla* (pinnacle) is a lightweight child,

Castellers building an impressive *castell* (human castle) in front of the Ajuntament

the *anxaneta,* who scrambles up the structure to the top and waves his/her hand to indicate the castell has been completed. The anxaneta then scuttles back down and each level lowers itself by sliding down the lower stories. A castell that is successfully disassembled wins greater admiration than one that collapses.

Some teams aim to make broad, squat castells (like *nou de set,* or seven stories of nine people each), while others try for slender *torres* (levels of two people) or *pilars* (levels of one); the latter two rarely rise beyond six levels.

More Places to Visit in Barri Gòtic

Església de la Mercè

One of Barcelona's few baroque houses of worship, this church is also home to the image of Nostra Senyora de la Mercè (Our Lady of Mercy), the city's co-patron. She was elevated to this exalted role when, it is said, she single-handedly warded off a bout of the plague in 1637. More curious still, Our Lady was made commander-in-chief of the city's defenses toward the end of the siege that ended the War of the Spanish Succession, and Catalonian autonomy, in 1714. She was forgiven this failing and is the religious focal point of the city's biggest annual party, the Festes de la Mercè, held in late September. The church is actually a curious mix: A Renaissance flank on Carrer Ample accompanies the main baroque facade. The edifice was built over an earlier Gothic structure.

🅰 Map p. 59 ✉ Plaça de la Mercè 1 🕐 Closed 1–6 p.m. Mon.–Sat., 1:30–7 p.m. Sun., & holidays 🚇 Metro: Línies 3 (Drassanes) & 4 (Jaume I)

Església de Santa Anna

Back in 1141, members of the military order of the Holy Sepulchre began construction of a monastery dedicated to St. Anne. It lay beyond the Roman walls, which still served as the city's northern defense perimeter, and a small "suburb" soon grew around the church. The church you see today is largely Gothic, although some Romanesque elements are visible, and the shady if somewhat unkempt Gothic cloister comes as a lovely surprise. The complex is hidden away on a little square off Carrer Comtal and much ignored by the passing tourist trade and frenzied shoppers.

🅰 Map p. 59 ✉ Plaça de Ramon Amadeu 🕐 Closed 1–6 p.m., from 1 p.m. Sun., & holidays 🚇 Metro: Línia 3 (Catalunya)

Església de Sant Felip Neri

Again, hidden away from the main stream of visitors to the city, but barely a hop, skip, and jump from the Catedral, this modest baroque church was built in the mid-18th century. Look for the damage in the wall: In one of the city's sadder chapters, a bomb was dropped here in 1938 during the civil war, killing 42 people, mostly children. The square was once a medieval cemetery; looking onto it is the Gremi de Sabaters, the medieval cobblers' guild—look for the stone standard depicting the lion of St. Mark, the shoemaker's patron saint. Inside today is the curious **Museu del Calçat,** or Shoe Museum *(closed Mon. & from 2 p.m. Tues.–Sun.),* where you can see everything from Roman sandals to a giant shoe made for Columbus on his statue.

🅰 Map p. 59 ✉ Plaça de Sant Felip Neri 🕐 Closed p.m. 🚇 Metro: Línies 3 (Liceu) & 4 (Jaume I)

Església de Sants Just i Pastor

Recent archaeological finds suggest that this church, which is claimed to be the oldest in Barcelona, dates to the fourth century, like the Catedral. The present structure was raised eight centuries later in typical Catalan Gothic style. To this church was accorded an unusual privilege: From the 11th to the 15th century, court cases that could not be resolved by standard judicial process could be dealt with in a Trial of God. The two parties would come to the church and vow to fight it out according to the rules stipulated by this privilege. God ensured that the guilty party lost.

At the junction of narrow streets that forms Plaça de Sant Just in front of the church is a medieval fountain. If you follow the dead-end Carrer del Bisbe Caçador to the end and find the gates open, you can enter the magnificent Gothic courtyard of **Palau Requesens,** also known as Palau de la Comtessa de Palamós. Look up at the narrow windows; some of them are Romanesque and others are Gothic.

🅰 Map p. 59 ✉ Plaça de Sant Just 🕐 Closed 2 p.m.–5 p.m. Mon.–Fri. & from 1 p.m. Sun. 🚇 Metro: Línia 4 (Jaume I)

La Rambla—Barcelona's main boulevard and its center stage—plus El Raval, a multicultural enclave of Gaudí fantasy, modern art, and late-night watering holes

La Rambla & El Raval

Introduction & Map   86–87

Walk: Rambling Along La Rambla   88–91

Palau Güell   92–93

Feature: From Xino to Boho   94–95

Experience: Enjoy Barcelona's Bar Scene   95

Museu d'Art Contemporani de Barcelona (MACBA) & CCCB   96–97

More Places to Visit in La Rambla & El Raval   98

Hotels & Restaurants   249–251

A permanent resident peers out from the front of a house in La Rambla.

La Rambla & El Raval

La Rambla undergoes five name changes along its length, suggesting that more than a little history lies behind the impassive hotel facades and colorful street theater of Barcelona's best known avenue. The broad pedestrian-only promenade, which runs southeast toward the old port from central Plaça de Catalunya and is flanked by two narrow (and often choked) traffic lanes, bubbles with activity.

Many distractions await pedestrians along La Rambla's central section.

During their short stay in eighth-century Barcelona, the Muslims applied the Arabic name *al-raml* (stream) to the rivulet that dribbled into the Mediterranean beyond the city's western wall. By the time Jaume I raised new walls alongside it in the mid-13th century, that stream was reduced to a stinking sewage ditch. Beyond it sprawled the fetid mess of El Raval, an early shantytown.

Jaume's wall was thus deprived of its defensive intent, and in its shadow La Rambla gradually took shape. First, starting in the 1530s, came convents and churches. Later, nobles built mansions here. When the wall was finally pulled down in the mid-19th century, the gaps were filled with new housing.

What stretches before us now is a year-round carnival. Daytime strollers, tourists, and three-card tricksters are replaced at night by hedonists, hookers, and one or two petty thieves. In the predawn hours the pleasure-seekers wend their animated way past news-stands, to Plaça de Catalunya for a cab home.

To the west of La Rambla lies El Raval. Poorest of the Old City's quarters and home to what remains of the down-at-heel red-light district of Barrio Xino, the area is changing fast. New streets have been laid out, and buildings are being restored. A wave of migrants has altered the face of El Raval. With the creation of the MACBA modern art museum, the CCCB, and other galleries, an infusion of young blood has reinvigorated what was long a neglected slum. A host of new bars, cafés, restaurants, and clubs attests to the trend. Many tourists fail to move beyond Gaudí's extraordinary Palau Güell, just off La Rambla, but other lesser known gems, some admittedly still in need of a polish, await discovery. For all its roughness, a wander around El Raval adds a rewarding dimension to knowledge of the city. ■

NOT TO BE MISSED:

A stroll along La Rambla 88–91

Early Gaudí at Palau Güell 92–93

The cutting-edge Museu d'Art Contemporani de Barcelona 96–97

Enjoying a dance or cinema festival at the CCCB 97

The evocative air of the Antic Hospital de la Santa Creu 98

The Romanesque cloister of the Església de Sant Pau del Camp 98

A Catalan meal in Casa Leopoldo 250

Sipping a thick chocolate *suisso* in Granja Viader 251

Discover La Sagrada Família & L'Eixample

⬌ Getting There & Away

○ **Metro** Four Metro lines criss-cross L'Eixample, three stopping at Passeig de Gràcia for the Manzana de la Discordia. Línia 3 stops at Diagonal for La Pedrera, while Línies 2 and 5 stop at Sagrada Família.

○ **Train** FGC lines from Plaça de Catalunya take you one stop to Provença, in the heart of L'Eixample.

◎ Sights

L'Esquerra de L'Eixample

Casa Amatller   Architecture

Map p136 (☎ 93 487 72 17; www.amatller.org; Passeig de Gràcia 41; tour €10; ☺ tour Sat; Ⓜ Passeig de Gràcia) FREE One of Puig i Cadafalch's most striking bits of Modernista fantasy, Casa Amatller combines Gothic window frames with a stepped gable borrowed from Dutch urban architecture. But the busts and reliefs of dragons, knights and other characters dripping off the main facade are pure caprice.

The pillared foyer and staircase lit by stained glass are like the inside of some romantic castle.

The building was renovated in 1900 for the chocolate baron and philanthropist Antoni Amatller (1851–1910) and it will one day open partly to the public. Renovation – still continuing at the time of research – will see the 1st (main) floor converted into a museum with period pieces, while the 2nd floor will house the Institut Amatller d'Art Hispanic (Amatller Institute of Hispanic Art).

For now, you can wander into the foyer, admire the staircase and lift, and head through the shop to see the latest temporary exhibition out the back. Depending on the state of renovation, it is also possible to join a 1½-hour guided tour of the 1st floor, with its early-20th-century furniture and decor intact, and Amatller's photo studio. These are generally held on Saturdays; check the website for details.

Amatller was a keen traveller and photographer (his absorbing shots of turn-of-the-20th-century Morocco are

Casa Amatller

Bell towers

The towers (eight completed) of the three facades represent the 12 Apostles. Lifts whisk visitors up one tower of the Nativity and Passion Facades (the latter gets longer queues) for fine views.

③

Completed church

Along with the Glory Facade and its four towers, six other towers remain to be completed. They will represent the four Evangelists, the Virgin Mary and, soaring above them all over the transept, a 170m colossus symbolising Christ.

Glory Facade

This will be the most fanciful facade of all, with a narthex boasting 16 hyperboloid lanterns topped by cones that will look something like an organ made of melting ice cream.

⑦

Museu Gaudí

Jammed with old photos, drawings and restored plaster models that bring Gaudí's ambitions to life, the museum also houses an extraordinarily complex plumb-line device he used to calculate his constructions.

Escoles de Gaudí

⑤

④

② ⑥

Crypt

The first completed part of the church, the crypt is in largely neo-Gothic style and lies under the transept. Gaudí's burial place here can be seen from the Museu Gaudí.

Passion Facade

See the story of Christ's last days from Last Supper to burial in an S-shaped sequence from bottom to top of the facade. Check out the cryptogram in which the numbers always add up to 33, Christ's age at his death.

La Sagrada Família

A TIMELINE

1882 Francesc del Villar is commissioned to construct a neo-Gothic church.

1883 Antoni Gaudí takes over as chief architect, and plans a far more ambitious church to hold 13,000 faithful.

1926 Death of Gaudí; work continues under Domènec Sugrañes. Much of the **apse** ❶ and **Nativity Facade** ❷ is complete.

1930 **Bell towers** ❸ of the Nativity Facade completed.

1936 Construction is interrupted by Spanish Civil War; anarchists destroy Gaudí's plans.

1939-40 Architect Francesc de Paula Quintana i Vidal restores the crypt and meticulously reassembles many of Gaudí's lost models, some of which can be seen in the **museum** ❹.

1976 Completion of **Passion Facade** ❺.

1986-2006 Sculptor Josep Subirachs adds sculptural details to the Passion Facade, including the panels telling the story of Christ's last days, amid much criticism for employing a style far removed from what was thought typical of Gaudí.

2000 **Central nave vault** ❻ completed.

2010 Church completely roofed over; Pope Benedict XVI consecrates the church; work begins on a high-speed rail tunnel that will pass beneath the church's **Glory Facade** ❼.

2026–28 Projected completion date.

TOP TIPS

» **Light** The best light through the stained-glass windows of the Passion Facade bursts through into the heart of the church in the late afternoon.

» **Time** Visit at opening time on weekdays to avoid the worst of the crowds.

» **Views** Head up the Nativity Facade bell towers for the views, as long queues generally await at the Passion Facade towers.

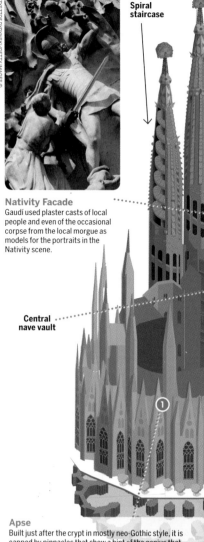

Spiral staircase

Nativity Facade
Gaudí used plaster casts of local people and even of the occasional corpse from the local morgue as models for the portraits in the Nativity scene.

Central nave vault

Apse
Built just after the crypt in mostly neo-Gothic style, it is capped by pinnacles that show a hint of the genius that Gaudí would later deploy in the rest of the church.

The Design

Gaudí devised a temple 95m long and 60m wide, able to seat 13,000 people. It was to have a central tower 170m high above the transept (representing Christ) and another 17 of 100m or more. The 12 towers along the three facades represent the Apostles, while the remaining five represent the Virgin Mary and the four Evangelists. With his characteristic dislike for straight lines (he said there were none in nature), Gaudí gave his towers swelling outlines inspired by the weird peaks of the holy mountain Montserrat outside Barcelona, and encrusted them with a tangle of sculpture that seems an outgrowth of the stone.

Building planners estimate that the church will be completed in 2026, roughly 140 years after construction began. Already, some of the oldest parts of the church, especially the apse, have required restoration work.

The Interior

Inside, the roof is held up by a forest of extraordinary angled pillars. As the pillars soar towards the ceiling, they sprout a web of supporting branches, creating the effect of a forest canopy. The tree image is in no way accidental – Gaudí envisaged such an effect. Everything was thought through, including the shape and placement of windows to create the mottled effect of sunlight pouring through the branches of a thick forest.

Visiting La Sagrada Família

Although essentially a building site, the completed sections and the museum may be explored at leisure. Fifty-minute guided tours (€4.50) are offered. Alternatively, pick up an audio tour (€4.50). Enter from Carrer de Sardenya and Carrer de la Marina. Once inside, €4.50 will get you into lifts that rise up the towers of the Nativity and Passion facades. These two facades, each with four sky-scraping towers, are the sides of the church. The main Glory Facade, on which work is underway, closes off the southeast end on Carrer de Mallorca.

1 **PASSION FACADE**
Among the *Fachada de la Pasión*'s stand-out features are the angled columns, the dramatic scenes from Jesus' last hours, an extraordinary rendering of the Last Supper and a bronze door that reads like a sculptured book. But the most surprising view is from inside the door on the extreme right (especially in the afternoon with the sun in the west).

2 **MAIN NAVE**
The majestic *Nave Principal* showcases Gaudí's use of tree motifs for columns to support the domes. But it's the skylights that give the nave its luminous quality, with light flooding into the apse and main altar from the skylight 75m above the floor.

3 **SIDE NAVE AND NATIVITY TRANSEPT**
Although beautiful in its own right, this is the perfect place to view the sculpted treelike columns and get an overall perspective of the main nave. Turn around and you're confronted with the inside of the Nativity Facade, an alternative view that most visitors miss. The stained-glass windows are superb.

4 **NATIVITY FACADE**
The *Fachada del Nacimiento* is Gaudí's grand hymn to Creation. Begin by viewing it front-on, then draw close (but to one side) to make out the details of its sculpted figures. The complement to the finely wrought detail is the majesty of the four parabolic towers, which are topped by Venetian stained glass.

5 **MODEL OF COLÒNIA GÜELL**
The most interesting model in the Museu Gaudí is the church at Colònia Güell. It's upside down because that's how Gaudí worked to best study the building's form and structural balance.

Don't Miss
La Sagrada Família

If you have time for only one sightseeing outing, this should be it. La Sagrada Família inspires awe by its sheer verticality and magnificently elaborate design – inside and out. It may be unfinished, but it attracts over 3 million visitors a year and is the most visited monument in Spain. There's much to explore here – symbol-rich facades, an other-worldly interior and the on-site Museu Gaudí, which houses materials on the master's life and work.

Map p136

☎ 93 207 30 31

www.sagrada familia.org

Carrer de Mallorca 401

adult/child under 10yr/senior & student €13/ free/11

🕓 9am-8pm Apr-Sep, to 6pm Oct-Mar

Ⓜ Sagrada Família

scales and bonelike columns) and an abstract St George (the swordlike chimney) slaying the dragon (the scaly roof).

4 Fundació Antoni Tàpies

Just around the corner is another of Domènech i Montaner's fine works, which today houses the **Fundació Antoni Tàpies** (p135). The symmetrical brick exterior shows Muslim influences, while the wiry sculpture on the roof is a Tàpies creation and represents a chair jutting out of a cloud.

5 La Pedrera

Up the road is Casa Milà, better known as **La Pedrera** (p142) for its grey grey stone facade. The undulating walls and rippling wrought-iron balconies show organic influences. Up top stand the famous stone chimneys that resemble helmeted warriors, but you'll have to pay to see them.

6 Casa Thomas

Casa Thomas was one of Domènech i Montaner's earlier efforts. The ceramic details are a trademark and the massive ground-level wrought-iron decoration is magnificent. Wander inside to the Cubiña design store to admire his interior work.

7 Casa Llopis i Bofill

Casa Llopis i Bofill is an interesting block of flats designed by Antoni Gallissà. The graffiti-covered facade is particularly striking. The use of parabolic arches on the ground floor is a clear Modernista touch, as are the wrought-iron balconies.

8 La Sagrada Família

Strolling around **La Sagrada Família** (p130), you'll notice the wildly different styles of the Nativity Facade, completed during Gaudí's lifetime, and the Passion Facade, designed by Josep Maria Subirachs in the 1980s. Other key things to look for: the Risen Christ teetering halfway up the Passion Facade, eight completed belltowers with a different apostle seated at each and the image of Gaudí himself in the Passion Facade.

 ## The Best…

PLACES TO EAT

Tapaç 24 Innovative chef Carles Abellàn creates some of Barcelona's best tapas. (p140)

Cerveseria Catalana Great-value neighbourhood haunt that draws crowds any time of day. (p143)

Cinc Sentits Tasting menus that showcase the best of Catalan cooking. (p148)

Cata 1.81 Lovely setting for gourmet tapas and wines by the glass. (p146)

PLACES TO DRINK

Monvínic Enchanting setting amid one of Spain's best wine bars. (p150)

La Fira Funhouse ambience and a staggering drinks selection. (p150)

Les Gens Que J'Aime Stylish but unpretentious gem in L'Eixample. (p151)

Dry Martini Classy bar serving Barcelona's best gin and tonics. (p149)

PLACES TO SHOP

Vinçon Beautifully designed furniture and housewares in a Modernista building. (p152)

El Corte Inglés Sprawling department store that often has unbeatable sales. (p153)

El Bulevard dels Antiquaris Dozens of antique shops. (p152)

Spanish-style antipasto

La Sagrada Família & L'Eixample Walk

L'Eixample is packed with Modernista treasures. Start with the three unique buildings of the Manzana de la Discordia and end at La Sagrada Família.

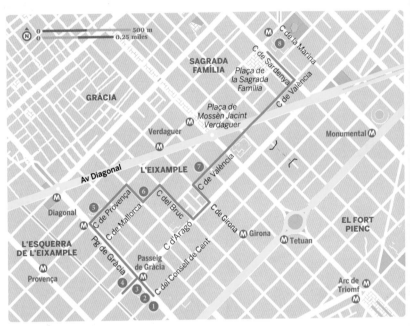

WALK FACTS

- **Start** Passeig de Gràcia
- **Finish** La Sagrada Família
- **Distance** 3km
- **Duration** 1.5 hours

① Casa Lleó Morera

Near Carrer del Consell de Cent, have a look at the heavily ornamented facade of **Casa Lleó Morera** (p135), designed by Domènech i Montaner. Note the fine-featured sculptures of maidens holding the latest in early 20th-century technology: the telephone, the phonograph, the telegraph and the camera.

② Casa Amatller

A few doors up, you'll see Puig i Cadafalch's **Casa Amatller** (p134), which has a stepped Flemish Renaissance roof and a medievalesque facade adorned with whimsical statuary. Near the entrance portal, St George is impaling the dragon and there are more curious creatures on the second floor, including a monkey hammering on a forge.

③ Casa Batlló

Casa Batlló (p147) shimmers in Gaudíesque extravagance. Its symbolic meaning is open to interpretation but is undoubtedly connected with Catalan identity: a Carnaval celebration (the masklike balconies, the facade glittering like confetti), a fish (with

La Pedrera (p142)

CULTURA TRAVEL/QUIM ROSER/GETTY IMAGES©

One of Passeig de Gràcia's most captivating Modernista structures, La Pedrera is in the top tier of Gaudí's achievements. Officially called Casa Milà after its owners, it was nicknamed La Pedrera (The Stone Quarry) by bemused locals who watched Gaudí build it from 1905 to 1910. Conceived as an apartment block, it bears all the trademarks of Gaudí: swirling staircases, hallucinogenic curves and not a straight line in sight.

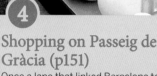

Shopping on Passeig de Gràcia (p151)

Once a lane that linked Barcelona to the village of Gràcia, the elegant, tree-lined Passeig de Gràcia has metamorphosed into the city's most opulent boulevard. Heaving with posh hotels and punctuated with architectural nods to Catalonia's Modernista movement, it is feted most for its shopping. Luxury labels share space with the odd indie fashion guerrilla.

Above: Vinçon (p152)

Manzana de la Discordia (p128)

One block on Passeig de Gràcia is embellished with buildings by the three enfants terribles of early-20th-century Modernisme. Each building has a unique style. Puig i Cadafalch's Casa Amatller (p134) is gabled and faintly Dutch, Domènech i Montaner's Casa Lleó Morera (p135) has a regal quality and Gaudí's Casa Batlló (p147) is downright other-worldly.

Above: Casa Amatller; architect: Josep Puig i Cadafalch

La Sagrada Família & L'Eixample Highlights

La Sagrada Família (p130)

Spain's biggest tourist attraction, La Sagrada Família, is a unique, extraordinary piece of architecture. Conceived as atonement for Barcelona's sins of modernity, this giant church became Gaudí's holy mission and, in medieval fashion, is still under construction 100 years after its inception. At once ancient and thoroughly modern, La Sagrada Família is packed with religious iconography and symbolism, and leaves no one unmoved.

Fundació Antoni Tàpies (p135)

Take a pioneering Modernista building by architect Luís Domènech i Montaner and stuff it with works by one of Spain's great painters, Antoni Tàpies. This collection showcases hundreds of pieces of the Catalan painter, sculptor and theorist, from surrealist works of the 1940s to imaginative sculpture-like pieces of 1970s Abstract Expression.

KRZYSZTOF DYDYNSKI / GETTY IMAGES ©

La Sagrada Família & L'Eixample

By far the most extensive of Barcelona's districts, this sprawling grid is full of subidentities. Almost all the city's Modernista buildings were raised in L'Eixample. The pick of them line Passeig de Gràcia, but hundreds adorn the area. Work on Gaudí's La Sagrada Família church continues.

As Barcelona's population exploded, the medieval walls were knocked down by 1856. In 1869, work began on L'Eixample (the Extension) to fill the open country that then lay between Barcelona and Gràcia. Building continued until well into the 20th century. Well-to-do families snapped up prime plots and raised fanciful buildings in the eclectic style of the Modernistas.

Shoppers converge on Passeig de Gràcia and La Rambla de Catalunya. At night, mainly from Thursday to Saturday, Carrer d'Aribau and nearby streets are home to a buzzing nightlife scene. The 'Gaixample', around Carrer del Consell de Cent and Carrer de Muntaner, is the centre of gay nightlife.

Casa Batlló (p147)

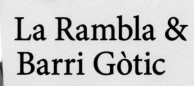

La Rambla & Barri Gòtic

Packed with historic treasures, Barri Gòtic is one of Europe's most atmospheric neighbourhoods. Its tangle of narrow lanes and tranquil plazas lie amid Roman ruins, medieval churches and converted palaces, with history lurking around every lamplit corner. There are swarms of tourists afoot, but these cobbled streets have plenty of local character, with first-rate restaurants, creative boutiques and a vibrant nightlife keeping things buzzing until early in the morning.

Nearby, La Rambla is Spain's most talked-about boulevard. It certainly packs a lot of colour into a short walk, with flower stands, historic buildings, a sensory-rich food market, overpriced beers, tourist tat and a ceaselessly changing parade of people from all corners of the globe. Once a river and sewage ditch on the edge of medieval Barcelona, it still marks the southwest flank of Barri Gòtic.

Plaça Reial (p59)

La Rambla & Barri Gòtic Highlights

Strolling La Rambla (p52)

Snaking its way through the Ciutat Vella (Old City), this 1.2km-long boulevard is always awhirl with activity. There are street performers, food and drink stalls, souvenir stands and a pastiche of architectural intrigue lining both sides of the street. Come early in the morning to see La Rambla at its most serene, then return later to the people-packed lane to see it in all its carnivalesque glory.

Plaça Reial (p59)

The elegant Plaça Reial is wonderfully recuperative after wandering the narrow, sometimes pungent streets of the medieval quarter. Outdoor cafes and restaurants set beneath the arcades draw a relaxed crowd by day, while after dark the plaza becomes a hidden hive of candlelit restaurants and clubs. A trickling fountain, intricately sculpted street lamps and occasional live music sets the scene. Left: A restaurant on Plaça Reial

JEAN-PIERRE LESCOURRET/GETTY IMAGES ©

Museu d'Història de Barcelona (p67) ③

More subterranean adventure trail than stash of dusty exhibits, this museum takes visitors on a journey through time. Start in ancient Roman-era Barcino and stroll past fragments of old bathhouses, laundrettes and wine-making stores. Then wind your way up through the centuries past Visigothic ruins, picture-perfect Gothic halls and medieval chapels.

La Catedral (p52) ④

La Catedral de la Santa Creu i Santa Eulàlia is a riot of Gothic and gargoyles, high altars and murky crypts, Catalan legends and 13 resident geese. Like many Spanish churches, it is a hybrid – the 14th-century shell has been overlaid by a 19th-century neo-Gothic facade – a factor that makes it all the more fascinating and enigmatic. Don't miss the superb view from the rooftop.

Plaça de Sant Jaume (p58) ⑤

The epicentre of the historic Ciutat Vella (Old City), this plaza has been an essential part of civic life since the Romans erected a forum here 2000 years ago. Several key government buildings continue to play a role in political affairs, including the Ajuntament, where Barcelona's first ruling council met in the 1300s. By day, the buzzing plaza brings a mishmash of bureaucrats, protestors and gawking tourists.

Above: Plaça de Sant Jaume during Festes de la Mercè (p41)

La Rambla & Barri Gòtic Walk

This scenic walk through the Barri Gòtic will take you back in time to the early days of Roman-era Barcino. Amid architectural treasures from previous centuries, you'll pass picturesque plazas, looming Gothic churches and an atmospheric quarter once the centre of a medieval Jewish quarter.

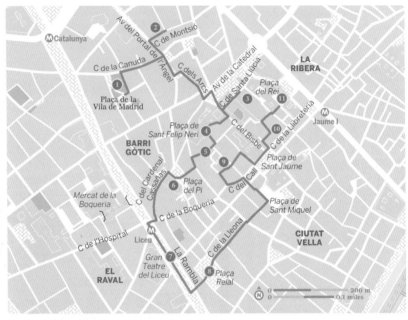

WALK FACTS
- **Start** Plaça de la Vila de Madrid
- **Finish** Plaça del Rei
- **Distance** 2.5km
- **Duration** Two hours

1 Roman Tombs
On Plaça de la Vila de Madrid is a sunken garden with various **Roman tombs** (p63). It was customary to line highways leading out of cities with tombs and it's believed this road connected Roman Barcino with the Via Augusta, which linked Rome and Cádiz.

2 Els Quatre Gats
Next, head over to one of the few Modernista buildings in the Gothic quarter. **'The Four Cats'** restaurant, started life as Casa Martí. From 1897 to 1903, it was the hang-out for bohemians and artists, including Picasso.

3 La Catedral
Head down Avinguda del Portal de l'Angel to the magnificent **cathedral** (p56). Before entering, look at the three Picasso friezes on the building facing the square.

4 Plaça de Sant Felip Neri
Enter the former gates of the ancient fortified city and turn right into **Plaça de Sant**

Felip Neri. Note the shrapnel-scarred walls of the **old church**, damaged by pro-Francist bombers in 1939.

⑤ Santa Eulàlia

Head out of the square and turn right. On this narrow lane, you'll spot a small **statue** of Santa Eulàlia (p205), one of Barcelona's patron saints. Martyred by the Romans, she allegedly suffered numerous tortures.

⑥ Església de Santa Maria del Pi

Make your way west to the 14th-century **Església de Santa Maria del Pi**, which is famed for its magnificent rose window. Adjacent to the church are two serene plazas with outdoor cafes.

⑦ La Rambla

Continue west to Barcelona's liveliest **pedestrian boulevard** (p52). As you stroll south, you'll walk over a striking **Miró mural** and pass the **Gran Teatre del Liceu**, Barcelona's famous opera house.

⑧ Plaça Reial

Turn down the small lane leading into **Plaça Reial** (p59), one of Barcelona's prettiest squares.

⑨ Sinagoga Major

Make your way northeast to the atmospheric, narrow lanes of **El Call**, the medieval Jewish quarter until a bloody pogrom of 1391. The **Sinagoga Major** (p62), one of Europe's oldest, was discovered in 1996.

⑩ Roman Temple

Head across Plaça de Sant Jaume and turn left after Carrer del Bisbe. You'll soon pass the remnants of a **Roman temple**, with four columns hidden in a small courtyard.

⑪ Plaça del Rei

The final stop is **Plaça del Rei**. The former palace houses a superb **history museum** (p67), which boasts significant Roman ruins underground.

 The Best...

PLACES TO EAT

Pla Mouth-watering fusion fare in a spacious medieval dining room. (p65)

La Vinateria del Call An atmospheric setting for classic Catalan and Mediterranean cooking in El Call. (p64)

Koy Shunka Artfully prepared Japanese cuisine is worth a splurge – especially the 11-course *menú degustación*. (p65)

PLACES TO DRINK

Salterio Medieval ambience in the picturesque quarter of El Call. (p66)

Ocaña Stylish spot with a beautifully designed interior. (p65)

Sor Rita Join festive crowds in a whimsical Almodovar-esque world. (p65)

HISTORICAL TREASURES

Temple Romà d'August Mighty columns from a once great empire. (p63)

Via Sepulcral Romana Funereal markers from the days of Barcino. (p63)

Sinagoga Major A tiny medieval synagogue attests to a once flourishing Jewish quarter. (p62)

Els Quatre Gats

Don't Miss
La Rambla

Flanked by narrow traffic lanes and plane trees, the middle of La Rambla is a broad pedestrian boulevard, crowded every day until the wee hours with a cross-section of *barcelonins* (people of Barcelona) and out-of-towners. Dotted with cafes, restaurants, kiosks and news stands, and enlivened by buskers, pavement artists, mimes and living statues, La Rambla rarely allows a dull moment.

Map p58

Ⓜ Catalunya, Liceu or Drassanes

La Rambla de Canaletes

The stretch from Plaça de Catalunya is La Rambla de Canaletes, named after an inconspicuous turn-of-the-20th-century **drinking fountain**, the water of which supposedly emerges from what were once known as the springs of Canaletes. It used to be said that *barcelonins* 'drank the waters of Les Canaletes'. People claim that anyone who drinks from the fountain will return to Barcelona. Delirious football fans gather here to celebrate whenever the main home side, FC Barcelona, wins a cup or the league premiership.

Església de Betlem

Just north of Carrer del Carme, this **church** was constructed in baroque style for the Jesuits in the late 17th and early 18th centuries to replace an earlier church destroyed by fire in 1671. Fire was a bit of a theme for this site: the church was once considered the most splendid of Barcelona's few baroque offerings, but leftist arsonists torched it in 1936.

Palau Moja

Looming over the eastern side of La Rambla, **Palau Moja** is a rare pure neo-classical pile. Its classical lines are best appreciated from across La Rambla.

Palau de la Virreina

The **Palau de la Virreina** is a grand 18th-century rococo mansion (with some neoclassical elements) that houses a municipal arts-and-entertainment information and ticket office. It's home to the **Centre de la Imatge**, which has rotating photography exhibits. Admission prices and opening hours vary.

Mosaïc de Miró

At Plaça de la Boqueria, where four side streets meet just north of Liceu Metro station, you can walk all over a Miró – the colourful **mosaic** in the pavement. Miró chose this site since it's near the house where he was born on the Passatge del Crèdit. The mosaic's bold colors and vivid swirling forms are instantly recognisable to Miró fans,

but plenty of tourists stroll right over it without noticing it. Near the bottom of the work, there's one tile signed by the artist.

La Rambla dels Caputxins

Named after a now nonexistent monastery, this stretch of La Rambla runs from Plaça de la Boqueria to Carrer dels Escudellers. The latter street is named after the potters' guild, founded in the 13th century, whose members lived and worked here. On the western side of La Rambla is the Gran Teatre del Liceu (p59). Further south on the eastern side is the entrance to the palm-shaded Plaça Reial (p59).

La Rambla de Santa Mònica

The final stretch of La Rambla widens out to approach the Mirador de Colom overlooking Port Vell. La Rambla here is named after the Convent de Santa Mònica, which once stood on the western flank of the street. It has since been converted into an art gallery and cultural centre, the **Centre d'Art Santa Mònica**, which tends to exhibit modern, multimedia installations; admission is free.

Civil War & La Rambla

La Rambla saw action during the Civil War. In *Homage to Catalonia*, George Orwell described the avenue gripped by revolutionary fervour in the early days of the war: 'Down the Ramblas, the wide central artery of the town where crowds of people streamed constantly to and fro, the loud-speakers were bellowing revolutionary songs all day and far into the night... There was much in it that I did not understand, in some ways I did not even like it, but I recognised it immediately as a state of affairs worth fighting for.' Later in the war, heavy street fighting took place on La Rambla. Anarchists shot at Orwell as he dashed across La Rambla.

La Rambla

A TIMELINE

Look beyond the human statues and tourist-swarmed restaurants, and you'll find a fascinating piece of Barcelona history dating back many centuries.

13th century A serpentine seasonal stream (called ramla in Arabic) runs outside the city walls. As Barcelona grows, the stream will eventually become an open sewer until it's later paved over.

1500–1800 During this early period, La Rambla was dotted with convents and monasteries, including the baroque **Església de Betlem ❶**, completed in the early 1700s.

1835 The city erupts in anticlericism, with riots and the burning of convents. Along La Rambla, many religious assets are destroyed or seized by the state. This paves the way for new developments, including the **Mercat de la Boqueria ❷** in 1840, **Gran Teatre del Liceu ❸** in 1847 and **Plaça Reial ❹** in 1848.

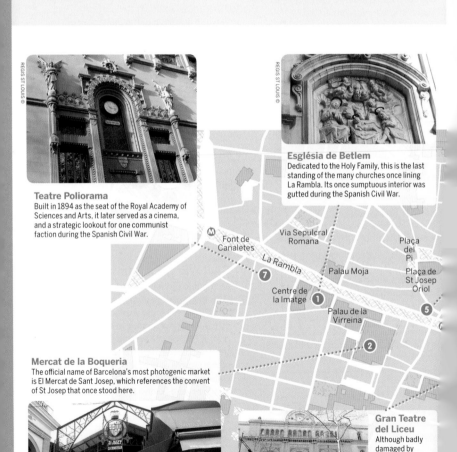

Teatre Poliorama
Built in 1894 as the seat of the Royal Academy of Sciences and Arts, it later served as a cinema, and a strategic lookout for one communist faction during the Spanish Civil War.

Església de Betlem
Dedicated to the Holy Family, this is the last standing of the many churches once lining La Rambla. Its once sumptuous interior was gutted during the Spanish Civil War.

Font de Canaletes

Via Sepulcral Romana

Plaça del Pi

La Rambla

Palau Moja

Plaça de St Josep Oriol

Centre de la Imatge ❶

Palau de la Virreina

❼

❺

❷

Mercat de la Boqueria
The official name of Barcelona's most photogenic market is El Mercat de Sant Josep, which references the convent of St Josep that once stood here.

Gran Teatre del Liceu
Although badly damaged by fire in 1994, this gorgeous opera house was restored and reborn in 1999, and remains one of Europe's finest theatres.

1883 Architect Josep Vilaseca refurbishes the **Casa Bruno Cuadros** ❺. As Modernisme is sweeping across the city, Vilaseca creates an eclectic work using stained glass, wrought iron, Egyptian imagery and Japanese prints.

1888 Barcelona hosts the Universal Exhibition. The city sees massive urban renewal projects, with the first electric lights coming to La Rambla, and the building of the **Mirador de Colom** ❻.

1936–39 La Rambla becomes the site of bloody street fighting during the Spanish Civil War. British journalist and author George Orwell, who spends three days holed up in the **Teatre Poliorama** ❼ during street battles, later describes the tumultuous days in his excellent book, *Homage to Catalonia*.

Casa Bruno Cuadros
The Casa dels Paraigües (House of Umbrellas) – as it's known locally – prominently advertised its wares, with wall-mounted parasols and an ornate Chinese dragon.

REGIS ST LOUIS ©

REGIS ST LOUIS ©

Plaça Reial
Just off La Rambla lies one of Barcelona's prettiest plazas, home to outdoor cafes and bars, palm trees, a gurgling fountain and some unusual lampposts designed by a young Antoni Gaudí.

Mirador de Colom
Southern anchor of La Rambla, this Columbus monument was dedicated in 1888 as part of the Universal Exhibition. You can enjoy fine views from its 60m lookout.

REGIS ST LOUIS ©

BARRI GÒTIC

❹

La Rambla

❸

Palau Güell

La Rambla

Centre d'Art Santa Mònica

Ⓜ

❻

EL RAVAL

Don't Miss
La Catedral

Approached from the broad Avinguda de la Catedral, Barcelona's central place of worship presents a magnificent image. The richly decorated main (northwest) facade, laced with gargoyles and the stone intricacies you would expect of northern European Gothic, sets it quite apart from other churches in Barcelona. The facade was actually added in 1870, but it's based on a 1408 design. The rest of the building was built between 1298 and 1460. The other facades are sparse in decoration, and the octagonal, flat-roofed towers are a clear reminder that, even here, Catalan Gothic architectural principles prevailed.

Map p58

☎ 93 342 82 60

www.website.es/catedralbcn

Plaça de la Seu

admission free, special visit €5, coro admission €2.20

🕒 8am-12.45pm & 5.15-8pm Mon-Sat, special visit 1-5pm Mon-Sat, 2-5pm Sun & holidays

Ⓜ Jaume I

Choir

In the middle of the central nave is the late-14th-century exquisitely sculpted timber *coro* (choir stalls). The coats of arms on the stalls belong to members of the Barcelona chapter of the Order of the Golden Fleece. Emperor Carlos V presided over the order's meeting here in 1519. Take the time to look at the craft up close; the Virgin Mary and Child depicted on the pulpit are especially fine.

Rooftop View

With so much going on inside, it's easy to forget the outside. The roof is notable not just for the views of medieval Barcelona but also for the opportunity to evaluate the cathedral's huge footprint from above. Access to the higher echelons is gained via a lift from the Capella de les Animes del Purgatori near the northeast transept.

Geese

The Tower of London has ravens; Barcelona's Catedral has geese. The 13 birds in the leafy *claustre* (cloister) supposedly represent the age of Santa Eulàlia at the time of her martyrdom and have, generation after generation, been squawking here since medieval days. They make fine watchdogs!

Crypt

Here lies the hallowed tomb of Santa Eulàlia, one of Barcelona's two patron saints, more affectionately known as Laia. The reliefs on the alabaster sarcophagus, executed by Pisan artisans, recount some of her tortures and, along the top strip, the removal of her body to its present resting place.

Baptismal Font

Columbus purportedly kidnapped two dozen North American Indians from the Caribbean island of Hispaniola after his first voyage and brought them back to Spain. Only six survived the journey and, according to legend, they were bathed in holy water at this font just left from the main entrance.

1 CRYPT OF SANTA EULÀLIA

References to the patron saint of Barcelona can be found all over the cathedral but nowhere is as striking as in the crypt. In the centre, an Italian 15th-century alabaster sarcophagus stands where Eulàlia's remains supposedly still lie within. The crypt only opens on the 12 February, Saint Eulàlia's Day, but you can take a peek from the outside. Add 50 céntimos to the box and let the place light up for a more intimate experience.

2 MAIN NAVE

If there is an organ concert going on, sit down on one of the benches, relax and wonder at the magnificence of this Catalan Gothic stone masterpiece. The sounds from the 15th-century carved wooden organ surround the whole place with magic and mystery.

3 THE CHOIR

In 1519, the Order of the Golden Fleece, the elite of Europe's nobility, were invited to Barcelona by the king of Spain, Charles I. A visit to the cloister is a voyage to old times with the coat of arms of each participant painted on the back of the chairs. Try to find Henry VIII of England!

4 CLOISTER

A glimpse of Paradise where the 13 geese in honour of Saint Eulàlia live. While you walk around, look at the tombstones on the floor and find shoes, scissors and the different symbols of the medieval guilds (including shoemakers, tailors and carpenters). If you are here during the Corpus Christi, marvel at one of Barcelona's most popular traditions: the *Ou Com Balla* (dancing egg).

5 EXTERIOR GARGOYLES

There are 160 different gargoyles in the cathedral. Always a good excuse to lift your eyes to the sky and discover not only the obvious dragons and mythological beasts, but also elephants, unicorns and medieval warriors. Great for the young ones and for the not so young.

Discover La Rambla & Barri Gòtic

Getting There & Away

- **Metro** Key stops near or on La Rambla include Catalunya, Liceu and Drassanes. For Barri Gòtic's east side, Jaume I and Urquinaona are handiest.

- **Bus** Airport and night buses arrive and depart from Plaça Catalunya.

- **Taxi** Easiest to catch on La Rambla or Plaça Catalunya.

Carrer dels Comtes, Barri Gòtic
MANFRED GOTTSCHALK/GETTY IMAGES ©

◎ Sights

La Rambla   Street
See p52

La Catedral   Church
See p56

Palau del Lloctinent   Historic Site
Map p60 (Carrer dels Comtes; ⏰10am-7pm; Ⓜ Jaume I) **FREE** This converted 16th-century palace has a peaceful courtyard worth wandering through. Look upwards from the main staircase to admire the extraordinary timber *artesonado,* a sculpted ceiling made to seem like the upturned hull of a boat. Temporary exhibitions, usually related in some way to the archives, are often held here.

Museu Diocesà   Museum
Map p60 (Casa de la Pia Almoina; ☎93 315 22 13; www.arqbcn.org; Avinguda de la Catedral 4; adult/child €6/3; ⏰10am-2pm & 5-8pm Tue-Sat, 11am-2pm Sun; Ⓜ Jaume I) Next to the cathedral, the Diocesan Museum has a handful of exhibits on Gaudí (including a fascinating documentary on his life and philosophy) on the upper floors. There's also a sparse collection of medieval and romanesque religious art usually supplemented by a temporary exhibition or two.

Plaça de Sant Jaume   Square
Map p60 (Ⓜ Liceu or Jaume I) In the 2000 or so years since the Romans settled here, the area around this square (often remodelled), which started life as the forum, has been the focus of Barcelona's civic life. This is still the central staging area for Barcelona's traditonal festivals. Facing each other across the square are the Palau de la Generalitat

(seat of Catalonia's regional government) on the north side and the *ajuntament* (town hall) to the south.

Ajuntament
Architecture

Map p60 (☑ 93 402 70 00; www.bcn.cat; Plaça de Sant Jaume; ☉ 10.30am-1.30pm Sun; Ⓜ Liceu, Jaume I) FREE The *ajuntament*, also known as the Casa de la Ciutat, has been the seat of power for centuries. The Consell de Cent (the city's ruling council) first sat here in the 14th century, but the building has lamentably undergone many changes since the days of Barcelona's Gothic-era splendour.

Palau de la Generalitat
Palace

Map p60 (www.president.cat; Plaça de Sant Jaume; Ⓜ Liceu, Jaume I) Founded in the early 15th century, the Palau de la Generalitat is open on limited occasions only (the second and fourth weekends of the month, plus open-door days). The most impressive of the ceremonial halls is the **Saló de Sant Jordi**, named after St George, the region's patron saint. To see inside, book on the website.

Museu d'Idees i Invents de Barcelona
Museum

Map p60 (Museum of Ideas and Inventions; ☑ 93 332 79 30; www.mibamuseum.com; Carrer de la Ciutat 7; adult/child €8/6; ☉ 10am-2pm & 4-7pm Tue-Fri, 10am-8pm Sat, to 2pm Sun; Ⓜ Jaume I) This small museum's collection makes for an amusing browse over an hour or so. You'll find both brilliant and bizarre inventions: square egg makers, absorbent pillows for flatulent folks, a chair for inserting suppositories, as well as more useful devices like the Lifestraw (filters contaminants from any drinking source) and gas glasses (adaptive eyecare for any prescription).

Plaça de Sant Josep Oriol
Square

Map p60 (Ⓜ Liceu) This small plaza flanking the majestic Església de Santa Maria del Pi is one of the prettiest in the Barri Gòtic. Its bars and cafes attract buskers and artists and make it a lively place to hang out. It is surrounded by quaint streets, many dotted with appealing cafes and shops.

Plaça Reial
Square

Map p60 (Ⓜ Liceu) One of the most photogenic squares in Barcelona, the Plaça Reial is a delightful retreat from the traffic and pedestrian mobs on the nearby Rambla. Numerous eateries, bars and nightspots lie beneath the arcades of 19th-century neoclassical buildings, with a buzz of activity at all hours.

Gran Teatre del Liceu
Architecture

Map p60 (☑ 93 485 99 14; www.liceubarcelona. com; La Rambla dels Caputxins 51-59; tour 20/80min €5.50/11.50; ☉ guided tour 10am, short tour 11.30am, noon, 12.30pm & 1pm; Ⓜ Liceu) If you can't catch a night at the opera, you can still have a look around one of Europe's greatest opera houses, known to locals as the Liceu. Smaller than Milan's La Scala but bigger than Venice's La Fenice, it can seat up to 2300 people in its grand horseshoe auditorium.

Mirador de Colom
Viewpoint

Map p116 (☑ 93 302 52 24; Plaça del Portal de la Pau; lift adult/child €4.50/3; ☉ 8.30am-8pm; Ⓜ Drassanes) High above the swirl of traffic on the roundabout below, Columbus keeps permanent watch, pointing vaguely out to the Mediterranean. Built for the Universal Exhibition in 1888, the monument allows you to zip up 60m in the lift for bird's-eye views back up La Rambla and across the ports of Barcelona.

Església de Sants Just i Pastor
Church

Map p60 (☑ 93 301 74 33; www.basilicasantjust. cat; Plaça de Sant Just 5; ☉ 11am-2pm & 5-8pm Mon-Sat, 10am-1pm Sun; Ⓜ Liceu or Jaume I) This somewhat neglected, single-nave church, with chapels on either side of the buttressing, was built in 1342 in Catalan Gothic style on what is reputedly the site of the oldest parish church in Barcelona. Inside, you can admire some fine stained-glass windows. In front of it, in a pretty little square that was used as a set (a smelly Parisian marketplace) in 2006 for *Perfume: The Story of a Murderer,* is what is claimed to be the city's oldest Gothic fountain.

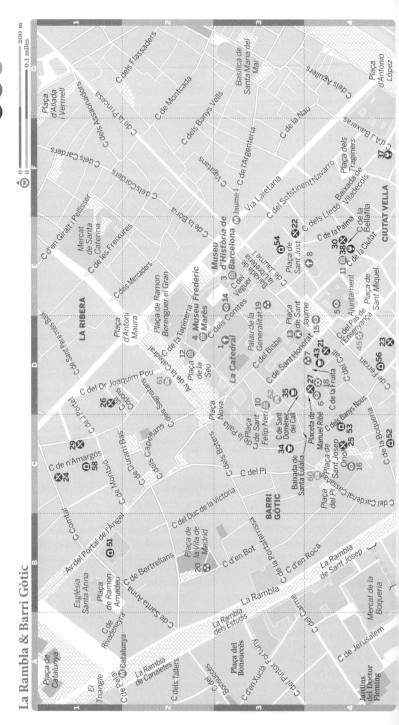

La Rambla & Barri Gòtic

LA RAMBLA & BARRI GÒTIC

200 m
0.1 miles

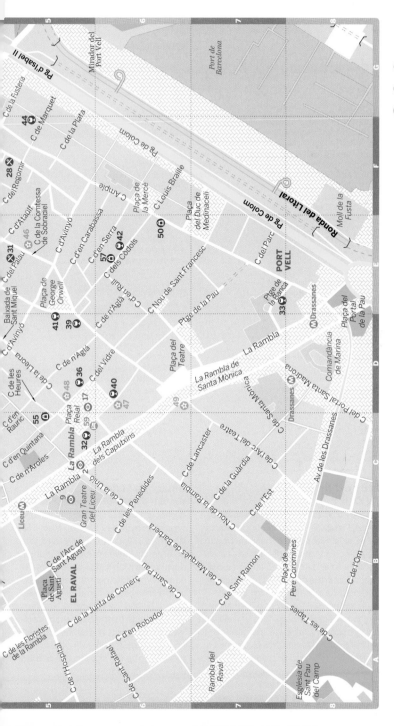

La Rambla & Barri Gòtic

Don't Miss Sights
1 La Catedral D3
2 La Rambla C5
3 Museu d'Història de Barcelona E3
4 Museu Frederic Marès D2

Sights
5 Ajuntament E4
6 Centre d'Interpretació del Call D4
7 Domus de Sant Honorat D4
8 Església de Sants Just i Pastor E4
9 Gran Teatre del Liceu C5
10 Museu del Calçat D3
11 Museu d'Idees i Invents de
    Barcelona E4
12 Museu Diocesà D2
13 Palau de la Generalitat D3
14 Palau del Lloctinent E3
15 Plaça de Sant Jaume D4
16 Plaça de Sant Josep Oriol C4
17 Plaça Reial D5
18 Sinagoga Major D4
19 Temple Romà d'August E3
20 Via Sepulcral Romana B2

Eating
21 Allium D4
22 Cafè de l'Acadèmia E3
23 Cereria D4
24 Cerveceria Taller de Tapas C1
25 Cerveceria Taller de Tapas C4
26 Koy Shunka D1
27 La Vinateria del Call D4
28 Milk F5
29 Onofre C1
30 Pla E4
31 Rasoterra E5

Drinking & Nightlife
32 Barcelona Pipa Club C5
33 Bosc de les Fades E7
34 Caelum C3
35 Čaj Chai D3
36 Karma D5
37 La Cerveteca F4
38 L'Ascensor E4
39 Marula Cafè D5
40 Ocaña D6
41 Oviso D5
42 Polaroid E6
43 Salterio D4
44 Sor Rita F5

Entertainment
45 El Paraigua D4
   Gran Teatre del Liceu .... (see 9)
46 Harlem Jazz Club E5
47 Jamboree D6
48 Sidecar Factory Club D5
49 Teatre Principal D6

Shopping
50 B Lab E6
51 El Corte Inglés B1
52 El Ingenio C4
53 Empremtes de Catalunya C4
54 Fires, Festes i Tradicions E3
55 Herboristeria del Rei C5
56 La Manual Alpargatera D4
57 La Talenta E6
58 Taller de Marionetas Travi C1

Sleeping
59 DO C5
60 El Jardí C4
61 Hotel Colón D2
62 Hotel Neri D3

Centre d'Interpretació del Call
Historic Site

Map p60 (☎ 93 256 21 22; www.museuhistoria. bcn.cat; Placeta de Manuel Ribé; ⏱ 11am-2pm Tue-Fri, to 7pm Sat & Sun; Ⓜ Jaume I or Liceu) FREE Once a 14th-century house of the Jewish weaver Jucef Bonhiac, this small visitors centre is dedicated to the history of Barcelona's Jewish quarter, El Call. Glass sections in the ground floor allow you to inspect Bonhiac's former wells and storage space. The house, also known as the Casa de l'Alquimista (Alchemist's House), hosts a modest display of Jewish artefacts, including ceramics excavated in the area of El Call, along with explanations and maps of the one-time Jewish quarter.

Sinagoga Major
Synagogue

Map p60 (☎ 93 317 07 90; www.calldebar- celona.org; Carrer de Marlet 5; admission by suggested donation €2.50; ⏱ 10.30am-6.30pm Mon-Fri, to 2.30pm Sat & Sun; Ⓜ Liceu) When an Argentine investor bought a run-down electrician's store with an eye to converting it into central Barcelona's umpteenth bar, he could hardly have known he had stumbled onto the remains of what could be the city's main medieval synagogue (some historians cast doubt on the claim). A guide will explain what is thought to be the significance of the site in various languages.

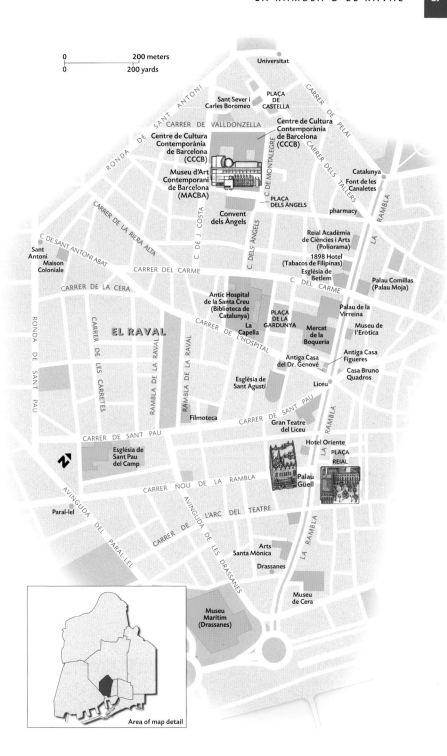

0 ———————————— 200 meters
0 ———————————— 200 yards

Universitat

Sant Sever i
Carles Boromeo

PLAÇA
DE
CASTELLA

CARRER DE PELAI

CARRER DE SANT ANTONI

RONDA DE SANT ANTONI

CARRER DE VALLDONZELLA

Centre de Cultura
Contemporània
de Barcelona
(CCCB)

Centre de Cultura
Contemporània
de Barcelona (CCCB)

C DE MONTALEGRE

CARRER DELS TALLERS

Museu d'Art
Contemporani
de Barcelona
(MACBA)

PLAÇA
DELS ÀNGELS

Catalunya
Font de les
Canaletes

pharmacy

LA RAMBLA

Convent
dels Àngels

C. DE J. COSTA

C. DELS ÀNGELS

Reial Acadèmia
de Ciències i Arts
(Poliorama)

1898 Hotel
(Tabacos de Filipinas)

Església de
Betlem

Palau Comillas
(Palau Moja)

CARRER DE LA RIERA ALTA

Sant
Antoni
Maison
Coloniale

C DE SANT ANTONI ABAT

CARRER DEL CARME

C. DEL CARME

Palau de la
Virreina

Museu de
l'Eròtica

CARRER DE LA CERA

Antic Hospital
de la Santa Creu
(Biblioteca de
Catalunya)

PLAÇA
DE LA
GARDUNYA

La
Capella

CARRER DE L'HOSPITAL

Mercat
de la
Boqueria

Antiga Casa
Figueres

Antiga Casa
del Dr. Genové

Casa Bruno
Quadros

EL RAVAL

RONDA DE SANT PAU

CARRER DE LES CARRETES

RAMBLA DE LA RAVAL

RAMBLA DE LA RAVAL

Església de
Sant Agustí

Liceu

LA RAMBLA

Filmoteca

CARRER DE SANT PAU

Gran Teatre
del Liceu

Església de
Sant Pau
del Camp

CARRER NOU DE LA RAMBLA

Hotel Oriente

Palau
Güell

PLAÇA
REIAL

AVINGUDA DEL PARAL·LEL

Paral·lel

CARRER DE LES DRASSANES

AVINGUDA DE

L'ARC DEL TEATRE

Arts
Santa Mònica

Drassanes

Museu
de Cera

Museu
Marítim
(Drassanes)

Area of map detail

Rambling Along La Rambla

La Rambla is Barcelona's drawing room. For more than a century, townspeople have gathered along the lively pedestrian boulevard to chat, stroll, or duck into a café to pass the time. Unofficially divided into five segments (which is why some call it Las Ramblas), its colorful parade of flower stalls, artists, and posing human statues also makes it a popular first stop for visitors.

On Sunday morning the market comes to Plaça Reial, where people can sell and trade stamps, coins, and an assortment of knickknacks.

They say that if you slake your thirst from the **Font de les Canaletes,** the late 19th-century drinking fountain at the top end of La Rambla, you will surely return to Barcelona. This initial stretch, known as **La Rambla de Canaletes,** was the last to be cleared in the second half of the 19th century, when the final vestiges of

NOT TO BE MISSED:

Palau de la Virreina • Mercat de la Boqueria• Gran Teatre del Liceu • Cafè de l'Òpera• Hotel Oriente

See also area map p. 87
► Plaça de Catalunya
🕐 0.75 mile (1.25 km)
🕐 1 hour
► Museu de Cera

Jaume I's wall were demolished and new housing was raised. Some of those buildings remain, such as Nos. 134–136, which stand next to where the Santa Anna gate once stood, and Nos. 125–129 across the road. The **pharmacy** ❶ at No. 121 retains its distinctive modernista decor.

La Rambla dels Estudis

The second stage of the street is known as La Rambla dels Estudis, after the early 16th-century academic institute, the Estudis Generals, that occupied the area until 1844. Several striking buildings line this part of La Rambla. No. 115, the **Reial Acadèmia de Ciències i Arts (Poliorama)**, was established as a seat of learning during the Enlightenment in the 18th century and received its present look in an 1883 makeover. A little farther down at No. 109 is the large, imposing 19th-century **Tabacos de Filipinas** building, the headquarters of the company in control of Philippine tobacco imports and now home to the luxurious Hotel 1898. Next door is the baroque **Església de Betlem** ❷, part of a 16th-century Jesuit compound that included a religious college. The present church dates from the end of the 17th century and is one of a few outstanding examples of baroque architecture in the city. The interior decoration was lost when anarchists torched the church in the Spanish Civil War in 1936.

Across La Rambla is one of three grand private residences built along the boulevard in the late 18th century, **Palau Comillas (Palau Moja).** You can see temporary exhibitions here and peer into the courtyard from the main entrance on Carrer Portaferrissa. This street takes its name from the Iron Gate, a city gate that once stood here. It was so called after the iron bar used to close it at night. The same bar had a double function as one of the official yardsticks of medieval Barcelona. This section of La Rambla is also known as La Rambla dels Ocells (Birds), because until recently caged birds and exotic animals were sold here.

La Rambla de Sant Josep

Next, the street comes to be known as La Rambla de Sant Josep, after a Carmelite convent that stood here until the mid-19th century. Flower stands abound, explaining the second sobriquet of La Rambla de les Flors. **Palau de la Virreina ❸**, another fine mansion begun in 1772 and named after the widow of the Viceroy of Peru, fronts it. One of the most outstanding baroque residences in Barcelona, it is now used in part to stage temporary photographic exhibitions. On the first floor you'll find an information and ticket office for cultural events around the city.

Next door spreads the grand expanse of the **Mercat de la Boqueria ❹**, a modernista palace of metal and light, and a colorful place to do some grocery shopping, for a picnic maybe, in one of Barcelona's parks or quieter squares. It stands on the site of a Carmelite convent founded in 1586. Farther down at No. 83 is yet another modernista delight, **Antiga Casa Figueres,** adorned with marvelous mosaic

and stucco ornamentation and selling exquisite chocolates. A couple of other extraordinary buildings from the same period are the narrow, blue-tiled **Antiga Casa del Doctor Genové** at No. 77 and the former umbrella-makers' house, **Casa Bruno Quadros,** clad with model umbrellas, at No. 82.

INSIDER TIP:

To enjoy fresh seafood *a la plancha* and to truly be a part of Barcelona's ambience, there is no better place than the Mercat de Sant Josep (La Boqueria).

—CHRISTEL CHERQAOUI
Director of Promotions, National Geographic Books

La Rambla dels Capuxins

A Joan Miró mosaic in the pavement marks Plaça de la Boqueria, the convergence point of a couple of streets with La Rambla. This also indicates the next stage of the avenue, La Rambla dels Caputxins, named after Capuchin monks who had a monastery here. Most interesting now is the **Gran Teatre del Liceu ❺** (see p. 98 & Travelwise p. 263), the city's premier lyric theater that was reopened in late 1999 after suffering bad fire damage several years earlier. Various elements of the original modernista

Ruta del Modernisme Pack

Here's a money-saving idea for every traveler in Barcelona: Rather than paying for each modernista sight as you go, consider picking up a Ruta del Modernisme pack *(rutadelmodernisme.com).* For €12 (about $16) you will receive a guide to 119 modernista buildings great and small, a map, and discounts of up to 50 percent on the main modernista sights in Barcelona. What's more, the discounts are valid for one year. You can pick up the pack at the main tourist office at Plaça de Catalunya 17 or the Pavellons Güell in Pedralbes.

decoration have been retained and the best way to see them is to enjoy a high-quality opera or ballet performance during your stay in town.

Be sure to drop in at the atmospheric **Cafè de l'Òpera** ❻ opposite the opera house. Dating from 1929 it is a favorite for morning coffee or a drink before the performance.

A little farther down on the right at Nos. 45–47 is the **Hotel Oriente** ❼.

(see pp. 92–93). From here onward, the avenue gets decidedly seedier. Late into the night, groups of unhappy-looking hookers huddle among a couple of sad strip clubs, strangely out of place amid the bustle of the street stands on the pedestrian strip that runs down the middle of La Rambla.

You pass another theater, the **Teatre Principal,** and a nondescript square of

La Rambla, Barcelona's famous pedestrian street, is a people-watcher's paradise.

Once a Franciscan religious college, the building was converted into a hotel in the middle of the 19th century. The former cloister and refectory have been preserved and lend much to the faded elegance of the place.

Virtually opposite the hotel is the entrance to the 19th-century **Plaça Reial** (see p. 81). Off to the west down Carrer Nou de la Rambla is **Palau Güell**

the same name as the street enters its final incarnation as **La Rambla de Santa Mònica,** named after the convent that has now been converted into a creative center, **Arts Santa Mònica.**

Across La Rambla and down an alley is the last attraction before you reach the end, the **Museu de Cera** ❽, a wax museum featuring figures ranging from Salvador Dalí to Don Quixote.

Palau Güell

One of Gaudí's earliest masterpieces stands just off La Rambla. His main patron, the wealthy industrialist Eusebi Güell i Bacigalupi (1846–1918), commissioned the building in the early 1880s as an annex to his prime residence on La Rambla. The result is a typically bizarre stylistic mix, as Gaudí looked to past conventions (especially Gothic and Islamic art) to inspire his fresh modernista take.

Four parabolic arches soar three stories high inside one of Gaudí's masterpieces, Palau Güell.

The audio guide takes you first down a ramp to the stables below ground level. Exposed bricks, often seen in his later work, lend warmth to the slightly bizarre landscape of columns with mushroom-like capitals where horses were tethered and the stable boys slept. The area is cleverly ventilated from the interior patio and the street. A spiral ramp winds back up to the vestibule. The pavement appears to be brick but in fact the "bricks" are made of red pinewood, which deadened the clatter of horses' hoofs so as not to disturb the family above. Again the walls are largely unclad brick, unusual at the time when this was considered an ignoble and ugly material. Gaudí had earthy but innovative taste, hence the extensive use of black wrought iron throughout. Another odd feature here is the use of ceramic tiles to clothe the ceiling.

The tour continues up a rather gloomy gray marble stairway. After passing through a small chamber, the **Escala d'Honor,** or principal stairway, leads up to the main floor of the house.

Here a series of three **ante-chambers** looks onto the street and screens off the central salon where the Güell family would receive visitors before ushering them farther into the house. Again the wrought iron is of note, particularly the lamps. Remember to look up, especially in the tiny third room, as the ceilings are magnificent constructions of timber and iron.

The **central salon,** entered through splendid doors, is a curious space indeed. On a square base, four parabolic arches soar three stories and end in a dome, giving the sensation of being in a very small cathedral. It was here that the Güell family held chic parties and occasional political meetings. Sometimes the room even became the family chapel; its altar was destroyed during the civil war.

From the salon a passage leads to the **dining room,** a sumptuous affair of walnut paneling and furniture. The space next door to the dining room is dominated by a tribune fronted by four parabolic arches atop columns. It pushes outward from the rear of the building in a semicircular balcony whose ceramic decoration can be admired from the little **terrace** that opens out from the dining area.

Pass through the private chamber of the family, including a space where they could discreetly view who was in the salon below. From there service stairs climb up onto the **roof** of the building.

Palau Güell

Map p. 87

Carrer Nou de la Rambla 3–5

93 472 57 75

Closed Mon. from 5:30 p.m. Nov.–March, from 8 p.m. April–Oct.

Metro: Línia 3 (Liceu)

palauguell.cat

INSIDER TIP:

The audio guide to Palau Güell, included in the entrance fee, reveals key features of Gaudí's techniques.

—JUSTIN KAVANAGH
National Geographic Travel Books editor

On the way you can peer down into the central salon from several different angles. The roof itself presents the kind of weirdness one expects from Gaudí. Ranks of bizarrely shaped chimney pots, some coated with a dazzling and fragmented array of brightly colored tiles, leave you guessing as to whether Gaudí was giving in to a childlike playfulness or had other more complex intentions. No two chimney pots are alike—each is a separate work of art.

From the roof you can gaze across the Old City's rooftops west toward Palau Nacional (see pp. 186–190) on Montjuïc and east toward the Catedral (see pp. 60–65) and Església de Santa Maria del Mar (see pp. 131–132). ∎

From Xino to Boho

Today's El Raval is fast morphing from notorious neighborhood into hip new boho district with top cultural facilities, artists' studios, vintage shops, and loft living. Yet it retains its edge and colorful overtones, which stem from the district's decadent roots. Known for most of the 20th century as the Barrio Xino (Chinese District), not because of its inhabitants but rather its seedy side as a red-light district favored by bohemian artists and foreign sailors in from the port, it is now a successful product of the municipal urban regeneration policies of the 1980s and 1990s.

The Raval cat, by Colombian sculptor Fernando Botero, a favorite selfie spot with kids

Some streets still have cramped housing filled with floods of migrants from North Africa, Pakistan, and Bangladesh and petty drug traffickers who hawk their wares on some street corners to the excitement of eager visiting students. In the darker alleys the unwary or unlucky may be relieved of their wallets and purses. And although the sex trade is now largely carried on elsewhere in the city, a small group of diehards plies the lower half of the district by day and La Rambla by night. There are still some shops where transvestites can buy their high heels and dresses, though the clubs where they used to hang out are dying fast.

These remnants of the neighborhood's shady past fit well with its multicultural atmosphere and new residents, preventing it from excessive gentrification and making it appealing to a young crowd. The urban regeneration instigated by the enlightened city council in the post-Franco democracy had a heyday in El Raval, resulting in the new cultural centers of MACBA and CCCB (see pp. 96–97), as well as university faculties. A major project involved the demolition of a whole street of housing to create the broad boulevard Rambla del Raval. This new space lined with palm trees, a towering hotel with an inviting roof bar, and every possible kind of restaurant has brought light and life into this formerly dense area.

On weekends a trendy craft market and a Moroccan tent serving mint tea share the space with Botero's jolly, rotund cat sculpture as locals of many nationalities stroll up and down enjoying the new space. At the slightest excuse a stage is erected at one end for live concerts, celebrating Barcelona's patrons or a Sikh festival.

Just off this new Rambla, the film theater, Filmoteca de Catalunya, opened a striking new headquarters in the Plaça Salvador Seguí in 2012. Here you can catch original language films at a reasonable price or enjoy the café. In keeping with the true color of this barrio, prostitutes sometimes loiter in the shade provided by its overhanging designer roof before disappearing down the streets Robadors or Sant Ramon with their prey.

The world's oldest trade is still practiced nightly in the Barrio Xino.

EXPERIENCE: Enjoy Barcelona's Bar Scene

You can still experience the essential flavor of the Barrio Xino with a nocturnal tour of some of the establishments that have survived despite the influx of tourists and increasing rents. Trendy new watering holes abound for the fainthearted.

Some of the bars in Barcelona keep comfortingly late hours and even retain just a whiff of the old spirit—indeed, those that existed back in the day probably saw the likes of Hemingway, Dalí, and Picasso pass through their doors.

Back in 1820, **Bar Marsella** *(Carrer de Sant Pau 65)* opened its doors, and it seems barely anything has changed since. It serves *absenta* (absinthe), once a beverage hard to find because of its supposed narcotic qualities. The drink is a complicated aniseed affair into which you melt sugar cubes with water to produce the full pleasing effect.

One of Picasso's personal favorites was the century-old **London Bar** *(Carrer Nou de la Rambla 36)*, with its modernista decor. People have been cramming in here since 1909.

Another classic nearby, **Kentucky** *(Carrer de l'Arc del Teatre 11)* flourished in the 1950s and 1960s, when U.S. Navy personnel called in to Barcelona on frequent R & R stops.

A more conspiratorial air pervades in the claustrophobic **Bar Pastís** *(Carrer de Santa Mònica 4)*, in business off and on since the end of World War II. French singer Edith Piaf is the mascot. If they aren't playing her songs, there is plenty of live music from singer-songwriter to tango.

Museu d'Art Contemporani de Barcelona (MACBA) & CCCB

Never let it be said that art and the real world have nothing to do with one another. In 1995 this inspired dazzling repository of contemporary art was opened as part of a plan to breathe new life into the top half of El Raval. The result has been spectacular. Tourists and art lovers flock to the museum, and the area has shaken off its seediness without losing the charm.

The startling white facade of MACBA was designed to help lift El Raval out of its economic misery.

The bright white architectural knight was designed by American Richard Meier. Neither as ambitious or outlandish as Paris's Pompidou Center, Meier's creation still shows functional panache. The main entrance is a pleasing interplay of vertical planes, while a curvaceous bulge caps the opposite end and juts into the square. Skateboarding kids animate the area in front; serious art lovers prowl around inside.

The structure and idea are simple. On the first, floor an ever changing arrangement of the gallery's permanent collection forms the core and expresses the museum's aims: to present an international sketch of modern art trends with a strong Barcelona spin. A spiral staircase and graceful ramps for the disabled lead up to two floors above, reserved for temporary exhibitions.

The permanent collection, in

constant rotation, dates from the late 1940s to the present day. The early period covers the Dau al Set movement in Catalonia founded by visual poet Joan Brossa (whose sculpted letters spell Barcino in the cathedral square) and involving artists like Tàpies and Modest Cuixart. Closely related to Surrealism and Dadaism, their informality, a reaction to the restraints of the Franco dictatorship, manifested itself by spontaneous, unstructured creation. You can also see examples of the more order-seeking constructivists like Madrid's Pablo Palazuelo. The collection encompasses European pop art and the avant-garde artists of the 1960s and 1970s through to anti-minimalist sculptures of the 1980s up to recent video and digital installations.

One permanent installation is Tàpies's "Rinzen," a hospital bed hanging dramatically from the wall in the entrance. Made for the Venice Biennale in 1993, when nearby Bosnia was at war, it echoes the suffering of the conflict.

MACBA always has a busy program of dynamic temporary exhibitions and other activities as well as late-night summer events.

Check what's on in their exhibition space housed opposite in the superb 16th-century Convent dels Àngels *(Carrer del Àngels 3–7),* an amazing architectural contrast.

Centre de Cultura Contemporània de Barcelona

Make your way up the street to find the Centre de Cultura Contemporània de Barcelona (CCCB), another striking architectural feat. This 18th-century poorhouse was converted by local architects Piñón and Viaplana in the 1990s into a contemporary cultural center. It hosts a changing program of exhibitions and other activities—seminars, film festivals, concerts—related to contemporary issues around cities, particularly on the new digital challenges of the 21st century.

Recent successes have included Poetry Slam, spoken-word performances, and a series of electronic brunches on Sundays. During the summer months it screens films in its central patio to an audience lounging in deck chairs under the night sky. One side of the patio is a glass wall tilted at an angle at the top giving an unusual panoramic view of the city beyond. ∎

Museu d'Art Contemporani de Barcelona (MACBA)

- Map p. 87
- Plaça dels Àngels 1
- 93 412 08 10
- Closed Tues. & from 3 p.m. Sun.
- $$
- Metro: Línies 1 & 2 (Universitat)

macba.cat

Centre de Cultura Contemporània de Barcelona (CCCB)

- Map p. 87
- Carrer de Montalegre 5
- 903 306 41 00
- Closed Mon.
- $

cccb.org

Cool Art & Café Circuit

The arrival of MACBA and the CCCB has attracted an arty crowd to this part of El Raval. Some have opened small private galleries or trendy boutiques in the area, particularly on Carrer Pintor Fortuny, Carrer dels Àngels, and Carrer del Doctor Dou. Others just come to drink and chat, and they have a growing choice of places in which to do so. For coffee or cocktails a hot spot is **Dos Trece** *(Carrer del Carme 40).* Just west of MACBA on Carrer de Joaquín Costa are lots of options for late-night post-gallery repose. **Casa Almirall** at No. 33 is a fine modernista relic. **Benidorm,** at No. 39, is a lounge-style favorite for local journalism students. Other good options include **Negroni,** at No. 46, and **Betty Ford's,** at No. 56.

More Places to Visit in La Rambla & El Raval

Antic Hospital de la Santa Creu

As early as the 12th century, ailing locals were treated in a hospice here. By 1401 it had been decided to unite all Barcelona's medical centers under one roof. The new buildings were raised around a central cloister (1417) so the dominating style is Catalan Gothic, but with additions from the 16th and 17th centuries. In its heyday, the hospital was said to be one of Europe's finest. Gaudí died here in 1926.

The Gothic chambers now house the **Biblioteca de Catalunya** (Catalonia's national library), which contains the single most complete collection of documents tracing the region's history.

The west side of the complex is home to the **Institut d'Estudis Catalans** (IEC; Institute for Catalan Studies), in the former 17th-century hospice where patients from the hospital would recover. Its cloister is finely decorated with ceramics. The library reading rooms can be seen in library hours. The IEC sometimes opens for temporary exhibitions. In one corner of this peaceful complex, an outdoor café serves light snacks and drinks.

On Carrer de l'Hospital is **La Capella,** the former hospital chapel, now used for temporary art exhibitions focusing on new creative talent. There is an organ above the entrance to this bare, single-nave affair, which preserves a couple of the chapel's richly decorated niches.

🅰 Map p. 87 ✉ Carrer de l'Hospital
🕐 Library: Closed from 2 p.m. Sat. & Sun. Chapel: Closed Mon. 2–4 p.m., Tues.–Sat. & from 2 p.m. Sun. 🚇 Metro: Línia 3 (Liceu)

Església de Sant Agustí

When the Augustinian friars' monastery was demolished to make way for the Ciutadella after the War of the Spanish Succession, they set to building a replacement in El Raval in 1728. The style is a restrained baroque, along classical lines, but the facade was never completed. Indeed much of the exposed side of the church is more akin to a demolition site than a monumental house of worship. Nevertheless, it is one of Barcelona's few examples of baroque architecture. Inside you'll find some exquisite artwork by Italian artist Claudio Lorenzale. The church comes to life during Easter when many Holy Week processions originate here.

🅰 Map p. 87 ✉ Plaça de Sant Agustí 2
🕐 Closed 2–4 p.m. 🚇 Metro: Línia 3 (Liceu)

Església de Sant Pau del Camp

Now surrounded by the inner-city bustle and housing of El Raval, the Romanesque Church of St. Paul in the Fields seems incongruously named. When it was built, though, in 1117, it was well out of town. What makes this somewhat run-down relic interesting today is the exquisite little cloister, whose twin sets of slender columns are topped by unusual lobed arches vaguely resembling clover leaves. The Visigothic ornamentation around the main entrance was probably a leftover from an earlier church.

🅰 Map p. 87 ✉ Carrer de Sant Pau 101
🕐 Closed from 1 p.m.–4 p.m. Mon.–Sat.
🚇 Metro: Línies 2 & 3 (Paral-lel)

Gran Teatre del Liceu

Built in 1847, Barcelona's magnificent opera house was destroyed by fire in 1994 and resurrected five years later. If you can't catch a night at the opera, try to make a day visit to admire the **Salò dels Miralls** (Hall of Mirrors) and its beautiful marble staircase, dominated by Venanci Vallmitjana's modernista sculpture "Al egoria de la Música." liceubarcelona.cat

🅰 Map p. 87 ✉ La Rambla dels Caputxins 51–59 ☎ 93 485 99 00 🕐 Guided tours 10 a.m.; unguided 11:30 a.m., 12 noon, 12:30 p.m., & 1 p.m. 💲 $$ 🚇 Metro: Línia 3 (Liceu)

A busy entertainment complex, maritime and history museums, and seaside warehouses, where once there was only neglect and decay

The Waterfront

Introduction & Map   100–101

Museu Marítim (Drassanes)   102–104

Port Vell   105–109

Feature: When Columbus Sailed
    the Ocean Blue   110–111

La Barceloneta   112–113

Feature: Life's a Beach   114–115

Experience: Spread Your Sails   114

More Places to Visit on the Waterfront   116

Hotels & Restaurants   251–252

The Torre de Jaume I and World Trade Center in Port Vell

The Waterfront

They used to say that Barcelona had turned its back on the sea. Strangely for a seafaring city, a defensive *muralla de mar* (seawall) was raised in the 16th century, shutting off the citizens from the Mediterranean.

With no natural harbor at its disposal, Barcelona had always had to satisfy itself with an imperfect artificial port. Nevertheless, it grew to be one of the great maritime trading cities in medieval Mediterranean Europe. Decline set in from the 16th century, but new wind filled Barcelona's sails from the late 18th century on, when transatlantic trade boomed. As this ebbed in the early 20th century, a morose air of slow decay descended upon the waterfront. However, a visitor to the city in the 1970s would not recognize its coastline

today, such has been the waterfront's phoenix-like rise from the half-abandoned industrial gloom that long preceded the city's frenetic bout of urban renewal.

While the area's commercial operations have been relocated away from the center down along the coast to the southwest, extending as far as the mouth of the Llobregat River, Port Vell (Old Port) has been transformed into a showcase for contemporary Barcelona. Wandering around it can be rewarding.

Passeig de Colom, the busy boulevard along

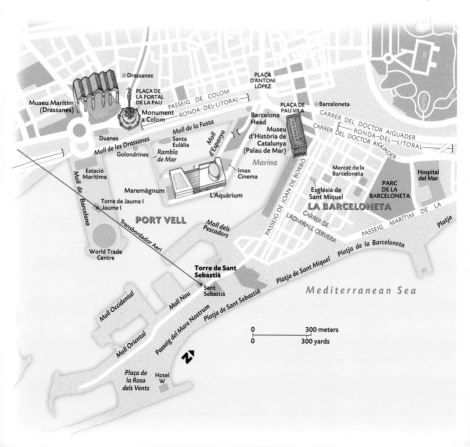

whose length once stood the seawall, has been cleared of all the industrial clutter that once blighted the waterfront. A forest of pleasure boat masts sways in front of landscaped Moll de la Fusta (Timber Dock). On the other side of the Rambla de Mar pedestrian bridge looms the

INSIDER TIP:

Barcelona's Port Vell is a great place for a stroll and to fantasize about the lifestyles of the rich and famous while ogling boats big enough to have their own helicopter.

—ZACHARY BRISSON
National Geographic contributor

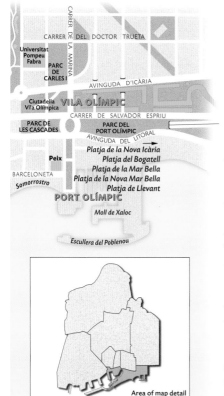

Area of map detail

NOT TO BE MISSED:

The Museu Marítim in Barcelona's royal shipyards   **102–104**

The circling sharks of L'Aquàrium, one of Europe's biggest aquariums   **106–109**

Museu d'Història de Catalunya and a harborside seafood lunch downstairs   **112–113**

Walking or cycling along the beaches north of Port Olímpic   **114–115**

The Museu Blau in the modern Edifici El Fòrum   **116**

Catching the Transbordador Aeri for bird's-eye views of Barcelona   **116**

A night out at CDLC, a beachside lounge bar   **261**

Maremàgnum complex, with bars, restaurants, stores, movie theaters, and a shark-infested aquarium that will thrill the kids.

The water no longer laps at the slipways of the Drassanes Reials (royal shipyards), now home to an engaging maritime museum, but none of the building's splendor has been lost. Nearby, the Monument a Colom (statue of Christopher Columbus) keeps watch over it all from his high perch at the end of La Rambla.

Farther north, just before the tight lanes of 18th-century La Barceloneta, stand former warehouses that today house seafood restaurants and an intriguing museum dedicated to the history of Catalonia. From the towering W Hotel, marking the southernmost point, you can stroll along the different city beaches way beyond the Olympic Port. Once filthy, these beaches nowadays fill to the brim with sun-worshipping locals. The beaches peter out where the new high-rise area known as El Fòrum (see p. 116) sprang up for the 2004 Forum of Cultures. The great news for sun-seekers is that there are plenty more fine sandy strands, easily reached by train, along the coast to the north and south of the city. ∎

Museu Marítim (Drassanes)

In 1570 a grand new galley slid down the slipway of the Drassanes Reials, Barcelona's Royal Shipyards. This jewel of naval production, 197 feet (60 m) long and carrying a crew of 400, would serve as the flagship of Don Juan of Austria in the classic sea battle of Lepanto in 1571. This reconstructed vessel alone makes a visit to this outstanding museum worthwhile.

Extraordinary maritime memorabilia lies beneath the arches of Barcelona's royal shipyards.

Museu Marítim de Barcelona

🅰 Map p. 100

✉ Avinguda de les Drassanes s/n

☎ 93 342 99 20

💲 $$

Ⓜ Metro: Línia 3 (Drassanes)

mmb.cat

The **Drassanes** are a singular work of old civic architecture. Construction of the shipyards began here in the reign of Pere II in the 13th century, soon after the Venetians began building their famed Arsenale. All the great maritime cities developed shipyards at about this time, but few are this impressive.

Expansion came in the late 14th century under Pere IV. At the time, the sea washed up at the entrance to the parallel halls of the yards, lightly inclined so that completed vessels could be easily let down slipways into the water. Additions were made in the 15th and 16th centuries, and the whole area was fortified around the end of the 17th century. In the 18th and 19th centuries the shipyards passed into the hands of the army, which used them for artillery production and training. In 1941 the army handed the structure over to civilian authorities, and the idea of a naval museum was born.

Rewriting History

The Maritime Museum has been closed intermittently for major restoration work over 25 years but reopened in 2013, proudly showing off its cathedral-like proportions with eight soaring naves under majestic arches. Part of the 13th-century city wall has been exposed, and archaeological work revealed a Roman necropolis (1-6 A.D.) indicating a hitherto unknown route out of Roman Barcino. Remains of 13th-century pillars found during the work show that the original Gothic construction was demolished and the building we see today was built in the same style but in the 16th century. It is still breathtaking and worth a visit.

Visiting the Museum

There are plans to relaunch the museum with a new permanent exhibition, raised walkways, and a new entrance, but they are currently on hold. The idea is to give a broad view of the history of maritime culture and the relationship between mankind and the sea, but with 21st-century museum technology and interactive displays. Watch out for its inauguration as it promises to be a fascinating presentation. Until then this magnificent building displays part of its huge collection and holds regular all-encompassing temporary exhibitions on subjects related to the sea, like "The Vikings," an exploration into these intrepid seafarers, which was held for six months in 2014, or "The Antarctic," which gave chilling insight into what is involved in scientific expeditions to the South Pole.

Garden Display: The current entrance is through a shady courtyard where the museum's excellent-value restaurant, Norai

(closes 8 p.m.), has outdoor tables by a pond. Pause here to enjoy the flora and fauna, including what looks like a timber sunfish. It is in fact a life-size model of the Ictineo I, an early submarine created by Barcelona inventor Narcis Monturiol in 1859. He sunk his life savings into this and a second, bigger version (which stands outside near the IMAX cinema in Maremàgnum), but eventually went broke in the effort.

Another interesting nautical remnant in the garden is the bridge of Sayremar I. It used to be part of the schooner *Santa Eulàlia,* now moored at the Moll de la Fusta (see p. 105), when this

(see p. 105)

INSIDER TIP:

For a budget tour, take the no. 24 bus past key Gaudí buildings in Passeig de Gràcia as far as Park Güell, or the no. 17 from uptown to the harbor at Barceloneta.

—ANNIE BENNETT
National Geographic author

was commandeered as a working vessel. Have a glimpse through the porthole to see a slice of a sailor's life at sea.

Inside the Museum: Once inside the building, apart from the temporary exhibition of the moment you will see various cabinets displaying part of the collection such as handsome models of steamships, from the earliest belchers to transatlantic liners. These range from the grand "Royal Edward," built in Glasgow shipyards in 1908 for a Canadian company to one of the modern fast ferries that today zip between Barcelona and the Balearic Islands.

The centerpiece of the museum is the full-scale replica of Don Juan of Austria's flagship,

---

Don Juan of Austria

Half-brother of King Philip II of Spain, Don Juan (John) of Austria (1547–1578) was a military man with a mission. When he drew up his forces to face the Turkish armada off Lepanto in Greece in 1571, it was largely his will to win that kept the allies together and led to victory. Had Philip not been so distrustful of the allies, they and Don Juan might have gone on to overthrow Ottoman Turkish power in the Mediterranean. Instead, Don Juan ended up as governor of Spain's rebellious Dutch provinces until his death.

---

which carried the Christian allies to victory over the Turks in 1571 in the last sea battle dominated by galleys. This brings to life the appalling conditions in which the galley crews lived. Made up of slaves, prisoners, and even the occasional unwitting volunteer, this 200-strong crew of oarsmen remained chained to benches, three or four across, for the duration of their time at sea. They rowed during battle, when

the ship had to make complex maneuvers, or when there was no wind. They ate, drank, and slept where they sat. Legend has it that you could smell a galley from miles away.

Artworks: Until the new exhibition is launched pieces from the museum's prized collection will be rotated, so you may see some fascinating charts such as the 1439 Vallseca one used by Florentine explorer Amerigo Vespucci (1454–1512), where the Red Sea is colored red and Ireland is green. One of the earliest is a parchment copy of Abraham i Jafuda Cresques's 1375 chart. Or you may see *mascarons,* wooden figureheads, which for centuries adorned the bows of vessels. These grew out of the custom of painting eyes on ships' prows, still common on small fishing boats. The belief was that these figures, like the eyes would help guide and protect both vessel and crew from the cruel hazards of sea and war.

Floating Museum

Wander down to the quayside near the Rambla de Mar which leads to Maremàgnum to see the floating part of the museum. With your museum ticket you can board the elegant *Santa Eulàlia,* (closed Mon. & Sat. a.m.; see sidebar p. 107), a restored 1918 three-masted schooner. Its most important role is on the eve of Epiphany (Jan. 5) when it brings the Wise Kings from across the seas to land in the port of Barcelona to deliver their gifts to wide-eyed children. ■

Port Vell

Nowadays if you stand in the shadow of the Monument a Colom and look toward the Mediterranean, the view is very different from that of pre-Olympics Barcelona. Back in the 1980s, Port Vell (Old Port) was a disastrous tangle of half-abandoned warehouses, dumps for empty containers and rusty scrap metal, and creaking rail yards. The 1992 Games provided the city fathers with the excuse they needed to give the waterfront a face-lift. They succeeded.

The modern waterfront of Port Vell

Across the partly subterranean Ronda del Litoral freeway, the pedestrianized Moll de la Fusta (Timber Quay) looks onto a revamped parking lot for yachts, the Port de Barcelona. Luxury yachts that are part of the annual Boat Show, or yachts waiting to sail off to a regatta are often moored at this quayside. Their proud crews will often be happy to share seafaring stories with admiring passersby.

In the middle of the harbor looms a modern pleasure center built on Moll d'Espanya (Spain Dock). To get to it, cross the stylish **Rambla de Mar bridge** (it opens up occasionally to let yachts pass), its wavy design nicely in keeping with the water it spans. Thousands stroll across here every day to crowd into **Maremàgnum**, an inviting cornucopia of stores, eateries, and bars. Across the water to the south, Barcelona's

L'Aquàrium

🅰 Map p. 100

✉ Moll d'Espanya

☎ 93 221 74 74

💲 $$$$

🚇 Metro: Línies 3 (Drassanes) & 4 (Barceloneta)

aquariumbcn.com

snazzy World Trade Center is a hive of activity.

Behind Maremàgnum (to the north) is a movie theater complex and then the star of the show, L'Aquàrium. Beyond that stands the city's wide-screen IMAX theater.

L'Aquàrium

The Aquarium is an extraordinary sea show and makes a pleasing diversion from the city's grand monuments, museums, and galleries. Those who don't have the chance to dive in the Mediterranean, Red Sea, Caribbean, or Great Barrier Reef are compensated here with the 21 tanks that make up this underwater world for landlubbers. Open since 1995, it is one of Europe's largest aquariums and home to some 11,000 fish comprising more than 400 species. A dozen sharks are among the star guests.

The tanks contain about 1.3 million gallons (4.9 million L) of seawater, regularly filtered, treated, and topped off. Artificial lighting, controlled by a central computer, is adjusted constantly to reflect as closely as possible what happens in nature. New fish, when introduced to the aquarium, are not simply thrown in the deep end; they go through a quarantine period in which they are checked for disease and given time to grow accustomed to a new diet. More than two tons of feed (fish, shellfish, plankton, vitamins, and seaweed) is on the marine menu every week.

The Tanks: With your ticket in hand, you head down a series of ramps to the tanks. Before doing so you may wish to buy the detailed and colorful "Guide—L'Aquàrium," a useful illustrative handbook to what you are about to see. Less detailed labeling in Spanish,

Thousands of fish, including several shark species, patrol the tanks of L'Aquàrium.

Catalan, and English appears throughout the display.

The first ten tanks re-create various Mediterranean environments. Indeed, it is claimed that the collection of Mediterranean species here is the most extensive in Europe. **Tank 1** simulates a shallow-water rocky area just off the coast, characterized by transparent water and lots of light, which fuels the growth of algae the purple dye for their togas.

Tank 3 re-creates the specific environment of the Ebro Delta, in southern Catalonia, where freshwater from the river mixes with seawater in extensive lagoons. The fish that live in these waters have evolved in such a way that they can cope with varying levels of salinity. Among them are gilthead bream, corb, sole, and meagre. Eels, which breed in the

Grande Dame of the Sea

Docked by the Rambla de Mar bridge that links the Port Vell shoreline to Maremàgnum, a tall three-master rides at anchor. Restored by the Museu Marìtim in the late 1990s, the *Pailebot de Santa Eulàlia* was launched in 1918 under the name *Carmen Flores*. For decades, it operated from Catalonia and in the Balearic Islands. Today, the ship is used for a variety of events in and beyond Barcelona. When it is docked at home, you can climb aboard *(closed Mon. & Sat. a.m.)* and inspect the rigging at close quarters. Drop belowdecks to the sleeping quarters in the aft, feel the water lapping against the sides of the hull, and admire photos of an era long past.

and other vegetation. Fish here seek out protection among the rocks, although some, such as the black scorpion fish, have different defense methods (the scorpion fish has nasty spikes). Other common inhabitants include sea bass and two-banded bream. A nastier customer is the moray eel, which delivers a mean bite to anything that disturbs it. The Romans used to use the toxins in moray blood to make poison.

Tank 2 is dedicated to sandy coastal areas. Various kinds of rays dominate, along with several species of fish that bury themselves in the sand, such as the wide-eyed flounder. You can also see an assortment of crustaceans and snails, including the *Spinus murex*, from which the Romans extracted Sargasso Sea, also migrate in and out of the area.

Next, in **Tank 4** is a rocky environment made up of tunnels and caves. Several species of fish favor this dark ambience, and crustaceans, such as hermit crabs, lobsters, and prawns, simply love it.

Tank 5 is dominated by algae and various fish breeds, such as the ornate wrasse, that prefer a weedy environment. A couple of smaller tanks next to it contain shark eggs, crabs, and sea horses.

The following five tanks are dedicated to a variety of Mediterranean environments ranging from shallow plains reaching out from the shoreline to the mid-sea depths. Everything from striped red mullet to the big, spiny St. Peter's fish inhabits these waters.

Some, like the pilot fish, happily swim around the depths without ever having to explore the seafloor.

Things get a good deal more colorful in the next two tanks. Beautiful red coral, found in many parts of the Mediterranean, dominates **Tank 11.** Swimming around in here are cardinal fish and a few other species. Whitetip and blacktip sharks, common in tropical waters, swim about in **Tank 12,** along with all other tropical fellows, like the Napoleon fish.

All sorts of beautiful coral and shoals of brightly colored little fish dominate **Tank 13.** Yet another carnival of color is presented in **Tank 14,** dedicated to the Caribbean, containing yellow surgeonfish, French angelfish, royal gramma, and sergeant majors.

Then comes a taste of the tropical waters of Australia's Great Barrier Reef in **Tank 15.** Residents are a mixed bunch, with such eye-catching members as imperial

angelfish and harlequin tuskfish. **Tank 16** contains a Red Sea environment, and its inhabitants are a riot of color, from the bright yellow butterfly fish to the Arabic angelfish and various types of surgeonfish. Small whitetip reef sharks are in perpetual motion, and for good reason—otherwise they would drown from lack of oxygen. If you look closely, you can also make out at least one giant clam.

Tank 17 is altogether another story, taking you to murkier depths where more dangerous fellows lurk. They include the ugly rockfish, several species of scorpion fish, and other poisonous critters.

Next comes the star attraction, the Oceanarium, with its 263-foot-long (80 m) **tunnel** that leads you through this huge tank full to brimming with all sorts of

All at Sea

While at the waterfront, it is tempting to get a seaward perspective on Barcelona. The traditional Golondrina excursion boats (tel 93 442 31 06; lasgolondrinas.com) **have been sailing from Moll de les Drassanes in front of the Monument a Colom since 1888. A trip to the breakwater** (rompeolas) **and lighthouse** (faro) **on the seaward side of the harbor takes about 40 minutes. Or try the longer sailing on a glass-bottom catamaran around to Port Olímpic and the Forum, which takes 90 minutes. Departures are more frequent in summer. The lighthouse run normally leaves hourly when there is demand.**

Mediterranean deep-sea species. These range from menacing sandbar sharks and majestic rays to the enormous and oddly oval-shaped sunfish. This tank and tunnel afford the opportunity to observe these grand creatures up close and from just about every conceivable angle. What better view of a shark's sharp dental set than from below?

The next couple of tanks can be viewed about halfway through the tunnel. The first concentrates on a coralline environment similar to that of the Illes Medes, or Medes Islands, off the Costa Brava north of Barcelona. The area is a popular dive spot, and here you can see a few of the fish species encountered in the protected marine reserve—among them conger eels, scorpion fish, grouper, and trigger fish.

Tank 20 plumbs the depths to visit the few species of fish that live on the Mediterranean seafloor. You can't always see a great deal in this tank as the lighting is kept low to simulate the deep-sea conditions. You should be able to witness the antics of octopuses.

When you finally emerge from the tunnel, one tank awaits inspection, this time the re-creation of an atoll in the South Seas. In its warm waters gathers a predictably colorful assortment of little fish. After the blue-water magnificence of the shark tunnel, this seems to serve as a sweetener to bring you back down to Earth before heading upstairs.

Planeta Agua: The fun is not quite over, for an interactive zone called Planeta Agua (Planet Water) upstairs is worth some time. Here you can see families of penguins in a peaceful

The Maremàgnum complex, full of restaurants, shops, and bars, provides striking views across the harbor to the city.

Antarctic setting; one can only wonder what they make of their human observers. A series of tanks re-creates mangrove swamps and other freshwater environments in which a variety of water creatures circulate, including a couple of versions of the famed piranha. Children will enjoy the open tank full of rays. An aquarium guide will give you rubber gloves and supervise as you caress the rays as they swim lazily around the tank. Lastly, several interactive displays reveal the weird and wonderful, such as the weedy sea dragon (a bizarre relative of the sea horse) and lumpy rockfish. Inside a whale diorama are models of truly odd deep-ocean creatures and some huge crabs. ■

When Columbus Sailed the Ocean Blue

Christopher Columbus (1451–1506) must have been exultant on the day in January 1492 when he received the order to attend an audience with the Catholic Monarchs of Spain, King Ferdinand and Queen Isabella. Having just taken Granada, the last Moorish stronghold in the country, they were in high spirits. Columbus now finally heard the words he had longed to hear: The monarchs announced they would back his plan to search for a western ocean route to India and Cathay (China).

Columbus set out from Spain convinced he would find a new sea route to India.

Columbus was born in Genoa, northern Italy. An avid fan of the adventures of Marco Polo, he moved to Portugal as a young man and became a senior navigator. From 1486 onward he was based in Spain, and he set out from Palos in August 1492 with his little fleet of three ships, the *Santa Maria, Pinta,* and *Niña.*

Controversy

Ever since that first voyage, controversy has surrounded Columbus. A brilliant navigator, he was also an autocratic and ruthless commander, and his almost mystical religiosity and inflexibility won him few friends. Columbus discovered Cuba and other Caribbean islands but was convinced he had crossed the seas to Cathay: He refused to countenance the possibility that he had discovered hitherto unknown lands.

INSIDER TIP:

Why not take one of the chartered boats or sailboat tours available along the waterfront? Use the statue of Columbus as your reference point and set sail in a spirit of discovery.

—ZACHARY BRISSON
National Geographic contributor

Second & Third Voyages

In mid-1493 Columbus arrived in Barcelona to report to the Catholic Monarchs, who happened to be in residence at the time (at this stage they had no fixed court). It was a lively exercise in show-and-tell—his display of gold, spices, exotic birds, and some captive natives left Ferdinand and Isabella suitably impressed. They immediately authorized a second voyage, which, with 17 ships and 1,500 sailors and passengers (including friars and investors), set sail in September of the same year.

This and a third voyage kept Columbus busy until 1500, by which time he had explored more of the Caribbean and landed on the South American mainland (Venezuela). Although he may by then have realized that he had discovered a new world, he insisted otherwise. Meanwhile, the Spaniards had colonized Hispaniola (modern Haiti and the Dominican Republic) and, under Columbus's brothers who were in charge on land, were making themselves unpopular as they extracted gold and reduced the local populace to slavery. Their

methods were so harsh that a commission of inquiry arrested Columbus (who was ultimately responsible for his brothers' excesses) and sent him back to Spain. Exonerated, he was sent on one last mission of exploration, but this proved largely a failure. His last years in Spain were ones of sad decline. He died in Valladolid but was buried in Seville: Later his remains were moved to Santo Domingo in Hispaniola.

In 1888 the tall **Monument a Colom** was opened on Plaça del Portal de la Pau (Gate of Peace Square) in the presence of town officials from Barcelona and Genoa. At the time, a popular line of thinking claimed Columbus was actually a Catalan, and even today some historians maintain this is the case. You can take an elevator to the top for panoramic views.

Day and night, Columbus's stoic figure gazes out to sea from its perch at the foot of La Rambla.

La Barceloneta

The narrow streets and apartment blocks of "Little Barcelona" were first designed by French military engineer Prosper Verboom in 1715, but his plans were not carried out until 1753 by Spanish engineer Juan Martín Cermeño.

Tempting seafood restaurants flank the former warehouses that now contain a museum of Catalan history.

Aimed at relocating dispossessed citizens from La Ribera after construction of the Ciutadella fortress (see pp. 133–135), the area became a poor if ebullient quarter housing mostly sailors, fishermen, and their families. Even today, it is said the city's best fish is served here.

Originally, streets of consistently uniform, two-story houses (so as not to obstruct the firing line of cannon in the Ciutadella) were quickly built. With time and a growing population, they were subdivided into as many as four tiny apartments, and a few of these still remain today. Higher apartment blocks (up to five stories) gradually replaced the smaller houses and gave the quarter the slightly claustrophobic feel it has today.

A wander around the inner part of La Barceloneta, whose centerpieces are the baroque **Església de Sant Miquel** (built in 1755 on Plaça de Sant Miquel) and the renovated market, **Mercat de la Barceloneta** (on Plaça de la Font), is to step a little out of time, for the place retains the lively community feeling of the old fishermen's quarter with some traditional old bars still surviving.

Barcelona's dwindling fishing fleet ties up at nearby **Moll del Rellotge** (Clocktower Wharf), opposite the promenade known as Passeig de Joan de Borbó, which is, appropriately, lined with seafood restaurants.

Overlooking the newly developed super-yacht marina is the fine Magatzem General de Comerç, the last of the old port's warehouses, now home to the Museu d'Història de Catalunya, an introduction to the history of Catalonia.

Museu d'Història de Catalunya

The museum's permanent exhibition is spread out over the third and fourth floors; temporary exhibitions are occasionally held, too. It is worth picking up a returnable guide in your language at the ticket desk, as most of the explanations throughout the museum are in Catalan only.

On the **third floor** you start with simple implements from prehistoric times. There are Bronze Age bracelets, coins, and household objects from Iberian tribes as well as from Greek and Roman settlements. Maps and illustrations accompany the recounting of ancient history in Catalonia, and displays include life-size cutaway remakes of a Roman boat and the atrium of a Roman house.

Next are displays dedicated to the rise of Christianity and the Visigothic period, followed by the arrival of the Muslims in Catalonia. The story continues with the Middle Ages: Models of churches and castles are accompanied by explanations of monastery life, a mock-up of Jaume I's field campaign tent, and accounts of Catalonia's expansion in Spain and the Mediterranean. You can even try on some armor.

Other sections are devoted to Romanesque and Gothic art, Jewish and Muslim communities in Catalonia, and the region's gradual absorption into the Spanish Crown. You finish up at the War of the Spanish Succession with scenes of the siege of Barcelona. The city's surrender to the Bourbon king Philip V marks the end of autonomy for Catalonia.

Up on the **fourth floor** the story continues with industrialization in the 18th and 19th centuries and the Napoleonic wars. Photos from late in the 19th century onward shed light on what Barcelona must have been like more

than a hundred years ago and help trace the most recent stages in the city's history. They touch on themes such as modernisme, child factory labor, internal migration from the rest of Spain, and the growth of Catalan nationalism in the run-up to the civil war.

Old typewriters, cameras, and phones are on display, as well as newspapers from prewar years. Next come the horrors of the civil war, so you can take cover in a Barcelona air raid shelter. Or you can see newsreels in a postwar, Franco-era movie theater. Or sidle up to a bar and watch 1950s TV.

Roy Lichtenstein's Head

Just off Plaça d'Antoni López at the end of Via Laietana stands Roy Lichtenstein's "Barcelona Head" sculpture. An abstract painter of America's pop art movement, Lichtenstein (1923–1997) made a hit with his enlarged comic-strip characters, characterized by black-rimmed primary colors and the Ben Day screen dots simulated with a stencil. His sculpture bears many of the traits of this comic-strip painting.

The display finishes in the declaration of Catalonia as an autonomous region and a review of contemporary Catalonia. After all this history, why not try the terrace restaurant-bar on the same floor with a great view of the port? ■

Museu d'Història de Catalunya

- 🅰 Map p. 100
- ✉ Palau de Mar, Plaça de Pau Vila 3
- ☎ 93 225 47 00
- 🕐 Closed Mon. & from 2:30 p.m. Sun. & holidays
- 💲 $$
- 🚇 Metro: Línia 4 (Barceloneta)

mhcat.cat

Life's a Beach

Until the late 1980s, Barcelona's beaches were fairly awful. Lined with rubbish and lapped by polluted water, they were hardly inviting, although hardier locals refused to be deterred. Amid the neglect was some cheer, however. The two beaches lining La Barceloneta's seaward side, Platja de Sant Sebastià and Platja de la Barceloneta, were long famed for their *chiringuitos,* little makeshift seafood eateries. Some were so close to the water that you got your feet wet while you ate!

All good things come to an end, though, and the chiringuitos disappeared along with all the garbage that the town authorities removed in a drive to remake the face of the waterfront. Today, the beaches are kept immaculate and the water, although not transparent, is much cleaner than it was not so long ago.

Palms have been planted and a pleasant pedestrian-only promenade takes you to Port Olímpic and beyond to farther city beaches. Strollers mix with seemingly suicidal in-line skaters, street performers, and a cheerful assortment of locals and visitors. On midsummer weekends the beaches around Barcelona tend to be packed.

Stretching beyond the bar-lined mooring for expensive yachts that is Port Olímpic (see p. 116) is a string of four more beaches, each separated from the other by moles (breakwaters). **Platja Nova Icària** and **Platja del Bogatell** are family beaches. Where the latter joins **Platja de la Mar Bella** there is a small nudist strip, although sunbathers who prefer to keep one or two items of clothing about them mingle in freely enough with the in-the-altogether crowd. The northern end of the beach and its neighbors, **Platja de la Nova Mar Bella** and **Platja de Llevant,** tend to be less crowded than the others, if only because they are slightly less accessible by public transportation. Since 2002, a string of hip chill-out bars (offering a limited menu of food) have appeared along these beaches. They keep a hedonistic, suntanned crowd drinking cocktails, chatting, and dancing from the afternoon well into the Barcelona night. These *xiringuitos* (beach bars) are generally open from about 10 a.m. to 1 a.m., from Easter until October, depending on the weather.

This is only a taste of the local beach scene. Beyond Barcelona to the southwest and northeast lie strings of wonderful beaches. Indeed, the entire Catalan coast is festooned with them. The most accessible lie on *rodalies,* which are local suburban train lines. Trains run

EXPERIENCE: Spread Your Sails

Sitting on one of the city beaches gazing out to sea, you might feel inclined to do something more strenuous than turn over and over improving your suntan. Ever wanted to learn windsurfing? You can do so here—and meet locals in the process—by heading to the **Base Nàutica Municipal** *(Avinguda Litoral s/n, tel 93 221 04 32, basenautica.org),* on the north end of Platja del Bogatell. Tuition in windsurfing costs €200 for 8 hours. All the equipment is provided. There are other opportunities, too. The same place offers courses in catamaran sailing, kayaking, and sailing of light vessels. As a rule, classes take place a couple of times a week, so you are looking at a minimum of two weeks' commitment. Windsurfers and kayaks are also available for renting if you can prove your skills. The terrace bar is a good spot for a snack, open to all.

A much needed cleanup that began in the 1980s has given La Barceloneta a fine beach.

with surprising frequency from, among other stops, Plaça de Catalunya to the Maresme coast just north and to the south from Passeig de Gracia and Sants to beaches at **Sitges** (see pp. 216–218) and beyond at **Vilanova i la Geltrú** and at **Calafell.**

Heading north there is a long succession of beaches along the rail line to **Blanes.** These beaches tend to be narrower, but in general they are clean and all have showers. Most are within about an hour's rail travel of central Barcelona.

More Places to Visit on the Waterfront

Diagonal Mar & El Fòrum

A modern high-rise residential and commercial district has arisen in the city's northeast corner. Known as Diagonal Mar, its core is **El Fòrum,** an open area dominated by the triangular Edifici Fòrum, designed by Swiss architects Herzog & de Meuron. Its navy blue flanks are gashed by great mirror strips. It now houses the Museu Blau, part of the Natural History Museum *(museu ciencies.cat, closed Mon.)*, showing some of the four million species in its collection.

INSIDER TIP:

Capture the best views of the city from Torre de Jaume I at the midway point of the cable car ride that runs between Barceloneta and Montjuïc.

—ANNIE GRIFFITHS BELT
National Geographic photographer

Nearby are a conference center, shopping mall, and apartment blocks. Local architect Enric Miralles designed **Parc Diagonal,** with Mediterranean plant species, ponds, and innovative kids' play area. Also close to the Edifici Fòrum, in the shadow of a huge photovoltaic panel, is the **Zona de Banys,** a protected swimming area and another marina.
Map inside front cover

Port Olímpic

Perhaps the most astounding thing about Port Olímpic and the residential area surrounding it, Vila Olímpica (the athletes' village during the 1992 Games), is what you can no longer see.

The creation of the new pleasure port for the sailing events in the Olympic Games and the village next door were only part of a much broader urban renewal program.

Nowadays, expensive yachts from all over the world call in at Port Olímpic either for brief stays or complete refits. Awaiting their crews along the landward side of the port is a line of restaurants, eateries, and bars.

Behind the port rise two landmark skyscrapers, the Torre Mapfre office block and the chic, high-rise Hotel Arts Barcelona (see Travelwise p. 251). Below them a couple of discos, a casino, and restaurants are fronted by the striking bronze-colored sculpture known as **"Peix"** ("Fish"). This scaly contribution to Barcelona's seaside is the handiwork of Frank Gehry.

After the athletes left, the housing in Vila Olímpica was sold off as private apartments. The quality of the apartments, it turns out, was not always of the highest, but the surrounding redevelopment revolutionized this part of the city. Before, the working-class Poble Nou district straggled down to the seaside in what had been known to Spaniards since the mid-19th century as the Catalan Manchester. Beneath the now established neighborhood of Vila Olímpica lies buried the memory of another world: chemical and alcohol factories, docks, warehouses, and railway lines which made this area one of the least appealing of the city.
Map p. 100

Transbordador Aeri

Looking like some creaking old remnant of a bygone industrial age, an imposing metal tower rises high above Barcelona's old port inland from Platja de Sant Sebastià. This is **Torre de Sant Sebastià,** the start/end point for an aerial excursion linking the sea with Montjuïc (see pp. 183–202). The **cable car** that goes over the water from the tower passes a second tower, **Torre de Jaume I,** by the **World Trade Center,** and continues to the Miramar observation point on Montjuïc. The views are spectacular. Round-trip tickets cost only marginally more than one-way trips.
Map p. 100

The eastern wing of the Old City, watched over by the Gothic Santa Maria del Mar and showcasing Picasso, an 18th-century archaeological site, and the modernista fantasy of the Palau de la Música Catalana

La Ribera

Introduction & Map   118–119

Palau de la Música Catalana   120–121

Experience: Take in the Full Palau Experience   121

Feature: Young Picasso   122–123

Experience: Tracing Picasso's Early Years   123

Carrer de Montcada   124–129

Experience: Try Bubbly, Baroque, & Basque   129

El Born   130–132

Experience: Hit the High Notes in High Church   132

Parc de la Ciutadella   133–135

Feature: To Market, to Market   136–137

Experience: Taste the Magic of Chocolate   137

More Places to Visit in La Ribera   138

Hotels & Restaurants   252–254

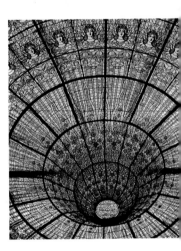

The modernista skylight of the Palau de la Música Catalana

La Ribera

Centuries ago, the Mediterranean ate much deeper into Barcelona's land than today. Nowhere was this more the case than in La Ribera (The Shore), the logical center of international medieval trade as vessels from around Europe called in to do business.

Bars and restaurants now line Passeig del Born, once the scene of jousts and executions.

The first settlement, beyond the then city walls, clustered around the original Església de Santa Maria del Mar as early as the tenth century. It came to be known as Vilanova de Mar—Newtown by the Sea. Farther inland, another satellite of the city, Vilanova de Sant Pere, grew around the monastery of Sant Pere de les Puelles, and the two nuclei grew in tandem. While tradesmen, artisans, and storekeepers concentrated around what is today Carrer de la Princesa, seafarers and businessmen with trade interests abroad moved into Vilanova de Mar. By the 13th century much of the wealth pouring into the city as a result of Jaume I's conquests and the rapid growth in sea trade was ending up in what by then had come to be called La Ribera.

As early as the 13th century, the denizens of La Ribera had acquired a measure of independence from the city's mayoral control. Toward the end of that century, Carrer de Montcada—soon to be the wealthiest address in town—was carved out to link Vilanova de Mar with the burgeoning commercial district inland. A century later the increasing opulence of La Ribera made the soaring Gothic remake of

Santa Maria del Mar almost inevitable.

The good times continued into the 16th century, but things began to turn sour as the Atlantic gained in importance over the Mediterranean and Barcelona was completely excluded from American trade. Worse was to come. When Philip V of Spain brought Barcelona into submission at the end of the War of the Spanish Succession in 1714, he pulled down more than a thousand houses in La Ribera to make way for a huge fortress, the Ciutadella, whose guns were to be trained on the rebellious city. This odious symbol of central control was destroyed and replaced in the late 19th century by what is now Parc de la Ciutadella. During recent excavations the demolished houses have been exposed, forming part of the striking Born Cultural Center.

Modernista Palau de la Música Catalana is a central pillar in the city's cultural life, while once moneyed Carrer de Montcada has become an

NOT TO BE MISSED:

A concert in the modernista marvel of the Palau de la Música Catalana **120–121**

Perusing Picasso's early works in the Museu Picasso **125–129**

The Església de Santa Maria del Mar in El Born, attending a recital, followed by cocktails in Collage **131–132, 262**

Rowing a boat in the verdant Parc de la Ciutadella **133–135**

Experiencing a key part of Catalonia's history in the Born CC **135**

Discovering the history of chocolate at the Museu de la Xocolata **138**

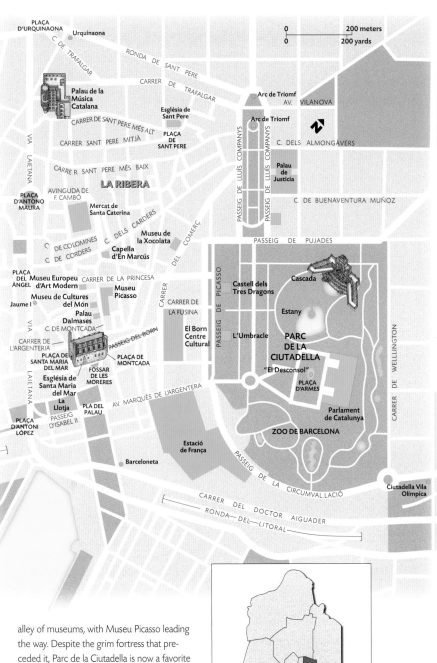

alley of museums, with Museu Picasso leading the way. Despite the grim fortress that preceded it, Parc de la Ciutadella is now a favorite for weekend fun: A zoo, and, ironically, the Catalan regional parliament are now located at the heart of the park. ■

Area of map detail

Palau de la Música Catalana

Declared a World Heritage site by UNESCO in 1997, this remarkable theater is not only one of the best places in Barcelona to attend performances of classical and choral music; it is also a sumptuous high point of modernista architecture and art.

Palau de la Música Catalana

- Map p. 119
- Carrer Palau de la Música 4–6
- 93 295 7200
- Closed from 3:30 p.m. Sept.– June; guided tours every half-hour
- $$$
- Metro: Línies 1 & 4 (Urquinaona)

palaumusica.cat

Even as you approach this extraordinary building, you cannot help being taken aback: Indeed, it is barely contained by the narrow medieval streets it dominates. Here among the many stores dedicated to the wholesale rag trade, it beckons the great and the good from across the city to its concerts.

The "palace" figures quite prominently in the memory of the city and is by no means merely a music hall. Built between 1905 and 1908 by Lluís Domènech i Montaner, it amply demonstrates that Gaudí had no monopoly on the fanciful during this exciting period of artistic fervor in Barcelona. A battalion of the best artisans joined with Domènech i Montaner to create a decorative homage to Catalonia. Commissioned by the Orfeó Català choral society, the building symbolized a reawakening in Catalan nationalism, at the time embodied in the Renaixença (see pp. 31 & 33). The Orfeó had emerged late in the 19th century out of a desire to marry popular Catalan song with classical music and to awaken broad interest in homegrown production, while elevating it to international levels. Its founders also wanted to bring the greatest classical music from all over Europe to audiences in Barcelona.

From the outside, the building is almost too rich in detail and is difficult to appreciate in its cramped location. In the decades after it was built, many critical voices opined it was so gaudy that only the wrecking ball could remedy the situation. Thankfully, no one paid any heed.

Exposed brick and mosaics are decorative constants. The voluptuous climax is in the sculpture that bulges from the corner of the building, as if leaning over a balcony. It is a modernista allegory for popular song: a nymph

Notoriously poor acoustics don't deter music lovers from concerts at the Palau de la Música Catalana.

EXPERIENCE: Take in the Full Palau Experience

Every half hour groups of visitors troop through the extravagantly decorated interior of the **Palau de la Música Catalana** in tours given in many languages. You begin in the Orfeó Català's rehearsal room, passing through the Sala Lluís Millet—where you can step onto the iconic balcony on the facade and inspect the floral mosaic columns. The visit winds up in the Sala de Concerts, the main auditorium. For the full experience, nothing equals attending a performance. To sit under the hall's dazzling skylight, absorbing its intricate details while being elevated by world-class music is magical.

The Palau has a packed program ranging from intimate piano recitals and chamber music to full-blown symphony orchestras and baroque ensembles. Stars from the international musical firmament light up the busy calendar: Alfred Brendel played the penultimate concert of his final tour here. If classical music is not your thing, the wide-ranging program offers more: Flamenco or Spanish guitar gigs, key concerts in the International Jazz Festival every fall, and perennial favorites such as Marianne Faithfull. Reserve ahead online *(palaumusica.cat)*. Allow time for a preshow cava in the foyer bar, or tapas in the interval, so as to enjoy the bustle of variegated spectators in this monument to modernisme, still a stronghold of its loyal Catalan bourgeoisie.

surrounded by representatives of the people. Complementing this are busts of composers, mosaic-clad columns, and a ceramic frieze of singers of the Orfeó.

Inside, the theater is all light and color. The low-slung arches, reminiscent of Catalan Gothic, lend a slightly more sober air to the building, but don't be deceived. As you ascend the stairs, the almost serpentine qualities of Domènech i Montaner's inventive decoration are in evidence everywhere.

However, nothing can really prepare you for the **auditorium,** consisting of stalls and two circles that seat about 2,000 people. The walls are made up substantially of sheets of vividly colored stained glass; unfortunately this has made the hall poor in terms of acoustics, as has been universally recognized since the Palau opened in 1908. (A smaller second stage with better acoustics, the Petit Palau, was added to the building in 2004.) An enormous shimmering skylight appears to drip down from the ceiling, resembling a work in progress on a potter's wheel. Where there is no room for glass, the walls have a layer of glazed ceramics, whose dominating feature is a series of floral motifs.

Amid all the decoration, the proscenium, framing the stage, is a metaphor for the universal genius of music and Catalan resurgence. Above a bust of Beethoven on the right explodes a vast sculpture of Richard Wagner's Valkyries.

The back of the stage, above which is mounted an organ, is a symphony of *trencadís* (mosaic of pottery fragments, a common device in modernista decoration) in shades of red and orange. Growing out of them are 18 sculptures of young maidens playing instruments, sculpted by Eusebi Arnau. It is as though the music never stops. ∎

Young Picasso

With his piercing dark eyes and voracious appetite for work, women, and life, the young Picasso was a live wire and lost no time in becoming acquainted with all sides of city life—and painting them.

Els Quatre Gats tavern, where Picasso used to hang out with other avant-garde artists

Born in Málaga, southern Spain, the precocious Pablo Ruiz Picasso (1881–1973) began demonstrating his talent early on. His father, José Ruiz Blasco (1838–1913), had a respectable job as a drawing teacher in the town's school of fine arts until he transferred to a similar post in the northwestern city of La Coruña in 1891. A handful of young Pablo's earliest efforts from Málaga survive, but his potential became apparent during the family's four years in La Coruña. José could smell genius and enrolled his son in art school.

When his father moved to Barcelona in 1895 to teach drawing at that city's fine arts school in La Llotja (see p. 138), the teenage Picasso followed the rest of the family and was signed up at the same school. They moved into a flat on

what is now Carrer de la Reina Cristina, near the old port, before shifting to Carrer de la Mercè 3. Pablo displayed prodigious capabilities, portraying family members (including his mother, from whom he took his preferred surname, Picasso) and churning out the academic work of model portraiture. In 1896 his father rented a small studio space for him in Carrer de la Plata (a restaurant now occupies the spot).

Growing Pains

Packed off to Madrid in 1897 to study at the Acadèmia de Bellas Artes de San Fernando, the teenager quickly tired of school and, conveniently out of reach of the family, gave free rein to his own instincts. Picasso's school became the Prado art gallery, where he studied and aped grand masters such as Velázquez and

El Greco. He took to the streets, painting the faces and scenes that came to him, and acquired a taste for taverns and brothels, which provided entertainment *and* material.

In Picasso's mind, however, the following six-month sojourn spent staying with a friend in the village of Horta de Sant Joan, in southern Catalonia, was the most fruitful period in his apprenticeship. There he submerged himself in the light and color of the countryside and broke with the constraints of academic painting.

Portrait of Picasso as a young man

Back in Barcelona in early 1899, Pablo rented studio space on Carrer dels Escudellers Blancs, just behind Plaça Reial, but he moved often in the ensuing years. He immersed himself in the bohemian, avant-garde world of Els Quatre Gats tavern, the favored haunt of leading modernistas and other artistic types, and the scene of Picasso's first exhibitions.

With these like-minded souls he whiled away moments of diversion in the bars and brothels of the Barrio Xino, especially along Carrer Nou de la Rambla, where for a while in 1902 he had a studio at No. 10. He also was very fond of the sailors' brothels of Carrer d'Avinyò, said to have inspired his very famous 1907 painting, "Les Demoiselles d'Avignon."

As Barcelona's artists looked to Paris, it was only a matter of time before Picasso would try his luck there. The first trip came in 1900, followed by a brief stint in Madrid and repeat trips to Paris until, in April 1904, he moved to France for good.

In the following years he returned several times to Barcelona, the last being the summer of 1934. The civil war and Franco's victory meant that the strongly anti-Franco Picasso would never again set foot on Spanish soil.

EXPERIENCE: Tracing Picasso's Early Years

Picasso will always be a Parisian fixture. The city is where he first found acclaim, and it sustained his talent for more than half a century. However, Barcelona was the backdrop of the painter's early days, and it left an indelible mark on the young Picasso and his work. Barcelona allows you to appreciate the artist in a more immediate fashion. The **Museu Picasso** (see pp. 125–129) is one of the most visited art museums in the world, with more than a million annual visitors. Although it might seem like a good idea to save a few euros, don't plan on visiting the first Sunday of the month when the museum is free. If you do, you will find a long line.

An alternative idea: The **Icono Serveis**

Culturals (Avinguda Portal de l'Angel, 38, tel 93 410 14 05, iconoserveis.com, $$$$$) offers, among other interesting routes, an unrivaled bespoke Picasso walking tour. The tour follows boulevards and alleys that inspired his artistic greatness. It begins with a site relevant to Picasso's rowdy group of friends, the restaurant Els Quatre Gats, on Carrer Montsió. The path winds through the side streets, stopping at studios, galleries, and legendary haunts.

The tour gives you a clear picture of Barcelona's tumultuous shift into the modern day through the art and life of Picasso. It wraps up at the Museu Picasso after about 90 minutes. Tickets to the museum are included in the cost of the tour.

Carrer de Montcada

This medieval street has been prime real estate several times over. It started when Count-King Ramon Berenguer IV ceded land to Guillem Ramon de Montcada in the mid-12th century. Montcada created a road linking Vilanova de Mar with today's Carrer de la Princesa. By the early 14th century it was flanked by mansions. Decline came in the 19th and 20th centuries, but a revival has seen its mansions now housing grand museums and sophisticated bars.

Formerly one of the top addresses in Barcelona, Carrer de Montcada is a museum alley today.

The northern end was marked by the small Romanesque **Capella d'En Marcús,** on the corner of Carrer dels Carders and Placeta d'En Marcús. The main body of the street was cut off from this wayside chapel when Carrer de la Princesa was built in 1853. Back in 1166, when the chapel was built, Carrer dels Carders was the main road out of town, having left the eastern city gate (where Plaça del Àngel is today) well behind. The chapel was part of a larger complex financed by a prominent citizen, Bernat Marcús, but the pilgrims' hostel, hospital, poorhouse, and cemetery have long since disappeared. In the 14th century the "runners' fraternity," or postmen, would call in here for blessing before setting out; their patron remains the Mare de Déu (Mother of God) housed here. A simple structure in the sober Lombard style (see p. 36), the chapel was restored in 1980.

Museu Picasso

South across Carrer de la Princesa lies what is, for most, the star attraction of the street—the Museu Picasso. The collection concentrates on Picasso's early years, roughly until the time he left Barcelona, but important additions over the years have broadened the display, which is frequently complemented by temporary exhibitions.

The museum spreads across five principal mansions dating from medieval times and a couple of other buildings. These and other residences along Carrer de Montcada make the street one of the most important living documentations of civic Gothic construction in Barcelona. Although Gothic at heart, most of these buildings underwent changes over time, with many baroque and even neoclassical alterations and additions. These stout stone houses tend to have an internal courtyard off the street, with a grand external staircase sweeping up to the second floor, where the master of the house resided. The ground floor was reserved for stables, kitchens, and storehouses.

Thus, on entering the Museu Picasso by Palau Meca (Carrer de Montcada 19), this is what you see, with stores and other conveniences occupying the ground floor. Head up the stairs to view the collection, which begins through a door to the right and

runs chronologically. Occasionally pieces are loaned out, used in the temporary exhibitions, or removed for conservation work, so the itinerary may differ slightly.

Rooms 1 to 3: After a biographical introduction, in **Room 1** you are at first immersed in the mist-bound world of La Coruña, the northwest coastal town where Picasso lived from the age of 10 to 14. In the small countryside scenes and images of local people we see an already accomplished artist. The "Home amb Boina" ("Man in a Beret," 1895) reveals an uncommon sensitivity to

INSIDER TIP:

Early Picasso works at the Picasso Museum include "First Communion," a girl in a luminous lace dress, painted by the artist at age 15 when he still painted eyes and noses in their usual places.

—JERRY CAMARILLO DUNN, JR.
National Geographic author

light and a capacity to lend life to his subjects. The same room also covers the years 1895–1897 in Barcelona. On show are three small portraits of Picasso's father, one of which demonstrates that Picasso already had a sure hand and was dabbling in ideas beyond the norms of academic painting, in this case the use of monochrome.

Museu Picasso
Map p. 119
Carrer de Montcada 15–23
93 256 30 00
Closed Mon.
$$$, $$$$ with temporary exhibitions
Metro: Línia 4 (Jaume I)
museupicasso.bcn.cat

The contemplative "Retrat de la Mare" ("Portrait of Picasso's Mother") is outstanding. This portrait shows a mastery of draftsmanship and a will to capture the human essence of

his models. A series of mischievous self-portraits, including one of him wearing a wig, is amusing.

The following room, related to the same period, offers quite a mix. In one cabinet is a series of small day-to-day scenes of Barcelona, almost all of them done with oil on wood. "La Ona" ("The Wave") is an absorbing work in which the young artist manages to capture a sense of movement and liquid. Others are less generic, with curious snapshots of La Barceloneta and its beach as they were more than a century ago, and various urban perspectives. Up on the walls are several nude studies done at art school. They give insight into Picasso's formal training and amply demonstrate his technical abilities.

Continuing in the vein of rural scenes is a series of views from

around Picasso's native Málaga. Southern sunlight suffuses these images. They seem to take inspiration from the Impressionists, with thick, short brushstrokes in pieces such as "Paisatge Muntanyenc" ("Mountain Landscape," 1896).

The room is dominated by two key works. "Tía Pepa" ("Aunt Pepa") is possibly his most striking early portrait of a family member. His ability to capture a certain world-weariness in his aunt's eyes is remarkable. "La Primera Comunió" ("First Communion," 1896) is one of the artist's earliest grand canvases. It is an utterly conventional religious and moral work typically in vogue at the time. For any doubters who might be tempted to see the artist's later work as childish squiggles, this is formidable evidence of his academic training and capacity.

In **Room 3** comes the still more important "Ciència i Caritat" ("Science and Charity," 1897), on the right as you enter. In it, Picasso's father poses as a doctor at the bedside of a sick woman. Again, the artist marches to the beat of somebody else's drum, but this grand canvas shows he could easily have been a successful society artist. In the same room, to your left as you enter, you can inspect three of his initial sketches for the final work. On the same wall follows an assortment of scenes from Madrid and nine views of rural Horta de Sant Joan (in southern Catalonia), including "El Mas del Quiquet" (1898), a sun-drenched farmhouse.

Rooms 4 to 7: Next up in **Room 4** is a curious mix of material done in Barcelona from 1899 to 1900. "Carrer de la Riera de Sant Joan" (1900), depicting a lane where Picasso had a studio, reveals major change in the young artist's approach. Viewers are invited to look through the window onto a busy street. Here Picasso displays some liking of the abstract: The carefully accurate recording that dominates many of his more youthful works is absent here. Minimal but sure brushstrokes render human figures, a cart, and buildings across the way. The image is positive and light. Other scenes from Barcelona figure here, along with half a dozen portraits that by now have left academic rigor behind in favor of a more playful style. They include two of his sister Lola and a brooding image of his close friend Carles Casagemas. A striking one is his haunting "Retrat d'un Desconegut a l'Estil d'El Greco" ("Portrait of an Unknown Person in El Greco's Style").

Rooms 5 to 7 are dominated by works from Picasso's first Paris sojourn in 1900–1901. The artist's penchant for louche nightlife is evident, and, although his use of color is quite different and the element of caricature is not as predominant, these paintings remind one of Toulouse-Lautrec, another aficionado of nightclubs. This is especially the case with the "La Fi del Número" ("Curtain Call," 1901). In "Margot" and "La Nana" ("The Dwarf"), ugliness and beauty are easily confounded, if only through a joyous summer splurge of color.

Sala G & Rooms 8 to 11: As you emerge from Room 7, you could head across the corridor for a room marked **Sala G.** Four rooms here are filled with some dramatic prints that Picasso worked on much later. Subjects include busts of his lover, Jacqueline, a series of delirious takes on Manet's "Le Déjeuner sur l'Herbe," and "Home amb

Ordering tapas and a glass of *cava* in El Xampanyet, a classic champagne bar on Carrer de Montcada.

Gorgera, Segon El Greco" ("Man with Ruff, El Greco-Style"), with numerous studies done prior to achieving the final result.

Back in Barcelona, Picasso embarked on the first of his many "periods," in this case the Blue Period (1901–1904). **Room 8** and an annex are dedicated to paintings from this time. Their melancholy may have been due in part to the suicide of Casagemas (1880–1901). Themes range from eerie moonlit scenes like "Terrats de Barcelona" ("Barcelona Rooftops," 1903) to portraits. Among the more unsettling of the latter is "El Foll" ("The Madman," 1904).

Room 9 contains a couple of items from the following period variously known as the Pink or Rose Period. Overshadowing the odd self-portrait is the striking "Retrat de la Senyora Canals" ("Portrait of Mrs. Canals," 1905).

Rooms 10–11 are devoted to paintings Picasso did during his final stay in Barcelona, in 1917. Of the two in Room 10, the more powerful by far is "Cavall Banyegat" ("Gored Horse"), the extreme lines of which presage the cubism evident in the seven works hanging in Room 11.

More Salas

Opposite Room 8 you can pop over to the **Espai Sabartés,** dedicated to Sabartés, Picasso's personal secretary. In the first part are playful collage sketches by Picasso of Sabartés next to photos of pinup girls. You then pass into the **Sala Neoclàssica,** whose décor lends insight into the lifestyle of Barcelona's elite

"Las Meninas No. 31," 1957 (oil on canvas), by Pablo Picasso

in the 19th century. Next you loop through the second part of the Sabartés display.

Rooms 12–15 are devoted to two main themes. The first is Picasso's re-examination of Velázquez's masterpiece "Las Meninas." Through a deforming and sometimes cubist prism, Picasso re-creates this classic of Spanish art and then takes it apart to section out single portraits of each figure in the original. The other theme (Room 15) is pigeons

(see p. 170). These magnificent palaces with medieval origins, the Palau de Marquès de Llió and its neighbor the Palau de Nadal, have been renovated to house the new **Museu de Cultures del Món** (Museum of World Cultures), which is due to open in early 2015. Its display will include more than 2,000 fascinating pieces from the Folch collection as well as non-European pieces from the Ethnological Museum on Montjuïc. This

Museu de Cultures del Món
- Map p. 119
- Carrer de Montcada 12–14
- Closed Mon.
- $$
- Metro: Línia 4 (Jaume I)

EXPERIENCE: Try Bubbly, Baroque, & Basque

Wandering down Carrer de Montcada in the evening can be as rewarding as cruising its museums by day. Try the bar **El Xampanyet,** at No. 22, where you can indulge in a glass of *cava*, the Catalan version of champagne. It is the standard tipple in this, one of the city's oldest and best known cava bars. Pick out a couple of the many *tapas* (bar snacks) on offer.

Later in the evening, the baroque **Palau Dalmases** next door is another world altogether. Drop by for a glass of wine or a cocktail and, with luck, live classical music, opera, or flamenco in what feels like an 18th-century salon.

Too refined (or pricey)? Saunter on to the **Centre Cultural Euskal Etxea** *(Placeta de Montcada 1)* for a rowdy taste of Basque Country with its exquisite tapas, cider, and white wine *(txacoli).*

---

in "Pichones," a celebration of Mediterranean light.

Finally, head along the gallery of the Gothic courtyard to a display of 36 ceramic pieces and three paintings from the final years of Picasso's life. Temporary exhibitions are held in **Palau Mauri** and **Palau Finestrelles.**

Other Sights

Across Carrer de Montcada from the mansions making up the Museu Picasso are some further fine Gothic-baroque houses. The first used to house a textile museum that has now relocated to the Design Museum's state-of-the-art building in Glòries

private collection comprising ceremonial sculptures, jewels, ceramics, and art was the result of journeys through the Far East, Africa, Central and South America, and Oceania by Albert Folch and several other explorers. This global collection will be complemented by temporary exhibitions on related subjects, starting with an intriguing presentation about written texts in ancient cultures.

Heading south toward Passeig del Born, Carrer de Montcada is lined with more mansions, many of them art galleries. Look inside **Palau dels Cervelló,** at No. 25, and **Palau Dalmases,** at No. 20, two of the finer examples. ∎

El Born

Closed off at its western end by the apse of the mighty Església de Santa Maria del Mar and at the other end by the Centre Cultural Born, a former market, broad Passeig del Born (Borne in Spanish) has a special place in the hearts of locals. An old saying affirms: *"Roda el món i torna al Born*—Go around the world and come back to the Born." Once a commercial sector, it has recently experienced a comeback as a popular haunt for hedonistic barhoppers and shoppers.

The Església de Santa Maria del Mar was built in thanks for the conquest of Sardinia by the Catalan merchant empire.

In the 13th century, what is now a long pedestrian-only island flanked by two traffic lanes was a grand square in the middle of Vilanova de Mar. Many of Barcelona's foreign-trade deals were executed here, and the square became a natural hub. El Born, as the square and its immediate surrounds are known, literally means "limit" or "barrier," and refers to a space cordoned off for tournaments. Try to imagine the long square surrounded by tribunes for the city's gentry raised above crowds of onlooking commoners, their attention fixed on the colorful spectacle of the joust, with banners fluttering and the clash of lances against shields and armor. El Born was the city's main site for weapons practice and tournaments of all sorts from at least the 14th century; the first documented joust took place in 1372.

But El Born was not the exclusive preserve of dashing knights: All manner of popular festivals and processions took place here. In later years, trade fairs (especially of silver and glassware) were held regularly. From the end of the 15th century, the Inquisition chose El Born as the stage for its autos-da-fé, the gruesome punishments, including burning at the stake, meted out to heretics by the Holy Office. Non-religious public executions also took place here until 1723. From then on, the prime function of the square was as a market. The fine metal structure at the far end was raised in 1876 and remained in use as a food market until 1971. After extensive excavations, the site has come back to life as the dazzling Born CC, a cultural center (see p. 135).

Most of the housing that flanks Passeig del Born dates from the 19th and, in some cases, 18th centuries. Only No. 17, heavily restored, survives from the 14th century. Once dedicated to all manner of activities (Carrer dels Sombrerers was Milliners' Street, Carrer de la Vidrieria was Glass-makers' Street, and so on), the narrow streets woven around El Born have been revived since the mid-1990s by a growing battalion of bars, chic little restaurants, and bijou stores.

Església de Santa Maria del Mar

Bulging out into the western extreme of Passeig del Born is the apse of the single most majestic example of Catalan Gothic in Barcelona, Església de Santa Maria del Mar (Church of St. Mary of the Sea). Earliest evidence of the existence of a church on this site dates from 998. Legend has it that the remains of Santa Eulàlia (see p. 63) lay in a church here after her supposed martyrdom in the twilight years of the Roman Empire. Although more likely fiction than fact, the story has made the present church a symbol of Catalan nationalist identity, so much so that even the Spanish royal family has on at least one occasion been politely told that it could not celebrate a wedding here!

By the time this architectural gem of gray Montjuïc stone was completed (in the record time of 54 years from 1329), its surround-ing parish (El Born) had become one of Barcelona's most impor-tant. Many writers have asserted that, had they not seen the Catedral beforehand, they would have taken this for the city's main place of worship.

Flanking the entrance on the broad, unfussy west face of the church are statues of Saints Peter and Paul, and above them is a 15th-century rose window, the original having been destroyed in an earthquake in 1428, the princi-pal source of light into the central nave. Around the sides stout but-tresses hold up the structure.

The church's splendor becomes fully apparent once you are inside. Gutted during the civil war, the interior is devoid of embellishment; the central choir stalls and virtually all its works of art were destroyed, but to some this only serves to emphasize the exquisite harmony of line and

Església de Santa Maria del Mar

- 🅼 Map p. 119
- ✉ Plaça de Santa Maria del Mar
- 🕐 Closed 1:00–4:30 p.m.
- Ⓜ Metro: Línia 4 (Jaume I)

Kingly Magic

Although white-bearded Santa Claus is making inroads into the con-sciousness of people the world over, for Spanish children Christmas is a bore. In Spain, the holiday marks Christ's birth and is a time for quiet family meals. The gifts don't come until the visit of the Three Wise Men (known to the Catalans as Els Reis Mags) on the eve of January 6 (Epiphany). The fun happens when the kings arrive by boat in Port Vell and then embark on a parade finishing up in Montjuïc. They are greeted by throngs of chil-dren, who are bombarded by volleys of candy along the whole route.

magnitude. Alongside the wide nave run two aisles, and between them slender octagonal pillars rise up between arches to the filigree delicacy of the vaults. Nowhere is this lacework more finely executed than in the narrow arcade that carves its way around the inside of the apse. You are drawn to look upward as if in contemplation of the Almighty, but unlike in many claustrophobic northern Gothic churches, the generous, open width of the Catalan version invites you to look around as well. It is an earthy, human touch. The windows along the sides feature captivating

nearby alleys (home to a couple of wine bars) form the best-preserved corner of the bustling medieval commercial quarter that once occupied much of El Born. The square boasts a restored Gothic fountain, while lanes like Carrer dels Caputxers (Hoodmakers' Street) and Carrer dels Canvis Nous and Canvis Vells (New and Old Money Changers' Streets) have remained largely unchanged, retaining features in their higgledy-piggledy style such as the upper floors jutting out on heavy timber barbicans, a typical medieval space-creating trick in Spain.

EXPERIENCE: Hit the High Notes in High Church

The Gothic **Església de Santa Maria del Mar,** something of a symbol of Catalan identity and a building of extraordinary power and harmony, is also a unique setting for concerts of baroque and classical music. Catalan conductor and virtuoso player of the viola da gamba Jordi Savall (*jordisavall.es*) has probably done more than any other musician in the world to recover the "lost" music of the baroque and earlier periods. With the three ancient music ensembles he founded with his wife, soprano

Moutserrat Figueras (1942–2011), he occasionally gives concerts in the Església de Santa Maria del Mar. Their children, Arianna and Ferran, often perform with him. The acoustics in a space like this church are difficult, but the setting is romantic and suits the music perfectly. You need to keep your eyes open for announcements of the concerts, which tend to be repeated two or three evenings in a row. They are irregular, although in the run-up to Christmas or Easter they are more common.

stained glass dating from the 18th century, and in some instances from the 15th century.

To see the church's interior illuminated, attend Mass or one of the occasional classical music concerts that are staged here at night (see sidebar above).

The irregular little square in front of the church, **Plaça de Santa Maria del Mar,** and the

Opposite the south flank of Santa Maria del Mar is the **Fossar de les Moreres,** site of a cemetery located on what had in early medieval times been a hillock covered in mulberry bushes. Heroes who died in the defense of Barcelona during the siege of 1714 were buried here, and a flame constantly burns in their memory. ∎

Parc de la Ciutadella

Central Barcelona's main green lung, century-old Parc de la Ciutadella, is laden with heavy symbolism for Catalans—and home to several attractions. As the stage for the 1888 Universal Exhibition, it also has some interesting modernista morsels.

Gaudí assisted with the design of the Cascada in Parc de la Ciutadella, one of his earliest assignments.

In the 1880s, the Ajuntament (City Hall), industrialists, and businessmen of Barcelona were in high spirits. The city was in the vanguard of a slow process of industrialization in an otherwise pitifully backward Spain. Transatlantic trade was booming, and many Catalan families were doing nicely out of cash crops harvested largely by slave labor in Cuba. That Cuba and Spain's other remaining colonies would be lost in ignominious battle to the United States in 1898 could hardly be predicted when, in 1885, the Ajuntament determined to hold a Universal Exhibition in 1888.

The site chosen was the gaping hole left behind after the demolition of the notorious and much hated Ciutadella. This fortress that had kept watch over Barcelona, and in which its more rebellious citizens had frequently been jailed and executed, since defeat in the siege of 1714. It had been built under Spain's Philip V after he marched into the city on September 11, 1714, ending the War of the Spanish Succession.

Park for the People

Work to turn the area into a public park began in 1872 and progressed slowly. Then came the decision of 1885, and the city set about with feverish activity to erect the necessary pavilions and other facilities. Entering by the main entrance off Passeig de Picasso, you soon arrive at a cluster of buildings from the original Ciutadella. A small chapel and school stand close by one another; the latter once served as the Governor's Palace. Just east is the **Plaça d'Armes,** its oval pool overlooked by **"El Desconsol"** ("Disconsolate," 1907), by modernista sculptor Josep Llimona.

Behind stands evidence of what may be interpreted as a nice sense of irony on the part of the Catalans: **Parlament de Catalunya,** housed in the Ciutadella's arsenal. Between 1939 and 1980, it was a barracks, but the regional parliament returned when Catalonia's autonomy statute came into effect.

A symbol of Catalan identity, the Parlament is on occasion open for visits. You will be led up the sweeping Escala d'Honor (Stairway of Honor), through solemn halls to the Saló de Sessions, the auditorium where parliament sits.

The Zoo & Around

While strolling around the park's southern end, take time out to see some live works of art at the **Zoo de Barcelona**. Around 7,500 animals represent about 400 species, ranging from elephants to black-tailed prairie dogs, from Cuban flamingos to Humboldt penguins. You can also recoil in horror at the boa constrictor and crocodiles, or enjoy the dolphin show.

Directly north of Plaça d'Armes spreads the pleasant **Estany,** or artificial lake. Sitting by the water or having a picnic here makes for a pleasant diversion. You can also rent rowboats. Facing the lake on the north side is the park's most lavish object, the immense **Cascada** (Waterfall) by the Passeig de Pujades entrance. A creation of Josep Fontsère, the man behind the park, it took six years to build and was completed in 1881. Fontsère was assisted by a young Antoni Gaudí in his creation with its high central arch, flanking staircases, and overcrowded company of neo-baroque statues.

A model mammoth watches over rowers enjoying a pleasant afternoon on the Estany, or artificial lake.

Modernista Landscape

Although most of what was hastily built for the 1888 Universal Exhibition was not designed to last, a few sturdy buildings have survived.

INSIDER TIP:

The municipal "bicing" red-and-white bikes are not for tourists, but you can tour the park by renting a four-seater bike at Bicitram [Passeig de Picasso, 46] outside the main gate.

—LARRY PORGES
*National Geographic
Travel Books editor*

The most intriguing is the **Castell dels Tres Dragons** at the top end of the park on the Passeig de Picasso side, a medieval-style caprice that sprang from the mind of Lluís Domènech i Montaner. Conceived as a café-restaurant for the exhibition, it was a statement of intent by the architect. The use of unclad brick on an iron frame, with exposed wrought iron became a standard feature of the modernistas' work. The building creates the impression of a fairy-tale castle with an Islamic air. Its battlements, faced by fictitious coats of arms, are topped by ceramic crowns.

Until recently the building served as the **Museu de Zoologia,** along with the nearby **Museu de Geologia** and its exposition of rocks, minerals, and fossils. Both buildings are now used to store collections and for research.

Their former contents are in the Museu Blau (see p. 116). Next door is **L'Hivernacle,** a 19th-century hothouse. Beyond is **L'Umbracle,** recreating a tropical jungle *(closed afternoons).*

El Born Centre Cultural

A block southwest of the Parc de la Ciutadella, the hulk of the once-busy **Mercat del Born** might seem to have nothing to do with the park. But there is a close link. During its renovation, a network of cobbled streets was unearthed that was until the early 18th century a medieval neighborhood. More than 1,000 buildings were demolished to make way for the Ciutadella fortress, built after the city's surrender to the Bourbon monarch, Philip V. Today's fine Born Centre Cultural (Born CC) is a testament to that devastating era in Catalan history. It opened on September 11, 2013, to commemorate the beginning of the three hundredth anniversary of the siege which ended with Barcelona falling on September 11, 1714.

You can walk from the park through this huge space back into Passeig del Born. Beneath the tiled roof observe the well-preserved streets and ruined houses below. Exhibition rooms explain the history of the siege and daily life in late 17th- early 18th-century Barcelona. Check the busy program of events for talks or shows, or have a snack in its Espai Gastronòmic. This complex has become emotionally bound to the Catalan independence movement as the outsize Catalan flag outside suggests. ∎

Zoo de Barcelona
- ⬛ Map p. 119
- ✉ Parc de la Ciutadella
- ☎ 93 225 67 80
- 💲 $$$$
- Ⓜ Metro: Línia 4 (Barceloneta or Ciutadella)

zoobarcelona.cat

El Born Centre Cultural
- ⬛ Map p. 119
- ✉ Plaça Commercial 12
- ☎ 93 256 68 51
- 🕐 Closed Mon.
- 💲 $
- Ⓜ Metro: Línia 4 (Jaume I or Barceloneta)

elborncentrecultural .bcn.cat

To Market, to Market

Most Barcelona *barris* (neighborhoods) have their own food market—with Mercat de Santa Caterina, Mercat de la Boqueria, and Mercat de Sant Antoni among the best. They all tend to be open Monday through Saturday, although some close for a few hours at 2 p.m. A colorful array of street markets complement them.

Mercat de la Boqueria is a hive of colorful activity and tempting fresh produce.

While in El Born be sure to visit the city's first "designer market," **Mercat de Santa Caterina** (St. Catherine's Market), a bustling market with a long history and sparkling new clothes. Look out for a small, glassed-over corner of ancient foundations, all that remain of the 15th-century Monestir de Santa Caterina, a powerful Dominican monastery. Fruit gardens and fields of crops that the monks tended were spread out all around it. The monastery was torn down in 1838 to make way for a market, which in turn was swept away in 1999 to be replaced by its bright successor in 2005. Local architect Enric Miralles (1955–2000) designed the new location, with its wavy roof scintillating

in bright color. Propped up by tufts of twisting gray steel bamboo-like trunks, the roof is lined with timber on the underside. All around, the densely packed housing is a strange mix of the old and the new, pulsating with the life of a melting pot of locals, Latin Americans, and a host of North African migrants.

The best known and most central produce market is the historic **Mercat de la Boqueria,** on La Rambla (see p. 90). Its name comes from *boc* (goat), because goat meat was sold around here outside the then city walls from the 13th century onward. Simply wandering between the fish and seafood stands, the fruit and vegetable sections, and all the other food stands and bars is a heady experience. Although some parts remain open until well into the evening, the best time to come is the morning, especially on Friday and Saturday.

Not far from the Mercat de la Boqueria at Carrer del Comte d'Urgell 1 is another excellent neighborhood market and one of Barcelona's biggest, **Mercat de Sant Antoni** (St. Anthony's Market). Built in 1882 (and currently closed for a major refit), it is a classic example of the wrought-iron construction so much in vogue at the end of the 19th century. On Sunday mornings, vendors specializing in old maps, stamps, books, and cards replace the fishmongers and fruit purveyors. In the surrounding streets, others sell clothes and leather goods—though they are largely of indifferent quality.

Of all the different street markets, the biggest is the **Els Encants Vells** (closed Tues., Thurs., & Sun., metro: Glòries) flea market, literally meaning "old charms." Also known as Fira de Bellcaire, it has been doing business next to the Plaça de les Glòries since 1928, but has recently moved into an architect-designed space nearby, losing much of its shabby charm

in the process. You'll find every conceivable kind of item, from antique furniture to ancient magazines. Clearly a lot of it is junk, but it's fun just to wander around and barter.

Several specialist markets enliven the squares of the Barri Gòtic. In Plaça de Sant Josep Oriol, an art market takes place on weekends, while on neighboring Plaça del Pi you'll occasionally get the chance to sample all sorts of local food and produce, ranging from tasty cheeses to delicious honeys. On Thursdays an antique market sets up along Avinguda de la Catedral, while a coin and stamp collectors' market brings an unusually congenial air to Plaça Reial on Sunday mornings.

In the weeks before Christmas, a market sets up directly in front of the Catedral. You can buy figurines to make your own nativity scene.

INSIDER TIP:

Mercat de la Boqueria is a perfect place to take pictures of food, but it's advisable to buy something first!

—TINO SORIANO
National Geographic photographer

EXPERIENCE: Taste the Magic of Chocolate

Those with an eye for the good things in life will notice all sorts of tempting chocolate shops dotted about town, from traditional like **Escribà** (La Rambla 83) to state-of-the-art like **bubó Born** (Carrer Caoutxes, 10). There's even a museum dedicated to the history of this delicious substance (see p. 138). Apart from visiting the exhibition there, it's possible to sign up for various activities. Most of them are directed at groups of local schoolchildren, but some are open to all, like pairing of wines and cavas with chocolate, which are strictly for adults. **Coquus** (Carrer Ferrer de Blanes 7, tel 93 368 02 29, coquus.es, $$$$$) sometimes offers courses

on the art of cooking up chocolate dessert storms. Truly serious chocolate buffs, including professional pastry cooks, need to head out of town to **Gurb**, on the N152a road to Vic from Barcelona. **Chocolate Academy** (Carretera N-152, tel 93 889 34 19, chocolate-academy.com, $$$$$) is a major chocolate factory where serious three-day general courses on the making of chocolates are held. These hands-on courses are aimed at professionals and amateurs, and you'll find yourself making anything from chocolate cakes to creative dessert decorations. The courses, which are offered in Catalan and/or Spanish, are held irregularly.

More Places to Visit in La Ribera

Arc de Triomf

The hastily prepared Universal Exhibition of 1888 needed (at least the city fathers believed) a suitably grand and welcoming entrance. And so architect Josep Vilaseca (1848–1910) set about creating this highly unusual triumphal arch. Eschewing classical models and the use of stone, Vilaseca turned instead to the Islamic traditions implanted in Spain centuries before and made his arch of brick. His grand idea of flanking the arch with towers was scrapped. Nevertheless, a flurry of Catalan sculptors came together to decorate the arch.
🅰 Map p. 119 ✉ Passeig de Lluís Companys 🚇 Metro: Línia 1 (Arc de Triomf)

Església de Sant Pere de les Puel.les

One of the earliest churches to be raised in what was in the early Middle Ages countryside beyond the innermost line of city walls, St. Peter of the Maidens was one of the most important convents in Barcelona. The Greek-cross floor plan has been preserved, along with a few Romanesque and Gothic traces, such as the 12th-century dome. It has not been the luckiest of locations. Sacked in 985 by a marauding Muslim force that massacred or enslaved the nuns, the site has been damaged several times since. Opening hours are somewhat erratic.
🅰 Map p. 119 ✉ Plaça de Sant Pere 🚇 Metro: Línia 1 (Arc de Triomf)

La Llotja

The western end of Plaça del Palau is closed off by the formidable 18th-century neoclassical facade of La Llotja, which hides a prized interior of Catalan Gothic civil architecture. It was here that the likes of Picasso and Miró went to art school as youngsters (see p. 122). Picasso's father taught here, too, in the Acadèmia de Belles Artes de Sant Jordi, which occupied part of the building from 1847 until the 1980s. Perhaps more significantly for Barcelona, it was the home of the city's stock exchange from the late 14th century to the late 20th century. La Llotja was the first such trading house on the Iberian Peninsula. The medieval interior of Gran Saló, made up of three aisles separated by lofty rounded arcades, is where trading went on. Currently home to the Chamber of Commerce, it is sadly not open to the public.
🅰 Map p. 119 ✉ Consolat de Mar 2–4 🚇 Metro: Línia 4 (Barceloneta)

Museu de la Xocolata

Some would say divine inspiration led the town to install a museum dedicated to chocolate on the site of the beautiful former Convent de Sant Agustí. Displays trace the history of this fundamental foodstuff, but the place abounds in the sticky stuff, too. Visitors see what pre-Columbian societies did with cacao and how it arrived in Europe in the 16th century. Audiovisual displays provide more material. The **Sala Barcelona** contains chocolate models of everything from literary figures to city sights. You can see machines used for making chocolate, too. In the **Obrador** (Workshop), you might be lucky enough to catch chocolate tasting classes if you reserve a week in advance via the website.

The museum is also home to the *mona* competition, which celebrates chocolate as art. Monas, a unique Catalan tradition, are ornate chocolate figurines depicting everything from cartoon characters to fashion styles. The competition is held during Holy Week, and it can be fierce! *museuxocolata.cat* 🅰 Map p. 119 ✉ Comerc 36 ☎ 93 268 78 78 🕐 Closed from 3 p.m. Sun. 💲 $$ 🚇 Metro: Línies 1 (Arc de Triomf) & 4 (Jaume 1)

Intriguing modernista mansions along one of the city's most fashionable boulevards, high-end shopping, and the Fundació Antoni Tàpies, a contemporary art lover's dream come true

Passeig de Gràcia

Introduction & Map   140–141

Illa de la Discòrdia   142–143

Experience: Learn to Cook Catalan Cuisine   143

Fundació Antoni Tàpies   144

La Pedrera (Casa Milà)   145–151

More Modernisme Walk   146–148

Experience: Getting Inside Modernisme   150

Gràcia   152–153

More Places to Visit in Passeig de Gràcia   154

Hotels & Restaurants   254–256

Rooftop detail of Gaudí's Casa Batlló

Passeig de Gràcia

Lined by chic stores, crowded tapas bars, slick hotels, and high-rent offices, Passeig de Gràcia is one of the most sought-after addresses in town. Starting at Plaça de Catalunya, it links the old city with Gràcia, a separate village until the Eixample filled up the intervening countryside in the last decade of the 19th century.

The *modernisme* (art nouveau) theme starts with the street itself, which boasts a series of elegant wrought-iron street lamps erected in 1906. Most Barcelonans think Gaudí designed the lamps with their built-in *trencadís* (mosaic) benches, but they are in fact the work of a lesser known colleague, Pere Falqués Urpí (1850–1916).

It is little wonder that some of Barcelona's wealthiest and showiest families should have acquired property here around the turn of the 20th century and sought to outdo one another by taking on the biggest names in architecture.

These were boom times in the housing construction business. By the 1850s it had become clear the Old City could no longer contain its burgeoning population, so the city walls were knocked down and competitions held for urban expansion plans. The winner was Ildefons Cerdà, whose idea for the Eixample (Extension) entailed a grid pattern of streets spreading

inland from the old city. Blocks at regular intervals were to be set aside as parks, but property speculation meant that these areas were sold off as building plots.

Into this atmosphere stepped a gallery of the most daring architects the city had ever seen. And just as they had no fear of convention or of deploying all their imagination, so their patrons seemed addicted to eclecticism.

Gaudí's two contributions alone, the wavy La Pedrera and dragon-backed Casa Batlló, demonstrate the impossibility of pinning down modernistas to any set of rules. Contributions by his most outstanding contemporaries, Puig i Cadafalch and Domènech i Montaner, created a series of discordant houses.

The latter designed another building just off Passeig de Gràcia, destined to become home to

NOT TO BE MISSED:

More Gaudí fantasy inside Casa Batlló 142–143

Casa Amatller, a modernista house full of playful pseudo-Gothic touches 143

Modernisme meets contemporary art in the Fundació Antoni Tàpies 144

The science-fiction roof of La Pedrera (Casa Milà) 145 & 149–151

A wander around the streets and squares of Gràcia 152–153

Palau Baró de Quadras, another strange modernista gem 154

0 — 500 meters
0 — 500 yards

Mercat Lesseps
JARDINS MENÉNDEZ PELAYO
PLAÇA DE LESSEPS
TRAVESSERA DE DALT

VIA AUGUSTA
Casa Vicenç
PLAÇA DE ROVIRA I TRIAS
JARDINS DE MORAGAS
CARRER DE LES CAROLINES
GRÀCIA
Mercat Galvany
CARRER DELS MADRAZO
Fontana
PLAÇA DEL DIAMANT
Església de Sant Josep
PLAÇA DE CARDONA
Mercat Llibertat
PLAÇA DE LA VIRREINA
PLAÇA DE FRANCESC MACIÀ
TRAVESSERA DE GRÀCIA
PLAÇA DE LA LLIBERTAT
PLAÇA DEL SOL
TRAVESSERA DE GRÀCIA
PLAÇA DE LA VILA DE GRÀCIA
Mercat Abaceria Central
AVINGUDA DIAGONAL
Casa Sayrach
Hotel Casa Fuster
JARDINS DE SALVADOR ESPRIU
PARÍS
CARRER DE PARÍS
PLAÇA DE JOAN CARLES I
Universitat Industrial
CARRER DE CÒRSEGA
CARRER DE CÒRSEGA
Hospital Clínic
Diagonal
Casa Comalat
CARRER DEL ROSSELLÓ
Hospital Clínic i Provincial
Casa de les Punxes
Parc Bombers
CARRER DE PROVENÇA
La Pedrera (Casa Milà)
Palau Baró de Quadras
AVINGUDA
Verdaguer
Mercat Porvenir-Ninot
CARRER DE MALLORCA
Casa Enric Batlló
Casa Thomas
PLAÇA MOSSÈN JACINT VERDAGUER
Fundació Antoni Tàpies
Palau Montaner
DIAGONAL
C. DE VALÈNCIA
Casa Viuda Marfà
Museu Egipci de Barcelona
Casa Batlló
Passeig de Gràcia
CARRER D'ARAGÓ
Casa Amatller
Casa Lleó i Morera (Illa de la Discòrdia)
CARRER DEL CONSELL DE CENT
Girona
Museu del Modernisme Català
Urgell
Universitat de Barcelona
Fundació Francisco Godia
L'EIXAMPLE
Tetuan
CORTS CATALANES
PLAÇA DE LA UNIVERSITAT
GRAN VIA DE LES CORTS CATALANES
PLAÇA DE TETUAN
Universitat
Cases Rocamora
CARRER DE CASP
Sant Antoni
Casa Pascual i Pons
Casa Calvet
Cases Cabot
Catalunya
RONDA DE LA UNIVERSITAT
PLAÇA DE CATALUNYA
PLAÇA D'URQUINAONA
RONDA DE SANT PERE
Catalunya
Urquinaona
Mercat de Sant Antoni

the Fundació Antoni Tàpies. Tàpies was one of Barcelona's most celebrated contemporary artists until his recent death, and it is apt that his work should hang in a building that reminds us of the glory days of architectural creativity in the city.

After seeing the cream of the crop, enthusiasts can put together any number of itineraries, especially in the Eixample, in an effort to slake their *modernista* thirst. ∎

Area of map detail

Illa de la Discòrdia

In the years 1898 to 1906, three mansions on one block of Passeig de Gràcia (between Carrer del Consell de Cent and Carrer d'Aragó) were given modernista overhauls in what seems in retrospect like a divine contest between the three greatest names in modernisme: Gaudí, Domènech i Montaner, and Puig i Cadafalch.

Resembling some bizarre aquatic creature, the Casa Batlló facade is one of Gaudí's most outlandish creations.

Casa Batlló

- 🅰 Map p. 141
- ✉ Passeig de Gràcia 43
- ☎ 93 216 03 06
- 💲 $$$$$
- 🚇 Metro: Línies 2, 3, & 4 (Passeig de Gràcia)

casabatllo.es

The results are so utterly disparate that this block came to be known as Illa de la Discòrdia, *illa* being the Catalan word for the Eixample blocks, and in this case with three discordant styles.

By far the most extraordinary house is Gaudí's **Casa Batlló** (completed in 1906) at No. 43, which happily is now open to the public. It is worth paying the high entrance charge for such a spectacle. Gaudí retained the original structure of the 1877 building but completely recast the exterior and interior design. As always, he

avoided straight lines and right angles. The facade undulates and shimmers with its *trencadís* coat, while the second floor (the main floor in Barcelona mansions) is fronted by what seems to be a series of melting cavern entrances. The stone and glasswork are of a singular beauty.

Balconies resembling jawbones of prehistoric beasts (some liken them to Carnival masks) jut out from the upper floors. Finally, the six-story building is capped by what is doubtlessly the strangest roof in all of Barcelona. Said to represent St. George and the dragon, its tiles do indeed appear to be the scales of a mythological beast. It is capped by a tower with the customary four-arm cross that appears on Gaudí constructions elsewhere.

Inside, the entrance halls are pleasingly simple, with vaguely rippling ceilings and curvaceous balustrades. Everything, from the elevator doors and balconies on the stairwell down to the tiniest details like ergonomic handrails and doorknobs, received his full attention. The rooms on the main floor, with their swirling ceilings and blob-like window-panes, are remarkable.

Walk to the rear terrace and then catch the elevator up to the roof. You will notice the blue tile decor darkens in tone as you head up. Apart from a behind-the-scenes look at the extraordinary roof, the views are great.

For a free rear view of these amazing houses pop up to the garden department on the third floor of Servei Estació [Aragó 270], a store with access to the inner patio of the Block of Discord.

—JUSTIN KAVANAGH
National Geographic Travel Books editor

More Modernista

The other two objects of discord may not speak to your fantasy the way Casa Batlló does, but they are fine, original buildings. Puig i Cadafalch completed the remake of **Casa Amatller,** next door to Casa Batlló, in 1900, and it is possibly his most exuberant creation. The facade is largely inspired by religious and civic Catalan Gothic, but with playful touches, such as the twin entrance of differently sized and shaped doorways, dripping with sculptures that include St. George and the dragon, and a woman in art nouveau style.

Topping the building is a gabled conceit straight out of Amsterdam, coated in ceramics that exude a mildly metallic sheen. Part of the house is due to open to the public, but you need to reserve in advance *(casessingulars .com)*. If not peep inside the main entrance, which gives you an idea of the internal decoration, rich in vividly colored tiles, fine timberwork, and stained glass.

On the corner of the block at No. 35 is Domènech i Montaner's curious **Casa Lleó i Morera** (1905; *casalleomorera.com*). Topped by fanciful battlements, the facade fascinates with its variety of windows and bulging balconies. It has recently opened the main floor, the *principal*, but visits are limited. Reserve in advance online to see the wonderful ceramic work and stained glass inside. ∎

EXPERIENCE: Learn to Cook Catalan Cuisine

Barcelona was always considered one of the most pleasant places for a good meal in Spain—Catalan cuisine is hearty and mixed, one of the richest in the country.

Since the early 1990s, the city has been catapulted to the forefront of the international stage with a phalanx of new-wave cooks who have decidedly closed the breach with their rival French sophisticates to the north.

One of the first stops on any foodie's tour of Barcelona is the **Mercat de la Boqueria** on La Rambla (see pp. 136–137). This marvelous produce market is overflowing with edible goodies, and many of the city's top chefs shop here. If you find yourself wanting to learn how to make classic Spanish and Catalan dishes, contact **Escuela Cuina Boqueria** (*escuela cocinaboqueria.com*) in the market itself or **Cook & Taste** (*cookandtaste.net*), who will take you on a tour of the Boqueria and then get you busy in the kitchen. All sorts of options are available.

Fundació Antoni Tàpies

In 1984 Barcelona's signal avant-garde artist, Antoni Tàpies (1923–2012), launched this foundation not only as a place to exhibit key examples of his own work but also as a research center and exhibition space for the promotion of contemporary art. It opened in 1990.

Fundació Antoni Tàpies

🅜 Map p. 141
✉ Carrer d'Aragó 255
☎ 93 487 03 15
🕐 Closed Mon.
💲 $$
🚇 Metro: Línies 2, 3, & 4 (Passeig de Gràcia)

fundaciotapies.org

Before rushing inside, those with an interest in architecture will want to take some time to study the outside of this early Domènech i Montaner creation. Built in 1880 to house the publishing company Editorial Montaner i Simón, the edifice is an important precursor of *modernisme*. In its time, the use of brick and an eclectic mix of styles was innovative. It is crowned with Tàpies's own work "Núvol i cadira ("Cloud and chair," 1990), a striking sculpture inviting contemplation. The chair is a recurring symbol in his work.

The interior has been substantially reordered to cope with the Fundació's requirements, but a few original elements remain. In the center of the top floor yawns a huge rectangular gap creating a sense of space below. Domènech i Montaner opted to use slender pillars of iron rather than stone, another novelty at the time.

Tàpies mixed up materials and paints to create physical effects, often working on wood rather than canvas. A selection from the huge collection is put on display on a rotating basis several times a year so you may see prints, sculptures, or works like "Armari" ("Wardrobe," 1973), a stack of clothes tumbling out of a closet, or "Terra sobre Tela" ("Earth on Canvas," 1983), literally a pile of mud on canvas. More works hang in the basement, mostly from the 1940s and 1950s, when Tàpies was in a playful painting mood.

Those unfamiliar with Tàpies's work may find it inaccessible, but exhibitions are accompanied by enlightening videos in Espai C. The rest of this fine space is decked with temporary exhibitions by other artists. These can be hit or miss in terms of quality. Be sure to visit the newly-opened terrace at the top of the building where Tàpies's controversial sculpture "Mitjó" ("Sock," 2010) presides over the peace of an Eixample inner patio. ∎

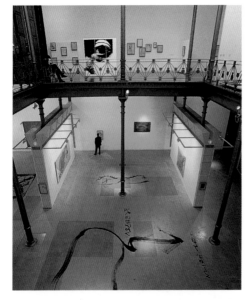

The grand space at the center of the Fundació Antoni Tàpies is a *modernista* relic.

ARTUR DEBAT/GETTY IMAGES ©

Don't Miss
La Pedrera

This undulating beast is another madcap Gaudí masterpiece, built in 1905–10 as a combined apartment and office block. Formally called Casa Milà, after the businessman who commissioned it, it is better known as La Pedrera (the Quarry) because of its uneven grey stone facade, which ripples around the corner of Carrer de Provença.

The Fundació Caixa Catalunya has opened the top-floor apartment, attic and roof, together called the Espai Gaudí (Gaudí Space), to visitors. The roof is the most extraordinary element, with its giant chimney pots looking like multicoloured medieval knights.

One floor below the roof, where you can appreciate Gaudí's taste for parabolic arches, is a modest museum dedicated to his work.

The next floor down is the apartment (El Pis de la Pedrera). It is fascinating to wander around this elegantly furnished home, done up in the style a well-to-do family might have enjoyed in the early 20th century. The sensuous curves and unexpected touches in everything from light fittings to bedsteads, from door handles to balconies, might seem admirable to us today, but not everyone thought so at the time. The story goes that one tenant, a certain Mrs Comes i Abril, had complained that there was no obvious place to put her piano in these wavy rooms. Gaudí's response was simple: 'Madame, I suggest you take up the flute.'

On summer evenings, La Pedrera usually stages a series of concerts on the roof.

NEED TO KNOW
Map p144; Casa Milà; ☎ 93 484 59 00; www.lapedrera.com; Carrer de Provença 261-265; adult/student/child €16.50/14.85/8.25; ☺9am-8pm Mar-Oct, to 6.30pm Nov-Feb; Ⓜ Diagonal

Mediterranean touch, so you'll get things like sardine tempura with an aubergine, miso and anchovy puree, or *tataki* (lightly grilled meat) of *bonito* (tuna) with *salmorejo* (a Córdoban cold tomato and bread soup). This is fusion at its very best.

Granja Petitbo
Mediterranean €€

Map p144 (📞93 265 65 03; www.granjapetitbo. com; Passeig de Sant Joan 82; sandwiches €5-6, menú del día €12.90; ⏰8.30am-10pm Mon-Wed, 8.30am-midnight Thu, 8.30am-1am Fri, 10am-1am Sat, 10am-5pm Sun; 📶; MGirona) High ceilings, battered leather armchairs and dramatic flower arrangements set the tone in this sunny little corner cafe, beloved of local hipsters and young families, who up until now have been ill-served in this part of town. As well as an all-day parade of homemade cakes, freshly squeezed juices and superior coffee, there's a brunch menu at weekends, and a *menú del día* (daily set menu) during the week.

Casa Amalia
Catalan €€

Map p144 (📞93 458 94 58; Passatge del Mercat 4-6; mains €8-17; ⏰1-3.30pm & 9-10.30pm Tue-Sat, 1-3.30pm Sun; MGirona) This very local restaurant is popular for its hearty Catalan cooking that uses fresh produce, mainly sourced from the busy market next door. On Thursdays during winter Casa Amalia offers the mountain classic, *escudella* (soup). Otherwise, you might try light variations on local cuisine, such as the *bacallà al allioli de poma* (cod in an apple-based aioli sauce). The three-course *menú del día* is exceptional lunchtime value at €12.

Casa Alfonso
Spanish €€

Map p144 (📞93 301 97 83; www.casaalfonso. com; Carrer de Roger de Llúria 6; tapas from €4, mains €18-28; ⏰8am-1am Mon-Sat; MUrquinaona) In business since 1934, Casa Alfonso is perfect for a morning coffee or a tapas stop at the long marble bar. Timber panelled and festooned with old photos, posters and swinging hams, it attracts a faithful local clientele at all hours

141

La Pedrera (Casa Milà)

One of Gaudí's less charitable colleagues was once heard to say, "If I had designed Casa Milà I wouldn't sleep easy at night." The building that came to be known as La Pedrera (Stone Quarry) elicited a range of responses, with cartoonists depicting it variously as a bizarre fortress, with cannon poking out of every opening, and as a science-fiction port for flying machines.

Barcelona satirists never tired of poking fun at Gaudí's curiously undulating residence.

The building, with its undulating facade, is considered by most critics to be more significant still than Casa Batlló (although for sheer weirdness the latter makes a greater initial visual impact). Most significantly, the latter project involved renovation of an existing building, while the existing constructions on the corner of Passeig de Gràcia and Carrer de Provença were bulldozed to make way for La Pedrera. The new block was commissioned in 1906 by wealthy businessman Pedro Milà i Camps, who once remarked that he was less likely to run out of cash for the costly project than of patience for the time it was taking to finish (work finally ended in 1912).

(continued on p. 149)

La Pedrera (Casa Milà)

Map p. 141

Carrer de Provença 261–265

902 20 21 38

$$$

Metro: Línies 3 & 5 (Diagonal)

lapedrera.com

More Modernisme Walk

The inevitable theme of any stroll around the Eixample will be modernisme. This is a short tour of some striking examples of the style (of which there are hundreds in the city) beyond the key sights mentioned in this and other chapters. Often you can peek inside the entrance halls, but if not, observing the exteriors reiterates just how eclectic were the tastes and fantasy of this brief but exuberant period.

Casa de les Punxes (The House of Spikes), Josep Puig i Cadafalch's Gothic jewel in Barcelona

Gaudí's **Casa Calvet,** at Carrer de Casp 48, is curious above all for its restraint. The architect completed the building in 1899, only a year before he finished the much more fanciful Palau Güell (see pp. 92–93). The house has a baroque flavor, particularly in the wavy crest that tops the facade

NOT TO BE MISSED:

Casa Viuda Marfà • Palau Montaner • Casa de les Punxes • Casa Comalat • Hotel Casa Fuster

and also in the two sets of protruding wrought-iron balconies.

Around the corner, Josep Vilaseca designed two contiguous buildings, the **Cases Cabot,** for the same family. They were his first fully modernista constructions. The outstanding element is the doorway to the one on the left *(Carrer de Roger de Llúria 8–10),* its tympanum's oriental flavor made singular by the dense floral ornament. The hallway is also worth inspecting for its modernista decor. From here walk down to Ronda de Sant Pere, turn right, and head for Plaça de Catalunya.

Casa Pascual i Pons & Beyond

Soaring up across from the northeast corner of Plaça de Catalunya is the impressive bulk of **Casa Pascual i Pons ❶,** at Passeig de Gràcia 2–4. Designed by Enric Sagnier Villavecchia (1858–1931), this stone palace is an airy burst of Gothic-inspired modernisme, finished in 1891. The tracery on the second-floor windows, trefoil decoration on the top-floor windows, towers, and other elements are all medieval throwbacks.

Across Carrer de Casp at Passeig de Gràcia 6–14 is another well-known Barcelona facade, equally inspired by the Gothic but with a heavy French leaning and not completed until 1920 by the brothers Joaquim (1854–1938) and Bonaventura Bassegoda Amigó (1862–1940). The **Cases Rocamora** stand out for their conical tower and the crowning

elements of the window galleries that jut out from the facade.

Manuel Comas i Thos (1855–1914) reached further back into the Middle Ages for his **Casa Viuda Marfà ❷,** at Passeig de Gràcia 66, finished in 1905. What most attracts the eye is the neo-Romanesque

> 🅰 See also area map p. 141
> ▶ Casa Calvet
> ↔ 2.7 miles (4.25 km)
> ⏱ 2 hours
> ▶ Casa Sayrach

arches that mark the entrance and the neo-Gothic gallery above.

A block farther north, Josep Vilaseca completed the elegant facade of **Casa Enric Batlló,** now part of the Condes de Barcelona Hotel, at Passeig de Gràcia 75 in 1896.

Exquisitely ornate windows of Casa Comalat, designed by Salvador Valeri Pupurull

His use of brick, wrought iron, and ceramic ornament (the latter on the top floor) are all signs that Vilaseca was moving toward modernisme.

Domènech i Montaner was busy in Carrer de Mallorca (turn to the right), having a hand in his cousin's **Palau Montaner** ❸ at No. 278 and **Casa Thomas** at Nos. 291–293. The former has a Florentine Renaissance ring to it and seems quite out of place, standing apart and with just three

stories, although the use of ceramic decor on the top floor facade and floral ornament elsewhere are clear signs of modernista handiwork. Domènech i Montaner created the first and second floors of Casa Thomas in 1898. Fourteen years later the upper floors and towers were added, respecting but not imitating the original architect's style. You can see more interior detail by visiting the furniture store in the basement.

More Modernisme

Possibly the best known of Puig i Cadafalch's works in Barcelona is **Casa de les Punxes** ❹, at Avinguda Diagonal 416–420, named for the conical points that crown the six towers. The whole looks like a combination of northern European mansion and Loire Valley château and features florid ornament in the balconies and the galleries.

Imitation is the best form of flattery, and Gaudí gets his in **Casa Comalat,** at Carrer de Còrsega 316. Designed by Salvador Valeri Pupurull (1873–1954), the building's main facade swirls uncomfortably between two stock-standard Eixample blocks. However, although the first floor mirrors elements of Gaudí's Casa Batlló, the upper levels are highly original. The interlocking windows form an armored casing that resembles the shell of an armadillo.

Another classic Domènech i Montaner mansion, **Hotel Casa Fuster** ❺ crowns the top end of Passeig de Gràcia (No. 132). Now a luxury hotel, it bursts with variety in its tower, balconies, galleries, trefoil windows, and broad arches. For more Gaudiana, you need to tramp a few blocks west along Avinguda Diagonal until you reach **Casa Sayrach** ❻ at Nos. 423–425, by Manuel Sayrach Carreras (1886–1937). The sinuous mansard level clearly takes its cue from La Pedrera, and every inch inside has been exploited to the full. Finished in 1918, it seems almost like a tribute to the master.

Gaudí closely directed every element of construction and decoration and was profoundly disappointed when the owner rejected the crowning glory, a massive bronze sculptural group depicting the Virgin of the Rosary flanked by archangels Gabriel and Michael. After the events of the Setmana Tràgica in 1909 (see p. 33), when many churches were attacked and religious images destroyed, Senyor Milà didn't want to attract such trouble to his house. Gaudí bailed out of the project in its last stages over a contractual misunderstanding in which his chosen interior decorator was replaced by another.

The gray stone (from the Garraf and Penedès areas) used to create the facade flows around the corner of the intersection like a wave in continuous motion. The eye is so caught up in this movement that the serried ranks of windows, buried deep in the folds of the stone, appear almost as afterthoughts. Like drifts of algae on the wave's surface, ribbons of interwoven wrought iron are draped in front of many of them to form balconies. Across the top is spread the inscription in Gaudí's fanciful script: "Ave Gratia Plena Dominus Tecum—Hail, Full of Grace; the Lord Is with You," the archangel Gabriel's words to the Virgin Mary.

At ground level, Gaudí's deliberately uneven pillars extend the erratic, sinuous surface to the pavement. When the building was complete, municipal inspectors told Gaudí that, since some pillars jutted out farther than others, they were in

contravention of city ordinances. He said that, if they insisted, he could remove the pillars, but since they supported the building, he would not be responsible for the results. He heard no more about it.

Two separate and unconnected entrances lead into the building, one on the street corner and the other on Carrer de Provença, by which you enter the building proper. The motion-filled design continues in the internal layout, consisting of two separate internal courtyards, one circular and the other a long oval. The apartments and offices of the building swirl around them like river water

INSIDER TIP:

If you can't face the line for La Pedrera, linger over a coffee or a gourmet lunch under the wavy ceiling and Gaudíesque columns of Café de la Pedrera: It's in the mezzanine, overlooking Passeig de Gràcia.

—LARRY PORGES
*National Geographic
Travel Books editor*

around boulders. The internal facades are more sober affairs, but the external stairways seem to ripple upward.

Access is available only to the rooftop, the top floor, the attic, and the two first-floor patios. Sometimes you can visit temporary art exhibitions on the first floor.

EXPERIENCE: Getting Inside Modernisme

Those with a yen to get to know Barcelona's extraordinary art nouveau building heritage could start with the **Ruta del Modernisme** pack (*rutadelmodernisme.com*; see sidebar p. 90). Or use this listing to create your own tour.

The tourism office offers a two-hour walking tour in English that takes in some of the key works of this time. It starts at their office on Plaça de Catalunya (*4 p.m. Fri.–Sat. Oct.–May, 6 p.m. June–Sep.*).

It is possible to join specific tours of some of the highlights of modernisme. In the temple of Gaudí genius, **La Sagrada Família** (*Plaça Sagrada Família, 3, tour: $$$$$; see pp. 158–162*), for example, a 50-minute guided tour sets off up to four times a day. (Reserve ahead online at *bcnshop.barcelonaturisme.com*).

Alternatively, you can go it alone with an audio tour (*$$*).

You can also join a tour of the nearby **Hospital de la Santa Creu i Sant Pau** (*Carrer de Sant Antoni Maria Claret 167, tours in English: 12 p.m., 1 p.m., & 4 p.m. Mon.–Sat.; 12 p.m. & 1 p.m. Sun., $$$$; see p. 163*).

An audio guide is included in the ticket price for **Casa Batlló** (see pp. 142–143) and **Palau Güell** (see p. 92–93). Next door to Casa Batlló, in **Casa Amatller** (see p. 143), there will soon be tours of the foyer, the main floor, and the photo studio of the building's onetime master, Antoni Amatller (1851–1910).

Over in Pedralbes, guided tours of the **Pavellons Güell** (*tours in Eng.: 10:15 a.m. & 12:15 p.m. Sat.–Sun.; see pp. 177–178*) are available.

You will be guided to an elevator. Get out at the **Pis de la Pedrera** (alternatively, you can walk down the stairs from the attic). This top-floor apartment has been beautifully restored and furnished in much the way it probably was early in the 20th century. As is to be expected with Gaudí, the interior of the house is almost as curvaceous as the exterior. Where possible, he eliminates the straight line in the ceilings, walls, and doors. The succession of rooms—kitchen, bedrooms, dining area, bathrooms, and so on—takes you right around a circuit of the larger of the internal courtyards. Some of the decorative details and furnishings, along with the wrought-iron balconies, were actually designed by one of Gaudí's right-hand men, fellow architect Josep Maria Jujol. The view down Passeig de Gràcia, combined with the simple elegance of the furnishings, is enough to make your heart jump with joy. You may even find yourself saying, as many have when they visit, "I want to live here!"

Unfortunately that isn't an option. So the only thing to do

Music on the Roof

There is no shortage of distractions on the long, hot summer nights in Barcelona. One of the more surreal options is heading up to the hauntingly illuminated La Pedrera roof to listen to jazz concerts, (held from mid-June to mid-Sep.; $$$$$), occasionally accompanied by a glass of cava.

is move up to the next floor, the remarkable brickwork attic of the building. Fascinating in itself for its rib cage of parabolic arches, the attic has been turned into the **Espai Gaudí**, a museum-style review of all the master's work. Models of his buildings are interspersed with photos and videos about the man, his life, and his works. You can also see examples of the lead-and-string structural models he used to solve load-bearing and engineering conundrums in a way that allowed him you for the bizarre sight that awaits you. It is not hard to see why some saw La Pedrera as a fortress, for the array of chimney pots and other structures looks like a brigade of soldiers or robots recently disembarked from the imagination of George Lucas. The great squat structures might be watchtowers, while others, dotted with curious openings, seem like space-age pillboxes. More slender types, clustered together in groups and each topped with a menacing helmet, are the storm troopers

Fanciful chimney pots atop La Pedrera look like science-fiction warriors.

to pursue his ideal of mimicking the wonders of nature. These models hang upside down; by placing a mirror under them you can see an image of the sought-after structure.

Access to the rooftop is from the attic, and little can prepare manning this fantastical roof. They look like so many pieces ready to move on some strange, intergalactic board game. If you can drag your eyes away from these strange objects for just a moment, you can enjoy some magnificent views across central Barcelona. ∎

Gràcia

While on the lookout for more modernista caprices, you may end up in the tangle of narrow streets and charming squares that make up Gràcia. Gaudí completed one of his earliest commissions, the Casa Vicenç, up here back in the 1880s.

The fashionable Passeig de Gràcia, once a rural road

Gràcia

🅰 Map p. 141

🅱 Metro: Línia 3 (Fontana)

The area is worth experiencing for the atmosphere of what was until the end of the 19th century a separate village. With few tourists about, the sense of a genuinely Catalan environment is all the stronger.

By the time Barcelona absorbed Gràcia in 1897, it was a busy industrial center, and its 60,000 souls were a feisty lot. In the 1870s, several uprisings were launched here, and by the 1890s Gràcia was a hotbed of liberal, Republican, radical Catalanist, and left-wing activity. In the 1960s and '70s it became *the* place to be for intellectuals and bohemians. That spirit has ebbed, but local house prices reflect the fact that Gràcia still carries a certain cachet.

In 1883, when Gràcia was still a separate entity, Gaudí was asked to build a secluded private residence for a ceramics manufacturer. The result was **Casa Vicenç** (*Carrer de les Carolines 18–24*), which, although it doesn't display the fluidity of Gaudí's better known later works, is eye-catching amid the apartment blocks that surround it. Chessboard–style green and white tiles are a prominent decorative touch, and the wrought-iron fence and window grilles are also fine. With its towers, windows, and other openings, the house exudes the air of a mini-castle. Visitors are not permitted inside.

Four blocks south of Casa Vicenç, on the rousingly named Plaça de la Llibertat (Liberty

Square), is a fine late 19th-century wrought-iron market (Mercat Llibertat) designed by Francesc Berenguer (1866–1914), one of Gaudí's closest assistants; on Berenguer's death Gaudí exclaimed that he had lost his right hand. The heart of the area is, however, on the right side of Carrer Gran de Gràcia, the narrow and often traffic-choked extension of Passeig de Gràcia and the main shopping street.

Among the many squares where locals delight in sitting over coffee, or something stronger, some stand out. **Plaça de la Vila de Gràcia** is dominated by a clock tower that dates from 1862; hence it is known to most locals as the Plaça del Rellotge (Clock Square). In the 1870s it was a rallying point for revolutionaries and several small uprisings began here.

Three blocks north is the liveliest square in Gràcia, **Plaça del Sol.** Ringed by bars and cafés, it is wonderful for the hedonists but not so good for long-suffering residents, especially during the August Festa Major de Gràcia, one of the best of the city's fiestas, when it becomes a focal point for raucous street partying.

A more tranquil spirit reigns on **Plaça de la Virreina,** three blocks northeast. The square, presided over by the modest 17th-century Església de Sant Josep, offers a rare treat: trees. Together with a couple of welcoming cafés, they make it one of the most pleasant spots in Gràcia for a drink. Two blocks west is **Plaça del Diamant,** setting for the eponymous book by Mercè Rodoreda (1909–1983), one of the most popular Catalan novels of the 20th century, translated as *The Time of the Doves.*

A few blocks farther northeast is **Plaça de Rovira i Trias,** dedicated to Ildefons Cerdà's rival for the Eixample urban expansion plan in the 1860s. Antoni Rovira's plan is laid out beneath his statue here. Judge for yourself whether he or Cerdà deserved the commission. ∎

The Miracle of the Beans & a Saintly Procession

On March 3 each year, a singular procession of faithful on horseback, in horse-drawn carriages, and on floats winds through the streets of Gràcia and on to the districts of Sarrià, Sant Gervasi, Sants, and Montjuïc. They do so to honor a local martyr, Sant Medir *(santmedir.org)*, and at 8 p.m. the parade concludes along Carrer Gran de Gràcia. Legend recounts that, in A.D. 303, under the anti-Christian reign of Roman emperor Diocletian, Barcelona's local bishop, Sever, fled Barcelona in fear of his life. On the road to Sant Cugat del Vallès, he met a farmer, Medir, planting beans. Having explained his situation, he asked the farmer to tell his pursuers the truth, that Sever had passed by and was not far on down the road. Medir followed the bishop's wishes, and the beans he had just planted suddenly blossomed. Irritated by this evident miracle, the soldiers arrested Medir and, shortly after, Sever. Both were tortured and died martyrs.

More than 1,500 years later, a Gràcia baker named Josep Vidal swore he would make an annual pilgrimage to the saint's chapel in the Collserola mountains if his shaky health recovered. It did, and Vidal made his first trip in 1830. In following years, he was joined by others, who formed an association *(colla)*. Today, 28 colles join the processions on March 3.

More Places to Visit Around Passeig de Gràcia

Fundació Francisco Godia

This private foundation was set up in 2000 to display the private collections of a Catalan industrialist, Francisco Godia (1921–1990). Godia's tastes were wide-ranging, but the core of his collection is made up of Romanesque and Gothic art, including paintings and sculpture mostly from Spain. The mid-13th-century painting (thought to have been executed in León) depicting the taking down of Christ from the Cross is remarkable for its allegorical density and its brilliant color. Godia also collected fine medieval ceramics and paintings from the 19th and 20th centuries. The collection is located in a majestic modernista building designed by Enric Sagnier. Temporary exhibitions are held regularly. *fundacionfgodia.org* ⓜ Map p. 141 ✉ Carrer de la Diputació 250 ⏰ Closed Tues. & Sun. from 3 p.m. ⓜ Metro: Línies 2, 3, & 4 (Passeig de Gràcia)

Museu Egipci de Barcelona

This private collection is the only museum in Spain devoted to ancient Egyptian artifacts. Spread across two floors, the extensive display gives a taste of the wonders of Egypt and the pharaohs. Just past the ticket desk is a row of stone and basalt figures, followed by the colorful sarcophagus of an eighth-century B.C. noblewoman. Circling the first floor counterclockwise you will see jewelry (including a striking little gold figurine of the god Osiris), ceramics, alabaster jars, and funerary objects. In among the sarcophaguses, death masks, and mummies of humans are several belonging to animals, too. The Egyptians believed that certain animals, such as the cat and the falcon, were the earthly incarnations of the gods. Standing to attention upstairs is an array of statuettes and figurines made of bronze, stone, wood, and other materials.

Other curious items include a large stone sculpture of a baboon, Ptolemaic- and Roman-era coins, and fragments from a tomb. The top floor is taken up by a pleasant café and terrace. *museuegipci.com* ⓜ Map p. 141 ✉ Carrer de València 284 ☎ 93 488 01 88 ⏰ Closed Sun. from 2 p.m.; Mon.–Sat. 2 p.m.–4 p.m. except mid-summer & Dec. 💲 $$$ ⓜ Metro: Línies 2, 3, & 4 (Passeig de Gràcia)

Museu del Modernisme Català

Located in a modernista house, this museum gives an insight into the kind of art, furniture, and adornments the bourgeois Catalan families would have chosen to decorate their sumptuous homes in the late 19th and early 20th centuries, with works by Gaudí, cabinetmaker Gaspar Homar, sculptor Eusebi Arnau, and other leading artists of the period. *mmcat.cat* ⓜ Map p. 141 ✉ Carrer de Balmes 48 ☎ 93 272 2896 ⏰ Closed from 2 p.m. Sun. 💲 $$ ⓜ Metro: Línies 2, 3, & 4 (Passeig de Gràcia)

Palau Baró de Quadras

Palau Quadras is a modernista folly that is worth checking out even though it can not be visited. As the overburdened mock-Gothic facade suggests, it is the handiwork of Puig i Cadafalch. Note the square fish figures bearing the whole load. Peep inside the entrance, and don't forget to see the rear facade on Carrer Rosselló. ⓜ Map p. 141 ✉ Avinguda Diagonal 373 💲 $ ⓜ Metro: Línies 3 & 5 (Diagonal)

INSIDER TIP:

Take a wander down Rambla de Catalunya, a boulevard with all the elegance of the parallel Passeig de Gràcia, but less frantic and lined with cafés; not to be confused with its more notorious cousin downtown.

—JUSTIN KAVANAGH
National Geographic Travel Books editor

Gaudí's genius in his mighty Sagrada Família church and his whimsical Park Güell—the city's most famous icons

La Sagrada Família to Park Güell

Introduction & Map   156–157

La Sagrada Família   158–162

Sant Pau Recinte Modernista   163

Feature: Gaudí & Güell   164–165

Experience: Biking the Parks & More   165

Park Güell   166–167

Feature: Breaking New Ground   168–169

More Places to Visit Around La Sagrada Família & Park Güell   170

Hotels & Restaurants   256–257

Entrance pavilion at Park Güell

La Sagrada Família to Park Güell

The rapidly changing skyline in this area goes from renovated 19th-century industrial chimneys in Poble Nou to the 21st-century architecture of the Torre Agbar and the Museu del Disseny in Plaça de les Glòries, heralding the new business district known as 22@. And dominating the entire city skyline of Barcelona, of course, is the ever evolving architectural wonder of La Sagrada Família.

Looking toward the hill, the eight completed towers of La Sagrada Família church make it look something akin to the superstructure of a science-fiction battleship steaming majestically across the urban sea that surrounds it. For many first-time visitors to the city, it is the one thing they know of Barcelona, and frequently it is their first port of call. This unique temple is a magnificent, yet-to-be-finished architectural symphony.

When construction began in the 1880s, the area around it was mostly open land, for building in the Eixample (Extension)—the grid-plan expansion of the city beyond the confines of the medieval walls—had barely begun. It would be decades before this part of town would fill up with the housing that you now see. And in theory, it will be another decade from now before this most unusual of parish churches is finally completed, 100 years on from Antoni Gaudí's death in 1926. Thanks to some surviving drawings, photos, and models, architects have been able to get a reasonable idea of how Gaudí intended to complete the church. Computer studies have confirmed his daring structural calculations, and private donations keep the cranes and workshops busy.

Heading north from the church, a broad avenue bearing the name of the genius behind La Sagrada Família leads to a lesser known but in many respects equally important example of modernista building by one of Gaudí's most esteemed peers, Lluís Domènech i Montaner. If La Sagrada Família was built as a thing of beauty for God, the Hospital de la Santa Creu i Sant

Pau (Holy Cross and St. Paul's Hospital) was designed as a thing of beauty for the people, but with a practical purpose.

It lies on a slight rise in the city. About a mile (1.6 km) to the west, that rise is much more marked and has long been known to locals as "la Muntanya" (the Mountain). A mountain it isn't, but it is a steep walk up to the 50-acre (20 ha) block bought by Eusebi Güell late in the 19th century to create a garden city residential zone. The climb probably deterred potential buyers, but didn't stop Gaudí from laying out the gardens in his fanciful way. The result was that the citizens of Barcelona inherited this Gaudí gem as a stunning public park. ∎

NOT TO BE MISSED:

Exploring La Sagrada Família, a giant work of architectural art, perpetually in progress 158–162

A visit to the Sant Pau modernista complex, Domènech i Montaner's house of healing 163

A stroll and a picnic in the fable-like, almost psychedelic surrounds of Park Güell 166–167

The Torre Agbar, lit up at night 169

Viewing the instruments in the Museu de la Música, followed by a concert in l'Auditori 170

Interacting with the light installation 'BruumRuum' outside the Museu del Disseny 170

Casa Trias
Sala Hipòstila
PARK GÜELL
Casa Museu Gaudí

EL CARMEL

Hospital de L'Esperança

Lesseps (Metro)

TRAVESSERA — DE — DALT

CARRER DE L'ESCORIAL

PLAÇA DE LA FONT CASTELLANA

PARC DE LES AIGÜES

Alfons X

RONDA

C. DE CARTAGENA

MARE — DE — DÉU DE MONTSERRAT

DEL GUINARDÓ

Guinardó

Joanic

C. DE SARDENYA

JARDINS DEL PRÍNCEPS DE GIRONA

C. DE PADILLA

Sant Pau Recinte Modernista

TRAVESSERA — DE — GRÀCIA

C. DE SANT ANTONI MARIA CLARET

LA SAGRADA FAMÍLIA

CARRER DE CÒRSEGA

Sagrada Família

Verdaguer

PLAÇA MOSSEN JACINT VERDAGUER

PLAÇA DE LA SAGRADA FAMÍLIA

La Sagrada Família

AVINGUDA — DE — GAUDÍ

PLAÇA DE GAUDÍ

C. DE PADILLA

CARRER DE LA INDÚSTRIA

Hospital de Sant Pau

Camp de L'Arpa

CARRER DE CÒRSEGA

CARRER DE PROVENÇA

CARRER DE MALLORCA

C. DE VALÈNCIA

LA DRETA

C. D'ARAGÓ

L'EIXAMPLE

PLAÇA DE PABLO NERUDA

Encants

CARRER DE VALÈNCIA

CARRER D'ARAGÓ

AVINGUDA — MERIDIANA

Clot

PASSEIG DE SANT JOAN

C. DE SARDENYA

C. DE LA MARINA

Plaça Monumental dels Braus

Monumental

PLAÇA DE TETUAN

GRAN VIA DE LES CORTS

Els Encants

Teatre Nacional de Catalunya

PLAÇA DE LES GLÒRIES CATALANES

CATALANES

L'Auditori (Museu de la Mùsica)

Glòries

DHUB (Museu del Disseny)

AVINGUDA MERIDIANA

AVINGUDA DIAGONAL

Torre Agbar

Estació del Nord

PARC ESTACIÓ DEL NORD

22@ EL POBLENOU

Marina

CARRER DELS ALMOGÀVERS

CARRER DE PERE IV

CARRER DE LA MARINA

CARRER DE PALLARS

Bogatell

RAMBLA DEL POBLENOU

Llacuna

Universitat Pompeu Fabra

CARRER DEL DOCTOR TRUETA

Area of map detail

0 ————— 500 meters
0 ————— 500 yards

La Sagrada Família

Like the grand Gothic cathedrals that in part inspired it, La Sagrada Família church has been more than a century in the making. In spite of repeated setbacks, this dizzying modernista temple continues to rise slowly to the heavens, almost 90 years after the death of the man who designed and nurtured it in its early decades—Antoni Gaudí.

Looking up toward the ceiling of La Sagrada Família, the traveler is awestruck by the scale of Gaudí's ambition.

A trip to the Temple Expiatori de la Sagrada Família (Expiatory Temple of the Holy Family) is a visit to a puzzle and a work in progress. Much of the shell is now complete, and the most intense work is going on inside the church. Optimistic estimates suggest it may be completed by 2026. Some would argue it should not be completed at all. By the time of Gaudí's death in 1926, one facade (minus three towers), the crypt, and the apse were finished. Lack of funds had slowed construction to a snail's pace, and the political upheavals of the 1930s, civil war, and the difficult years of the 1940s and '50s brought building to a halt. Since then another facade has been raised, the central nave has been roofed over, and work on the main facade has begun.

Neo-Gothic Origins

The foundation stone of what was initially conceived as a neo-Gothic church was laid in 1882, almost two years before Gaudí took over the project. It was the fruit of a plan by an arch-conservative society dedicated to St. Joseph to turn what it considered Barcelona's increasingly lax citizens back toward the glory of God.

Gaudí would dedicate much of the rest of his life to this, his most extraordinary creation. Influenced though he may have been by his Gothic predecessors, he sought much of his inspiration in nature. The sinewy, twisting, bulbous forms that inform his planning drafts, models, and completed construction are unique. Although most of his plans and models were destroyed by fire in the civil war, what survived (along with clues provided by some of his other buildings) gave his successors strong hints as to how he might have proceeded.

Towering Heights

Gaudí's plans changed as he proceeded, but the final version envisaged a temple 310 feet (95 m) long by 197 feet (60 m) wide, with a central tower 560 feet (170 m) high and another 17 of 329 feet (100 m) or more. It will seat 13,000 people. Twelve of the towers (four on each facade) represent the Apostles (eight have been built), while five others symbolize the four Evangelists and the Virgin Mary, now under construction. Soaring above them, the central tower will represent Christ. Each of the three facades was planned to tell a story: the Nativity, Passion, and Glory of Christ.

Visiting La Sagrada Família

Enter by the Passion facade, which architects began to raise in 1954. While it largely respects its designer's original wishes, it is clearly different from the Nativity facade that was mostly built in Gaudí's lifetime.

In 1987 sculptor Josep Maria Subirachs (1927–2014) started work on the sculptural sequence that depicts the last two days in the life of Christ. His work is designed to be "read" from left to right, describing an "S" from bottom to top and ranging from the Last Supper to end in the top right corner with Christ's burial.

Symbolic Facade: At the table of the Last Supper, St. John in his grief rests his head on the table while the other Apostles look on in sadness. To the left of the depiction of Judas's kiss of betrayal is a cryptogram—from its numbers 310 combinations can be made to arrive at 33, Christ's age when he died. In front of the central door is depicted the flagellation of Christ. Other episodes that follow include Christ before Pilate, Peter's denial, and Veronica wiping Christ's face. Next to her (strangely faceless as she holds out the veil marked with the bloody image of Christ) stand soldiers whose helmets are a deliberate reference to the strange chimney pots of Gaudí's La Pedrera (see pp. 145 & 149–151). To the left of Christ crucified, the Virgin Mary, Mary Magdalene, and St. John stand in helpless sorrow. To the right yawns open the entrance to his burial place.

La Sagrada Família

- Map p. 157
- Plaça de la Sagrada Família
- 93 513 20 60
- $$$$–$$$$$ Audio guides and English-speaking guides available
- Metro: Línies 2 & 5 (Sagrada Família)

sagradafamilia.cat

Can You Say GATCPAC?

The Museu de les Arts Decoratives housed in the new Museu del Disseny (see p. 170) has a good amount of work from members of GATCPAC, translated as Group of Catalan Artists and Technical Experts for the Progress of Contemporary Architecture. Somewhat of a Catalan Bauhaus, GATCPAC began in the 1920s and stood for functionality and simplicity. Perhaps in response to the frivolity of Gaudí's modernisme, the work of these designers wasn't afraid of using a straight line or two. On display: a prototype of the famous BKF "butterfly" chair.

La Sagrada Família
Four towers on each facade, represent the 12 Apostles.

Tree of Life

Nativity facade

Main entrance

Bird's-Eye View: Having marveled at the towers from below, you can now go in the right-hand entrance of the Passion facade and take the elevator up the rightmost tower. Follow the signs when you reach the top to climb stairs and ramps in this and the adjacent tower. From up here the views across the city are spectacular. You can take the elevator back down or follow the arrows to walk downstairs

Inside the Church: Once back on solid ground, you enter the church proper. In 2000 the central nave stretching to Carrer de Mallorca was roofed over, and it is now possible to see the uncommon genius of Gaudí. Using photos, models, and computer simulations to test the master's calculations, today's architects have erected faithfully the most extraordinary array of pillars to hold up the roof. At their base, they have the appearance of straightforward Doric columns, but they culminate in strangely spherical capitals from which further branches sprout toward the ceiling. Each of these branches, together giving the impression of a high forest canopy, has been designed to share in the load bearing. The tribunes set high above the aisles were able to

host a choir of 1,500 when Pope Benedict XVI consecrated it as a Basilica in 2010.

Most of the nave and transept area is now a busy work site: You can peer into workshops at the end of the nave along Carrer de Mallorca. The external walls of the nave are lined with spires topped by what look (quite intentionally) like piles of brightly colored wild fruit. Gaudí's plans for the **Glory facade** give it the appearance of a distorted, massive church organ. In it will be represented creation, the virtues, angels announcing the Last Judgment, and the Holy Trinity, with God the Father presiding. Work started on this in 2004.

INSIDER TIP:

Professionals love to photograph monuments at night. When the sky is black, a little touch of red, yellow, or green will give more visual impact to your architecture pictures, like those of Sagrada Família.

—TINO SORIANO
National Geographic photographer

Nativity Facade: The marked path winds around the nave to the inside of the Nativity facade. Step outside to admire it. The busy, swirling, and curvaceous facade stands in stark contrast to the bleak, angular nature of the Passion facade. The joyousness of the one occasion is thus differentiated from the pain of the other. As on the Passion facade, the huge bulging bell towers soar into the sky, topped by mosaic-bedecked structures representing the symbols of the bishop: the cross, the ring, the miter, and the crosier.

Three portals culminating in acute spires make up the facade, and behind them are four bell towers. Dominating the central portal are the figures of the Holy Family, flanked by the adoring Magi and shepherds. Above them angels announce the birth of Christ. A twisting pinnacle of stone draws one's gaze up to the star that guided Christ's adorers to Bethlehem. The left door is decorated with sculptures recounting the wedding of Joseph and Mary, the flight to Egypt, and Herod's slaughter of the innocents. Episodes in the young Jesus's life, such as his appearance among the doctors and his presentation in the temple, are depicted around the right door. A striking element of the facade is the luxuriant floral decor. Palms, wheat, a cypress, and other plants are topped by layers of what look like tightly packed dripping stalactites.

On either side of the Nativity facade's portals are halls designed to be part of a series that will encircle the church. If the church were a courtyard, these halls would be the passageways of the cloister. Gaudí completed the portal dedicated to Our Lady of the Rosary and of Montserrat in the building to the right of the facade. The decoration is laden with symbols. Note the serpent (the devil) handing an anarchist a bomb, illustrating the temptation of humankind to do evil.

Museum, Workshop, and Chapel: Beneath the church, an extensive **crypt** stretches between the Nativity and Passion facades. It hosts the **Museu Gaudí,** showing drawings for the original project before Gaudí took over, as well as photos of various Gaudí works around Spain and the raising of the Nativity facade. You then enter the main aisle by striding beneath a plaster model of the church's central nave. About two-thirds of the way along the aisle to the right, you can look at the workshop where models are still being made. Toward the end of the crypt is a series of Subirach's preparatory sketches for his Passion facade sculptures, as well as a mock-up of the same facade.

INSIDER TIP:

A good place to enjoy a snack is at one of the sidewalk cafés lining the pedestrian Avinguda Gaudí.

—CAROLINE HICKEY
*National Geographic
Travel Books editor*

Opposite the workshop is a room that leads to a viewing point of the **Chapel of El Carmen,** where Gaudí lies buried. Campaigners for the miraculous architect's beautification hope it will happen in 2016. ∎

Sant Pau Recinte Modernista

Until 2009 this extraordinary modernista complex, the largest in Europe, was a working hospital, Hospital de la Santa Creu i Sant Pau. After several years of major renovation it has been born again as a knowledge center, housing institutions involved in health, education, and sustainability such as the World Health Organization and UN-Habitat. Now more dazzling than ever, this World Heritage site can and should be visited *(santpaubarcelona.org)*.

The hospital was designed by leading modernista architect Domènech i Montaner, and work on it began in 1902. The building was completed in 1930 by his son Pere Domènech i Roura. The patients from the 500-year-old Hospital de la Santa Creu in the Old Town (see p. 98) were transferred to this revolutionary complex where different pavilions, underground walkways, and landscaped gardens were all designed to contribute to the healing process of ailing Barcelonans.

The main entrance, as was often the case in Domènech i Montaner's projects, was clearly inspired by Gothic models. Grand but not overpowering, it is adorned with statuary, ceramic coats of arms, and several mosaics.

Each of the pavilions was dedicated to various specialties, but the emphasis is very much on the human dimension of the buildings. Clad in warm brick, they seem more like imaginative country houses, topped by tiled domes with a vaguely Byzantine look. That Levantine element continues in the domes on the church and of Casa de Convalescència at the eastern end of the compound.

Throughout the hospital, the ceramic and mosaic decoration, designed by artist Francesc Labarta (1887–1963) and executed by

The modernista facade reflects its Gothic inspiration.

Italian Mario Maragliano (1864–1944), is subtle but constantly pleasing. Particularly beautiful are the glazed tiles that adorn the center of the building at the end of the promenade.

A brand new Hospital Sant Pau, located to the north of the complex, has taken over all the clinical work of the old hospital. ■

Sant Pau Recinte Modernista

- 🅰 Map p. 157
- ✉ Carrer de Sant Antoni Maria Claret 167
- ☎ 93 268 24 44
- 🕐 Closed from 4:30 p.m. Nov.–Mar., from 6:30 p.m. Apr.–Oct.
- 🚇 Metro: Línia 5 (Sant Pau–Dos de Maig)
- 💲 $$, $$$ with guide

Gaudí & Güell

The day wealthy industrialist Eusebi Güell i Bacigalupi (1846–1918) wandered into the Spanish pavilion at the Paris Universal Exhibition in 1878 was one of the most decisive in Gaudí's career. The young architect had designed a storefront for a Barcelona glove retailer with a stand at the exhibition, and Güell was so impressed by its vitality and originality he sought out its creator upon his return to Barcelona.

During Güell's lifetime, Gaudí was rarely unemployed, with such projects as Park Güell and Colònia Güell to keep him busy.

Güell liked the man as much as the work and soon began to regale Gaudí with commissions of ever increasing importance. It was the beginning of a lifelong and fruitful relationship.

Güell became so confident in the capacity of Gaudí not only to construct sound and original buildings but also to express through them their shared Catalanist sentiments, that he commissioned Palau Güell, which was built on Carrer Nou de la Rambla in El Raval between 1886 and 1889 (see pp. 92–93). Here Gaudí began to give freer rein to his architectural expression. The result was a gamble that paid off. One day the two men were observing work to place a great coat of arms on the facade. A couple of passersby looked up and decried the "weird things" being added to the building. Güell, it is said, turned to his protégé and said: "Mr. Gaudí, now I like you even more!"

By the turn of the 20th century, Gaudí was involved in two far more ambitious projects for his benefactor. The first was a church for the Colònia Güell (see p. 238) just outside the city, a self-sufficient village for textile workers, devised in the best traditions of the enlightened magnate. While other architects built the houses, Gaudí set to raising the church. However, he only managed to finish the crypt (1915) before Güell abandoned the project due to lack of funds. The crypt, at Santa Coloma de Cervelló, provides important clues to Gaudí's groundbreaking structural ideas on weight distribution, vaulting, and other dilemmas.

At the same time, Gaudí set about developing Park Güell as a garden city (see pp. 166–167). His patron gave him a free hand in this project, and Gaudí gladly accepted it. For 14 years he worked on it, but the land parcels put up for sale failed to attract buyers, and Güell had to admit the idea had been a failure.

While some architects were full of praise for Gaudí's unique work, critics abounded too, dubbing Gaudí a *somnia truites*—an omelette dreamer—meaning someone who dreams up many crazy things. In one magazine a commentator observed, "Some say that in Park Güell all he is doing is spending all his money on making monumental omelettes. The fact is, however,

Portrait of Eusebi Güell, Antoni Gaudí, and Torras i Bages (Ricardo Opisso Sala, turn of the 20th century)

that Güell is the one who has to pay for all the eggs!" Well, Gaudí had always insisted that the best way to know a man was to spend his money!

Güell's death was a great personal loss to Gaudí, for whom the patron had also become a friend. By that time he had stopped taking on any projects, preferring to concentrate on La Sagrada Família (see pp. 158–162).

EXPERIENCE: Biking the Parks & More

The best way to see a city is by bike. It's quicker than walking, yet you still can grasp the minutiae that you'd miss from inside a cab or metro. And with 112 miles (180 km) of bike lanes in Barcelona, the scope is now endless (and safer).

The city has a variety of bike rental companies, some of which offer tours. At €3 ($4) an hour, **Barceloneta Bikes** (*Carrer de l'Atlàntida, 49, tel 93 177 11 19, barcelonetabikes.com*) is the best deal, but it doesn't offer tours. **Biking in Barcelona** (*Passeig Marítim de la Barceloneta 33, tel 932 219 778*) is more

expensive, but it offers a variety of specialized tours. The international **Fat Tire Bike Tours** (*Carrer de Sant Honorat 7, tel 933 013 612*) offers four-hour tours (*$$$$$*). It's a great company and has just brought out an e-bike tour of the hill of Montjüic (*$$$$$*). For a charge, **Bike Rental Barcelona** (*Carrer de Montserrat 8, tel 666 057 655, bikerentalbarcelona .com*) will deliver the bike to you. It's a bit pricier, but the service is convenient and the bikes are new. It even offers a modernisme tour that starts at Park Güell, so it's downhill all the way.

Park Güell

You could be forgiven for thinking, when you reach the main entrance to Park Güell, that you have landed on the set for a Disney fairy tale. The two stone pavilions flanking the wrought-iron gates look like a pair of gingerbread houses topped with generous servings of icing frozen into the most curious shapes.

Park Güell is a surreal outdoor experience in a city of constant architectural surprises.

Such is the popularity of this landmark park that a small entry charge is now made to the core "monumental area," and numbers are reduced so reserve your slot online in advance.

The original concept behind this and the remaining 50 acres (20 ha) of what is one of the world's most singular public parks was rather more prosaic.

The industrialist and Gaudí's patron, Eusebi Güell, who owned the land, yearned to create an English-style garden city, hence the spelling of "park," that would host some 60 houses for the well-to-do. He commissioned Gaudí, who set about the work in 1900 with characteristic gusto, employing several outstanding contemporaries (Josep Maria

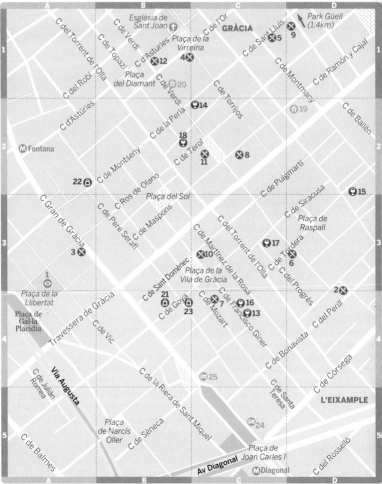

was first opened to the public in 1983 and is now a museum of monastic life (the few remaining nuns have moved into more modern neighbouring buildings). It stands at the top of Avinguda de Pedralbes in a residential area that was countryside until the 20th century, but which remains a divinely quiet corner of Barcelona.

Camp Nou
Stadium

Map p186 (📞902 189900; www.fcbarcelona. com; Carrer d'Aristides Maillol; adult/child €23/17; ⏱10am-7.30pm Mon-Sat, to 2.30pm

Sun; MPalau Reial) Among Barcelona's most-visited sites is the massive stadium of Camp Nou (which means New Field in Catalan), home to the legendary Futbol Club Barcelona. Attending a game amid the roar of the crowd is an unforgettable experience. Football fans who aren't able to see a game can get a taste of all the excitement at the museum, with its multimedia exhibits, and can also go on a self-guided tour of the stadium.

Bellesguard
Architecture

Map p186 (📞93 250 40 93; www.bellesguard-gaudi.com; Carrer de Bellesguard 16; admission €7; 🕙10am-7pm Mon-Sat Apr-Oct, 10am-3pm Mon-Sat Nov-Mar; 🚃FGC Avinguda Tibidabo) This Gaudí masterpiece was recently rescued from obscurity, and opened to the public in 2013. Built between 1900 and 1909, the private residence (still owned by the original Guilera family) has a castle-like appearance with crenellated walls of stone and brick, narrow stained-glass windows, elaborate ironwork and a soaring turret mounted by a Gaudian cross. It's a fascinating work that combines both Gothic and Modernista elements.

Jardins del Palau de Pedralbes
Park

Map p186 (Avinguda Diagonal 686; 🕙10am-8pm Apr-Oct, to 6pm Nov-Mar; Ⓜ Palau Reial) FREE A few steps from busy Avinguda Diagonal lies this small enchanting green space. Sculptures, fountains, citrus trees, bamboo groves, fragrant eucalyptus, towering cypresses and bougainvillea-covered nooks lie scattered along the paths criss-crossing these peaceful gardens. Among

the little-known treasures here are a vine-covered parabolic pergola and a gurgling fountain of Hercules, both designed by Antoni Gaudí.

Observatori Fabra
Observatory

Map p186 (📞93 431 21 39; www.fabra.cat; Carretera del Observatori; admission €10; 🚋tramvia blau, 🚃FGC Avinguda Tibidabo then) Inaugurated in 1904, this Modernista observatory is still a functioning scientific foundation. It can be visited on certain evenings to allow people to observe the stars through its grand old telescope. Visits, generally in Catalan or Spanish (Castilian), have to be booked. From mid-June to mid-September an option is to join in the nightly **Sopars amb Estrelles** (Dinner under the Stars; 📞93 327 01 21; www.soparsambestrelles.com).

Museu-Monestir de Pedralbes
Monastery

Map p186 (📞93 256 34 34; www.bcn.cat/monestirpedralbes; Baixada del Monestir 9; adult/child €7/5, free 3-8pm Sun; 🕙10am-5pm Tue-Fri, to 7pm Sat, to 8pm Sun; 🚌22, 63, 64 or 75, 🚃FGC Reina Elisenda) This peaceful old convent

Discover Park Güell, Camp Nou & La Zona Alta

🔀 Getting There & Away

● **Metro** Take Metro Línia 3 toward Canyelles for Gràcia (Fontana stop) and Park Güell (Vallcarca stop). Take Línia 3 toward Zona Universitària to reach Palau Reial de Pedralbes or Camp Nou (Palau Rail stop).

● **Train** FGC trains are handy for getting near Tibidabo (Tibidabo stop), Sarrià (Sarrià stop) and Museu-Monestir de Pedralbes (Reina Elisenda stop).

● **Tram** Outside Avinguda de Tibidabo station, the tramvia blau runs to Plaça del Doctor Andreu, where you can catch an onward funicular up to Tibidabo.

◎ Sights

Gràcia

Park Güell   Park
See p178

Mercat de la Llibertat   Market
Map p182 (📞93 217 09 95; www.mercatllibertat.com; Plaça de la Llibertat 27; ⊘8am-8pm Mon-Fri, 8am-3pm Sat; 🚊FGC Gràcia) **FREE** Built in the 1870s, the 'Market of Liberty' was covered over in 1893 in typically fizzy Modernista style, employing generous whirls of wrought iron. It got a considerable facelift in 2009 and has lost some of its aged charm, but the market remains emblematic of the Gràcia district: full of life and all kinds of fresh produce. The man behind the 1893 remake was Francesc Berenguer i Mestres (1866–1914), Gaudí's long-time assistant.

La Zona Alta

CosmoCaixa   Museum
Map p186 (Museu de la Ciència; 📞93 212 60 50; www.fundacio.lacaixa.es; Carrer de Isaac Newton 26; adult/child €4/free; ⊘10am-8pm Tue-Sun; 🚌60, 🚊FGC Avinguda Tibidabo) Kids (and kids at heart) are fascinated by displays here and this science museum has become one of the city's most popular attractions. The single greatest highlight is the recreation over 1 sq km of a chunk of flooded Amazon rainforest (Bosc Inundat). More than 100 species of Amazon flora and fauna (including anacondas, colourful poisonous frogs and caymans) prosper in this unique, living diorama in which you can even experience a tropical downpour.

Bellesguard
JOSÃ© FUSTE RAGA/GETTY IMAGES ©

Background

Park Güell originated in 1900, when Count Eusebi Güell bought a tree-covered hillside (then outside Barcelona) and hired Gaudí to create a miniature city of houses for the wealthy in landscaped grounds. The project was a commercial flop and was abandoned in 1914 – but not before Gaudí had created 3km of roads and walks, steps, a plaza and two gatehouses in his inimitable manner. In 1922 the city bought the estate for use as a public park.

Much of the park is still wooded, but it's laced with pathways. The best views are from the cross-topped Turó del Calvari in the southwest corner.

Sala Hipóstila

The steps up from the entrance, guarded by a mosaic dragon/lizard, lead to the Sala Hipóstila (the Doric Temple). This forest of 88 stone columns – some of which lean like mighty trees bent by the weight of time – was originally intended as a market. To the left curves a gallery whose twisted stonework columns and roof give the effect of a cloister beneath tree roots – a motif repeated in several places in the park.

Banc de Trencadís

On top of the Sala Hipóstila is a broad open space whose centrepiece is the Banc de Trencadís, a tiled bench curving sinuously around its perimeter and designed by one of Gaudí's closest colleagues, architect Josep Maria Jujol (1879–1949). With Gaudí, however, there is always more than meets the eye. This giant platform was designed as a kind of catchment area for rainwater washing down the hillside. The water is filtered through a layer of stone and sand, and it drains down through the columns to an underground cistern.

Casa-Museu Gaudí

The spired house to the right is the Casa-Museu Gaudí, where Gaudí lived for most of his last 20 years (1906–26). It contains furniture he designed (including items that were once at home in La Pedrera, Casa Batlló and Casa Calvet) and other memorabilia.

Don't Miss List

BY GONZALO SALAYA VENTURA, TOURIST GUIDE AT ICONO SERVEIS CULTURALS

1 ENTRANCE PAVILIONS

The entrance to Park Güell is flanked by two pavilions, best viewed from the public square up above. Here you'll see classic Gaudí features – hyperbolic shapes, the use of brick and ceramic and cross-topped towers, plus the incredible decoration.

2 SALAMANDER

The most famous creation in the park is this striking, mosaic-covered creature – perhaps a depiction of the legendary salamander associated with medieval alchemy. Like so much of Gaudí's works, this sculpture serves both aesthetic and practical purposes by linking water from an underground reservoir to the (mostly unbuilt) homes.

3 SALA HIPÓSTILA

Located underneath the (planned) main public square, the One Hundred Columns' Room, aka Sala Hipóstila, has an incredible ceiling composed of broken bits of ceramic and glass, including bottles. Here Gaudí created organic forms – suns, waves and other nature-inspired shapes – while employing the innovative technique of *trencadis* (p217).

4 CARYATID COLUMN

Descending from the right stairs leading off the public square to the salamander, you can access a 'diagonal' porch. Here you see dramatically slanting columns, one of Gaudí's trademarks. Nearly concealed amid the columns is a caryatid (a sculpted female figure which serves as a support). It harks back to Ancient Greece, but Gaudí has given the figure the more contemporary appearance of a washerwoman.

5 TURÓ DEL CALVARI

Christian symbols figure heavily in Gaudí's work and Park Güell is no exception. Most obvious are the three crosses atop the Turó del Calvari, evoking the crucifixion of Christ and two thieves atop Mt Calvary. When you find the right perspective, you can appreciate the clever design as the three crosses become one.

Don't Miss
Park Güell

One of Antoni Gaudí's best-loved creations, Park Güell – a fantasy public park that was designed as a gated playground for Barcelona's rich – climbs a hillside north of the centre. This is where the master architect turned his hand to landscape gardening and the result is an expansive and playful stand of greenery interspersed with otherworldly structures that glitter with ceramic tiles. The lasting impression is of a place where the artificial almost seems more natural than the natural.

Map p184

☎ 93 413 24 00

Carrer d'Olot 7

admission free

🕙 10am-9pm Jun-Sep, 10am-8pm Apr, May & Oct, 10am-7pm Mar & Nov, 10am-6pm Dec-Feb

🚌 24, Ⓜ Lesseps or Vallcarca

③ Pavellons Güell

Over by Avinguda de Pedralbes are the stables and porter's lodge designed by Gaudí for the Finca Güell, as the Güell estate here was called. Known also as the **Pavellons Güell**, they were built in the mid-1880s, when Gaudí was strongly impressed by Islamic architecture. A magnificent wrought-iron dragon guards the gate.

④ Museu-Monestir de Pedralbes

A stroll uphill along tree-lined Avinguda de Pedralbes leads to an oasis of another time, the peaceful **Museu-Monestir de Pedralbes** (p181). This Gothic convent with its enchanting cloister provides a tantalising glimpse into the life of nuns down the centuries.

⑤ Parc de l'Oreneta

Just behind the Museu-Monestir de Pedralbes rise the green slopes of this somewhat scrubby **woodland**. You can walk amid eucalypts, pines and oaks in a park that attracts few visitors on weekdays. Weekend activities bring out families with pony rides and train rides on a miniature locomotive. Various lookouts provide views over Barcelona.

⑥ Sarrià

Go east along the peaceful Carrer del Monestir for a look at some of the elegant mansions dotting the neighbourhood. Turn right at Carrer Major de Sarrià, which leads you into the heart of what was once the medieval village of **Sarrià**. Wander the pleasant streets and squares in the immediate area and try the city's best *patatas bravas* (potato chunks in a slightly spicy tomato sauce) at **Bar Tomàs** (p185).

⑦ Vil·la Amèlia & Vil·la Cecilia Gardens

Further southwest, these two **gardens** were once part of a magnificent summer estate. Shaded pathways meander beneath cypress, date palms and magnolias, with statuary and pools lending an elegance to the greenery. The 19th-century Vil·la Amèlia today houses the Sarrià civic centre.

 The Best...

PLACES TO EAT

Vivanda Magnficent Catalan cooking with year-round garden dining. (p185)

El Glop A buzzing neighbourhood spot in Gràcia. (p183)

Les Tres a la Cuina Gràcia gem serving unique, Slow Food–minded dishes. (p183)

PLACES TO DRINK

Raïm A slice of old Havana with expert mojitos. (p188)

La Nena One of Gràcia's best-loved neighbourhood cafes. (p183)

Viblioteca A charming little nook for wine and cheese. (p188)

VIEWPOINTS

Parc de Collserola An 8000-hectare park in the hills. (p190)

Mirablau Fun crowd and panoramic views from its Tibidabo perch. (p189)

Temple del Sagrat Cor Giant Christ statue with lift to the top. (p190)

Torre de Collserola A 288m tower with a glass elevator to an observation deck. (p190)

Park Güell Architectural intrigue and breezy views over city and sea. (p178)

Torre de Collserola (p190)
FERAD ZYULKYAROV/GETTY IMAGES ©

Park Güell, Camp Nou & La Zona Alta Walk

This walk offers a window into centuries past when the Zona Alta was home to lavish summer estates, manicured gardens and sleepy age-old villages.

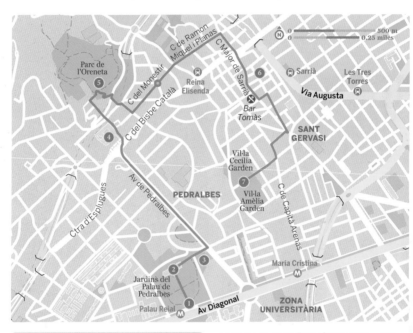

WALK FACTS

- **Start** Jardins del Palau de Pedralbes
- **Finish** Vil·la Amèlia & Vil·la Cecilia Gardens
- **Distance** 5km
- **Duration** Two hours

1 Jardins del Palau de Pedralbes

Although it's located on busy Avinguda Diagonal, this elegant little **park** (p181) feels like a peaceful escape from the bustling city beyond its gates. Pathways lead past manicured shrubbery, cedar and cypress trees, and a vine-covered pergola designed by Antoni Gaudí. A few sculptures dot the pathways, including a 17th-century urn and a nude by Enric Casanovas – one of the pivotal sculptors of the Noucentisme movement of the early 20th century.

2 Palau Reial de Pedralbes

At the north end of the park stands the **Palau Reial de Pedralbes**, an Italian neoclassical design built between 1926 and 1929. The estate belonged to the family of Eusebi Güell (Gaudí's patron) until it was handed over to the city to serve as a royal residence. King Alfonso XIII stayed here when visiting the city and in 1936 the *palau* became the official residence of Manuel Azaña, the last president of the Spanish Republic.

176

CosmoCaixa (p180)

This sprawling science museum, one of the largest in Europe, is packed with fascinating exhibits exploring the wonders of the natural world. You can wander through a mocked-up Amazonian rainforest, peer back in time at geologic formations and journey to the outer limits of the solar system. Interactive hands-on exhibits make CosmoCaixa a perennial kid-pleaser. It's easy to spend a half-day or more here.

FRANK WALDECKER/ROBERT HARDING ©

Museu-Monestir de Pedralbes (p181)

The city's periphery hides occasional oases of peace, including this impressive and beautifully preserved 14th-century Catalan-Gothic monastery. Highlights include the three-story cloister, a mural-filled chapel and a fascinating series of rooms that help conjure up life among the Poor Clares. The former sleeping quarters have been transformed into a gallery of religious art dating back to the 1500s.

Gràcia (p180)

Located halfway between L'Eixample and Park Güell, Gràcia was a separate village until 1897 and its tight, narrow lanes and endless interlocking squares maintain a unique, almost village-like identity to this day. In places bohemian, in others rapidly gentrifying, Gràcia is Barcelona at its most eclectic, its nooks and crannies home to everything from sushi bars to badly lit old taverns.

Park Güell, Camp Nou & La Zona Alta Highlights

Park Güell (p178)

Imagine a Disney fairy tale, scripted by Tolkien and filmed by Fellini, and you've conjured a picture of Park Güell. The park's construction was initiated in 1900 when Count Eusebi Güe bought a scrubby hillside and hired Antoni Gaudí to create a miniature city of posh houses landscaped grounds. The project was a commercial flop, but the abandoned site was saved in the 1920s and soon garnered a dedicated following.

Camp Nou (p182)

Spanish soccer is a sometimes bitter tal of two teams, Real Madrid and FC Barc lona, with the latter currently enjoying a spell as one of the best in the world, courtesy of such living legends as Lionel Messi and Xavi Hernández. The team's home stadium is the largest in Europe and its on-site museum is a manifestation of fervour, football and intense Catalan pride.

Park Güell, Camp Nou & La Zona Alta

The undulating terrain north of L'Eixample is dominated by the fairy-tale setting of Park Güell, one of Gaudí's most extraordinary creations. From its hillside perch, it has stellar views over Barcelona.

South of here is Gràcia, a separate village until 1897. It still has a distinct vibe and is home to artists, hipsters, expats and young families. Its pretty plazas are ringed with bars and cafes, and there's a plethora of restaurants, vintage shops and drinking dens in its narrow lanes.

West of Gràcia lies the vast Zona Alta, the affluent 'High Zone'. Scattered here are a handful of worthwhile sites, including the serene Pedralbes monastery and the charming neighbourhood of Sarrià. Further north is Tibidabo, the city's high point, with acres of green space, fine views and an amusement park. Further south, near the Sants neighbourhood is Camp Nou, the hallowed home stadium of FC Barcelona.

Park Güell (p178)

173

Jujol in particular) to help him. In the ensuing 14 years he managed to trace out the park and its installations. However, only two houses were built before interest in the idea waned, leaving the people of Barcelona with a bizarrely beautiful park, with glorious views across the city to the Mediterranean Sea.

The pavilions were designed to house the park's guardians and serve as a reception center for visitors to the residents. They are completely in keeping with Gaudí's insistence on the absence of

INSIDER TIP:

Walking through Park Güell is like taking a tour inside Gaudí's mind—part child, part genius.

—ANNIE GRIFFITHS BELT
National Geographic photographer

straight lines. Curvaceous ceramic layers culminating in unlikely towers top the rough local stone, and bloated wrought-iron grills protect the windows. One contains a shop of everything Gaudí, and the other, Casa Guarda, has an exhibition including Barcelona during the modernista period. The two houses serve as a frame for a grand staircase, and are flanked by low walls of *trencadís* ceramics, a visual spectacle of shattered patterns exuding color.

High up in the middle of it reigns a ceramic dragon, and beyond it more stairs lead up to the spectacular **Sala Hipòstila** (Hypostile Hall), a forest of 88

heavy pillars that support a huge platform above. The outer pillars lean inward and direct one's gaze up to the ceramic-covered ceiling.

The platform overhead is a broad observation point, overlooking the city and the shimmering Mediterranean on the horizon. The sparkling ceramic bench, designed by Jujol, resembles one long twisting serpent.

Casa-Museu Gaudí

As you head east, you reach the rose-colored Casa-Museu Gaudí, where he lived off and on from 1906 until he died in 1926.

You will guess from its sobriety that this is not a Gaudí design, but it is full of furnishings from other Gaudí houses. The most outlandish are perhaps the dining-room pieces for Casa Batlló (see pp. 142–143); the seats seem to have been cobbled together from wooden elephant ears. On the top floor you can see Gaudí's simple bedroom and office. A devout Catholic, he was also an ascetic, eschewing most comforts.

Other Park Sites

Leaving the house, follow the trail uphill, passing stone porticoes that blend into the mountainside. Their clusters of pillars leaning at strange angles and supporting higher levels of the path look like enchanted petrified trees. On the way up, you pass the only other house, **Casa Trias** *(closed to the public)*.

Tracks fan out across the park amid the trees planted here in the early stages of the park's development. A clearing by Casa Trias is a tranquil viewing point. ∎

Park Güell

⊠ Map p. 157

✉ Carrer d'Olot 7

☎ 93 409 18 31

$ $$

🚇 Metro: Línia 3 (Lesseps or Vallcarca) & a 10-minute walk following signs

parkguell.cat

Casa-Museu Gaudí

⊠ Map p. 157

☎ 93 219 38 11

$ $$

Breaking New Ground

At the extreme *dreta* (right) of the Eixample neighborhood, where once apartment blocks gave way to redbrick factories and smoking chimney stacks, a brand new phenomenon is emerging, launching Barcelona headfirst into the 21st century. This brave new development known as the 22@ Innovation district runs from Plaça de les Glòries to the Fòrum, between Avinguda Diagonal and the seafront.

The ever changing city skyline is being transformed by the 22@ scheme. Torre Agbar is on the right.

One of the largest urban regeneration projects in Europe, Barcelona's 22@ scheme is now transforming an obsolete industrial area with neglected housing into a new neighborhood and innovative knowledge-based business district. Hi-tech businesses, educational and research institutions, media groups, social housing, and green spaces are all playing a part in a cohesive effort toward sustainable city living. It also makes an interesting, alternative city walk.

Onward & Upward

The brainchild of the inspired city authorities in 2000, this cutting-edge business district has continued to attract interest and foreign investment despite the lean years of recession and financial crisis. International star architects like Jean Nouvel and David Chipperfield have left their mark as well as homegrown stars like Enric Ruiz-Geli, with his extraordinary, energy-efficient Media-TIC building, and Enric Massip-Bosch, whose

Torre Diagonal ZeroZero slices through the air where the Avinguda Diagonal meets the Fòrum.

Checkered Landscape

Plaça de les Glòries itself is being transformed from conflictive traffic junction into a huge park, ringed with landmark buildings like the Museu del Disseny, Torre Agbar, which will be a fancy hotel, and Els Encants, a flea market newly located under an eye-catching roof. The park will not see light until 2018, but it makes a good starting point to explore the 22@ development. The variegated mix of buildings profiles the theory behind it. Towering office blocks pose like a futuristic backdrop to former factories such as the handsome Ca l'Aranyó, an industrial complex impressively converted into a campus of the Pompeu Fabra University. Its renovated chimney is now used for the emissions of a new efficient energy system in the area. Nearby another smaller textile factory from the late 18th century has been converted into a fabulous ivy-covered art gallery, Can Framis (*closed Sun. from 2 p.m. & Mon.*), showing the Fundació Vilacasas' private collection of contemporary art. Adjacent to it is the Media-TIC building, housing part of the Open University and other information and communications technology organizations. A fenced-off derelict area near a smart energy plant announces an imminent communal allotment. This juxtaposition of skyscrapers with renovated factories and pockets of wasteland with graffitied walls makes a fascinating panorama.

Village Enclave

The original neighborhood of Poble Nou still has a village atmosphere with a bustling food market and local bars and restaurants. Its Rambla runs from the sleek refurbished Diagonal down to the sea, with terrace cafés and favorite haunts for ice cream like Tio Che (No. 44). Its modernista houses have been spared by the bulldozers, and former industrial buildings have been converted into libraries, cultural centers, and artists' studios. Beyond it begins the new residential area of Diagonal Mar; here impersonal high-rises shot up in 2004, but its designer parks are now well established and lush.

Torre Agbar: Barcelona's Multi-Hued Cucumber

Soaring upward into the sky above Barcelona, seemingly out of nothing, Torre Agbar (*Avinguda Diagonal 225, torreagbar.com, metro: Línia 1—Glòries*) has become the most visible—and most instantly recognizable—sight on the city's skyline since the spires of La Sagrada Família began their Gaudí-inspired ascent toward the heavens. The Torre Agbar is somewhat more prosaic, but no less remarkable in its own way.

Designed by French architect Jean Nouvel, this dazzling cucumber-shaped tower, inspired by the mountain of Montserrat, near Barcelona, stands barely half a mile (0.8 km) northwest of the Teatre Nacional. Originally owned by the city's water authority, Agbar, it will soon be transformed into a luxury hotel. The tower rises 34 stories aboveground (and dips four stories belowground), making it the third tallest building in the city (after the Arts Hotel and the Mapfre Tower, both 505 feet/154 m tall).

The Torre Agbar's environmentally friendly facade consists of nearly 5,000 glass windows, with temperature sensors that open and close them according to weather conditions in an attempt to reduce energy consumption. With the changing light of day the tower's coating of red and blue panels takes on many different hues, reflecting the mood of the skies above Barcelona. By night it is a spectacle, with special themes according to the fiesta of the moment.

More Places to Visit Around La Sagrada Família & Park Güell

Museu del Disseny

After years of anticipation, the new DHUB (Barcelona Design Hub) designed by the city's iconic architects MBM (Martorell, Bohigas, and Mackay), has landed in Plaça de les Glòries. It brings together various design organizations and decorative arts collections under one striking roof. Of most interest to the general public is the Museu del Disseny, comprising 70,000 pieces from the city's textile, ceramics, decorative arts, and graphic arts museums as well as temporary exhibits. Visit the whole of this extraordinary, sustainable building, including its landscaped surroundings with a lake. By night you can participate in a light installation on the esplanade entitled "BruumRuum!" that reacts to people's voices and city noise under the fluid, changing lights of the Torre Agbar. *museudeldisseny.cat* 🅜 Map p. 157 ✉ Plaça de les Glòries Catalanes 37–38 🕓 Closed Mon. until 4 p.m. ☎ 93 256 68 00 🚇 Metro: Línia 1 (Glòries)

Museu de la Música & L'Auditori

Part of the cultural complex near Glòries houses a fascinating music museum in the city's main classical music venue, L'Auditori. The building, designed by Rafael Moneo, is a strange ensemble of concrete blocks, russet-red steel panels, and open spaces. *www.museumusica.bcn.cat* 🅜 Map p. 157 ✉ Carrer Lepant 150 ☎ 93 247 93 00 🕓 Closed Mon. 💲 $$ 🚇 Metro: Línies 1 (Glòries) & 2 (Monumental)

Teatre Nacional de Catalunya

Opposite L'Auditori, the Teatre Nacional de Catalunya looks south like a cream-colored Parthenon. Lined by columns, the neoclassical theater by local architect Ricard Bofill opened in 1997. The entrance facade and tympanum is a curtain of glass. Upon entering, you see the walls of what could be a mini-Coliseum, which is the main stage, or Sala Gran. *tnc.cat* 🅜 Map p. 157 ✉ Plaça de les Arts 1 ☎ 93 306 57 00 🚇 Metro: Línies 1 (Glòries) & 2 (Monumental)

Bullfighting: A Dying Art

Barcelona is no longer somewhere to cry "Olé" as the *torero* swishes his brightly colored cape in front of a snorting bull. Nor will you find the much prized *toro de lidia*, beef fresh from the ring, in La Boqueria market as in the past. No, bullfighting is dead in Catalonia, deemed illegal by the Catalan parliament in 2010. The Catalans prefer to chase bulls in the street in festivals known as *correbous*.

Occasionally burning torches are attached to their horns weakening the argument that the ban is about cruelty to animals. It seems to be more about nationalism. The centuries-old ritual of bullfighting is considered a Spanish tradition and, as the oft repeated motto goes: "Catalonia is not Spain."

Of the last two remaining bullrings in Barcelona, one has been converted into a commercial center, Les Arenes (see p. 185) and the other La Monumental *(Gran Via de les Corts Catalanes 749, metro: Línia 1 for Glòries or Línia 2 for Monumental)* held the last *corrida* in Catalonia in 2011. This huge space, covering a whole block, today faces an uncertain future. Even if its bullfighting museum, Museu Taurí *(closed lunchtime and Sun. p.m.),* does not survive the building is worth a visit. Built in 1914 near Plaça de les Glòries, it has neo-mudéjar features mixed with modernista design.

The Jardins del Palau de Pedralbes, Tibidabo with its views and roller coasters, some lesser known Gaudí, and the magical, medieval aura of the Pedralbes convent

Northern Barcelona

Introduction & Map   172–173

Monestir de Santa Maria de Pedralbes   174–176

Experience: Learn the Lingo!   176

Jardins del Palau de Pedralbes & Pavellons Güell   177–178

Feature: F.C. Barca—More Than a Club   179

Tibidabo   180–181

More Places to Visit in Northern Barcelona   182

Experience: Enjoy Formula One Racing   182

Hotels & Restaurants   257

Camp Nou: the spiritual home of Catalonia

Northern Barcelona

For those who can afford to even think about it, Barcelona's northwestern edge, where the plain begins to give way to the chain of hills that cuts the city off from its hinterland, is prime real estate. In less than a century, farming country and villages have been swallowed up by a city whose appetite for land has been nothing short of voracious.

Like a fold in a map, Avinguda Diagonal, one of the city's great boulevards, cuts a swath across the city and funnels traffic out of Barcelona en route to Tarragona, the west, and ultimately Madrid. It might come as a surprise to find some of the city's unique attractions lying beyond this boundary, seemingly utterly disconnected from the rest of Barcelona.

Indeed, when the Pedralbes convent was raised on a slope northwest of the medieval polis in the 14th century, its founders required precisely that middle distance from the twisted and tangled maritime capital. Its nuns, many from wealthy and powerful families, were far enough away to keep out of trouble but not so far as to relinquish the influence such an institution could exercise over the earthly movers and shakers of the Aragonese Crown. Wandering through the atmospheric interior, you discover how nuns lived here down through the centuries—and still do today.

A short way down the road, Barcelona magnate Eusebi Güell commissioned Gaudí to build a grand entrance to his country estate. The old house on the grounds was remodeled into a palace used as a royal residence until 1931, then as a museum. Although no longer open to the public, its formal gardens make an attractive place for a walk and an apt venue for a smart summer music festival.

Farther to the north, the city's highest hill, Tibidabo, offers not only sweeping views of the entire city and surrounding countryside

NOT TO BE MISSED:

The Monestir de Pedralbes, a splendid Gothic convent 174–176

The pretty Jardins del Palau de Pedralbes and Gaudí's fantastical Pavellons Güell 177–178

Gaudí's Torre Bellesguard, a privileged visit to a family house 178

Taking in a soccer match at F.C. Barcelona's Camp Nou 179

City views and the roller coasters at Parc d'Atraccions 181

CosmoCaixa, an interactive science museum 182

The elevator up Torre de Collserola for sweeping Barcelona views 182

PLAÇA DEL MONESTIR

Monestir de Pedralbes

JARDINS DE TOQUIO

PEDRALBES

Palau Reial de Pedralbes

AVINGUDA DE PEDRALBES

JARDINS DEL PALAU DE PEDRALBES
Palau Reial

AVINGUDA DIAGONAL

Pavellons de la Finca Güell

PLAÇA DE PLUS XII

ZONA UNIVERSITÀRIA

CEMENTIRI DE LES CORTS

GRAN VIA DE CARLES III

Museu del FC Barcelona

Camp Nou FC Barcelona

Mercat les Corts

TRAVESSERA DE LES CORTS

LES CORTS

Les Corts

Collblanc

AVINGUDA DE MADRID

C DE BERLIN

CARRER DE LA RIERA BLANCA

CARRER DE RAMBLA DEL BRASIL

C DE BADAL

DE SANTS

JARDINS DE CAN MANTEGA

Plaça del Centre

Plaça de Sants

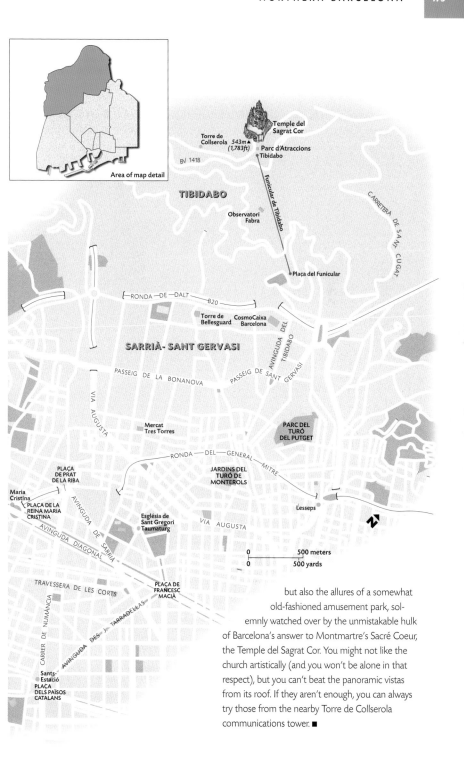

Area of map detail

Temple del Sagrat Cor

Torre de Collserola   543m ▲   (1,783ft)   Parc d'Atraccions Tibidabo

BV 1418

Funicular de Tibidabo

TIBIDABO

Observatori Fabra

Plaça del Funicular

RONDA — DE — DALT — B20

Torre de Bellesguard   CosmoCaixa Barcelona

SARRIÀ- SANT GERVASI

PASSEIG DE LA BONANOVA

PASSEIG DE SANT GERVASI

AVINGUDA DEL TIBIDABO

VIA AUGUSTA

Mercat Tres Torres

PARC DEL TURÓ DEL PUTGET

RONDA — DEL — GENERAL — MITRE

JARDINS DEL TURÓ DE MONTEROLS

PLAÇA DE PRAT DE LA RIBA

Maria Cristina

PLAÇA DE LA REINA MARIA CRISTINA

AVINGUDA DE SARRIÀ

Lesseps

Església de Sant Gregori Taumaturg

VIA AUGUSTA

AVINGUDA DIAGONAL

0   500 meters
0   500 yards

TRAVESSERA DE LES CORTS

PLAÇA DE FRANCESC MACIÀ

CARRER DE NUMANCIA

AVINGUDA DE J. TARRADELLAS

Sants-Estació

PLAÇA DELS PAÏSOS CATALANS

but also the allures of a somewhat old-fashioned amusement park, solemnly watched over by the unmistakable hulk of Barcelona's answer to Montmartre's Sacré Coeur, the Temple del Sagrat Cor. You might not like the church artistically (and you won't be alone in that respect), but you can't beat the panoramic vistas from its roof. If they aren't enough, you can always try those from the nearby Torre de Collserola communications tower. ∎

Monestir de Santa Maria de Pedralbes

When Queen Elisenda, fourth and last wife of the Count-King Jaume II, ordered in 1326 the foundation of the Monestir de Santa Maria de Pedralbes (from the Latin *pedras albas*, or white stones), it was located amid bucolic calm. Seven centuries later, the convent is an island of peace, surrounded by one of the more sought-after locations in suburban Barcelona.

The quiet, leafy cloister of the Monestir de Pedralbes contrasts with Barcelona's noisy chaos.

The complex was raised in record time (the church was finished within a year), which explains its remarkable unity of style. Soon thereafter, Clarissine nuns, among them daughters of several powerful Catalan families, took up residence. A dozen nuns still live here, but they have moved to quarters across the lane from the main entrance into the convent.

The simple, single-nave church (the entrance to which is just off Plaça del Monestir) is a minor gem of Catalan Gothic, broad, bare, and stout. Like so many churches in Barcelona, it was a victim of anarchist zeal during the first stages of the Spanish Civil

War in 1936. An impressive neo-Gothic retable that dominated the altar was destroyed. Untouched, however, was the tomb of Queen Elisenda de Montcada, located in the presbytery. The statue of the queen atop her tomb is presented in full regal splendor, with angels at her head and feet. Alongside the church, a typical octagonal bell tower stands watch.

Through the door to the left of the church is the way into the convent itself. You enter a **cloister** of singular elegance, its two Gothic stories topped by a third added in the 15th century. Cypresses and a tall palm preside over the immaculately kept grounds, in which the baroque well and medieval ablutions fountain are the most notable features.

Visitors follow a counterclockwise route along the lower gallery of the cloister. The first room open off to the right is the **Capella de Sant Miquel** (St. Michael's Chapel) or abbess's day cell, decorated with frescoes

in 1343–1346 by Ferrer Bassa, who was credited with having introduced the latest techniques of Italian Gothic painting to Catalonia. Among the scenes depicted are the birth of Christ and his preaching in the temple. At the end of the gallery is the entrance to a grand **upstairs hall** that served as the *dormidor*, or sleeping quarters. For centuries the walls were lined with the nuns' claustrophobic night cells. They have been stripped away and replaced by a modest collection of devotional art collected over the centuries.

There are some curious items in the collection. A stucco relief of hunting scenes (including a knight killing a dragon, which was a creature that people believed in then) is a rare piece of nonreligious Gothic art. Among the flood of Flemish art that managed to make its way into the convent is a false triptych with a beautiful Florentine *robbiana* (a Renaissance ceramic relief by Andrea della Robbia).

Monestir de Pedralbes

🅰 Map p. 172
✉ Baixada del Monestir 9
☎ 93 256 34 34
🕐 Closed Mon. and from 2 p.m. Tues.–Fri.; from 5 p.m. Sat. & Sun. Oct.–March; from 5 p.m. Tues.–Fri. & from 7 p.m. Sat.–Sun. Apr.–Sept.
💲 $$
🚇 FGC train (Reina Elisenda) then a 10-minute walk or buses Nos. 22, 64, & 75

monestirpedralbes .bcn.cat

Get Thee to a Nunnery

It was a common occurrence in medieval times for young girls, whose families had decided they should dedicate their lives to the faith, to be sent to a convent. Their hair was shorn and their civilian clothes replaced by shapeless habits. Soon they would take vows of poverty, chastity, and obedience, vows that were considered irrevocable and eternal.

At that point a class system intruded at every level. Nuns, seated in tiny cells around the cloister, spent their days embroidering vestments, painting saints' images, and studying religious texts. The latter was only for those who could

read—meaning the upper classes—and these sisters alone sang in the choirs and attained positions of power in the convent. Empowered by Queen Elisenda's legacy, the mothers superior maintained close links with the government of Catalonia.

Life was well ordered, with a rigorous canonical timetable starting well before dawn and ending after dark. Meals rarely included meat, and from September 8 until Easter the sisters were subjected to a regime of semi-fasting, eating only one full meal a day (except Sundays and holidays). And when they died, they were buried within the convent.

Allow time for coffee or lunch in nearby Sarrià, a charming village turned residential area. Bar Tomás [*Major de Sarrià 49*] has the best *patatas bravas* in town.

—JUSTIN KAVANAGH
National Geographic Travel Books editor

Other interesting objects include a couple of giant medieval choir songbooks and several nuns' personal treasure chests, such as one with Arabic touches that may have come from Granada, the southern Spanish city that was ruled by Muslims for eight centuries. Along this length of the cloister are the former botica (pharmacy) and a series of sparsely furnished day cells, where nuns would pass the time in prayer.

The third gallery of the first floor is taken up by the **refectory,** where the nuns would take their Spartan meals in silence while listening to readings from the scriptures. "Silentium" is inscribed solemnly around the refectory walls, along with other Latin exhortations such as "Audi tacens" ("Listen and keep quiet").

Behind the refectory is the extensive **kitchen.** Along the last leg of the cloister, you can inspect the rooms of the 16th-century **infirmary.** A display of the history of the convent and those who lived in it is in these rooms. Beyond it is the *sala capitular* (chapter house), where the nuns discussed issues affecting their community. ■

EXPERIENCE: Learn the Lingo!

It's one thing coming to admire the sights and enjoy the food and nightlife of Barcelona, but there's no better way to get under the skin of a city than by learning something of the language or, in this case, the languages.

Whether you're a beginner or already have a good level in Spanish, coming to town for a week or two of language class is a great way to meet people and "live" the city. Those with a taste for learning more about strictly local culture could opt for Catalan classes, although this option usually attracts only longer-term residents.

There is no shortage of language learning opportunities. Your first port of call could be the **Instituto Cervantes** (cervantes.es), Spain's international cultural institute, which can provide lists of schools in Barcelona and elsewhere in Spain. In the U.S. it has offices in New York City, Albuquerque, Chicago, and Seattle. Or try several tuition providers in Barcelona directly. The **Universitat de Barcelona** (www.eh.ub.edu) offers a variety of courses ranging from two weeks to a month. Longer semester courses are also possible. The university also offers Catalan tuition. A globally respected school is **International House** (ihes.com/bcn). Other well-known schools include **Don Quijote** (donquijote.org), with schools all over the country, and **Olé** (olelanguages.com).

The city abounds with language academies, so shop around. Many offer cultural packages combining language study with everything from cooking to diving. Most can help with accommodations, too, sometimes with host families.

The Gaudí designed dragon gates guard the Pavellons de la Finca Güell.

Torre Bellesguard

- Map p. 172
- Bellesguard, 16-20
- 93 250 40 93
- Closed Sun., from 2:30 p.m. Nov.–March
- $$ (exterior only with audio guide), $$$$ (complete guided visit)
- FGC (Avinguda de Tibidabo)

bellesguardgaudi.com

NOTE: Check the website for events like Nits de Gaudí at the Palau Reial de Pedralbes, a perfect place to chill out on hot summer evenings, sipping a cool cocktail in the night air.

and playful ceramics. Guided visits to the pavilions in English are available on weekends at 10:15 a.m. and 12:15 p.m.

Torre Bellesguard

Hidden from the public eye for more than a century, this barely known Gaudí house has just opened for visits, an interesting addition to the overexposed circuit of the genius' buildings. High up on the hillside among slick designer pads and 19th-century villas where wealthy Barcelonans summered in the cooler air, until now the curious could only peep through its gate to glimpse the garden. Part of the charm of Bellesguard is that it has been lived in as a family house since 1944, making this a privileged visit.

Torre Bellesguard was built between 1900 and 1909 for Jaume Figueras, a fervent Catalan, like Gaudí, who loved the historical significance of the location. Its origins date from around 1400, when Martí l'Humà (the Humane), the last of the Catalan kings, had a castle on the same

spot. The house was quite distinctive from other Gaudí works, and Figueras maintained the historic connection by giving the house a castle-like appearance behind its high walls. Despite its somber, straight lines you can still spot plenty of Gaudíesque elements, from ingenious solutions to bring natural light into the interior to decorated drainpipes and trencadís (mosaic) benches.

It is worth taking the guided tour to learn about its past and get inside to climb the narrow stairs up to the terrace with panoramic views living up to its name, Bell-Esguard meaning "beautiful lookout." Watch out for the hidden crouching dragon on the roof, a favorite symbol of Gaudí. The tour goes through what was to be the music room but was never finished, a distinctively Gaudí space with its exposed brick and parabolic arches. Finish off with a visit to the former stables, where children were sheltered during the civil war, before a cancer specialist opened the house as a hospital. His great grandchildren still live in the private areas of the house. ■

Jardins del Palau de Pedralbes & Pavellons Güell

For many years, whenever General Franco would come to town, he would stay in the Palau Reial, a neoclassical residence, surrounded by shady gardens and soothing fountains. Previously it had belonged to the wealthy Güell family, who then put it at the disposal of the Spanish king, Alfonso XIII. The building was converted into a palace in the mid-1920s, so the monarch, who abdicated in 1931, got precious little use out of it.

Enjoy the Jardins del Palau de Pedralbes, gardens fit for a king.

Although the building can no longer be visited the pretty gardens, bursting with bougainvillea, are open to the public. Their grand cedars and pines provide welcome shade, and various ponds and fountains help you to feel cooler. You can't miss the pergola designed by Gaudí, but you may have to hunt a bit to find his dragon-shaped fountain surrounded by bamboo which was lost in the undergrowth until 1984.

In 1883, Eusebi Güell commissioned his favorite architect to construct an entrance gate to his estate with two buildings known as the **Pavellons de la Finca Güell.** One was for the caretaker and the other destined to be the stables. These can now be admired from Avinguda de Pedralbes, just beyond the limits of the Palau Reial's gardens. The gate features a fantastical wrought-iron dragon, while the bright little pavilions are all twisting turrets, sunny brick,

Jardins del Palau de Pedralbes

- 🅰 Map p. 172
- ✉ Avinguda Diagonal 686
- 🕐 Closed from sunset
- Ⓜ Metro: Línia 3 (Palau Reial)

F.C. Barça—More Than a Club

One of the last professional sports clubs still owned by supporters, F.C. Barcelona's motto is *més que un club* (more than a club). To date, it has won four European Cups, 22 Spanish Championships, 26 Spanish Kings Cups, and two World Championships and its team glitters with soccer's biggest stars. But Barça's history is as much about what it represents off the field, as a shining symbol of Catalonia, as any sporting feats.

For many citizens of Barcelona, 1899 was a key date in the city's history. It was in that year that Fútbol Club Barcelona was formed by a Swiss sugar trader and a small fraternity of English expatriates. The club quickly came to embody a strong sense of loyalty to the Catalan cause and membership mushroomed throughout the following decades of political turmoil and civil strife. When the club's president, José Sunyol, was executed by fascist troops at the start of the Spanish Civil War, the club became a vehicle for political protest and the red and blue club colors became as much a symbol for Catalonia as the flag itself. As Spain fell under the repressive spell of Franco, the stadium became the one place where Catalans could gather to express their sense of collective identity without fear of arrest.

Brazilian Neymar Junior and his Barcelona teammates celebrate another Barça goal by Argentine Lionel Messi.

Camp Nou

The club today has about 170,000 members, more than enough to fill its Camp Nou (New Field) stadium, one of the world's great soccer cathedrals. Built in 1957 and expanded in 1982, it can hold 120,000 spectators, but may be extended further. Money is not an obstacle: The club is the world's second richest football club, with an annual turnover of $613 million.

Club Members

Despite its wealth, this is still a club very much of the people. Although it receives constant offers, it has long resisted the urge to sell: The club belongs, as it has since its inception, to its members, who have included Pope John Paul II and opera star José Carreras, and its president is chosen by election. Barcelona was one of the last professional clubs to refuse to sully its team jersey with sponsorship. This ended in 2006 when the club announced a deal to sport the UNICEF logo on its shirts.

Museu del F.C. Barcelona

If you can't see a game (see sidebar p. 18), visit the Museu del F.C. Barcelona at Camp Nou and muse over old trophies, photos, and videos. Barça's achievements in the years from 2008 to 2012, when coached by ex-player Pep Guardiola, are of special note: This team, featuring Argentine legend Lionel Messi alongside homegrown talents from the Barça academy such as Xavi and Iniesta, is considered one of the greatest in the history of the sport. Aficionados should go for the Camp Nou Experience, which includes a tour of the stadium (see map p. 172; *Carrer d'Aristides Maillol 12, tel 93 496 36 00 for tickets, $$$$$, fcbarcelona.com, Metro: Línia 5—Collblanc, Línia 3—Les Corts*).

Tibidabo

According to the Latin version of the Gospel of St. Matthew, the devil declared to Christ: *"Haec Tibi omnia dabo si cadens adoraveris me—*All this I will give you if you will fall down and worship me." At 1,783 feet (543 m), Tibidabo is the highest point overlooking Barcelona and, on a good day, affords views across the city and out to sea, as well as inland to Montserrat. The devil's pact would be a tempting deal.

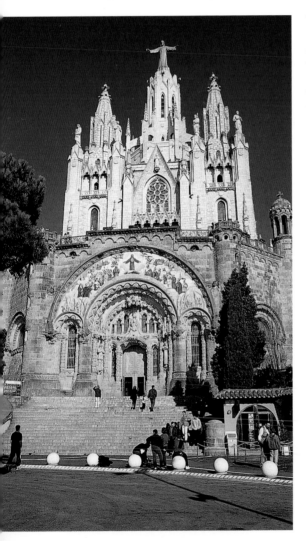

The Temple del Sagrat Cor is an odd mix, with its modernista lower half and wedding-cake crown.

The hill was developed as a public park in the early 1900s, and a private enterprise ran the Tramvia Blau (Blue Tram) and connecting funicular services that still link the summit with the city proper and are part of its fun. Later the Parc d'Atraccions (Amusement Park) and the Temple del Sagrat Cor were added.

The catechist Juan Bosco had already dedicated the hill to the Sacred Heart (Sagrat Cor), so it came as little surprise that the Church should be inspired to build a place of worship here. Enric Sagnier (1858–1931) was entrusted with the task and a year before his death had completed the eclectic mix that is the **Temple del Sagrat Cor.** Designed to rival the Sacré Coeur atop Paris's Montmartre district, the church is far from universally admired. The roughly hewn brownstone crypt is clearly of modernista (almost Gaudían) inspiration. Eusebi Arnau, one of the period's most important sculptors, was responsible for some of the statues adorning the crypt.

Inside the Church

Inside, the ceramic and mosaic decoration (finished in 1941) has some pleasing aspects. To the right, off the crypt, a door leads into a chapel dedicated to the Eucharist. Since June 1966, the chapel has been the scene of the permanent adoration of the Holy Sacrament. Although recruitment of the sufficiently faithful has not always proven easy, the chapel has never been left empty. Day and night at least one person has always been in attendance to worship. Each day, buses take up worshippers who, if their allotted hour falls during a night shift, sleep over in cells during their free time before being taken back to town the following day.

INSIDER TIP:

Barcelona is surrounded by mountains. You can take impressive shots of the city—especially at night—from the top of Montjuïc, Tibidabo, or from Parc del Guinardó.

—TINO SORIANO
National Geographic photographer

Stairs sweep up on either side of the crypt to the soaring gray hulk of the bare, neo-Gothic church proper. Some of the stained glass is fetching, but otherwise the building is bereft of significant ornament. From either the crypt or church, you can catch an elevator up to the roof, which can be decidedly windy. From there, stairs spiral up to the gold-tinted bronze statue of Christ that crowns the edifice. The other statues around the roof represent the Apostles. From anywhere up

here, the views across the city and the countryside are spectacular.

Parc d'Atraccions

For the majority of locals who make the effort to get up to Tibidabo, the main draw is the Parc d'Atraccions, the town's only remaining amusement park (one on Montjuïc was shut in the late 1990s). Although many new rides have been added in recent years, including a heart-stopping new roller coaster, the park has an old-fashioned flavor. A variety of tickets allows you the choice of simply entering and choosing one or two rides or settling in for the day to try everything.

One of the park's big favorites for those who like a fright is the seven-minute trip through the Hotel Krueger, a house of horrors in which everyone from Hannibal Lecter to Dracula attempts to scare the wits out of you. You might prefer the staid L'Avió, an aeroplane that has simply tootled around in circles since 1928, simulating flight. Other attractions include many of the old favorites: miniature trains, water rides, a fine old carousel, *autos de xoc* (bumper cars), and a historic museum of automatons with some pieces from the 19th century. Several shows are also staged, including a puppet performance in the Marionetarium.

Opening hours at the park can vary radically, so it is always worth making advance inquiries at the tourist office or on the website for the latest details. A number of restaurants and fast-food outlets are dotted about the amusement park. ∎

Temple del Sagrat Cor
- Map p. 173
- Plaça de Tibidabo
- 93 417 56 86
- $ (elevator)
- FGC (Avinguda de Tibidabo) & Tramvia Blau & Funicular or Bus: T2 (from Plaça de Catalunya)

Parc d'Atraccions
- Map p. 173
- Plaça de Tibidabo
- 93 211 79 42
- Open noon–10 p.m. Wed.–Sun. July–early Sept.; closes early Sat.–Sun. & holidays (check website)
- $$$$$
- FGC (Avinguda de Tibidabo) & Tramvia Blau & Funicular or Bus: T2 (from Plaça de Catalunya)

tibidabo.cat

More Places to Visit in Northern Barcelona

CosmoCaixa

Among the star attractions of this exciting, hands-on modern science museum, which kids love, is a 1,196-square-yard (1,000 sq m) reproduction of a flooded Amazon rain forest with more than 100 species of plants and animals. This is about as close as you can get to the real thing without going to Brazil. The **Mur Geològic** (Geological Wall) is another original element. Several different strata of rocks from different parts of Spain allow you to understand how such formations came to be through erosion, volcanic activity, glacial movement, and so on.

obrasocial.lacaixa.es 🅜 Map p. 173 ✉ Carrer Isaac Newton 26 ☎ 93 212 60 50 🕐 Closed Mon. 💲 $$; free for under 16 🚍 Bus: No. 196 or FGC (Avinguda de Tibidabo) & Tramvia Blau

---

EXPERIENCE: Enjoy Formula One Racing

In May, the superstars of Formula One (along with their entourages) descend on the city of Barcelona to fight out this stage in the annual Grand Prix championship at the Montmeló track, north of the city. This international glamour event has been staged here since 1991, and the locals embrace it with a passion. The track is surrounded by 17 grandstands from which to view the race. Also, more than 20 big-screen TV screens are scattered across the area, so you can catch all the action replays, too. If you buy tickets for the full three days, you'll have the opportunity to see the cars up close in the pit lane on the Thursday before the races begin. For information, get in touch with the **Circuit de Catalunya** race-track *(tel 93 571 97 70, circuitcat.com).*

Torre de Collserola

This slender communications tower, designed by Norman Foster and erected in the late 1980s, has become one of Barcelona's principal landmarks. At an impressive 947 feet (288 m) high, it dominates (along with the Temple del Sagrat Cor) the mountain ridge separating the city from inland Catalonia. The clever design is less of a draw than the elevator ride to the top for bird's-eye views.

The tower is surrounded by the most extensive park in the area, **Parc de Collserola.** Joggers, cyclists, and hikers flock here for a little peace and quiet (take the FGC train to Baixador de Vallvidrera). In the heart of the park you'll come across an 18th-century country house where Catalonia's famous poet, Jacint Verdaguer (1845–1902), passed the last days of his life.

torredecollserola.com 🅜 Map p. 173 ✉ Camí de Vallvidrera ☎ 93 211 79 42 🕐 Check website for closing information. 💲 $ 🚍 FGC (Peu de Funicular) & Funicular, then Bus No. 111

A mountain in continual renovation, showcasing grand art galleries and museums, an Olympic stadium and pool, a fortress, and magnificent gardens

Montjuïc

Introduction & Map   184–185

Museu Nacional d'Art de Catalunya
    (Palau Nacional)   186–190

Experience: Discover Barcelona at Your Feet   188

Pavelló Mies van der Rohe   191

Poble Espanyol   192–193

Anella Olímpica   194–195

Fundació Joan Miró   196–198

Gardens   199–200

Castell de Montjuïc   201

More Places to Visit in Montjuïc   202

Hotels & Restaurants   257

The futuristic Torre Calatrava on Montjuïc

Montjuïc

Thousands of years ago, household fires burned bright through the night among the huts of a Celt-Iberian tribe, Barcelona's first inhabitants. At least that's what the archaeologists surmise. When the Romans arrived, Montjuïc became a stage for religious rituals. At its base, it is believed, was the city's first ancient port.

Excepting the inland mountain range that culminates in Tibidabo and closes Barcelona off from the Catalan hinterland, Montjuïc is the city's only significant bump. Its role in the life of Barcelona's citizens has always been dual, as a source of recreation and escape from the urban squeeze below it and as a place of ceremony. A cemetery still occupies its southwestern flank.

In 1929 it was chosen to stage the ritual of the International Exhibition and in 1992 that of the Olympics. On weekends thousands now come up here to enjoy the gardens, swimming pools, museums, art galleries, and—a rare thing in Barcelona—fresh air and relative quiet.

That Montjuïc means Jewish Mountain seems demonstrated by the evidence of tombstones found in what appears to have been a Jewish cemetery here. However,

another theory claims the name evolved from Mons Jovis, a Roman temple to Jupiter.

Had initial plans for a follow-up to the 1888 Universal Exhibition been acted upon, the show might have taken place in 1907. Sanctioned by the Spanish dictator Gen. Miguel Primo de Rivera as a useful propaganda stunt, it finally occurred in 1929. The result changed this part of town completely.

The pompous Palau Nacional was built as the main seat of the exhibition and today houses a fine art museum. To its north, the grand Plaça d'Espanya traffic circle is

---

NOT TO BE MISSED:

The Romanesque frescoes in the Museu Nacional d'Art de Catalunya **187–188**

Seeing the diversity of Spanish architecture and culture in Poble Espanyol **192–193**

The Estadi & Museu Olímpic i de l'Esport **194–195**

Appreciating Miró's art at the Fundació Joan Miró **196–198**

A stroll through Montjuïc's gardens **199–200**

The views of the sea from the Castell de Montjuïc **201**

The art exhibitions and events at CaixaForum **202**

GRAN VIA

CARRER DE BADAL

PARC DE CAN SABATÉ

DE LA ZONA FRANCA

PASSEIG DE LA ZONA FRANCA

Auditori Sot del Migdia

FOSSAR DE LA PEDRERA

CEMENTIRI DEL SUD-OEST

RONDA DEL LITORAL

Area of map detail

Moll per a Petrolers

Montjuïc Walk

Montjuïc's pretty gardens and scenic views seem a world away from the bustle of downtown Barcelona. This leisurely stroll takes you from the Castell de Montjuïc on a winding (generally downhill) route toward the Font Màgica, passing by manicured flower-filled gardens. Bring along a picnic.

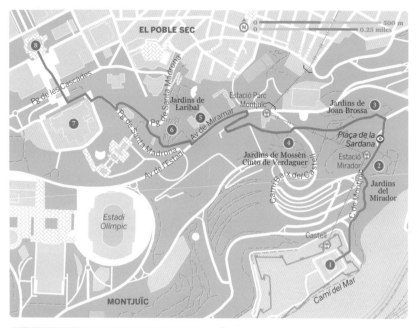

WALK FACTS

- **Start** Castell de Montjuïc
- **Finish** Font Màgica
- **Distance** 2.5km
- **Duration** 90 minutes

① Castell de Montjuïc

Long synonymous with oppression, the dark history of **Castell de Montjuïc** (p162) is today overshadowed by the fine views it commands over the city and sea. The Telefèric is the perfect way to get up and from there on it's all refreshingly downhill through amassing greenery.

② Jardins del Mirador

A short stroll down the road or the parallel Camí del Mar pedestrian trail leads to another fine viewpoint over the city and sea, the **Jardins del Mirador** (p168). Take the weight off your feet on one of the park benches, or pick up a snack and grab some reflection time.

③ Jardins de Joan Brossa

Further downhill is the multitiered **Jardins de Joan Brossa** (p168). The entrance is on the left just beyond Plaça de la Sardana, with the sculpture of people engaged in the classic Catalan folk dance. More fine city views can be had from among the many Mediterranean trees and plants.

Poble Espanyol (p163)

This microcosmic Spanish 'village' was the brainchild of Modernista architect Josep Puig i Cadafalch and is a bit like an all-Castilian Disneyland. Every region of Spain is architecturally represented, from Andalucía to the Basque Country. Village-like streets and plazas, full-scale replicas of famous buildings, craft workshops (pottery, glassmaking, textiles) and half a dozen restaurants (and a popular nightclub) mean you won't run out of things to do.

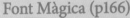

Font Màgica (p166)

If you take the dictionary definition of 'magic' as 'something that seems to cast a spell', Font Màgica is aptly named. A grandiose aquatic feature built for the 1929 International Exhibition, the fountain forms the centrepiece of a series of terraces and waterfalls cascading from the Palau Nacional. For full psychedelic effect, catch a nightly sound and light show.

Gardens of Montjuïc (p168)

Montjuïc is also home to large pockets of greenery. These lush environs harbour everything from fragrant botanical gardens planted with exotic species to manicured parks, dotted with sculptures, gurgling fountains and terraced lawns. The views are superb. To make the most of your time, bring a picnic (the Mercat de la Boqueria makes a fine stop before heading uphill).

Above: Jardins de Mossèn Cinto de Verdaguer

④ Jardins de Mossèn Cinto de Verdaguer

Exiting the Jardins de Joan Brossa at the other (west) side, cross Camí Baix del Castell to the painstakingly laid-out **Jardins de Mossèn Cinto de Verdaguer** (p168). This is a beautiful setting for a slow meander among the tulip beds and water lilies, which act as both relaxing and inspiration.

⑤ Fundació Joan Miró

Joan Miró left a broad collection of his works to the city in his specially designed hillside **foundation** (p167). You can discover his earliest, tentative artistic attempts and continue right through to the characteristic broad canvases for which he is known. Get close-up views of sculptures in the adjacent garden.

⑥ Jardins de Laribal

Dropping away behind the Fundació Joan Miró, the **Jardins de Laribal** are a combination of terraced gardens linked by paths and stairways. The pretty sculpted watercourses along some of the stairways were inspired by Granada's Muslim-era palace of El Alhambra. Stop for a snack and contemplate a Moorish paradise.

⑦ Museu Nacional d'Art de Catalunya

Whichever direction you are coming from, it is worth making the effort to reach this huge ochre beast of a **museum** (p160) to see one of Europe's finest collections of Romanesque art, salvaged from countless churches and chapels sprinkled over northern Catalonia. Further collections range from Gothic to Modernista.

⑧ Font Màgica

Descending from the museum past the Plaça de les Cascades to the **Font Màgica** (p166) is as magic as the name suggests, particularly if you've stretched this walk long enough (easily done) to arrive here after dark – in time for the rather splendid sound and light show.

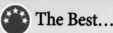

The Best...

PLACES TO EAT

Tickets Molecular gastronomy in all its glory. (p170)

Quimet i Quimet An old-time favourite with superb tapas. (p169)

Bodega 1900 Enticing tapas bar with refreshing vermouths. (p169)

Federal Excellent brunches and a small roof terrace. (p169)

Taverna Can Margarit Great old-fashioned ambience and classic Catalan fare. (p168)

PLACES TO DRINK

La Caseta del Migdia An open-air charmer hidden in the thickets of Montjuïc. (p170)

Tinta Roja A bohemian, cabaret-like atmosphere prevails at this Poble Sec bar. (p171)

La Terrazza Lovely summertime dance spot in Poble Espanyol. (p171)

VIEWS

Castell de Montjuïc The castle offers commanding views. (p162)

Miramar The first-rate cuisine is only slightly upstaged by the view. (p168)

Jardins de Mossèn Cinto de Verdaguer (p168)

Don't Miss
Museu Nacional d'Art de Catalunya

From across the city, the bombastic neobaroque silhouette of the Palau Nacional can be seen rising up from the slopes of Montjuïc. Built for the 1929 World Exhibition and restored in 2005, it houses a vast collection of mostly Catalan art spanning the early Middle Ages to the early 20th century. The high point is the collection of extraordinary Romanesque frescoes, which is considered the most important concentration of early medieval art in the world.

MNAC

Map p164

☎ 93 622 03 76

www.mnac.es

Mirador del Palau Nacional

adult/senior & child under 15yr/student €10/free/7, 1st Sun of month free

🕙 10am-7pm Tue-Sat, 10am-2.30pm Sun & holidays, library 10am-6pm Mon-Fri, to 2.30pm Sat

Ⓜ Espanya

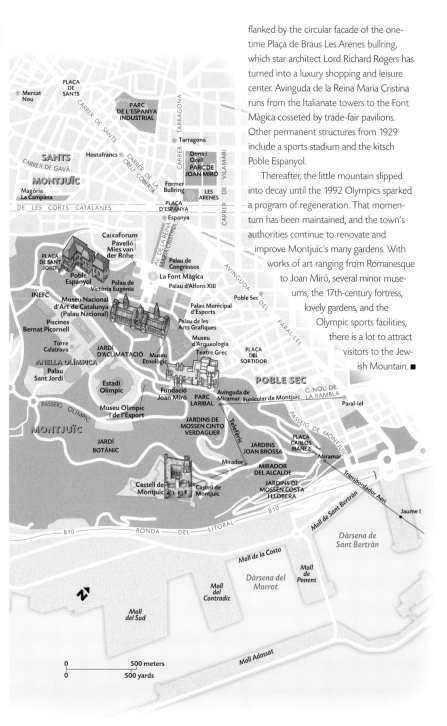

flanked by the circular facade of the one-time Plaça de Braus Les Arenes bullring, which star architect Lord Richard Rogers has turned into a luxury shopping and leisure center. Avinguda de la Reina Maria Cristina runs from the Italianate towers to the Font Màgica cosseted by trade-fair pavilions. Other permanent structures from 1929 include a sports stadium and the kitsch Poble Espanyol.

Thereafter, the little mountain slipped into decay until the 1992 Olympics sparked a program of regeneration. That momentum has been maintained, and the town's authorities continue to renovate and improve Montjuïc's many gardens. With works of art ranging from Romanesque to Joan Miró, several minor museums, the 17th-century fortress, lovely gardens, and the Olympic sports facilities, there is a lot to attract visitors to the Jewish Mountain. ∎

Museu Nacional d'Art de Catalunya (Palau Nacional)

Modernista architect Josep Puig i Cadafalch designed the Palau Nacional for the International Exhibition. By 1929, however, the exhibition had become an instrument of dictator Gen. Miguel Primo de Rivera, and Cadafalch's plan was turned into a mix of neoclassical and neo-baroque, to project an image of Spanish prowess. You'll find here the city's most important art displays.

The bombast of the building belies the beauty and importance of its art collection.

Museu Nacional d'Art de Catalunya (Palau Nacional)

- Map p. 185
- Palau Nacional, Parc de Montjuïc
- 93 622 03 76
- Closed from 3 p.m. Sun. & holidays, & Mon.
- $$$$
- Metro: Línies 1 & 3 (Espanya)

mnac.cat

The Museu Nacional d'Art de Catalunya contains a treasure trove of Romanesque frescoes and artworks transferred from churches around northern Catalonia. In addition it has an important collection of Gothic art, from Catalonia and other regions in Spain. From there the collections broaden out to the Renaissance and baroque. Two private collections, the Cambò bequest and the Thyssen-Bornemisza collection, are interspersed among the rest.

From the 19th century on, the collection again becomes almost exclusively Catalan, spanning the likes of Mariá Fortuny, modernisme, and noucentisme. Along with paintings and sculpture are displays of furniture and other applied art. Photography and coin collections round out the museum's treasures.

Winds of Change

The museum has a revolutionary master plan to roll out over the next few years aiming to make the collections more accessible to a wider audience. This will involve extending its pieces into the neighboring buildings, incorporating works from other collections in the city for themed exhibitions, and organizing multidisciplinary activities. This may mean changes to the current layout from time to time.

Romanesque Art

First comes the Romanesque collection, divided into 21 àmbits (rooms), many of them recreating interiors of 29 churches from where these extraordinary works were removed.

Àmbit 5 and Àmbit 7 contain some of the most extraordinary frescoes of all. The first were removed from the beautiful Església de Sant Climent de Taüll, in the Pyrenees, while the second came from the nearby Església de Santa Maria de Taüll.

In the case of the former, the main piece is the exquisite decoration from the central apse, in dominating colors of turquoise, ocher, and dull brick red. On high, as is usual for this kind of apse decoration, sits Christ in Majesty in his almond-shaped

cocoon. He appears seated on the throne, making the sign of peace and holding a piece of scripture (showing the words "Ego Sum Lux Mundi—I am the Light of the World"). In Romanesque iconography Christ is depicted surrounded by the tetramorph, the four Evangelists symbolized according to St. Jerome's explanation: the lion of St. Mark, the bull for St. Luke (in this case both are at Christ's feet), the angel for St. Matthew (to the left), and the eagle for St. John (to the right, the saint holds an eagle). On either side are seraphim with wings covered in eyes representing the all-seeing God.

Although Romanesque art tended to be rigid and seemingly expressionless, Christ's eyes here are enormously engaging. His depiction is deliberately symmetrical, and yet in the folds of his robes there is volume and movement. Below him and the Evangelists, separated by an elaborate dividing line, are various saints and Apostles, as well as Mary, Mother of God.

Mary is the principal figure in the apse of Santa Maria de Taüll. Mary is in typical pose with the

Fantastic Fountain

On certain evenings, the spectrally lit structure of Palau Nacional seems from its haughty position to be inspecting the broad sweep of Avinguda de la Reina Maria Cristina. A fan of searchlights pierces the night sky from behind the building. An expectant crowd gathers and, suddenly, a strange and colorful spectacle takes place on the terraces below.

La Font Màgica is a fantasia of light and water. In 15-minute bursts for a couple of hours *(7 p.m.–8:30 p.m. Fri.–Sat. Oct.–Apr., 9 p.m.–11 p.m. Thurs.–Sun. May–Sept.),* this "magic fountain" performs a sound-and-light show that can be truly moving. In time with the music, the water changes hue as jets rise and fall, plunge into one another, and ebb away. On the last night of the September Festes de la Mercè fireworks are thrown in too.

EXPERIENCE: Discover Barcelona at Your Feet

Barcelonan fitness jocks are joined by thousands of runners from around the world every March for the **Marató de Barcelona** (*zurichmaratobarcelona.com*). In all, some 16,000 people run the 26.2-mile (42 km) circuit, which starts and ends at Plaça d'Espanya at the foot of the Palau Nacional in Montjuïc.

This is a unique way of discovering the city's sights, as the circuit takes in many of Barcelona's key attractions. From Plaça d'Espanya you head for Camp Nou stadium and Pedralbes before turning back down to Gran Via de les Corts Catalanes. Then head for the city center, up Passeig de Gràcia past La Pedrera, by La Sagrada Família, and by a circuitous route that takes in Jean Nouvel's cucumber-shaped Torre Agbar, the Parc del Fòrum area, the waterfront, Parc de la Ciutadella, Plaça de Catalunya, the Barri Gòtic, and past Columbus on his column. Finally you head up Avinguda del Paral·lel to Plaça d'Espanya and the finish line. The Marató unites Barcelonans, Spaniards, and foreigners in a festive atmosphere.

Christ Child on her lap. Outside the encircling almond stand the Three Wise Men. On the south wall are various episodes from the New Testament.

In **Àmbit 8** is a rare 12th-century wooden crucifix that has retained much of its paint. An altar front in **Àmbit 10** shows the rather nasty martyrdom of four saints, whose equanimity in the face of awful deaths is exemplary (and an inspiration to the faithful). The paintings from the atrium of the Església de Sant Vicenç in Cardona occupy **Àmbit 14,** and in the last room, **Àmbit 21,** is the re-created chapter house of the Santa Maria de Sixena monastery in Aragón. The surviving frescoes (not destroyed when the monastery was torched in 1936) recount New and Old Testament episodes, and the genealogy of Christ.

Gothic Art

The Gothic collection is more wide-ranging. The first room, **Àmbit 22,** is devoted to nonreligious works, some depicting Jaume I's conquest of Mallorca.

Following are rooms with early Gothic works from Navarra, Aragón, Castile, and Catalonia, including remarkable alabaster statuary. In subsequent rooms the development of Gothic painting is traced. Italian painters had a huge influence on local production, the focus of which shifted to Valencia. By the start of the 15th century, artists from Italy, France, and the Low Countries were flocking here (**Àmbit 29).** They brought International Gothic, a pan-western European style that quickly caught on among locals, who spread the word throughout Catalonia (**Àmbit 30).** Works by the two most outstanding Catalan International Gothic masters, Bernat Martorell and Jaume Huguet, can be seen in **Àmbits 32** and **34**. The latter's "Consagració de Sant Agustí," part of a hagiographic series dedicated to St. Augustine, is extraordinary for its detail and expressiveness.

The Renaissance

The collection morphs from

the Gothic into the Renaissance. Two striking works are Valencian Pedro Berruguete's (1450–1504) doors for the grand retablo sequence in **Àmbit 44.** The scenes appear more akin to sketches Goya might have penned centuries later.

In the next hall is the **Cambò bequest,** a private, eclectic collection that mixes up Italian Renaissance, Spanish old master, and rococo. A smattering of works by such greats as Veronese (1528–1588), Titian (1490–1557), Rubens (1577–1640), and even Gainsborough (1727–1788) are among the treasures. In **Àmbit 48** you can enjoy an equally eclectic display, with the works of the **Thyssen-Bornemisza collection** that used to be in the Monestir de Santa Maria de Pedralbes. Before inspecting these, don't miss the El Grecos and Tintoretto hanging in **Àmbit 47.**

You will then pass into the great central hall, the **Sala Oval,** with bright ceiling frescoes and a café. Concerts, and even swing dance sessions, and yoga marathons, are held here occasionally. Head upstairs where you'll find yourself beneath the central dome; check out the views from the restaurant before continuing on your way. The next 12 rooms are a mishmash, with works ranging from Spain's golden century, including some by Francisco de Zurbarán (1598–1664), Claudio Coello (1642–1693), and José de Ribera (1591–1652) among the stars.

From **Àmbit 61** on, the collection fully returns to Catalonia. From here until the end of the main displays, works are concentrated on local painters, sculptors, and other artists from the early 19th to the mid-20th centuries.

After a little Romanticisme, we pass on to Catalan realisme (whose greatest exponent was Marià Fortuny) and then on

Demolished before the 1929 Exhibition, Puig i Cadafalch Quatre Columnes stand proudly among today's trade-fair buildings, re-erected as a statement of Catalan nationalism in 2010.

through anecdotisme, modernisme, and noucentisme (see pp. 36–53). Charging out at you from their central frame are the cavalry and foot soldiers depicted in Marià Fortuny's grand tableau, "Batalla de Tetuán" (1863), celebrating a battle fought out between the Spanish army and Moroccan forces.

In **Àmbit 65** Joaquim Vayreda (1843–1894) dominates with landscapes from around the region. More significant are the modernistas, of whom you'll find around a dozen paintings each by Ramon Casas **(Àmbit 71)** and Santiago Rusiñol **(Àmbit 72).** Among Casas' most captivating works are grand canvases reflecting the civil disorders in Barcelona toward the end

INSIDER TIP:

Watch an amazing light and music show at the Magical Fountain in front of the Montjuïc Palace on weekend evenings.

—ANNIE GRIFFITHS BELT
National Geographic photographer

of the 19th and early in the 20th centuries. "El Garrote Vil" and "La Càrrega," depicting an execution and police charge respectively, are insightful views into turbulent times. More lighthearted is the painting of the artist himself and his friend and fellow artist Pere Romeu on a tandem, originally painted for Els Quatre Gats Café, where these artists met in the Gothic quarter (see pp. 122–123). Among Rusiñol's better works is "Lecció de Piano."

Modernisme takes on a more tangible feel in the next room, which contains some fanciful furnishings from the modernista Casa Lleó i Morera (see p. 143). More furniture and applied arts in the same vein, including a private chapel, are worth close inspection in **Àmbit 75.** Timber chairs designed by Gaudí for Casa Battlló (see pp. 142–143) and Colònia Güell (see p. 238) are on show in **Àmbit 77.**

Isidre Nonell (see p. 50), whom some like to attribute to a symbolical branch of modernisme but is more typically lumped in with its successor, noucentisme, dominates **Àmbit 82.** The leading light of noucentisme, Joaquim Sunyer, follows in the next rooms, along with the much more abstruse Uruguayan, Joaquim Torres-García (1874–1949).

Of the final rooms, the most interesting is dedicated to the bronzes of Pau Gargallo (1881–1934), a sculptor who spent most of his life between Barcelona and Paris. His artistic contacts included the modernistas and Picasso.

For a change of pace, a photographic and coin collection round off a visit to this museum. The former is a mesmerizing stroll down photographic Memory Lane. The emphasis is on Catalan photographers, with one section ranging from the early days to the civil war period, and the second taking things to the present day. The numismatic collection ranges from the Greek colonies in Catalonia thousands of years ago to the introduction of the euro. Before leaving, pop up to the roof terrace, recently opened, to enjoy a privileged panoramic view. ■

Pavelló Mies van der Rohe

In 1929 the German government asked Ludwig Mies van der Rohe (1886–1969) to design the German Pavilion at that year's International Exhibition in Barcelona. He was at the forefront of the so-called modern movement, which gave rise to the influential International style.

Admirers of Mies van der Rohe's work re-created his German Pavilion in the 1980s.

The style sought to reflect a new age by creating "honest," functional buildings bereft of decoration and extraneous additions. Buildings that would exalt space and exploit materials such as concrete, glass, and steel. For Mies van der Rohe, who had worked alongside Walter Gropius and Le Corbusier, Barcelona was too good to pass up.

His design comprised an airy sequence of spaces on a travertine platform, defined by a series of planes: walls of marble, onyx, and frosted glass. It was partially covered by a thin roof, mirrored on the ground by a shallow pool.

The whole lot was destroyed after the exhibition, but was rebuilt, to the right of the Font Màgica in front of the Palau Nacional, in the 1980s by a society of Mies van der Rohe admirers. It bears its creator's name and represents a curious architectural anecdote at once out of place and out of time.

Mies van der Rohe left Germany after the rise of the Nazis and went to the United States, where in the next 30 years he deployed his talents in such masterpieces as the Seagram Building (designed with Phillip Johnson) in New York City. That austere skyscraper, clad in glass, marble, and bronze, is a perfect demonstration of its builder's adage: "Less is more." He might have said the same about his pavilion. ∎

Pavelló Mies van der Rohe

- 🄰 Map p. 185
- ✉ Avinguda Francesc Ferrer; Guàrdia 7
- 🕐 Guided visit in English 10 a.m. Sat.
- ☎ 93 423 40 16
- 💲 $$
- 🚇 Metro: Línies 1 & 3 (Espanya)

miesbcn.com

Poble Espanyol

This "Spanish Village," erected in just 13 months for the 1929 International Exhibition as a display of the country's architectural and cultural diversity, was destined to be torn down after the fair was over. Luckily that decision was rescinded, and today it makes an attractive entertainment venue for adults and kids alike, the fourth most visited site in Barcelona.

A team of two architects, one engineer, and an artist presented an ambitious project for Poble Espanyol in 1927. Not only would many types of architecture from across Spain's regions

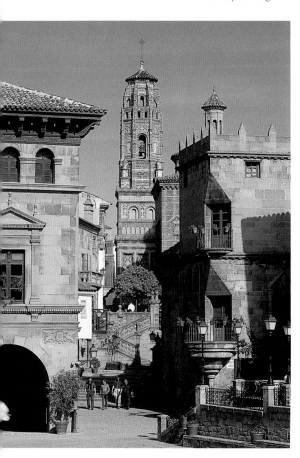

The re-creation of the magnificent Utebo bell tower can be seen from the Plaza Mayor.

be reproduced, the village would have its own central square, town hall, church, stores, bars, and eateries, joined much later by a couple of Barcelona's most popular discos, a club, and a flamenco *tablao,* so it is buzzing by day and night.

The main entrance takes you through the stout **Puerta de San Vicente,** a gate in the medieval walls of the Castilian town of Ávila. The original is one of the most complete sets of medieval walls in Europe. Poble Espanyol, too, is in part walled in.

Inside Puerta de San Vicente you arrive in **Plaza Castellana.** The western region of Extremadura inspired the buildings to the right around Calle de la Conquista, all mansions from cities like Cáceres and Plasencia. The exterior of the **Palacio del Maestrazgo** at No. 5 is emblazoned with its owners' coat of arms.

Next pass under the arches of **Ayuntamiento of Sangüesa** (No. 26), a town in the northern region of Navarra, and into spacious **Plaza Mayor.** This is the "Main Square," fronted by the thick-set **Ayuntamiento** (No. 21), an enlargement of the original in the Aragonese town of Vall-de-Roures, and duly lined with terrace cafés. Surrounding the square are buildings from Castilla y León, Madrid, Asturias, Cantabria, and

Aragón. In every "region" you will find representative craft shops and gastronomic goodies.

Along Calle del Alcalde de Zalamea and up the graceful Grados de Santiago (Steps of St. James, taken from Santiago de Compostela), you pass a series of houses from the northwestern region of Galicia, but more striking is the Aragonese composite before you. The baroque facade of **Iglesia de las Carmelitas** (No. 57), from Alcañiz, is imposing. But soaring behind it is the magnificent **Utebo bell tower** (No. 59). Raised in 1544, it is an exquisite mix of late Gothic and Mudéjar.

The Mudéjars were Muslims left behind in Christian territory as the Reconquista (Reconquest) rolled the Muslims out of Spain. They employed Arab techniques on their new masters' buildings, which are characterized by the use of slender brick, colored tiles, and geometrical decoration.

Behind the bell tower you arrive in Andalucía, identifiable by the whitewashed walls, arches, creeping vines, and Tío Pepe sherry ads of **Arcos de la Frontera** (No. 61). Here you can dine and witness an authentic flamenco evening at El Tablao de Carmen.

Beyond Plaza de la Hermandad, which lies in the middle of the Andalusian buildings, runs Calle de Levante, lined by specimens from the eastern regions of Spain: Valencia, Murcia, and the Balearic Islands. The bright Renaissance **Casa de Son Berga** (No. 69) represents the latter. More imposing is the Plateresque frontage of **Casa de los Celdrán** (No. 70), from Murcia.

Calle de Levante leads down to shady Plaça de la Font, where the buildings represent the Catalan provinces. To the right, rose-colored **Puerta de Prades** leads outside the walls toward a Romanesque monastery, **Monestir de Sant Miquel** (No. 116).

1929 Expo
The Universal Exhibition had already come to Barcelona in 1888; it was met with apathy. So in 1929, the city pulled out all the stops, as evidenced by Poble Espanyol. It was partly an exercise in propaganda for new dictator Primo De Rivera. He saw the Barcelona fair, and the concurrent Ibero-American Exposition (in Seville), as opportunities to show off his government. At the opening ceremony, 300,000 people marveled at the glory of modern Spain.

Back inside the walls, **Carrer dels Mercaders,** leading past a series of Catalan houses, feeds into Calle del Príncipe de Vergara, surrounded by fine houses from Navarra and the Basque Country. One element they share is the generous use of timber in balconies and awnings. **Calle de los Caballeros,** lined by Castilian mansions, is the last stretch that brings you back to where you started. While here, pop by the **Fundació Fran Daurel** (www.fundaciofrandaurel.com), a wide-ranging modern art exhibition covering anything from prints to tapestries, from Miró to Miquel Barceló. ■

Poble Espanyol
- Map p. 185
- Avinguda Francesc Ferrer i Guàrdia
- Closes midnight Tues.–Thurs. & Sun.; 3 a.m. Fri.; 4 a.m. Sat.; 8 p.m. Mon.
- 93 508 63 00
- $$$
- Metro: Línies 1 & 3 (Espanya)

poble-espanyol.com

Anella Olímpica

More than 20 years have passed, and they still talk about the 1992 Olympic Games in Barcelona. More than in many other cities where the games have been held, Barcelona took the event to heart with a determination to make them work for the city. Perhaps much of the urban renewal program would have been carried out anyway, but there seems little doubt that the Olympics were an excuse for Barcelona to get up to speed after the restrictive Franco years.

The focal point of the 1992 games was a stadium rebuilt inside the 1929 International Exhibition exterior.

Much of the activity took place around the central stadium, a 1929 International Exhibition inheritance that was modernized and around which new facilities and innovative structures were raised. The complex became known as the Anella Olímpica, or Olympic Ring.

At the heart of the ring is the **Estadi Olímpic** (Olympic Stadium), with a capacity of 65,000. This was the venue for the opening and closing ceremonies. The original 1929 exterior, an eclectic mix of styles, was retained, but the entire inside was redesigned and reorganized. The original main entrance is topped by two sets of equestrian bronzes.

For the Olympics the entrance was shifted to its present position on Avinguda de l'Estadi. To its left is the slightly bulging pillar atop which burned the Olympic flame. To light it, an archer had to shoot a flaming arrow up into the dish. This was a risky venture, but the authorities were prepared for a miss: The dish was full of inflammable gas, so that the arrow only had to pass within 6.5 feet (2 m) of it to ignite the flame. The archer did indeed miss, but managed to keep within the margin.

For years after the Olympics, the stadium was used only for occasional events. Then in the late 1990s, Espanyol, Barcelona's No. 2 soccer team, moved in while waiting for a new stadium, giving this one a temporary new lease on life. Every second weekend throughout most of the year the team's supporters converged on the hill to urge their team to victory.

Across the road from the Estadi is the **Museu Olímpic i de l'Esport**, an homage to the history of sport. From the ticket desk a ramp gradually winds its way downstairs past a series of displays starting with games of the ancient Greeks and Romans. From there on, you wander past sporting objects, from javelins to a Formula One racing car, with panels and touch screens explaining the history of the Olympic Games and other sports down the centuries.

The basement houses a section devoted to the 1992 Barcelona Olympics, where the games' mascot, Cobi, makes an appearance on all manner of gewgaws. Former head of the International Olympic Committee, Barcelona's Juan Antonio Samaranch, also donated his massive collection of Olympic mementoes and gifts, including a stamp collection.

Just west of the stadium sits what could be mistaken for a large UFO atop its landing pad. Actually, it's the shell-like roof of **Palau**

Sant Jordi, considered by the critics the most successful of the new Olympic buildings. Japanese architect Arata Isozaki designed it as a general indoor-sports, concert, and exhibition hall with a seating capacity of 17,000, a recent venue for the likes of Bruce Springsteen.

To the north of Palau Sant Jordi are the fine Olympic swimming facilities of the **Piscines Bernat Picornell,** open to the public. Between the pool and Palau Sant Jordi rises the brilliant white science-fiction telecommunications tower of the Spanish phone company, Telefónica. This structure has become a Montjuïc landmark to natives and visitors alike, and is now simply known as Torre Calatrava, after its Zurich-based Spanish designer, Santiago Calatrava.

INSIDER TIP:

Walk southwest from Estadi Olímpic to the Cementiri del Sudoest to visit family tombs stacked several stories high along tree-lined lanes.

—CAROLINE HICKEY
*National Geographic
Travel Books editor*

Beyond the circular arena west of the Olympic pool is the last of the main Olympic buildings. Created by leading Barcelona architect Ricard Bofill, the bright neoclassical structure houses the **Institut Nacional d'Educació Física de Catalunya** (INEFC), a sports university. ∎

Anella Olímpica
⬛ Map p. 185

Museu Olímpic i de l'Esport
⬛ Map p. 185
✉ Avinguda de l'Estadi, 60
☎ 93 292 53 79
$ Depends on tour & group size
🕐 Closed Sun. from 2:30 p.m. & Mon.; museum & museum/ stadium tours offered.

Fundació Joan Miró

It was fitting that the 20th century's most important Barcelona-born artist should present it with an inestimable gift—a gallery and archive dedicated primarily to his art. Designed by his longtime friend, architect Josep Lluís Sert (1902–1983), the building opened in 1975.

Sculptures dot the outdoor spaces of the Fundació Joan Miró.

The foundation's collection is made up of hundreds of Miró's paintings, sculptures, and other works, including thousands of sketches and drafts donated by the artist himself. Only a comparatively small part of this immense trove is ever on display, complemented by frequent temporary exhibitions of contemporary artists and new talent, notably in the Espai 13.

Sert, who had first worked with Miró in 1937 on the Republican Spanish pavilion at the Paris Universal Exhibition, placed an emphasis on light and space. The building's design around an internal courtyard and the bright whiteness of its interior and reinforced concrete exterior are two clear references to the artist's Mediterranean roots. The organization of exhibition areas, open spaces, and stairways ensures you need never go over territory already covered. Part of the top floor is an open-air walkway with Miró sculptures that nicely breaks the pace of the collection inside.

Fluidity of movement is a theme in the building, as indeed it is with the collection. While the permanent collection retains a simple chronological structure, beginning with Miró's early work on the first floor, the size of the collections is such that works on display are frequently rotated.

Through the Gallery

Visitors head first to various temporary exhibitions displayed in rooms to the right of the ticket desk before moving around to the beginning of the permanent collection.

In the first room of the latter hangs an enormous tapestry done in 1979 for the foundation, along with several of Miró's other later works. You then pass through a narrow gallery graced by Alexander

bronzes are also scattered about. His 1969 "Dona" ("Woman") is represented as an egg on a crate. A papier-mâché mock-up for statues of a couple of lovers (1975) in Paris's La Défense district marks the end of this room.

From here you turn left into the first room of the core collection. Dedicated to the art collector and Miró's friend, Joan Prat, the room (Sala Joan Prat) contains a cross-section of works from the artist's early years and into the 1920s.

"El Pedicur" ("The Pedicure," 1901) is one of the oldest surviving efforts by the artist. Although Miró doesn't display the same precocious genius of Picasso at this early age (he was eight when he drew this), the brightly colored drawing is nonetheless interesting for the caricatural traits it displays.

Fundació Joan Mir

- Map p. 185
- Plaça de Neptu
- 93 443 94 70
- Closed from 2:30 p.m. Sun. & holidays, & Mon. Open until 9 p.m. Thurs.
- $$$
- Metro: Línies 1 & 3 (Espanya) & Bus (No. 150 or No. 55); or Línia 3 (Paral-lel) & Funicular railway

fundaciomiro-bcn.org

The Public Face of Joan Miró

The diminutive, taciturn, and introverted Joan Miró got off to a slow and uncertain start in Barcelona. Born in 1893 on Passatge del Crèdit, just off Plaça de Sant Jaume in the heart of the old city, he was not allowed to attend art school and only began to go to classes at La Llotja while he was completing studies in commerce. But business was not for Miró: He fell ill while apprenticed to a store and afterward decided to dedicate all of his time to art.

Although Miró spent most of his adult life elsewhere, he never forgot his hometown. Several of his works are here, including the "Dona i Ocell" ("Woman and Bird," 1982) sculpture in the urban Parc Joan Miró near Plaça d'Espanya and a bronze statue, "Dona" ("Woman," 1983), on the first floor of the Ajuntament. There is a ceramic mural at Barcelona's airport (1970) and another Miró design in the pedestrian part of La Rambla by Mercat de la Boqueria (see p. 90).

Calder's "Font de Mercuri" ("Mercury Fountain"), created by the U.S. sculptor for the Paris exhibition in 1937, into a vast open space rising two floors. Here hang a couple of big canvases typical of Miró's later style—all primary colors and symbolic shapes. Some intriguing

There follow several sketches from the early 1900s of buildings and animals. The 1908 "Serp" ("Snake") is a striking exercise in design. By about 1915 Miró had developed a strong taste for experimentation, with his distorted female nudes and landscapes influenced by the fau-vists. One of the most memorable paintings of this period is "Retrat d'una Vaileta" ("Portrait of a Young Girl," 1919), an unsettling portrait of a young blond girl with feline blue eyes.

The beginnings of surrealism in mid-1920s Paris coincided with vast changes in Miró's objectives. He stepped radically away from depiction to a kind of reductionist poetry on paper. Boiled down to the barest bones, the paintings no longer suggest concrete images but invite onlookers to dream. You see this in "Ampolla de Vi" ("Bottle of Wine," 1924), in which the bottle floats in a barely noticeable dreamscape with an insect and serpent. Works of the

INSIDER TIP:

Book tickets online and check for forth-coming exhibits at fundaciomiro-bcn.org.

—ELIZABETH NEWHOUSE
National Geographic contributor

late 1920s develop the method. "L'Acomodador del Music Hall" ("Music Hall Usher," 1925) and "Arbre en el Vent" ("Tree in the Wind," 1929) convey simple but powerful imagery.

By the 1930s, the woman had become central to Miró's themes. In his bright "Flama en l'Espai i Dona Nua" ("Flame in Space and Nude Woman," 1932), the painter moves closer to his mature style, although the human figure of the woman remains instantly recogniz-able as such.

Miró's progress through the 1930s and '40s continues in the rooms above the Sala Joan Prat. Prior to World War II, Miró did etchings to illustrate the books of poets like Paul Eluard. Some of these are on display, as well as some of his paintings from the period. The latter include the bizarre figures of the less-than-poetically titled "Home i Dona davant un Munt d'Excrements" ("Man & Woman Before a Pile of Excrement," 1935).

The end of World War II signified for Miró a new begin-ning for the world, and his art became characterized by a search for light and harmony featuring women, birds, stars, the sun, and the moon. You pass from these rooms along a corridor toward an L-shaped hall dominated by paint-ings and sculpture from the 1960s and '70s.

Among these works are canvases on a grand scale. In the 1960s, while the underlying themes remained constant, Miró's expressive tools evolved. White and black became fundamental, otherwise dominated by primary colors, and, less frequently, greens. "Personatge davant el Sol" ("Person in front of the Sun," 1968) is a perfect example.

The exhibition closes with a series of photos of Miró and a series of works done from 1944 to 1973, on long-term loan from Gallery K in Switzerland. In the basement are two rooms with works that other artists have given in homage to Miró; they include Henry Moore, Marcel Duchamp, Max Ernst, and Eduardo Chillida. ∎

Gardens

When the idea for an International Exhibition on Montjuïc was first aired, plans were already afoot to reinvigorate the mountain. New gardens were laid out, and more extensive gardens have been created recently. For locals, the gardens are a refuge. Driving schools take advantage of the near-empty roads, and joggers, strollers, and lovers seek solace on garden paths.

Once downtrodden, Montjuïc's luscious gardens have been lovingly regenerated since the Olympics.

South across the Passeig Olímpic road from the Estadi Olímpic is the **Jardí Botànic** (Botanical Garden), landscaped into the hill by leading architect Carles Ferrater in the 1990s, containing plants that thrive in areas around the world with a climate similar to that of the Mediterranean.

Occupying a privileged position on one of the highest slopes on Montjuïc, the Jardí affords fine views back across the Olympic installations and beyond. The plants and trees on show come from the Eastern Mediterranean, Spain (including the Balearic and Canary Islands), North Africa, Australia, California, Chile, and South Africa. What the display demonstrates is the enormous diversity of plant life in these areas despite the similarity of climate. All the specimens are clearly labeled, and your ticket allows you to come back for a second visit free.

The former botanical garden, the curious **Jardí Botànic**

Jardí Botànic

- Map p. 185
- Carrer Dr. Font i Quer 2
- 93 426 49 35
- $
- Metro: Línies 1 & 3 (Espanya) & Bus (No. 13, 55, 150)

www.jardibotanic .bcn.es

Històric, has just reopened. Located in a quarry that provided the stone to build the Eixample, the garden has some immensely tall trees not found anywhere else in the city. This is due to its unique micro-climate. Its entrance is behind the Palau Nacional.

The **Jardins de Mossen Costa i Llobera,** stretch out on the south face of Montjuïc, over-

with its added attraction of innovative games for children.

Within the Anella Olímpica is another simple little garden, the **Jardí d'Aclimatació** (Acclimatization Garden). It grew out of a desire to import a broad range of foreign trees to the city, to be cultivated and observed in a controlled environment. The mixed bag of trees and shrubs comes

Mobile on Montjuïc

Getting to and around Montjuïc can take some time. Decide on where you want to start, as this will influence how you get into the area in the first place.

The nearest metro stops are Espanya, Paral-lel (which links directly with the funicular), and Poble Sec. With map in hand you can walk from these and follow

paths up the hill. A city tourist bus, the Bus Turístic, also gets around the main sights (see Travelwise p. 243). Buses No. 13 and 150 run all over the hill from Plaça Espanya.

The funicular goes up to the Parc de Montjuïc station and links with the cable car to take you as high as the Castell de Montjuïc.

looking the busy port and southbound highway. The main feature of the gardens, dedicated to exotic and desert plants, is the cactus, of which hundreds of fascinating species are represented.

Higher up, a more conventional garden space adorns **Mirador del Alcalde** (Mayor's Lookout), a pleasant spot with views over the city and port. It lies south off Carretera de Montjuïc, the road that leads to the Castell (see p. 201). Uphill are the picturesque **Jardins de Mossen Cinto Verdaguer.** Here the specialty is bulbs, and the place is densely packed with hyacinths, tulips, and narcissuses, plus various other species. The gardens lie on Camí Baix del Castell, a short walk east of the Fundació Joan Miró (see pp. 196–198). Farther south are the pleasant **Jardins Joan Brossa,**

from as far off as China, Australia, and South Africa.

Cascading down the northeastern side of Montjuïc below the Fundació Joan Miró is shady **Parc Laribal.** With its staircases, pergolas, statues, and fountains, it is a pleasant way to walk up into the heart of Montjuïc.

Dominating the southwest face of the mountain is **Cementiri del Sud-Oest,** also known as Cementiri Nou (New Cemetery). Opened in 1883, it is the resting place of several important Catalan figures and laden with ornate tombs. To the northwest is **Fossar de la Pedrera,** once a mass grave and now an extension of the cemetery. Lluís Companys, the Generalitat president executed by nationalists in 1940, is buried here. There is also a monument to the fallen in the 1936–1939 civil war. ■

Castell de Montjuïc

Built in the 17th century, ransacked by Bourbon troops in the 18th century, responsible for bombarding the city in the 19th and the scene of executions in the 20th, this mountain-top castle has a turbulent history. Understandably it is mostly remembered as a symbol of repression by the Catalans. However now in the 21st century it is opening up as a place for the people.

In its most recent incarnation the castle housed a sinister military museum, but during the civil war and the consequent dictatorship under Franco many prisoners were tortured and executed within its walls, most notably Lluís Companys, president of the Generalitat (1933–1940), shot here in 1940. A new era began when an equestrian statue of Franco was removed from the courtyard in 2001, followed by closure of the museum in 2009. In a symbolic gesture, the castle was handed back to Catalonia.

Castell de Montjuïc is now gradually being re-appropriated as an enjoyable space for leisure with a range of activities and exhibitions on the theme of historic memory, in order to remember and understand the tragedies of the recent past. For the moment it has a permanent exhibition entitled Montjuïc Castle. This is an exceptional viewpoint on the castle's history that incorporates an audiovisual presentation. Another exhibition explains the mountain's history, which dates back to pre-Roman times.

Most people enjoy coming up here for the spectacular views of city and sea from its nearly 600-foot (170 m) summit, where the air is wonderfully refreshing, especially after several days in the dense city below. The castle's deep moat, now landscaped with plants, and mighty buttresses and watch towers are also an imposing sight. The castle is at its best on summer evenings when it turns into an open-air cinema and people flock up with their picnics for a cool night under the stars, often with live music. It is also the starting point of the Camí del Mar, a path winding south around the hillside to the Mirador del Migdia, perfect for watching the sun go down. ∎

Castell de Montjuïc

- 🅐 Map p. 185
- ✉ Carretera de Montjuïc 66
- ☎ 93 256 44 40
- 🕐 Closed from 6 p.m. Oct.–March, 8 p.m. Apr.–Sept.
- 💲 $$
- 🚇 Metro: Línia 3 (Paral-lel) then Funicular railway & Montjuïc Teleféric or Línia 1 & 3 (Espanya) & Bus 150

The thick walls of Montjuïc Castle were built with invaders in mind.

More Places to Visit in Montjuïc

CaixaForum

Strangely, this striking brick structure, the Fàbrica Casaramona, started life as a factory. Beautifully restored with contributions from Arata Isozaki, this attractive building was designed by leading exponent of modernisme Puig i Cadafalch. It is owned by Spain's prime savings bank, la Caixa, which has an active welfare, cultural, and scientific program (see p. 182). Reincarnated as CaixaForum, it has become a focal point of the city's cultural scene, with revolving exhibitions coming from la Caixa's own art collections and touring shows. In 2014 these ranged from the work of Le Corbusier to an in-depth look at Mediterranean culture. Additional activities like concerts, talks, and films tie in with the exhibitions, and CaixaForum runs a busy program for kids. *fundacio .lacaixa.es* 🅰 Map p. 185 ✉ Avinguda Francesc Ferrer i Guàrdia 6–8 ☎ 93 476 86 00 💲 $ 🅼 Metro: Línies 1 & 3 (Espanya)

Museu d'Arqueologia de Catalunya

Set low down on Montjuïc, the city's archaeology museum is a mildly interesting detour for those with a special thirst for things ancient. The building itself is another remnant of the 1929 International Exhibition. The collection concentrates largely on finds unearthed in Catalonia and attempts to trace the remote past of the region. The first rooms cover prehistory with the predictable assortment of Stone Age fragments, ancient skulls, and the like. More interesting is the area (Rooms X to XIII) dedicated to finds from the Balearic Islands, among the most important of which is the jewel-studded bust of the Dama de Ibiza (Lady of Ibiza). *mac.cat* 🅰 Map p. 185 ✉ Passeig de Santa Madrona 39–41 ☎ 93 424 65 77 🕒 Closed from 2:30 p.m. Sun., & Mon. 💲 $, or with Arqueoticket (see sidebar p. 46) 🅼 Metro: Línies 1 (Espanya) & 3 (Espanya or Poble Sec)

Museu Etnològic de Barcelona (MEB)

A short walk down from the Museu Nacional d'Art de Catalunya is the Ethnological Museum. After a long period of being closed for renovation and restructuring, the MEB, the first purpose-built museum of the city, is to be born again in 2015. Its non-European collection will be housed in the Museu de Cultures del Món (see p. 129), leaving space here for in-depth exploration of Catalan culture and customs, using pieces from the museum's collection to make comparisons with other cultures that have left their mark in the region. Objects from daily life in town and country, from shepherds and blacksmiths to the wild creations used in popular festivals will be on display as well as a stimulating program of temporary exhibitions. *www.museuetnologic.bcn.cat* 🅰 Map p. 185 ✉ Passeig de Santa Madrona 16–22 ☎ 93 256 34 84 🕒 Closed Mon. 💲 $$ 🅼 Metro: Línia 3 (Espanya or Poble Sec)

Parc de Joan Miró

The park behind former bullring turned flamboyant shopping mall, Las Arenas, is still known to locals as Parc de l'Escorxador (Abattoir Park). When the bullring was in business, the animal carcasses ended up in the small abattoir here, their meat highly prized. The slaughterhouse is long gone, and in its place one of the first "urban parks" was created in 1983, in line with the newly democratic council's policy to use obsolete spaces for public use.

In the northwest corner rises the bright, spangly "Dona i Ocell" ("Woman and Bird"), one of Miró's most famous sculptures. To some, it's just plain phallic. Whatever way you see it, the original plan was for a forest of these sculptures to go up, but the artist's death put a stop to such extravagances. 🅰 Map p. 185 ✉ Carrer de Tarragona 🅼 Metro: Línies 1 & 3 (Espanya)

A former Roman city, grand monasteries, the fascinating work of Dalí, a bizarre mountain range, wine country, and a splendid stretch of coast, all within easy reach of the city

Excursions

Introduction & Map   204–205

Montserrat   206–209

Wine & Monasteries Drive   210–215

Sitges   216–218

Experience: Heat Up the End of Winter   218

Tarragona   219–223

Experience: Feasting at a *Calçotada*   222

Girona   224–227

Feature: Delirium Dalí   228–229

Figueres   230–233

Experience: Take a Hike!   232

Drive Along the Costa Brava   234–237

More Excursions From Barcelona   238

Vacationers flock to the Costa Brava.

Excursions

Barcelona is in some ways the least Catalan part of Catalonia, which, although it created a sea empire and enjoyed a degree of independence, never knew nationhood. Yet Catalans are highly conscious of their distinct identity, symbolized in the fantastical shapes and monastery of Montserrat, a mountain range outside Barcelona.

For almost a thousand years, a monastery has stood cradled below the strange, bare peaks of the "serrated mountain." In the days of the Renaixença around the turn of the 19th century, ardent nationalists would set out from Barcelona to hike amid the fantasyscape above the monastery. They were as much intent on gaining a deeper acquaintance with their region as getting a good few days' exercise. The proximity of these distinctive mountains to the capital and the long medieval tradition of pilgrimage to Montserrat have made the range one of Catalonia's national symbols.

Long before anyone had thought of raising a monastery there, Barcelona was a mere secondary town in the Roman territory of

Hispania Citerior, whose main capital was Tarraco (now Tarragona). Even today you can see parts of what was once the grand circus (where chariot races were staged), an amphitheater, the forum, and other key Roman buildings. Although eclipsed by Barcelona in the Middle Ages, Tarragona remained an important center, as its mighty Gothic cathedral indicates.

Stretching across an ever-changing landscape between Montserrat and Tarragona lies an array of sights and sensations. Only a short distance out of Barcelona along the AP-2 highway that leads to Madrid is the Penedès wine and *cava* district. Production of cava (Spanish champagne) is largely the preserve of wineries in this area, which also produce many notable whites and some decent reds.

The rocky coastline of the Costa Brava reaches its most southerly point at the town of Blanes.

Today, a small proportion of the grapes is still produced here by the monks of the greatest Cistercian monastery, the Reial Monestir de Santa Maria de Poblet. Its presence, along with two other once-powerful monasteries, is testimony to the extent of the power that once lay in the hands of the principal religious orders in medieval Catalonia. Poblet sits amid charming vineyards and gives access to the verdant territory around Prades. And nearby, as if in afterthought, stand the proud medieval walls of Montblanc. Down on the coast, the once tiny fishing town of Sitges is today one of gay Europe's preferred party stops, although it manages to retain a homey feel. The beaches are charming, the summer nightlife wild.

Northward is Girona, with a medieval center that gives a greater sense of completeness than that of Barcelona's. Its steep narrow streets around the cathedral and old Jewish district offer a joyous excursion back in time. Not a great deal farther up the highway toward France you are confronted with a rather more eccentric attraction—Salvador Dalí's museum theater and mausoleum in Figueres.

East of Girona and Figueres, Catalonia meets the Mediterranean with the fortress walls of the Costa Brava (Rugged Coast). Touring here brings you to enchanting coves and tranquil beaches, but can also lead to a breach in the natural defenses and the site of the ancient Greek and Roman cities at Empúries. ∎

NOT TO BE MISSED:

Hiking the mountain ridge at Montserrat   206–209

Reial Monestir de Santa Maria de Poblet, the greatest of Catalonia's Cistercian monasteries   214–215

Joining in the madness of Carnival in Sitges   218

The Roman remains of Tarragona   219–223

Girona's medieval core   224–227

Salvador Dalí's weird Teatre-Museu in Figueres   230–233

Tossa de Mar, a pretty Costa Brava town   234–236

Diving off the Illes Medes marine park   237

Montserrat

To some, it is the sacred site of Catalonia. To others it is the magic mountain that in the distance looks as the name suggests: a serrated edge of some supernatural saw. From Sant Jeroni, its highest point, you can gaze clear across Catalonia to the Pyrenees in the north. But for many, the principal object of a visit is the ancient Benedictine monastery.

Monastery buildings huddle beneath the sugarloaf formations of the Montserrat—a national symbol for Catalans.

This mountain range, dramatically rising out of the surrounding lowlands, 31 miles (50 km) northwest of Barcelona, seems, because of its abruptness, a great deal higher than it is. Just 6 miles (10 km) long and covering 17 square miles (45 sq km), it is the result of ten million years of geological upheaval and erosion on a conglomerate that once lay beneath the sea. It is frequently much colder here than in Barcelona, and often sea air meets mountain chill to create thick fog.

Archaeological finds in several caves reveal a human presence since neolithic times (about 4000 B.C.). But the real human story begins, at least according to legend, in A.D. 880 when, they say, the Virgin Mary appeared in a cave (known now as Santa Cova, or Holy Cave). The claim caused great excitement, and four small chapels were built in the area before the end of the century.

The Monastery

The Benedictine Monestir de Montserrat was founded in 1025 by Oliba, bishop of Vic and abbot of the grand monastery of Ripoll. During the 12th and 13th centuries a Romanesque church was built, and the black wooden image of the Virgin now on display was carved. Pilgrims began to make the arduous climb to the nascent monastery, located at an altitude of 2,384 feet (725 m). By the beginning of the 15th century, the complex was an independent abbey and its renown was spreading across Europe.

The Gothic cloister, some of it still standing, was begun in 1476, while the present church, a mix of Gothic and Renaissance, was consecrated in 1592. Disaster struck in 1811 and 1812, however, when Napoleon's troops destroyed much of the monastery, and in 1835 expropriation laws reduced the inhabitants of what remained to just one monk. Ten years later the Benedictines were back in force and the long process of reconstruction began. In 1881 the Virgin of Montserrat was declared Catalonia's co-patron along with Sant Jordi. During the civil war,

INSIDER TIP:

Spend a night or two at Cel.les Abat Marcet [tel 93 877 77 01], the former monks' cells converted into family apartments.

—JUSTIN KAVANAGH
*National Geographic
Travel Books editor*

the complex again came close to destruction and 23 monks were killed. Today about 70 monks live and work here.

No matter from which direction you approach the mountain, the unmistakable silhouette begins to work its strange magic from the moment you lay eyes on it. Whether you arrive by road or *cremallera* train, you will end up on a single road skirting the buildings until you reach the first of a couple of interlocking squares. From the second of these, the path bends back and leads into the broad esplanade, Plaça de Santa Maria, that precedes the basilica. To your left, facing the basilica, are buildings used to house and feed pilgrims. To the right an open wall has modern statues of the founders of various monastic institutions. On a clear

day you can see the Mediterranean from here.

Before entering the basilica, go down the steps to visit the **Museu de Montserrat,** an engaging display of art and artifacts *below* the esplanade. There are two main collections of paintings. The first spans the 13th to 18th centuries, mainly with works collected in Italy, including paintings by Tiepolo, Caravaggio, Giordano, Luca, and El Greco. The second collection covers roughly the mid-19th to the mid-20th centuries, with a heavy focus on Catalan artists, notably Dalí and Picasso. Beyond the Catalans there is an emphasis on French Impressionists such as Monet, Degas, Pissarro, and Sisley and more recently a collection of avant-garde and contemporary artists. Also taking pride of place is an exhibition on iconography dedicated to

Divine Voices

Apart from the monks, about 50 boys live in the monastery as members of the centuries-old Escolania, a kind of boarding school. Selection for entry is judged in large part on musical ability. It is said to be Europe's oldest music school (founded around 1223) and is renowned for its quality. You can hear the boys sing *(Mon.– Thurs. 1 p.m. & 6:45 p.m.; Fri. 1 p.m.; Sun 12 p.m. & 6:45 p.m.)* except late June –August and school holidays. Call to confirm as they also go on tour.

Montserrat (Monestir de Montserrat)

- Map p. 204
- 31 miles (50 km) NW of Barcelona
- By car: C-58 to C-16, take Montserrat exit then follow signs. By bus: Autocars Julià *(tel 93 261 5858)* from Sants (Viriat) at 9:15 a.m. daily, returning at 5 p.m. or 6 p.m. June–Sept. By train: FGC train (No. R5) hourly from Plaça d'Espanya station to Monistrol & from there rack and pinion *cremallera* train or cable car up from Montserrat-Aeri to monastery. The trip takes a little more than an hour.

Visitor Information

- Monastery complex
- 93 877 77 12

montserratvisita.com

Cambril de la Mare de Déu

🕐 Closed
10:30 a.m.–noon

Montserrat's Black Virgin, affectionately known to Catalans as La Moreneta (the Little Dark One). A separate display, the Espai Audiovisual, takes you on a journey through the monastery's history and the life of a monk.

Back on Plaça de Santa Maria, to the left you will notice two flanks of the original Gothic **cloister** tucked into the side of the modern basilica. Along with the 14th-century octagonal, flat-roofed **bell tower,** it is one of the oldest remnants of the medieval basilica. A modern five-door arcade leads to the courtyard. Go right, before walking into the courtyard proper, and you will see a well-worn **Romanesque doorway,** all that remains of the earliest buildings here. The marble floor of the **courtyard,** laid out in 1952, was inspired by the Campidoglio in Rome.

Inside, the **basilica** is in dazzling shape since its restoration in the 1990s. It dates from the second half of the 16th century and is a mix of late Gothic and Renaissance. The broad nave is typical of grand Catalan churches, with Gothic vaulting.

For pilgrims, the high point of a visit is to file past the Romanesque black statue of the Mare de Déu (Mother of God). Return to the courtyard and look for the sign to the **Cambril de la Mare de Déu** (Chamber of the Mother of God), a pre-modernista rearrangement of the area in the apse in which the young Antoni Gaudí had a hand.

The Hermitages

The compact mountains are crisscrossed by trails, some of which lead to a handful of the 13 hermitages built by solitary monks in precariously remote locations. They are largely in ruins, but add interest to the range of possible **walks,** many of them easily accessible to anyone of average fitness. The monastery tourist information office has a basic brochure detailing five such walks. Catch the **Funicular de Sant Joan** for the

first 822 feet (250 m) up from the monastery (departures every 20 minutes; the last one down leaves at 7 p.m.). Several walks are possible from here, including one of a little more than an hour to the highest peak, **Sant Jeroni.** Along the way you can enjoy fine views of some of the more bizarrely shaped peaks in the range and then drop down into woods. When you reach the little 19th-century **Capella de Sant Jeroni,** turn sharp left to rejoin the trail. The brief, last stretch to the top is the only steep part. ∎

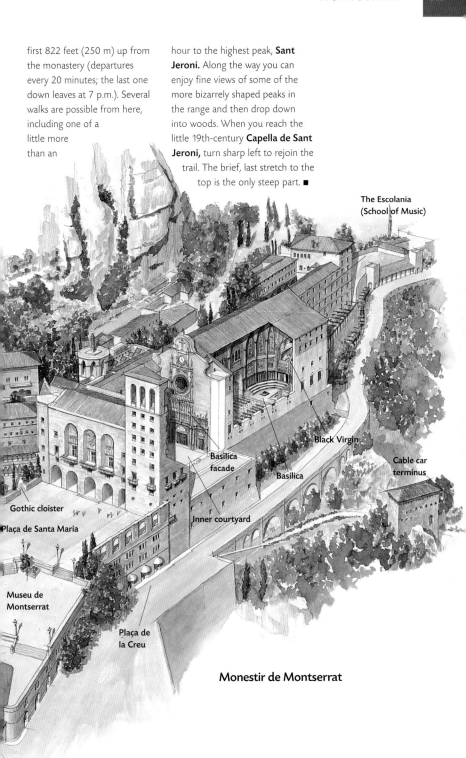

The Escolania
(School of Music)

Black Virgin

Cable car
terminus

Basílica
façade

Basílica

Gothic cloister

Plaça de Santa Maria

Inner courtyard

Museu de
Montserrat

Plaça de
la Creu

Monestir de Montserrat

Wine & Monasteries Drive

Barely an hour out of downtown Barcelona by car (or train), you can be in the heart of Catalonia's best known winemaking area, the Penedès. In addition to *cava*, the local version of champagne, vintners here also produce a fine range of quality non-sparkling whites and the occasional red. After thus treating with Bacchus, you may minister to the soul. A tour of three once-powerful Cistercian monasteries allows you to marvel at fine Gothic construction and enjoy the varied countryside.

The grapes of the lush green vineyards around the Reial Monestir de Santa Maria de Poblet end up in quality Torres wines.

Heading west from Barcelona, follow the signs for the AP-7 tollway toward Tarragona and Lleida. Take exit 27 for **Sant Sadurní d'Anoia,** a town of little grace but one emblematic in the wine business, or take the train from Plaça de Catalunya or Sants. Here you will find the modernista cellars (designed by Puig i Cadafalch) of the Codorníu label and their main competition, Freixenet. They are the two biggest names in cava production in Spain, although in Sant Sadurní alone another 20 or so wineries operate. You can visit **Codorníu** *(tel 93 891 33 42, visitascodorniu.com)* and **Freixenet** *(tel 93 891 70 00,* *freixenet.es*) for tours of their installations and tastings.

Back on the AP-7, the next stop is **Vilafranca del Penedès ❶,** in a sense the area's wine capital, 8 miles (13 km) to the southwest. Wine lovers should go to the tourist office (*Carrer Hermenegild Clascar 2, tel 93 818 12 54, turismevilafranca.com*) for tips on interesting wineries to visit all over the Penedès. In the town itself you could head to Plaça de Jaume I to visit the mostly Gothic **Basilica de Santa Maria** and, opposite, the **Vinseum,** a combined museum on the town and wine (*closed 2 p.m.–4 p.m. Oct.–May, Mon., & from 2 p.m. Sun.*).

The museum is housed in an impressive Gothic building, and a tour usually ends in a free tasting. One tip you may get from the Vilafranca tourist office is to head for the **Caves Romagosa Torné wine cellars** (*tel 93 899 13 53, reserve in advance for tour and tastings*) at Serra de Baix on the BP-2121 road from Vilafranca to Sant Martí Sarroca. Whether or not you drop in here for the wines, continue

A huge wood-and-stone winepress forms the centerpiece of the Museu del Vi in Vilafranca de Penedès.

to **Sant Martí Sarroca ❷.** Seated on a hill just outside the new part of town are two marvelous little Romanesque gems, a church and a castle. Anyone feeling hungry could try one of the small restaurants serving good Catalan cuisine located off the road up the hill.

Three Monasteries

A drive of about 19 miles (30 km) west cross-country takes you to the first of three extraordinary testaments to the power of medieval faith. **Reial Monestir de les Santes Creus ❸,** or Royal Monastery of the

---

NOT TO BE MISSED:

Wine-tasting in the Penedès area
• **Reial Monestir de les Santes Creus** • **Reial Monestir de Santa Maria de Poblet** • **Montblanc**

Bubbling Along Nicely

Way back in 1551, Jaume Codorníu was cultivating vineyards in the Penedès area, according to documents found. The business was a success, and for centuries Jaume's successors have made wine here. In 1872 the winery bottled its first ever batch of *cava*, a frothy, energetic, champagne-style wine.

Other winemakers such as Freixenet realized the Codorníu family was onto

something, and soon everyone in the region was making bubbly. Today, the small area around Sant Sadurní d'Anoia accounts for about 80 percent of national production. The method is the same used in the French Champagne district, but the French producers became indignant at the free and easy use of the term "champagne," so the Catalans chose the word "cava," which simply means "cellar."

Nuns still live in the Reial Monestir de Santa Maria de Vallbona de les Monges, deep in the heart of Catalonia.

great churches of Barcelona and elsewhere (such as Girona) couldn't be sharper.

After passing a huddle of houses, you arrive before a grand baroque portal that in turn leads into a somber, elongated square. Right before you, poised theatrically on a slight rise, is the mixed Romanesque and Gothic facade of the church that occupies the left wing of the complex. The entrance lies to the right of the building, and from the ticket desk you emerge into an exquisite Gothic cloister. The delicacy of the stonework complements the warmth of the sandstone. A peculiar element is the pavilion, with its fountain, jutting from one side into the garden. Off to the right of the cloister is the fine *sala capitular* (chapter house) and, above it, the monks' dormitory. Pass through to the second, older, and more disheveled

Holy Crosses (*closed Mon.*), suffered greatly during the 19th century and then in the civil war but remains a magnificent place. Founded in the 12th century by Cistercian monks from France, the structures show all the influence of that order's building style—transitional between Romanesque and Gothic, austere and imposing. Their churches—and the one here is no exception—boasted a tall central nave and aisles, and it is often claimed the Cistercians were responsible for the spread of the pointed Gothic arch across Europe. The White Monks, as they were also called, eschewed external decoration but otherwise the style of this and other monasteries of the order in Catalonia reflects French taste. The contrast with the broader, plain Catalan Gothic you see in the

🅰 See also area map p. 204
➤ Barcelona
🔁 102 miles (163 km)
🕒 Full day
➤ Montblanc

cloister, off which you can view the royal apartments, where the count-kings of the Crown of Aragón frequently stayed for Holy Week. In the stark church lie buried Count-Kings Pere II and Jaume II.

From Santes Creus, head north for El Pont d'Armentera and then west 4 miles (6 km) to El Pla de Santa Maria. From here you follow the TP-2311 country road northwest to **Sarral ❹**, a quiet rural town where you could stop to stretch your legs before proceeding 6 miles (9.6 km) northwest until you hit the C-14 road. Turn left onto this and within 0.6 mile (1 km) you will see a signpost to Vallbona de les Monges heading right (west). By now you are in the roasted ruddy hills of the Serra del Tallat. A 5-mile (8 km) drive brings you to one of those dusty, neglected country towns that signal you

are far away from the general tourist trail, which is probably just how the Cistercian nuns of **Reial Monestir de Santa Maria de Vallbona de les Monges ❺** *(closed Mon.)* prefer things. In its heyday, this was the most important Cistercian nunnery in Catalonia, and its political influence was immense. The convent is still home to a handful of nuns today, who apart

INSIDER TIP:

You can travel from the beaches of Barcelona to lush wine country dotted with vineyards in only 45 minutes.

—ANNIE GRIFFITHS BELT
National Geographic photographer

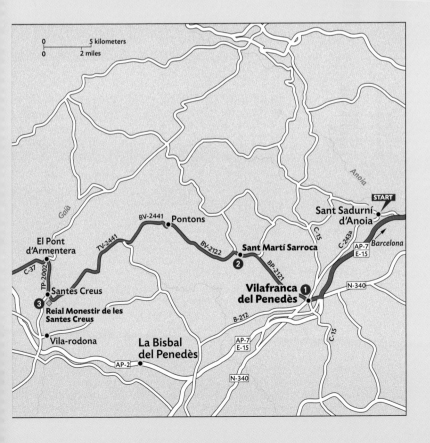

Reial Monestir de Santa Maria de Poblet, the most powerful monastery in Catalonia, still houses a magnificent pantheon of count-kings.

from their devotion to prayer also follow a sustainable lifestyle. They eat produce grown on the land, in keeping with Cistercian principles. The cloister can be seen up close, and the lofty church leaves its own haunting impression. During the civil war it was all but burned to a cinder.

Head back to the C-14 road and follow it south to Montblanc, where you will return presently. Six miles (9.6 km) west of this walled town stands the most impressive of the Cistercian monasteries, **Reial Monestir de Santa Maria de Poblet** ❻ *(closed 12:30 p.m.–3 p.m., tel. 977 870 089 to check on visiting times, www.poblet.cat).*

Penedès's Grapes

Wine has been produced in the Penedès region since ancient times. Indeed, the Phoenicians introduced Chardonnay vines in the sixth century B.C. During their occupation in the Middle Ages, the Moors conducted an extensive wine trade. Aside from the fact that *cava* reigns supreme here, the Penedès region, with its varied terrain, is conducive to growing a wide range of grape varieties.

In the humid, low-lying plains, you'll find the typical Spanish black grapes—notably Garnacha, Tempranillo, Cabernet Sauvignon, and Cariñene. White grapes dominate in higher elevations, including Xarel-lo and Macabeo, as well as Muscat d'Alexandrie, Riesling, and Gewürztraminer. The Alt Penedès, rising 2,600 feet (800 m), boast some of Europe's highest altitude wines, most notably the Parellada variety.

Aloof and self-sufficient behind the forbidding perimeter of its defensive walls, by the mid-19th century the whole site had been pillaged and left to its fate. Only in 1940, when four dedicated Italian Cistercians returned, did the arduous process of restoration begin.

Founded in the 12th century by Ramon Berenguer IV in territory recently retaken from the Muslims and donated to the Cistercians, the monastery grew rapidly to be the most important in Catalonia. This was the count-kings' spiritual center and pantheon. Contrary to the Cistercians' original rules, which forbade the accumulation of wealth, the abbots of Poblet came to be the masters of considerable territory and counselors to the count-kings. After the monks were unceremoniously evicted under expropriation laws in 1835, locals ransacked the place, destroying its immense library and carrying off other treasures.

You enter the monastery complex by the stout **Porta Reial** (Royal Gate), where you can either take a tour or go at your own pace. A Romanesque door leads into the extraordinary Gothic cloister, easily the most striking among the cloisters of the three monasteries with its pavilion, fountain, rows of arches and vaults,

and fine decoration. From here you enter the rear of the church, which houses a breathtaking array of alabaster: the immense *retablo* (altarpiece) and **Panteón dels Reis** (Pantheon of the Kings) made up of sarcophaguses of count-kings including Jaume I the Conqueror and Pere III. Afterward, you go upstairs to the dormitory and around the top of the cloister before heading through a series of halls and dependencies, including the onetime wine cellars. Nowadays, about 30 monks in residence raise grapes on a 30-acre (12 ha) property. The vineyards and nearby **Prades** hills give the countryside a special lilt; those with time could do worse than tour around the area.

When you are done at Poblet, head back to **Montblanc ⑦**, an intriguing medieval town surrounded almost completely by its 1.25 miles (2 km) of hefty 15th-century walls. Of the original 28 towers, 17 remain.

Inside the town gates, make for **Església de Santa Maria la Major,** a Gothic church with an elegant Plateresque (early Spanish Renaissance) entrance. Also worth a peek is the simple Romanesque **Església de Sant Miquel.**

From Montblanc you can pick up the AP-2 motorway for the trip back to Barcelona.

Wine lovers pour into Sant Sadurní d'Anoia to taste sparkling wine at the annual cava fair.

Sitges

Until the end of the 18th century, this cosmopolitan seaside resort town was basically a fishing village. The sudden influx of wealth came when Catalan merchants were finally permitted by Madrid, from 1778 onward, to trade directly with the American colonies. In the 1890s modernista artist Santiago Rusiñol, a cofounder of Els Quatre Gats, moved in, attracting the bohemian art world, which set the scene for the Sitges we know today.

Sitges, a half hour south of Barcelona, is a charming town with pleasant beaches and lots of great bars and restaurants.

Sitges

- 🗺 Map p. 204
- ✉ 19 miles (31 km) SW of Barcelona
- 🚗 By car: C-32 to exit 27 tollway. By train: Rodalies train from Barcelona Sants or Passeig de Gràcia stations to Sitges. The trip takes 30–45 mins.

Visitor Information

- ✉ Plaça Eduard Maristany, 2
- ☎ 93 894 42 51

Although in summer the population quadruples with the influx of well-heeled vacationers and hedonists, Sitges somehow manages to retain a relaxed small-town air. The area around the train station is lamentable, but development is controlled and the narrow streets near the waterfront make for very pleasant wandering.

The main city **beach** is kept silky clean and is reason enough for a trip down from Barcelona. As you approach its eastern end, you pass a brilliant white statue

of the 16th-century painter El Greco. You may be wondering what on Earth the Cretan master, who spent most of his working life in the central Spanish city of Toledo, has to do with Sitges. Nothing really, except that Rusiñol thought so highly of the artist that he hauled two of his paintings here (see p. 218) amid much public to-do in early 1894, and thus hoped to revive interest in his idol.

In front of you, dominating the bluff of land that jabs defiantly into the Mediterranean, is 17th-century **Església de Sant Bartomeu i Santa Tecla.** Inside are several baroque altars and an organ that dates from 1697. The church underwent considerable modification in the 19th century. A stroll around its seaward flank brings you to the most charming, albeit tiny, corner of town.

Three Museums

Two buildings confront you on the little square. The one on the right is the **Museu Maricel,** formerly a 14th-century hospice that now contains an eclectic collection of paintings, objets d'art, and other bits and pieces which run through the history of art, from Romanesque sculptures to 20th-century paintings. Charles Deering, an American collector, purchased the building toward the end of the 19th century and began to fill it with his expanding collection. Then he had the building renovated and across the lane built another edifice, similar in style, which became known as **Palau Maricel.** The two are connected by a lofty covered walkway.

As with the other museums in Sitges, this one is as interesting for the building as for the content. Nevertheless the collection, on view as a museum since 1970, is a curious mix. The first floor is filled with wooden religious sculptures ranging from the 12th to 15th centuries, some fine ceramics, and furniture of various epochs. One of the most striking items is the 14th-century Gothic fresco cycle depicting the martyrdom of St. Bartholomew (Sant Bartomeu in Catalan). It was transferred here from Belmonte de Calatayud, in Aragón. There are a number of modernista and *noucentista* statues in the glassed-in alcove that looks out over the sea, and on the third floor an eclectic mix of furnishings, porcelain, household items, and a pewter collection are on display.

On the top floor is the museum's **pinacoteca** (art gallery). The paintings hanging here include a half-dozen by Rusiñol. Also represented is his buddy, Ramon Casas, with one canvas. The noucentista Joaquim Sunyer has a couple of pieces here, too. Out in a back room is a collection of model sailing boats and seagoing paraphernalia.

You can get more insight into Rusiñol by visiting the **Museu Cau Ferrat,** next door to the Museu Maricel. Rusiñol bought two fishermens' houses and renovated them to his tastes to create what would for years thereafter be his home, studio, and private museum. Its doors were thrown open to the public in 1932, a year after the artist's death. The house alone is worth the entry price. The first floor is richly decorated with exquisite ceramic tiles. It contains the kitchen, an expansive fireplace, the artist's bedroom, and a hodgepodge of his collections. These range from porcelain, some of it dating from the 14th century, to a series of paintings by Rusiñol

Museu Maricel & Museu Cau Ferrat

✉ Carrer de Fonollar s/n

☎ 93 894 03 64

🕓 Closed Sun. p.m. & Mon.

💲 $$ (includes entry to Museu Romàntic)

museusdesitges.cat

Down on Sin Street

Not everyone in Sitges comes for culture. The real activity after a hard day on the beach and slipping from late lunches to even later dinners begins around midnight. Head down to Sin Street (Calle del Pecado). During the day this lane goes by the name of Carrer del 1er de Maig and has an air about it that reflects the hungover state of its nocturnal patrons. At night, a dozen disco bars thump and bump, accompanied by rather pricey drinks. There is a prominent gay scene, but straights mingle in well, and those with stamina have a choice of clubs where they can groove on from 3 a.m. until . . . well, whenever.

Museu Romàntic

- ✉ Carrer de Sant Gaudenci 1
- ☎ 93 894 29 69
- 🕐 Closed Sun. p.m. & Mon.
- 💲 $$ (includes entry to Museu Maricel & Museu Cau Ferrat)

museusdesitges.cat

and his pals, including four early works by Picasso.

Upstairs, the wrought-iron pieces that Rusiñol started collecting at the beginning of his artistic career dominate. They range from elaborate candelabra to an incredible assortment of keys. Tucked in among all the ironwork are the two El Grecos mentioned earlier, "Les Llàgrimes de Sant Pere" ("St. Peter's Tears") and "Santa Magdalena Penitent" ("Mary Magdalen Repentant"), and some copies of Italian masters by Rusiñol, including a couple of Giottos and Botticelli's "Birth of Venus." Of his originals, one of the best known is the rather sad "La Morfinòmana" ("The Morphine Addict").

The third in Sitges's trio of museums is the **Museu Romàntic,** a few blocks in from the

waterfront. Guided visits take about 40 minutes and start on the hour in various languages. The guided tour takes you through the refurbished 19th-century drawing rooms, ballroom, bedrooms (have a look inside the wardrobe of one of them), and so on. The spitoons that you'll see liberally sprinkled around the house were for the benefit of tobacco chewers.

On the top floor is a rather disconcerting collection of several hundred dolls, the oldest of which was made in the late 18th century. Most of these strange relics from another age are actually distressingly ugly.

You can also see a series of dioramas made in the 1950s to depict typical scenes in the life of the wealthy and not-so-well-off in 19th-century Sitges. ∎

EXPERIENCE: Heat Up the End of Winter

It is no secret that the once modest fishing village of Sitges is the gay party capital of Spain. There's plenty of hetero action, too, especially on Sin Street (see sidebar p. 217). Most of the partying happens in summer. In winter, Sitges can seem a placid backwater. That is, until Carnestoltes (Carnival, or Carnaval in Spanish) comes around.

As if shaking off the winter shivers, Sitges explodes in a week of colorful parades and partying. The celebration of Carnival has pagan roots. The general idea represents the inversion of the established moral order in a debauched celebration of winter's end and the coming of the new year. It kicks off on Dijous Gras (Fat Thursday), with the arrival of Carnestoltes (the King of Carnival), accompanied by the Queen and, a Sitges specialty since 2008, the Drag Queen!

There are dinners with traditional dishes and plenty of music. From the following Friday on, there are also activities involving the children, with His Majesty visiting schools and, later in the week, fancy dress afternoon parades for the little ones. At night, noisier parades, with over-the-top floats and a distinctly (but far from exclusively) gay flavor, pass through the town. The climax comes on Tuesday night. On Wednesday evening, with many still nursing hangovers, King Carnestoltes is "buried" in a sign that the old order is back for another year.

The best way to get involved is simply to be in the streets for the parades and head for the bars and clubs afterward as each night progresses. To learn more, visit *sitgestur.cat*.

Tarragona

You would never know it today, but in Roman times Barcelona was a bit of a backwater. The real power lay in Tárraco, capital of the Roman province of Hispania Citerior (subsequently Tarraconensis), a jurisdiction that covered two-thirds of the Iberian Peninsula, from Galicia in the northwest to Almería in the south.

Modern Tarragona is a more modest affair, but plenty of evidence of its splendor as a Roman city remains. The Scipio brothers founded Tárraco as a military camp when they landed in 218 B.C. to carry the Second Punic War into Carthaginian-held territory. The camp was built alongside the Celt-Iberian settlement of Kesse, of which nothing remains, which earned it the label of a World Heritage site in 2000. As the Romans consolidated their grip over the peninsula, Tárraco grew rapidly in importance as the provincial capital.

The end for the Romans came with the arrival of the Visigoths in A.D. 476, who were followed by the Muslims in 717. The latter razed the city, which remained largely abandoned until Christians returned to repopulate it at the end of the 11th century. Although an important port, it has played second fiddle to Barcelona ever since.

Second violin or no, Tarragona boasts the most extensive Roman remains in Catalonia, as well as the region's grandest cathedral. The bulk of the old city rests high above the shoreline, which is characterized at its northeastern end by a broad sandy beach, **Platja del Miracle,** the first of several

The largely Gothic cathedral at the heart of Tarragona is one of the most important in Catalonia.

strands on the way out of town.

To begin reconnaissance of Roman Tárraco, head for Plaça del Rei in the heart of the old town, or **Part Alta** (High Town). Two museums launch you into the ancient city and lie at what was the seaward, southeastern end of the provincial forum. This immense piazza (a few remains can be seen in Plaça del Fòrum) was the central meeting place for people from all over the province. To the northeast, where the cathedral now stands, was the temple to Jupiter.

Tarragona

- ⬛ Map p. 204
- ✉ 60 miles (96 km) SW of Barcelona
- 🚗 By car: C-32 then AP-7 W to exit 33. By train: Barcelona Sants or Passeig de Gràcia station to Tarragona. The trip takes 1.5–2 hrs.

Visitor Information

- ✉ Carrer Major 39
- ☎ 977 25 07 95
- **tarragonaturisme .cat**

Museu Nacional Arqueològic de Tarragona

⊠ Plaça del Rei 5
☎ 977 23 62 09
🕐 Closed Sun., Mon. p.m., & holidays
💲 $$
mnat.cat

The Amfiteatre

Museu Nacional Arqueológic de Tarragona

The Museu Nacional Arqueològic de Tarragona (MNAT) is the first port of call. Here are collected the best of the artifacts found in excavations around and beyond the city, discoveries that continue to be made today. The best known item on display is the extraordinary "Mosaic dels Peixos" ("Fish Mosaic"), which once decorated the floor of a Roman villa outside the city and now hangs on the wall by the stairs leading to the top floor. Judging by the 47 creatures depicted, the Mediterranean was a great deal more abundant in sea life than today. When you enter the museum, head downstairs to the basement, where you will see that the building bestrides part of what was the Roman defensive wall. On display around it are tombstones, columns, and statues, along with a limited collection of coins minted here and an audiovisual program recounting the history of the city.

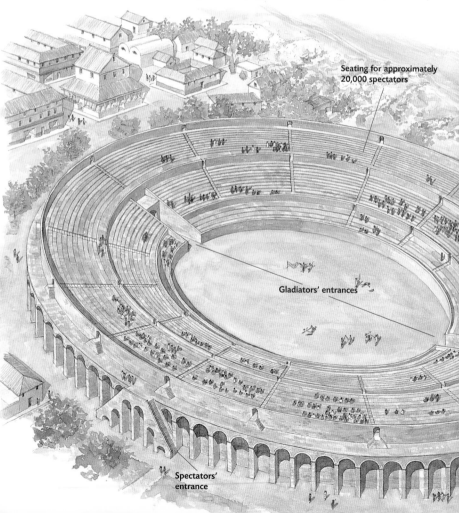

Seating for approximately 20,000 spectators

Gladiators' entrances

Spectators' entrance

The first floor is split into two parts. The main area is dominated by hefty pieces of statuary and architectural decoration, including columns, friezes, and two fine medallions depicting Jupiter. In the other area some mosaics retain spectacularly vivid color, notably the one of Medusa. More mosaics are on view on the next floor, as well as objects of daily life, ranging from amphorae, the Romans' standard storage vessel, through to bronzeware, ceramics, glass, and some interesting statuary, including one of a phallus (representative of the fertility deity Priapus). The top floor has more mosaics and statuary. Throughout the museum are handy returnable booklets in several languages.

Museu d'Història de Tarragona

Facing the museum on the same square is the entrance to the Museu d'Història de Tarragona (MHT), which administers several Roman sites across the city. What you enter here are the **Pretori i Circ Romans** (Roman Pretorium and Circus). The former, also known as the Torre de Pilat (Pilate's Tower), was built in the first century. Whether or not, as legend suggests, Pontius Pilate came from Tarragona will probably never be known. The tower was modified in later centuries, and by the 12th century it was known as the Castell del Rei (King's Castle). During Roman times, the 987-foot-long (300 m) circus was used for events ranging from chariot races (especially of *quadrigas,* chariots drawn by four horses) to the sacrificing of Christians and wild animals, a spectacle that was later transferred to the amphitheater. Stretching to the Ajuntament (Town Hall) building on Plaça de la Font, the circus could accommodate up to 23,000 cheering and jeering spectators.

On entering you will be directed to the elevator to the top of the tower (with wonderful views), from which you work your way downstairs. One level down is the **Sala Gòtica,** a medieval room that replaced the earlier Roman structure. The five broad arches are reminiscent of Barcelona's Saló del Tinell (see pp. 69–70). A long

Elliptical in shape

Spectators' entrance

EXPERIENCE: Feasting at a *Calçotada*

Perhaps the most peculiar food experience you can have in Barcelona is the unlikely sounding *calçot*. It is a long, tender spring onion harvested in winter and early spring, especially in the province of Tarragona, southwest of Barcelona.

Traditionally, groups of family and friends head to country restaurants for a big Saturday or Sunday *calçotada*—the calçot BBQ. The formula is simple enough. You are handed piles of the onions, which have been barbecued on roof tiles, and tubs of *romesco* (a scrumptious *nyora* pepper-and-almond-based sauce). Take a calçot, pull down the burned exterior from the head of the onion, revealing the soft, juicy interior, and dip in the sauce to eat. Yum! In addition, red wine is slurped in copious quantities from a *porrón*, a plump glass bottle with a long spout. You hold this high and away from your face, allowing the wine to squirt into your mouth.

When all have had their fill of calçots, stage two of this long lunch generally involves heading indoors for a feast of barbecued meats in several courses.

The best way to experience a calçotada is to join a group in reserving a place at restaurants scattered about Tarragona province, especially the area around the town of Valls.

staircase leads down to a bare, high-ceilinged space dominated by the remains of a pillar from the imperial temple that dominated the forum and stood some 53 feet (16 m) tall. Next door is the **Volta Superior,** or upper vault, which was part of the gallery that extended around the original forum.

The most intriguing part of the visit starts on the first floor. You first enter the **Volta Inferior** of the forum. This vaulted gallery was part of a structural support to level the enormous surface upon which the forum rested. From here turn back the other way and then right into the 306-foot-long (93 m) **Volta Longitudinal** of the Roman circus. It also served a structural purpose for the circus's upper levels. From one of the side rooms, you can see some of the original spectator seating. After retracing your steps, proceed outside through what was a monumental gateway to the next covered section. You are now at the point where the Porta Triumphalis was, the gate through which victors exited the arena. Passing under vaults, you walk through what was one of the main arena entrances, claustrophobically enclosed by city walls. Stairs (mostly restored) lead up to what was once the top level at the eastern end. Back down those stairs you can exit into La Rambla Vella.

More Roman Sites

A leaflet available at the tourist office, *Passejades per la Història (Walks Through History)* indicates a series of premises along Plaça de la Font and Carrer de Trinquet Vell where, with a little luck, proprietors won't mind you popping in to see other bits and pieces of the circus upon which their properties were subsequently built. The leaflet will also guide you through a medieval and modernista route.

Next head toward the coastline to visit the **Amfiteatre** (see illustration pp. 220–221), the

Roman amphitheater built in the second or third century (part of the Museu d'Història de Tarragona). In this elliptic enclosure locals enjoyed the clash of steel and the spilling of blood as gladiators hacked away at each other and at wild beasts. In the center of the arena are remains of a Romanesque chapel.

A wander back across the old town brings you to the entrance of the **Passeig Arqueològic,** a walkway along part of the perimeter walls. The inner line is predominantly Roman, while the outer walls were constructed by British military engineers during the War of the Spanish Succession.

INSIDER TIP:

From the Passeig Arqueològic, you will enjoy the third-century-B.C. ramparts, as well as a superb panorama of Tarragona.

—CHRISTEL CHERQAOUI
Director of Promotions, National Geographic Books

Yet another element of the museum is the remains of the **Fòrum Romà** on Carrer de Lleida. Among the ruins, several tall columns remain. A basilica where legal disputes were heard once occupied the north end of this forum, while the hub of public life was the lower southeastern part; the two are now linked by a footbridge.

Known popularly as the Pont del Diable (Devil's Bridge), the **Aqüeducte Romà** (Roman Aqueduct), 2 miles (3.2 km) from the center of town on the road to Valls, is impressive. What you see is the 540-foot-long (164 m) remains of a 20-mile (32 km) structure that supplied Tarraco with water.

Catedral de Santa Tecla

Where once Roman citizens prayed to Jupiter now stands one of the most remarkable cathedrals in Catalonia. Begun in 1171 on the site of the Roman temple, the predominantly Gothic **Catedral de Santa Tecla** incorporates some Romanesque elements, along with a few later baroque afterthoughts. It was completed in 1331.

The facade is an interesting mix. The two lateral doors are Romanesque while the main entrance, flanked by 22 statues of Apostles and prophets and split by a column graced with a statue of the Virgin and Child, is Gothic.

You enter the cathedral through the cloister. The 13th-century marble altar has reliefs recounting scenes of the life of St. Thecla. Four apses, three of them Romanesque, and one Gothic, grace the northern end of the church, which is more than 330 feet (100 m) long.

Fine Gothic arches line the four sides of the cloister, mounted on a total of 276 columns, whose capitals were mostly completed in Romanesque style and depict all sorts of scenes, from the biblical to the comic. One of the most famous illustrates the tale of a procession of rats celebrating a cat's funeral. The only hitch is that the said cat comes back to life!

Rooms off the cloister host the **Museu Diocesà,** which contains a host of religious art and some Roman artifacts. ■

Catedral de Santa Tecla

✉ Plaça Pla de la Seu

☎ 977 22 6935

🕐 Closed Sun. & holidays

$ $$

catedraldetarragona.es

Girona

Excavations have revealed that as early as the fifth century B.C. a settlement existed at the junction of the Onyar and Ter rivers. Phoenicians, Celts, and Celt-Iberians, to whom it was known as Geru Undar, later occupied it. It was only natural that the Romans should eventually waltz into what they called Gerunda, through which they laid the Via Augusta, the imperial road between Rome and Cádiz, in southeastern Spain.

Tightly packed lanes border the Riu Onyar.

Girona
- Map p. 224
- 57 miles (91 km) NE of Barcelona
- By car: AP-7 E15 to exit 7. By train: Barcelona Sants or Passeig de Gràcia station to Girona. Trip takes about 1.5 hrs. By AVE high-speed train from Sants (takes 40 mins.).

Visitor Information
- Rambla de la Llibertat 1
- 972 22 65 75

girona.cat/turisme

Conquered briefly by the Muslims in the eighth century, Girona was incorporated early on into the Count of Barcelona's territories. The city prospered in medieval times, but in later centuries Girona became a backwater: a feisty backwater, as its fierce resistance to Napoleon in two long sieges in 1808 and 1809 demonstrated.

Old Town

Stacked up against the right bank of the Riu Onyar, Girona's old city has a magical quality about it. Peppered with small boutiques

and charming restaurants, the narrow, twisting lanes, serpentine stairs, and closely huddled houses make it a wonderful place to discover at leisure.

Sooner or later you will end up walking along **Carrer de la Força,** which in Roman times followed the course of the Via Augusta through town. By the Middle Ages it was the main street of the Jewish quarter, the Call. Strung to either side was a web of narrow alleys, some of which (such as Carrer de Sant Llorenç) still exist. To become acquainted with the history of the Jewish community here, visit the **Museu d'Història dels Jueus de Girona,** in the much restored Centre Bonastruc Ça Porta. The house gives you an idea of how the better-off members of this community lived. Apart from explanatory panels and the like, little is on display except for a series of tombstones with inscriptions (the Jews buried their dead a few miles out of town at a place called Bou d'Or). Upstairs, however, interesting temporary exhibitions are frequently staged.

A little farther north along Carrer de la Força, you arrive in Plaça de la Catedral. Among the fine buildings around the square are the **Pia Almoina** (constructed over the 13th to 15th centuries as an almshouse), which is now home to an architects' society, and the 15th-century **Casa Pastas,** host to the city courts.

To your right, a grand 17th-century staircase sweeps regally up to the baroque facade (finished in 1733) of the **Catedral de Santa Maria.** Entry is off Plaça dels Apòstols through a Gothic doorway to the side of the church. Inside you are confronted by an enormous space of great austerity. Here the Gothic masters pushed the Catalan trend of creating broad, single-nave churches to its extreme; it is the widest Gothic nave in Europe.

Opposite the entrance, a shop gives access to the cathedral's cloister—a jewel of Romanesque architecture left over from the Gothic structure's predecessor—and its museum. The trapezoid shape of the cloister is unique, and the decoration of the capitals on the rows of columns that encircle the garden is exceptional. On the south side, friezes depict biblical episodes, including the stories of Cain and Abel, and Abraham and Isaac, along with another of the taking down of Jesus from the Cross. From the cloister you can see the 13th-century Torre de Carlemany bell tower.

In the museum, or Treasury, reached from the shop, you pass through several rooms full of religious works of art, silverware, and so on, but the real treat is waiting for you at the end—the early 12th-century Tapís de la Creació (Creation Tapestry), rich in color and iconography. Pick up an

INSIDER TIP:

If you like books, wander the quays of the Onyar River on April 23, the day of Sant Jordi, when lovers traditionally exchange books and roses. Dozens of booksellers set up stalls below the Jewish Quarter.

—ROBERT HOLMES
National Geographic photographer

explanatory booklet when you buy your admission ticket. Also significant is the 975 Beatus codex, a rare illuminated tome on display in the first room of the Treasury.

On exiting the church you can submerge yourself in more art in the **Museu d'Art,** housed in the

Museu d'Història dels Jueus de Girona

- ✉ Centre Bonastruc Ça Porta, Carrer de la Força 8
- ☎ 972 427 189
- 🕐 Closed from 2 p.m. Sun. & Mon. Sept–June
- 💲 $$

girona.cat/call

Catedral de Santa Maria

- ✉ Pujada de la Catedral
- ☎ 972 21 44 26
- 💲 $$

catedraldegirona.cat

Museu d'Art

- ✉ Plaça de la Catedral 12
- ☎ 972 20 38 34
- 🕐 Closed from 2 p.m. Sun. & Mon.
- 💲 $

www.museuart.com

Palau Episcopal (Bishop's Residence) next door to the cathedral. The second floor is the main area of interest, with a varied collection of paintings, frescoes, sculptures, and architectural touches such as columns and capitals. The first four rooms are dedicated to

nothing of particular note. The third floor also gives access to a onetime medieval prison—a large single room that, given the usual standards of the time, really wasn't too bad. The upper floors contain limited collections of art spanning the 17th to 20th centuries, including a couple

Girona's Jewish Quarter

Although the first Jews to reach Catalonia arrived after the destruction of Jerusalem, the earliest written records of their presence in Girona date from the late ninth century. At this time, they enjoyed the protection of the Catalan-Aragonese count-kings in return for financial aid. Girona's town authorities had no jurisdiction in the Jewish quarter, or Call, and this caused friction. Their privileged status and economic power frequently made the Jews the object of popular ire. But even in

the toughest times, the small community produced some of the Middle Ages' greatest Jewish thinkers, foremost among them Moshe ben Nahman (aka Nahmanides or Bonastruc de Porta), the Grand Rabbi of Catalonia in the early 13th century and author of the Iberian Peninsula's most ancient Cabbalistic poetry. It all ended with the 1492 order by the united Spain's Catholic Monarchs to expel all Jews who did not convert to Christianity.

the Romanesque period. Here the single most curious item is a column that once adorned a Girona street: A fanciful medieval lioness is scampering up it. The next four rooms are dominated by Gothic art and the last of them, a grand hall, is bedecked with enormous *retablos* (or retables), grand iconographic sequences that were painted on wood and placed behind altars. The most important of these are the "Retaule de Sant Miquel" (St. Michael) by Lluís Borrassà (1416) and, opposite, the "Retaule de Púbol" by Bernat Martorell (1437). Both are masterpieces of the International Gothic style.

A couple of rooms on the second and third floors are given over to a collection of 16th-century paintings by minor artists, with

of canvases by Santiago Rusiñol in Room 17 on the fifth floor.

Back down in Plaça de la Catedral, follow the main street to the brooding twin towers that make up the **Portal de Sobreportes.** Since the third century (plenty of changes were made between then and the 15th century) this has been the main gate into the old city. As if in defiance, the immense Gothic apse of the **Església de Sant Feliu** *(closed Sun. a.m.)* juts out in front of the gate. Dating from the 10th century when it was the cathedral, its nave has 13th-century Romanesque arches but 14th- to 16th-century Gothic upper levels. The northernmost chapel hosts the splendid alabaster Gothic sculpture of "Crist Jacent" ("Recumbent Christ"), executed by

Aloi de Montbrai (active in the 15th century).

A stroll down the street north from the Portal de Sobreportes will lead you to two little Romanesque gems, the **Capella de Sant Nicolau** (a diminutive 12th-century chapel) and the **Monestir de Sant Pere de Galligants** (a monastery built in the 11th and 12th centuries). The latter contains a modest archaeology museum (with artifacts ranging from Roman coins to Jewish tombstones) and a pretty cloister.

Circling back into the old town across the Riu Galligants, you again approach the old city. A couple of paths lead you on pleasant walks along the medieval city walls. But before embarking on these, there is one other stop worth making. On Carrer de Ferran el Católic are the so-called **Banys Àrabs**, or Arab Baths. Although it was modeled on Muslim and Roman bathhouses, with a changing room (*apodyterium*), a cold bath (*frigidarium*), a warm bath (*tepidarium*), a hot bath (*caldarium*), and a kind of steam bath known as the *hypocaust,* this public bathhouse was built in the 12th century. The frigidarium, with its shallow pool and slender columns, is particularly appealing.

New Town

Down in the new town is a museum for the modern age— the **Museu del Cinema.** This is a fascinating trip down filmmaking memory lane, put together from the vast collections of a Catalan cinephile, Tomàs Mallol.

The display begins on the fourth floor and continues on the third. Several shadow puppets dating from the 18th and 19th centuries get the ball rolling, while ensuing rooms explain the history of the camera obscura, the first attempt to project images onto a flat surface, and subsequent developments in the popular entertainment business, such as the magic lantern. The floor ends with the arrival of the first clunky still cameras of the late 19th century.

The third floor, progressing from still to moving pictures, is crowded with projectors, cameras, and other equipment from the 1920s on. Some of the earliest TVs (from the 1930s) are on display. On several, you can see some of the earliest golden moments of the silver screen. ∎

Banys Àrabs
- ✉ Carrer de Ferran el Catòlic
- ☎ 972 21 32 62
- 🕐 Closed from 2 p.m. Sun., holidays, & Oct.–Mar.
- 💲 $

Museu del Cinema
- ✉ Casa de les Aigües, Carrer Sèquia 1
- ☎ 972 41 27 77
- 🕐 Closed from 3 p.m. Sun & Mon (except July–Aug.)
- 💲 $$

museudelcinema.cat

The octagonal pool at the heart of the impressive 12th-century Banys Àrabs, built not by Arabs, but by Christians

Delirium Dalí

When the artist Salvador Dalí (1904–1989) found himself surrounded by flames in his fantasy castle-mansion, the Castell de Púbol, south of Figueres, in 1984, he must have thought all the psychedelic weirdness of his most nightmarish paintings was coming true. Ever since, a fire extinguisher has stood by the bed in his blue bedroom, although no one has slept there since the painter's death in 1989.

The courtyard of the Dalí Museum in Figueres

Dalí acquired the mansion for his headstrong Russian wife, Gala, subject of his obsessions and many of his later paintings. They had previously spent much of their time in his Port Lligat home near Cadaqués on the north Catalan coast. The parties they threw in the 1960s and '70s were legendary, as apparently was Gala's appetite for young men.

It had all begun modestly enough. As a young artist born in Figueres, Dalí came to the attention of Barcelona critics and was sent to study at Madrid's Escuela de Bellas Artes de San Fernando, where he met the likes of poet Federico García Lorca (1898–1936) and experimental film director Luis Buñuel (1900–1983). With the latter he would later make two key surrealist films,

Un Chien Andalou (An Andalusian Dog) and
L'Âge d'Or (The Golden Age).

Dalí was good and his range was broad.
Classic portraiture with a touch of the unreal,
a few stabs at cubism, and sunny urban and
country scenes were all accomplished with skill.
The deceptively simple but engaging "Noia a
la Finestra" of 1925 is a memorable work. But
he did not really find his voice until the late
1920s when, influenced by Freud's teachings
on the erotic and subconscious, he joined the
surrealist movement in Paris and embarked on
the most fecund period of his artistic life. Induc-
ing hallucinatory states in himself (by what he
dubbed his "paranoiacritical" method), he created, in minute detail, bizarrely mutated images.
Heavily erotic, sometimes violent, always
disturbing, his paintings took everyday people,
objects, and stances and transformed them into
irrational scenes. Objects and beings float, disin-
tegrate, and combine in an impossibly peculiar
way. During this time he met Gala, then married
to French poet Paul Eluard. They ran off to Paris
and stayed together for the rest of their lives,
although they did not marry until 1958.

U.S. Bound

Expelled from the surrealist movement
because of his thirst for commercial interests, Dalí and Gala moved to the United
States for most of the 1940s. French surrealist poet André Breton coined the anagram
Avida Dollars (meaning "avid for dollars")
from Dalí's name. It was apt, but probably left its target indifferent. Dalí's art was
popular in the United States, and he began
a campaign of purposeful eccentricity with
the aim of attracting publicity and money. It
seems to have worked. Moving around a lot,
he worked on movie sets (including scenes
from Alfred Hitchcock's *Spellbound*) and in
theater, wrote a couple of books, and generally sold his name to all comers. Meantime,
he abandoned the hallucinogenic painting
and returned to more classic lines, or what
he liked to refer to as his "mystical and
nuclear stage."

End of Life

By the 1960s (having returned to Europe in
1948), he was painting big canvases, often
with religious themes. Even after the death
of Gala in 1979 and the 1984 fire, he continued to paint, although he spent his last five
years as a recluse in the Torre Galatea, which
he bought along with the former theater
in Figueres. He converted the theater into
a museum of his work and chose it for his
burial place.

**Dalí, pictured here at his easel, churned out an
extraordinary quantity of art.**

Figueres

Its creator described it as a "gigantic surrealist object." Others might settle for just plain "strange." Whatever you think, a visit to the Teatre-Museu Dalí in the provincial northern Catalan town of Figueres, where Salvador Dalí began and ended his days, is a unique artistic experience.

Not surprisingly, eggs—frequent subjects in Dalí's work—feature on his museum-mausoleum.

One doesn't even need to go inside to realize that this former municipal theater, which Dalí transformed between 1961 and 1974, is off the wall; just look at the walls. Wine red, they are topped with a series of androgynous statues and what look like huge eggs, a recurring theme in some of Dalí's more nightmarish art.

Upon entering the building, you have before you a circular **courtyard** that was once the theater stalls, and you will hardly fail to notice the Cadillac that squats in the middle. It is said to have once belonged to gangster Al Capone. Be that as it may, it is a strange beast indeed. Near the front passenger door you can insert coins to trigger a rain shower *inside* the car, hence the title of this work, "Taxi Plujós" ("Rainy Taxi"). Suspended above this scene is a small fishing boat; why it should be there is anyone's guess.

In the so-called **Sala de les Peixateries** (Fish Shop Room) off the courtyard, you can wonder at Dalí's "Autoretrat Tou amb Tall de Bacon Fregit" ("Soft Self-Portrait with Fried Bacon"), in which you can barely make

INSIDER TIP:

Don't miss any of the four Salvador Dalí museums in the area. Dalí's wit and brilliance are exhibited on both the inside and the outside of the museums.

—ANNIE GRIFFITHS BELT
National Geographic photographer

out what appears to be a melted plastic death mask. His extremely unflattering "Retrat de Picasso" ("Portrait of Picasso") reveals all the bile Dalí apparently felt well up inside him at the mere mention of his rival's name.

Behind the courtyard is the former stage, now topped by a geodesic dome and dominated by a Dalían set (he contributed his skills to the theater on many occasions). Off to the left is the **Sala del Tresor** (Treasure Room), in which you will find some of Dalí's earlier works, like the bright, crisp, and somehow disquieting "Port Alguer" (a view of the Sardinian town of Alghero). Also on view are several portraits of Gala. Stairs to the right take you down to the crypt where Dalí is buried. Back upstairs you continue up another flight on the right of the stage to enjoy one of Dalí's games: The "furnishings" of the Sala Mae West make up her portrait. Climb the staircase and you will see how the sofa becomes her lips, the fireplace her nose, two paintings her eyes, and the curtains her hair.

The surrounding rooms and galleries above the courtyard are jammed in seemingly disorderly fashion with paintings and drawings by Dalí (such as his extensive series of lithographs on mythological themes) and others. Should you follow the museum layout, you will likely end up in the **Torre Galatea** (named after his beloved Gala and in which Dalí spent the last years of his life as a recluse) in the last stages of your tour. These rooms are dominated by the artist's later work, including "stereoscopic" paintings (works in repetition to be viewed simultaneously), mostly of Gala and himself. A separate entrance leads to **Dalí Joies,** the Owen Cheatham collection of 39 jewels in gold and precious stones designed by Dalí with his usual brio, as well as paintings and sketches.

Figueres

⚠ Map p. 204

✉ 80 miles (128 km) NE of Barcelona

🚗 By car: AP-7 E15 to exit 4. By train: Barcelona Sants or Passeig de Gràcia to Figueres via Girona. The trip takes about 2 hrs. By AVE high-speed train from Sants (53 mins.).

Visitor Information

✉ Plaça del Sol

☎ 972 50 31 55

visitfigueres.cat

Teatre-Museu Dalí

✉ Plaça Gala-Salvador Dalí 5

☎ 972 67 75 00

💲 $$$

salvador-dali.org

EXPERIENCE: Take a Hike!

Hiking has a long tradition in Catalonia. From the late 19th century, hiking groups were formed to make day trips around Barcelona, becoming a sort of pilgrimage to underline local Catalan identity. Particularly popular was Montserrat (see pp. 206–209), the Catalans' "holy mountain."

Now that Montserrat is a major tourist objective, Barcelonans with itchy feet head for the wilder **Parc Natural del Montseny**, 30 miles (50 km) northwest of Barcelona along the AP-7 motorway toward Girona. The highest point is the Turó de l'Home (1 mile/1,709 m), and there are plenty of trails. Of the villages, one of the prettiest to overnight in is **Arbúcies.** There are also some fine rural hotels scattered across the park, as well as camping options. Pick up the Editorial Alpina Montseny map from the Quera bookshop (see Travelwise p. 259).

Farther away, the Pyrenees mountain range and pre-Pyrenees areas offer boundless opportunities. The most striking park is **Parc Nacional d'Aigüestortes i Estany de Sant Maurici** (gencat.cat /parcs/aiguestortes), the only national park in Catalonia. You can get lost here for days, sleeping in a network of mountain huts (refugis).

For Catalan hikers, the symbolic peak is the **Pica d'Estats** (2 miles/ 3,143 m), the highest point in the Catalan Pyrenees. It lies on the French border in the northwest of the region. Getting up and back again is a beautiful all-day hike and not for the unfit. From Barcelona, you need to count on two nights away if you drive. On the Catalan national day, September 11, swarms of locals invade the mountain, many camping about halfway up the night before.

Museu de l'Empordà

✉ La Rambla 2
☎ 972 50 23 05
🕐 Closed Mon. & from 2 p.m. Sun. & holidays.
💲 $
museuemporda.org

Museu del Joguet de Catalunya

✉ Carrer Sant Pere 1
☎ 972 50 45 85
🕐 Closed from 2 p.m. Sun. & Mon. Oct.–May
💲 $$
mjc.cat

Other Attractions

A handful of items remain to be explored in this quiet town with its attractive rambla. Back in 1876, a local collector founded the **Museu de l'Empordà** (the northeastern part of Catalonia). It houses a collection of locally found artifacts from Celt-Iberian, Greek, and Roman times. You can expect to come across the usual kinds of things: personal effects, black-and-red Greek ceramics, and glass. The display continues with odds and ends ranging from column capitals taken from the Monestir de Sant Pere de Rodes (a monastery overlooking the northern Catalan coast) to minor paintings from the storerooms of Madrid's Prado gallery. Other sections are devoted to Catalan art from the mid-19th to early 20th centuries (Antoni Tàpies is

INSIDER TIP:

Figueres has come up with a tasty combo of food and fantasy called the Surrealist Tapas Festival from mid-June to mid-July [en.visitfigueres.cat].

—JUSTIN KAVANAGH
National Geographic Travel Books editor

among those represented) and strictly local painters.

A few doors down, the **Museu del Joguet de Catalunya**

is for many a great deal more captivating. With some 3,500 pieces, it's one of Europe's biggest toy museums. Housed in a late 18th-century mansion, the collection has a bit of everything: toy animals, soldiers, cardboard horses, planes, trains, cars, puppets, dolls, teddy bears, and tricycles, plus all sorts of other stuff. Mixed in with old photos of kids playing, this is a trip back through the years. A few of the toys belonged to such personalities as Joan Miró, Federico García Lorca, and Dalí himself.

To the north of town you'll find the **Castell de Sant Ferran,** an enormous star-shaped fortress built from 1750 to 1763 as a late reaction to the loss of territory known as "Catalunya Norte" (of which the main city is Perpignan) to the French by the Pyrenees Treaty of 1659. Built about a half mile (1 km) north of central Figueres according to the criteria of the famed French military engineer Sébastien Le Prestre de Vauban (1633–1707), it was at the time the second largest such fortification in Europe. Its walls are more than 5 miles (8 km) long, and it was said to be capable of resisting siege by a force of 8,000 soldiers and 500 horses for up to two years. They needn't have bothered. On the two occasions when the French invaded Spain (in 1793 during the French Revolution and again in 1808 under Napoleon), the fortress was surrendered without a shot—clearly it could not defend itself without a little help from the soldiers inside! Since then it has been a barracks, a

training ground, and a prison, but never has it been tested in siege. The Republican government held its last meeting here in early 1939, shortly before fleeing to France and thus signaling the end of the 1936–1939 civil war.

The fort, which now houses the contents of Barcelona's military museum (open Wed. & Fri. a.m. only; see p. 201), can be visited (with or without a guide). Special two-hour visits including a ride in a Zodiac in the huge subterranean cistern are another option. ∎

Castell de Sant Ferran

✉ Camì al Castell de Sant Ferran
☎ 972 50 60 94
🕐 Closed from 3 p.m. mid-Sept.–June
💲 $$

lesfortaleses catalanes.info

Dalí fever continues beyond his museum—Figueres cafés also adopt his distorted themes.

Drive Along the Costa Brava

Although speculators do their best to spoil things, the beauty of the Costa Brava (Rugged Coast) remains largely intact. To some, the name conjures images of budget package tourism, crowded beaches, and English-style pubs full to bursting with lobster-red revelers ferried in from northern climes. Apart from some infamous exceptions, the truth is thankfully rather different.

Dalí chose the quiet fishing town of Port Lligat, north of Cadaqués, for his coastal hideaway, now open to the public.

What follows takes in the best of the coast from Barcelona most of the way to the French border. It would be a stretch to do it in one day, but any given spot can easily be reached by car from Barcelona (taking the AP-7 tollway and cutting in to the coast at the appropriate point), with several stops along the way. Consider spending a night on the coast before returning to the big city.

From Barcelona, take the C-32 northeast. Where it ends inland behind Blanes, follow the signs along the coast road for Lloret and Tossa. **Lloret de Mar** is mentioned only in passing, for that is exactly what you will want to do. Just 39 miles (62 km) northeast of Barcelona, this sprawling mass of dormitory hotels, poor restaurants, and loud bars is the epicenter of the package tour. Hotels and apartment blocks

NOT TO BE MISSED:

Tamariu • Empúries • Parc Natural dels Aiguamolls de l'Empordà • Cadaqués's pretty harborside restaurants

creep up the hills behind what is, admittedly, a good beach. If anything, this marks only the beginning of the Costa Brava—and the end of its more lurid dimension. Our first stop is 8 miles (13 km) of winding road farther along, at **Tossa de Mar ❶**.

There's no shortage of summertime visitors here either, but the atmosphere is altogether different. Excavations show there has been a settlement here at least since Roman times, and

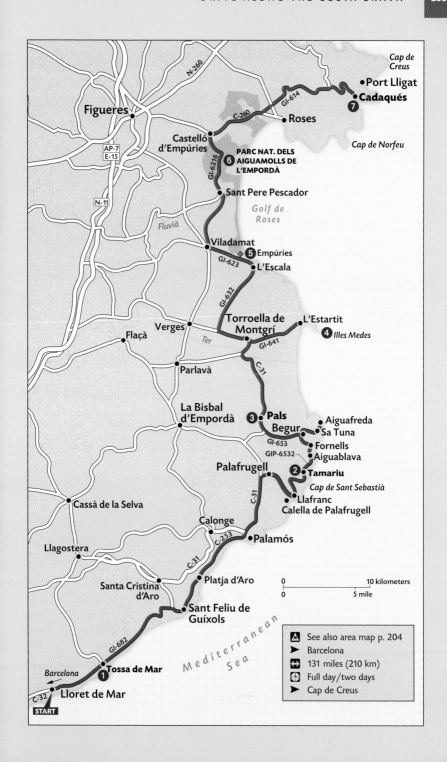

Cap de
Creus

• Port Lligat

Cadaqués

7

N-260

Figueres

GI-614

C-260

• **Roses**

Cap de Norfeu

AP-7
E-15

Castelló
d'Empúries

GI-6216

6 PARC NAT. DELS
AIGUAMOLLS DE
L'EMPORDÀ

N-11

• **Sant Pere Pescador**

Golf de
Roses

Fluvià

• **Viladamat**

5 Empúries

GI-623

• **L'Escala**

GI-632

Verges

Flaçà

**Torroella de
Montgrí**

L'Estartit •

4 Illes Medes

Ter

GI-641

• **Parlavà**

C-31

La Bisbal
d'Empordà

3 **Pals**

Begur

• Aiguafreda
• Sa Tuna

GI-653

• **Fornells**

GIP-6532

• Aiguablava

Palafrugell

2 **Tamariu**

Cap de Sant Sebastià

C-31

• **Llafranc**
Calella de Palafrugell

• **Cassà de la Selva**

Calonge

C-253

• **Palamós**

Llagostera

C-31

Santa Cristina
d'Aro

• **Platja d'Aro**

0   10 kilometers
0   5 mile

**Sant Feliu de
Guíxols**

Mediterranean
Sea

⛰ See also area map p. 204

▶ Barcelona

🔄 131 miles (210 km)

🕐 Full day/two days

▶ Cap de Creus

GI-682

Barcelona

Tossa de Mar **1**

C-32

Lloret de Mar

START

the *vila vella* (old town), with its twisting lanes and freshly painted houses, is a joy to explore. Up on a rocky, pine-stubbled promontory that closes off the southern end of the wide sandy beach, Platja Gran, a medieval watchtower stands guard over the coast and what remains of the 12th- to 14th-century city walls. Within them is a smattering of charming stone houses and a handful of bars and restaurants. The views and sunsets from up here are magical. In summer, glass-bottom pleasure boats set out from Platja Gran for tours of otherwise hard-to-reach beaches up and down the coast.

Leaving Tossa behind, the GI-682 road contorts itself on a series of winding climbs, mild switchbacks, and cliffside spurts along one of the most majestic stretches of the Costa Brava. The 13 miles (21 km) from Tossa to **Sant Feliu de Guíxols** is admirable, and along the way you'll see below you several tempting inlets and pretty little beaches. Development is taking place, but hopefully the steep terrain will hold it in check.

From Sant Feliu, not an unpleasant seaside town, the GI-682 coast road leads northeast to a couple of popular beaches. Among them is **Platja d'Aro,** a lively little resort that attracts foreigners and Spaniards alike.

Continue north to Palamós, exiting it northward along the C-31 inland highway (there's no choice). The next stop is **Palafrugell,** not in itself an objective but the hub from which three delightfully restrained beaches are reached. They are, from south to north, **Calella de Palafrugell, Llafranc,** and **Tamariu ❷.** The last is the quietest, a lovely beach with limpid water backed largely by thick woods and a few low-key hotels and restaurants. Calella, with its waterfront houses, restaurants, and fishing boats, has something of the feel of a Greek island town. Between them, Llafranc has a fishing harbor. From Tamariu, follow signs for Aiguablava, a pretty cove, along unnumbered roads. Continue on the GIP-6532 to Fornells,

INSIDER TIP:

Don't miss Parc Natural de Cap de Creus, where the axial zone of the Pyrenees meets the Mediterranean Sea. The region is geologically famous for its sheared granite outcrops.

—DECLAN G. DE PAOR
National Geographic field researcher

Capped at one end by a high promontory, Tossa de Mar is a delightful seaside village.

Diving the Illes Medes

The marine nature reserve of the Illes Medes is made up of seven tiny islets off the flat, arching coast town of L'Estartit. With nearly 1,400 species of animal and plant life and a labyrinth of underwater tunnels and caves, the isles have become one of Spain's favorite diving and snorkeling spots. Close to the surface and by the rocks you can see all sorts of fish, crabs, and octopuses. The deeper you go, the more interesting things get. About the deepest dive possible is 164 feet (50 m), where you may come across rays.

Other diving options on the Costa Brava include the Illes Formigues, rocky islets off the coast between Palamós and Calella de Palafrugell, with waters down to 148 feet (45 m), and Els Ullastres, three underwater hills off Llafranc with some sheer walls and depths to 178 feet (54 m).

L'Estartit is full of diving companies. Exercise some caution, however, as not all are top-notch: Equipment and safety measures could be found wanting.

another cove, and Begur, a bustling town with castle ruins.

From Begur, the GI-653 road heads west to meet the GI-650, which you follow for a few miles north to **Pals ❸**, with its Gothic defensive walls and handful of centuries-old mansions. From Pals, continue on the C-31 to **Torroella de Montgrí,** distinguished mainly for the castle ruins (accessible only on foot) that lie high up on a ridge above the town. From here divers may want to take the GI-641 east for 4 miles (6 km) to **L'Estartit,** to join groups diving off the **Illes Medes ❹** (see sidebar above).

Otherwise, head north for 7.5 miles (12 km) on the GI-632 to **L'Escala,** a pleasant seaside spot from where you can walk a couple of miles (or drive around the back) to the magnificent ancient site of **Empúries ❺**. This was a trading post and among the first of the Greek coastal settlements in Spain. The Greeks and indigenous Celt-Iberian tribes rubbed along in peace until the Romans landed in 218 B.C., beginning a long campaign to conquer the entire Iberian Peninsula. Today you can make out the Greek and Roman parts of the town— the latter is farther from the waterfront and reveals more detail, such as the forum, floor mosaics in private houses, and remains of the landward wall and amphitheater.

From L'Escala, the GI-623 cuts inland to Viladamat and then north via Sant Pere Pescador on the GI-6216 to **Castelló d'Empúries.**

This town has a pleasant old center dominated by the grand, Gothic Església de Santa Maria on Plaça de Jacint Verdaguer, retaining a fine Romanesque bell tower from an earlier church. Before Castelló, you may want to take a break in the **Parc Natural dels Aiguamolls de l'Empordà ❻** *(visitor information, tel 972 45 42 22).* This sanctuary is all that remains of the salt marshes that once lined the entire Golf de Roses (Roses Gulf). Although the best times for bird-watching in the park (there are marked trails and observation points) are the March to May and August to October migration periods, you can usually spot plenty of birds year-round. Of the more than 300 species here, resident and migratory, common birds include herons, terns, glossy ibis, and even the occasional black stork.

Some four miles (6 km) east of Castelló d'Empúries, the GI-614 road leads into the highlands of the Cap de Creus Peninsula and onto the chic coast town of **Cadaqués ❼.** Along with its neighbor around the next headland, **Port Lligat,** this was long a haunt of the rich and famous and retains a sophisticated air. The steep, narrow cobbled lanes of old Cadaqués are enchanting, as is the walk to Port Lligat, where you can visit the Casa-Museu Salvador Dalí, his old house *(tel 972 25 10 15, salvador-dali.org/museus, reserve ahead, closed Jan.– mid-March).* If time permits, drive out to **Cap de Creus,** Spain's most easterly point.

More Excursions From Barcelona

Cardona

It is worth considering taking the 56-mile (90 km) trip to this town near the Pyrenees to see the 18th-century **Castell de Cardona** and, within its walls, one of the grandest examples of early Romanesque church building in Catalonia. Protected by the three defensive walls of the hilltop castle—which has been converted into a Parador (state hotel)—the 11th-century **Església de Sant Vicenç** is splendid. Its nave and two aisles end in three proud apses and, unusually for a Romanesque structure, the ceiling is dominated by a central dome. Former salt mines underneath the hill can also be visited *(closed Mon.)*. The old town center has uneven lanes and a Gothic parish church. *cardonaturisme.cat* 🅜 Map p. 204 **Visitor Information** ✉ Avinguda del Rastrillo s/n ☎ 93 869 27 98 🚆 Rodalies train (Línia 4) from Estació de Sants & Plaça de Catalunya to Manresa, then Alsa bus to Cardona

Colònia Güell

Only 6 miles (10 km) west of Barcelona, reached via the C-32 and BV-2002, the sleepy hamlet of Santa Coloma de Cervelló hides one of Gaudí's last and least-known projects. Gaudí was to build the church for a Utopian village *(colònia)* to house textile factory workers. Financed by Eusebi Güell, the cottages were designed by other architects. Gaudí had finished only the crypt when finances ran dry in 1915. Now used as a chapel, it provides intriguing clues of what Gaudí's intentions had been for La Sagrada Família. The leaning pillars holding up the ribbed vaulting are reminiscent of an enchanted forest. *gaudicoloniaguell.org* 🅜 Map p. 204 ☎ 93 630 58 07 🕐 Closed from 3 p.m. Sat.–Sun. 🚆 FGC train (S4, S8, or S33) from Plaça d'Espanya to Colònia Güell station 💲 $$–$$$

Sant Cugat del Vallès

Once a summer getaway for Barcelonans, this town has little to offer except for the grand monastery from which it takes its name. Built near the site of its Visigothic predecessor, the present structure is interesting above all for the fine Romanesque first floor of its cloister. The upper level is Gothic, as is most of the church. The monastery, supposedly founded by St. Benedict, is named after a saint martyred in a Roman fort here in A.D. 303. *museu.santcugat.cat* 🅜 Map p. 204 ✉ Plaça Octavià ☎ 93 675 99 51 🕐 Closed 1:30 p.m.–3 p.m. Mon.–Sat., from 2:30 p.m. Sun., & holidays; church closed from noon–6 p.m. 🚆 FGC train (Nos. S1, S2, S5, or S55) from Plaça de Catalunya

Terrassa

Amid the high-rise suburbs lies an interesting old town center whose real treasure is a trio of pre-Romanesque churches. (They say Japanese urban planning students come here to learn how not to do things!) The **Esglésies de Sant Pere** (Churches of St. Peter) are actually dedicated to Sant Pere, Sant Miquel, and Santa Maria. The oldest elements date from the ninth and tenth centuries. Sant Miquel may be the most charming, with its square floor plan and pillars from Visigothic and Roman structures. A fine modernista factory, the Vapor Aymerich, is the center of Catalonia's Science and Technical Museums (MNACTEC), a fascinating insight into its industrial heyday *(xatic.cat)*.

Terrassa comes to life in early spring with its tremendous jazz festival. Spread throughout the town, the festival includes daily concerts as well as films, talks, and art exhibitions. Visit *jazzterrassa.org* for the latest information. 🅜 Map p. 204 **Visitor Information** ☎ 93 739 70 19 🚆 FGC train (S1) from Plaça de Catalunya, Provença, or Gràcia.

Travelwise

Planning Your Trip   240–241

How to Get to Barcelona   241–242

Getting Around   242–243

Practical Advice   243–246

Emergencies   246

Hotels & Restaurants   247–257

Shopping   258–260

Entertainment & Activities   261–263

Language Guide & Menu Reader   264

Barcelona's taxis are inexpensive by
European standards.

TRAVELWISE

PLANNING YOUR TRIP

Visiting Barcelona is an enriching and fun exercise. A modern, forward-thinking western city in most respects, it also has two millennia of history behind it and its own sometimes quirky ways. Things generally run efficiently, but often they run differently from how you might expect. The city is also bilingual, which on occasion can create confusion (especially if you are making some effort with one of the languages, probably Spanish). Still, so long as you are enjoying yourself, discovering how things are done can be a revealing part of the experience.

When to Go

The statistics speak for themselves. Year-round, Barcelona's hotels register 70–85 percent occupancy. The city is a 365-day destination, although clearly some times are busier than others. Peak periods include Easter week, Christmas to New Year's Day, the summer, and key trade fairs when hotel prices are known to rocket.

August is a funny month. Traditionally the time when most locals take their annual vacations to escape the strangulating heat, the city takes on a strangely empty air as many shops, restaurants, and bars close, though this custom is beginning to change. Banks and public offices work on reduced morning-only timetables. The vacuum is filled to some extent by foreign visitors undeterred by the thought of sizzling in the city and by Barcelonans who choose to stay behind to enjoy the relative peace, local beaches, or local street festivals. One of the biggest, the Festa Major de Gràcia, takes place in the middle of August. It is a weeklong

sweaty celebration of food, drink, music, noise, and community, preceded and followed by similar, though less hectic, versions in other *barris* (neighborhoods)

The best time to come is late April through June, when the weather is crisp and bright, and sometimes hot. February's Carnival (at its most raucous in Sitges—see sidebar p. 218) already marks the passing of the worst of winter, but March and April are unstable months, because you never know if it is going to be cold, wet, or hot!

The coolest and quietest period is from early December to late February (except Christmas and New Year's Day).

Some hotels drop prices in slacker periods best grabbed online.

Climate

Extremes of summer heat and humidity aside, Barcelona basks in a moderate Mediterranean climate. The hottest months of the year are July and August, when daytime temperatures reach the mid-90s°F (mid-30s°C). The city's location on the sea means that humidity can be high, but (if you're in the right place) you can sometimes benefit from soothing sea breezes. In summer you will need only light clothes (natural fabrics are best). Otherwise come prepared for changes in temperature. Even if it's hot during the day, the nights can cool off considerably, so a sweater and light jacket could come in handy.

Traditionally Barcelona gets a thorough bath in late September and well into October, while November, although cool, can be agreeably dry and sunny. Spring can have its wet moments, too, so you should bring an umbrella and possibly a raincoat.

Winters are chilly but not excessively cold. You will want a room

with heating and decent winter clothing for the evenings, but you could easily find yourself enjoying crisp, sunny days when you can eat outdoors. Temperatures hardly, if ever, go below freezing, and snow, is a rarity.

What to Take

Barcelonans tend to wear conservatively stylish dress. They don't have the same obsession with the latest fashion that many Italians do, but a certain Mediterranean desire to look good certainly pervades the atmosphere. Many younger people are pretty relaxed, however, and scathing about the upper middle-class pretensions of *pijos* (spoiled brats with classic clothes and cars).

If you intend to dine out in any style at all or go to concerts, you will want at least one set of casually elegant evening clothes. For tramping those city miles during the day, take a pair of sturdy shoes.

Other useful items include sunglasses (year-round), sunscreen lotion (spring and summer), and, for those sensitive to the sun, a hat. An under-the-clothes money belt or shoulder wallet is a good idea for keeping cash and documents out of sight.

Insurance

Comprehensive travel insurance is an essential investment and should cover you for theft, loss of possessions, emergency medical treatment, repatriation, and refund of flights and other travel should you be delayed by circumstances beyond your control, such as strikes or illness.

Passports

You need a valid passport. Keep a photocopy of the details pages in a separate location for ease of opicenme.

replacement in case of loss. Spain is part of the Schengen agreement, under which 26 European countries have dropped passport controls between them. U.S. and Canadian citizens do not need a visa to enter any Schengen country for up to three months. For longer stays, you will need to consider applying for a residence permit—a nightmarish process.

Further Reading

An excellent introduction to the history and art of Barcelona is Robert Hughes's witty and insightful *Barcelona* or *Barcelona: The Great Enchantress. Barcelona: The City that Reinvented Itself,* by Michael Eaude, paints the city with a broad brush, with knowledgeable insights, ranging from Gaudí to soccer. *Homage to Catalonia* is George Orwell's account of the 1936–1939 civil war in Catalonia, moving from the euphoria of the early days in Barcelona to disillusionment with the disastrous infighting on the Republican side. If you want a good general history of the war, get *The Spanish Civil War* by Hugh Thomas.

HOW TO GET TO BARCELONA

Most U.S. and Canadian citizens will fly to Barcelona. However, the city can be reached by rail from Madrid and other parts of Spain, as well as from France and the U.K. There are also high-class car-ferry services to Barcelona from Genoa and Civitavecchia near Rome in Italy.

Airlines

Air Europa (tel 902 401 501, aireuropa.com)
American Airlines (tel 902 115 570, aa.com)
Delta (tel 901 116 946, delta.com)
Iberia (tel 902 400 500, iberia.com)

United Airlines (tel 1-800-864-8335, united.com)
Vueling (tel 807-200-100, vueling.com)

American, United, and Delta have direct nonstop flights between several U.S. cities and Barcelona. You may also take Spain's national airline, Iberia, or another and go via Madrid or other European hub.

Iberia, Air Europa, and Vueling have extensive national networks. Flying within Spain is not always cheap, but can save lots of time between cities.

If flying from elsewhere in Europe, check out the many low-cost airlines (such as EasyJet, *easyjet.com,* and Ryanair, *ryanair .com*), along with other regular airlines and charter flights.

Airport

Direct flights between North America and Barcelona are available, but you will often find the best deals with routings through other European cities, possibly the Spanish capital Madrid but more than likely major hubs such as London, Paris, Amsterdam, or Frankfurt. Barcelona has one airport, El Prat (7.5 miles/ 12 km southwest of Barcelona; tel 902 404 704), which, while small for the volume of traffic it receives, functions relatively smoothly with two terminals (T1 & T2).

Getting into town is easy. The *Rodalies* (*Cercanías* in Spanish) local train service runs from a station about a five-minute walk along an overpass from T2, reached by a shuttle bus from T1. Main stops include Estació Sants and Passeig de Gràcia. Trains run every half hour from 5:42 a.m. to 11:38 p.m. (19 minutes to Sants; 24 minutes to Passeig de Gràcia). Departures from Sants to the airport are from 5:13 a.m. to 11:14 p.m.; from Passeig de Gràcia they're five minutes earlier. Tickets are available from the ticket office or a machine at the

station. Buy a T10 travel card which you can use on metro or bus (see p. 242).

The A1 (for T1) and A2 (T2) Aerobús service runs to Plaça de Catalunya via Plaça d'Espanya every 8–15 minutes from 6 a.m. to 1 a.m. Departures from Plaça de Catalunya are 5:30 a.m. to 12:15 a.m. The trip takes about 40 minutes, depending on traffic.

A taxi to downtown should not cost more than about €27.

By Car

The AP-7 E15 tollway takes you into Barcelona from the French border (and proceeds south to Tarragona and beyond along the entire Spanish Mediterranean coast). From Madrid you take the A2/E90 toward Zaragoza, which then becomes the AP-2 tollway.

By Boat

Daily high-speed ferries are run by Grandi Navi Veloci (*gnv.it*) between Genoa and Barcelona. The journey takes 18 hours. Book through local travel agents, online, or (if there is space) by turning up at Via Milano (Ponte Assereto) in Genoa or the port (Moll de San Beltran) in Barcelona. The same company runs summer ferries between Barcelona and Tangier (Morocco). Grimaldi Ferries (*grimaldi-ferries.com*) has similar services to Barcelona from Civitavecchia (for Rome, 20 hrs.) and Livorno (Tuscany, 19.5 hrs.) up to six days a week.

By Bus

Most national bus services arrive and depart from Estació del Nord (*tel 902 260 606, Carrer d'Alí Bei 80*). For travel along the Costa Brava, for instance, or farther afield, you generally have no option but to take the bus, as both areas are poorly served by train. International services depart from Estació d'Autobusos de Sants, alongside the

Estació Sants train station (tel 93 490 40 00).

By Train

The main station is Estació Sants, on Plaça dels Països Catalans. Trains fan out across Catalonia and the rest of Spain from here, as well as north into France. A bewildering variety of train types and classes confront the traveler moving around Spain, ranging from slow all-stops regionales to high-speed AVEs (and all their subvariants!). For information, call Renfe (the Spanish rail company, generally Spanish-speaking only; tel 902 24 02 02 or 902 243 402 international). You can book and check timetables at the station or on the website (renfe.es). For international services, book through selected travel agents or at the station direct.

GETTING AROUND
By Car
Car Rentals
In Spain:
Avis (Carrer de Còrsega 293–295, L'Eixample, tel 902 180 854, avis.es)
Europcar (Gran Via de les Corts Catalanes 680, tel 902 503 010, europcar.es)
Hertz (Carrer del Viriat 45, tel 902 402 405, hertz.es)
Atesa (Carrer de Muntaner 45, tel 902 100 101 www.atesa.es)
Sixt (Rambla de Catalunya, 74 tel 902 491 616, sixt.es)

A car is handy for making extensive trips beyond Barcelona (especially along the Costa Brava or if you want the liberty to move where and when you want), but not essential, as many day excursions are easily done by local transportation. A car in Barcelona itself is more trouble than it's worth (and a liability, as rental cars are frequently broken into and parking is a nightmare). It is cheaper to rent a car before you arrive in Barcelona.

Driving Regulations & Conventions

An international driver's license is not required for short-term visitors; your national license will suffice. When driving, carry all car documents (including insurance papers and at least a photocopy of your passport). Do not leave these documents (or anything else) in the car when you park.

Barcelona traffic may appear chaotic, but most drivers respect most rules. Locals have the habit of moving off at red lights just before they turn green—as though the extra second or two will help. Barcelona is full of motorcycles and mopeds. Watch these anarchic beasts, as their riders frequently run red lights and overtake on the right (your blind side). Parking illegally in Barcelona is commonplace, but the parking police can be ruthless. If you get towed away, call the Dipòsit Municipal (car pound; tel 901 513 151)—the staff may not speak English—to find out where to pick up the car (there are pounds scattered across town). The longer you leave your car in the pound, the more you will pay to release it—and the fees are high.

In built-up areas, the speed limit is between 30 kph (18 mph) and 50 kph (30 mph). Within city limits the maximum is 80 kph (50 mph), rising to 100 kph (60 mph) on major roads and 120 kph (75 mph) on autopistas and autovías (toll and toll-free motorways). Vehicles already in traffic circles have the right of way. The blood-alcohol limit is 0.5 g/liter of blood, and police checks are increasing. Motorcyclists must use headlights at all times. Crash helmets are obligatory on bikes of 125 cc or more.

Car Breakdown

Rental car companies will have their own emergency contact numbers. If you are driving your own car, make sure your insurers provide you with a number.

Public Transportation

Barcelona's buses, metro, trams, and suburban trains were integrated into a single ticket system in 2001 under the Autoritat del Transport Metropolità (ATM). The network extends well beyond the city in six zones, but for most people, all of interest is within zone 1. A single ride costs €2.15. Targetes are multiple-trip transport tickets sold at most city-center metro stations and some newspaper stands and can be shared. Targeta T-10 (€10.30) gives you 10 rides. You can catch a combination of metro, bus, tram and train within 1 hour and 15 minutes from the time you validate each ride on boarding. Targeta T-DIA (€7.60) gives unlimited travel for a day. The Targeta T-50/30 is for 50 trips within 30 days and costs €42.50. The T-Mes is a monthly pass offering unlimited journeys for the cost of €52.75.

For public transportation information, you can call tel 010 or tel 93 205 15 15 (for FGC trains). TMB, the public transit authority, (902 075 027), runs four customer service centers: in Estació Sants (the mainline Renfe station) and the metro stops of Universitat, Diagonal, and Sagrada Família.

Metro

Operates: 5 a.m.–midnight Sun. through Thurs.; 5 a.m.–2 a.m. Fri.; 5 a.m.–5 a.m. Sat. and public holidays. The metro has eight lines, numbered and color-coded, and it is the simplest way to get around town. Take care of your pockets on the metro, as pickpockets have been known to empty them, especially in a rush-hour crush.

FGC (Ferrocarrils de la Generalitat de Catalunya)

Operates: 5 a.m.–11 or 11:30 p.m. Sun. through Thurs., and 5 a.m.–2 a.m. Fri. and Sat. This is a supplementary suburban train system with a couple of lines through central Barcelona useful for uptown destinations.

Rodalies/Cercanías
Operates: 5 a.m.–11:30 p.m. (some lines close earlier), stopping at Sants, Plaça de Catalunya, Passeig de Gràcia, and some other stations. Run by Renfe, these trains fan out from the city to towns such as Sitges and Vilafranca del Penedès, as well as the Maresme beaches.

Bus
TMB (daytime service) Operates: 5 a.m.–11 p.m. (some services start later and end earlier)
TMB Nitbus (night service)
Operates: 11 p.m.–5 a.m. (some services end earlier)
The city is covered by an extensive bus network, although in general the metro is a faster and more convenient way of moving around. The night buses are a clear exception to that rule, but operate on limited routes, all of which start or pass through Plaça de Catalunya apart from NO (Pg. de Colom).

Taxis
Barcelona's black-and-yellow cabs are reasonably abundant and, by European standards, good value. Generally, taxi drivers follow the rules and turn on the meter. Note that the final fare may have extras thrown in (for instance, for large items of luggage). The rate to the airport is supposed to be standard (around €27). Fares go up marginally between 9 p.m. and 7 a.m. on weekends and on holidays. You can hail a cab on the street or pick one up at cab ranks. Look for a green light on the roof, which means the cab is free. Sometimes you'll also see a *lliure* or *libre* sign in the windshield (respectively Catalan and Spanish

for "unoccupied"). You can call a taxi at tel 93 225 00 00, 93 330 03 00, 93 300 11 00, or 93 420 80 88 for wheelchairs. General information is available at tel 010.

Tours & Organized Sightseeing
Bicycle Tours
You can get on your bike and indulge in any of several two-wheeled tours of the old center of town, La Barceloneta, and other parts of the city. Several organizations offer this sort of thing. They include Bike Tours Barcelona *(Carrer de l'Esparteria 3, tel 93 268 21 05, biketoursbarcelona.com)* (see sidebar p. 165).

Boat Tours
Forty-minute boat trips with the Golondrinas service *(tel 93 442 31 06)* chug out to the breakwater *(rompeolas)* and lighthouse *(faro)* from Moll de les Drassanes in front of the Monument a Colom (€7). The same people also organize a round trip to the Fòrum (€14.80, 90 mins.) on a glass-bottom catamaran (not that there is all that much to see down there!). The frequency of trips depends upon the season as well as the demand.

Bus Tours
The Bus Turístic service covers two circuits (37 stops) linking virtually all the major tourist sights (a third circuit of seven stops is added in the summer). It is not a tour as such but a handy way of covering the sights. You hop on and off as you please. Tourist offices, TMB offices, and many hotels have leaflets explaining the system. Tickets, available on the bus, are €27 for one day's unlimited rides, or €35 for two consecutive days. Find discounts online *(bcnshop.barcelona turisme.com)* plus details of other organized tours. Frequency of buses varies from 5 to 25 minutes,

depending on the season, from 9 a.m. to 8 p.m. Tickets entitle you to discounts on entry fees to more than 25 attractions, the Tramvia Blau, funiculars, and cable cars, as well as shopping discounts. To join daily city tours (half or full day) contact Barcelona City Tour (Balmes 5, *tel 93 317 64 54*) or Pullmantur (Gran Via de les Corts Catalanes 645, *tel 902 240 070*).

Independent Sightseeing
Really the best way to enjoy Barcelona is to get around it yourself and at your own pace. The metro and bus systems make it easy to cover a lot of ground, although inevitably some shoe leather will be involved, too. Be careful in pedestrian crossings, because many drivers seem to ignore their existence.

Walking Tours
A walking tour of the Barri Gòtic starts at 9:30 a.m. Sun.–Mon. (in English) at the Plaça Sant Jaume tourist office (Ciutat 2) for €15.50. The main tourist board also has similar tours covering modernista sights, walking in Picasso's footsteps, new architecture and a gourmet tour of specialty shops and markets *(barcelonaturisme.com)*.

PRACTICAL ADVICE
Communications
Post Offices
Main branch: Plaça d'Antoni López, 08002, tel 902 197197, metro: Línia 4 (Jaume I or Barceloneta), bus: 17, 19, 40, 45.
Open: Mon.–Sat. 8:30 a.m.– 10 p.m., Sun. noon–10 p.m.
Local branches: Mon.–Fri. 8:30 a.m.–2 p.m. A handful open Mon.–Fri. 8:30 a.m.–8:30 p.m., Sat. 9:30 a.m.–1 p.m.

Known in Catalan as *Correus* (*Correos* in Spanish), the Spanish postal service has branches across the city, although surprisingly few in central Barcelona. This is partly because, for ordinary mail, you can also buy stamps from *estancos* (tobacconists). Look for the yellow-on-maroon *tabacos* signs. Anything larger (like parcels) will oblige you to make a trip to the post office. Mail forwarded to you at the central post office should be addressed to you at Lista de Correos, 08080 Barcelona. Take your passport along as ID to pick up any mail.

Yellow *bústies/buzones* (mailboxes) are located at post offices and sprinkled liberally across town. Addresses in Barcelona can be quite complex, reflecting the location of apartments in various parts of any given building. "C/Carme 14, 3°D Int." probably looks utterly indecipherable. It means 14 Carme Street, 3rd floor, right hand *(dreta/derecha)*, interior (where there are several sets of floors, some might be well inside off the street and look onto an internal courtyard).

Telephones

All Spanish phone numbers have nine digits. The first two or three digits (93 in the case of Barcelona) indicate the province but must always be dialed, even if you are calling from next door. Numbers beginning with 6 are mobile phone numbers and suitably expensive. Toll-free numbers start with 900.

To call Spain from the United States, dial 011-34 (international dial out and Spanish country code) and the nine-digit number.

It is still possible to call from telephone booths in Spain, though increasingly hard to find one that works as they are rarely used now. Use coins or (preferably) buy a *tarjeta telefónica* (phone card), available in tobacconists and post offices. When you pick up the receiver, wait for a few seconds and then insert the card; the balance will be displayed on the screen, at which point you can dial your number. Increasingly all sorts of cheap-rate

(or supposedly cheap-rate) cards are available for long-distance calling to destinations outside Spain. Using your own mobile devices abroad depends on individual companies. Check out costs of roaming before traveling. Wi-Fi points are available across the city, even in some parks, or rent a "wifivox," portable internet supplier *(tel 937 370 0055, wifivox.com)*.

The access code for international calls from Spain is 00. Dial this, the country code, the area code, and the number you want. To make an international call from Spain, dial 00, followed by the country code (1 for the United States and Canada; 44 for U.K.), the area code (omitting the initial 0 if there is one), and the number. Calling home from Spain is easy. From public phones you can use coins or phone cards (€6 or €12) available from tobacconists and occasionally from newsstands. They also often sell a variety of cheap international phone cards. In areas like El Raval and Poble Sec there are many call centers, which can also work out more cheaply. Internet centers are increasingly equipped for voice calls (Skype and similar VOIP servers). You can dial free to an operator in your own country to make collect calls—remember to pick up the number before leaving home.

American long-distance operators include: **AT&T**: tel 990011; **Sprint**: tel 990013; and **MCI**: tel 990014.
Spanish directory assistance, tel 11811
International assistance, tel 11825 Services are charged.

Electricity

Spanish circuits (mostly) use 220 volts. American appliances need adaptor plugs, and those that operate on 110 volts will also need a transformer. These can be

bought in Barcelona but are easier to buy before you leave home.

Etiquette & Customs

It is not a bad idea to learn a few polite phrases in Spanish. No one expects you to know any Catalan though it will go down well if you try, even if many (perhaps more than half) people living in Barcelona are *not* Catalans. *Buenos días* (good day) and *buenas tardes* (good afternoon/evening—used after lunch) are standard greetings when entering and leaving shops. *Hola!* (Hi!) is also common. On leaving, it is customary to say goodbye. In Barcelona most people, Catalans or not, use the Catalan *Adéu!* (rather than the Spanish *¡Adiós!*). It may seem strange, given that the above greetings are more or less mandatory, that in Barcelona people are less concerned about their pleases and thank-yous. Overuse of *por favor* and *gracias* will be a sure sign that you are not a local!

Holidays

Some of these public holidays are celebrated in Barcelona or Catalonia alone; others are national: Jan. 1, Jan. 6, Good Friday, Easter Monday, May 1, Pasqua Granada (Monday after Pentecost Sunday), June 24, Aug. 15, Sept. 11, Sept. 24, Oct. 12, Dec. 6, Dec. 8, Dec. 25, & Dec. 26.

Media

Newspapers

Most *quióscos* (newsstands) in central Barcelona sell a broad range of English-language newspapers and magazines. In addition to the *International New York Times, Time,* and *Newsweek,* you will find a host of British dailies. Heading the list of Spanish national dailies is the middle-ground *El País,* excellent for broad coverage of foreign and local news. *El País* also has an excellent

English version online (elpais.com). Others include the conservative ABC and the right-wing paper, El Mundo. Important local papers are La Vanguardia and El Periódico (published in Spanish and Catalan editions). The main Catalan nationalist paper is El Punt Avui.

Radio

You can tune into the national network, Radio Nacional de España (RNE), on several stations: RNE 1 (738 AM; 88.3 FM in Barcelona) for current affairs; RNE 3 (98.6 FM) for jazz, rock, and world music; RNE 5 (576 AM; 99 FM) for sports and entertainment, and Catalunya Radio (101.5 FM) for classical. Among the most listened-to rock and popular music stations are 40 Principales (93.9 FM), Onda Cero (93.5 FM), and Cadena 100 (100 FM).

Television

Eight standard TV channels are available in Barcelona. TVE1 and La 2 are run by Spain's state television broadcaster, Televisión Española. There are five independent national stations: Antena 3, Tele 5, Cuatro, La Sexta, and Canal Plus (only available if the TV owner subscribes to Canal Plus). The Catalan regional government station is TV-3, which includes Canal 33 with interesting cultural programs and documentaries.

Money Matters

Interchange, La Rambla 74, tel 93 342 73 11. Metro: Línia 3 [Liceu]. For American Express clients only.

Barcelona is full of banks, in most of which you can change foreign currency (look for signs saying canvi or cambio, or displays with the day's exchange rates). As a rule, you are better off changing money in the banks, but if you need

cash outside of banking hours, currency exchanges abound in the center, especially along La Rambla. Always ask about the commission and confirm the day's exchange rate. Note that currency exchanges advertising "no commission" usually offer an inferior rate.

The currency of Spain is the euro, as in many other European Union member countries. Euros (€) come in coins of 1, 2, 5, 10, 20, and 50 cents and 1 and 2 euros. Bills are 5, 10, 20, 50, 100, 200, and 500 euros.

The best sources of currency with a credit/debit card are ATMs (caixer automàtic/cajero automático), outside many banks. Most major cards (Visa, MasterCard, etc.) will work, but you should check with your bank or credit card supplier that your PIN is valid overseas. ATMs offer information in various languages. Cash advances, whether obtained over the counter or by ATM, incur a transaction charge.

Opening Times

Bank opening times tend to vary considerably, but as a rule of thumb you should try to do your banking between 8 a.m. and 2 p.m. Mon.–Fri. Some banks stay open until 4 p.m. Virtually all close by 2 p.m. in the summer months.

Bar hours are more flexible, and the distinction between where you have a cup of coffee or settle in for a night's drinking is vague. Many bars aimed at daytime and after-work customers will be closed by 10 p.m. Many in the center stay open later, and in alcohol-oriented bars it is possible to get coffee, too. Restaurants are generally open 1 p.m.–4 p.m. and 9 p.m.–midnight.

Store hours vary, but many open Mon.–Fri. 9 or 10 a.m.–8 p.m., often closing around 2–4 p.m. for lunch. Many open on Saturdays, too, but sometimes only until 2 p.m. Department stores, malls and chains open until 9:30 or 10 p.m.

Time Differences

Like most of Europe from the last Sunday of October through the last Sunday of March, Barcelona is one hour ahead of Greenwich Mean Time; for the rest of the year (summer time) it is two hours ahead. If it's midnight in Barcelona, it is 6 p.m. in New York City and 3 p.m. in California.

Tipping

Spain does not have a big tipping culture, but it's usual to leave a little cash (5 percent is quite sufficient) if service is not included. Locals leave change at bars para el bote (for the common tips fund). You can tip hotel porters and maids at the end of your visit.

Travelers With Disabilities

Barcelona is improving quickly for wheelchair-bound, visual or hearing impaired visitors, who in general will still need to be accompanied. Only Línia 2 of the metro has elevator access to all stations, along with a few stations on other lines for the moment. Trains and many buses are accessible. You can reserve specially adapted taxis by calling 93 420 80 88. A good website on the subject is barcelona-access.com for travel, sites and hotels that are adapted to the needs of the disabled.

Visitor Information
Internet Sites

Turisme de Barcelona (barcelona turisme.com) is the city's official tourist office site, with interesting listings on what's going on in Barcelona and up-to-the-minute info on what to visit, as well as apps for do it yourself guides. The official site of the Ajuntament de Barcelona, the city's town hall (bcn.cat), is full of interesting information on the city, including zoomable maps and a virtual flight over the city. Freebie

English language magazine *Metro-politan (barcelona-metropolitan .com)* can be picked up in bars and shops. It's full of current Barcelona news and issues. The Generalitat de Catalunya's site *(gencat.net)* contains some interesting background material on the region in English.

Tourist Offices

Oficina d'Informació de Turisme de Barcelona (main city tourist office), Plaça de Catalunya 17-S (underground), tel 93 285 38 34. Metro: Catalunya. Open daily 8:30 a.m.–8:30 p.m. Aside from stacks of city information and a souvenir shop, you can book accommodations and theater tickets. A branch office operates in the Ajuntament (Town Hall), Plaça de Sant Jaume. (Carrer Ciutat 2) Metro: Jaume I. Open Mon.–Fri. 8:30 a.m.–8 p.m., Sat. 9 a.m.–7 p.m. Sun. 9 a.m.–2 p.m.

Palau Robert (Catalonia tourist office), Passeig de Gràcia 107, tel 93 238 80 91. Metro: Diagonal. Open Mon.–Sat. 10 a.m.–8 p.m., Sun. 10 a.m.–2:30 p.m.

There are other tourist offices at Estació Sants train station and the airport. For information on the rest of Spain visit tourspain.es.

EMERGENCIES
Consulates

Canadian Consulate, Plaça de Catalunya 9, 1° 2ª, tel 93 270 36 14, Metro: Línies: 1 & 3
United Kingdom Consulate, Avinguda Diagonal 477, tel 93 366 62 21, metro: Línia 3, bus: H8, 6, 7, 15, 33, 34, & 68
United States Consulate, Passeig de la Reina Elisenda de Montcada 23–25, tel 93 280 22 27, FGC: Reina Elisenda, bus: 22, 64, 68 & 75
Embassies & consulates in Madrid:
Canada, Torre Espacio, Paseo de la Castellana, 259D, tel 93 382 84 00, www.canadainternational.gc.ca
United Kingdom, Torre Espacio, Paseo de la Castellana, 259D, tel 91

714 63 00, ukinspain.fco.gov.uk
United States, Calle de Serrano 75, tel 91 587 23 03, embusa.es

Crime & Police

Barcelona is not a dangerous city. In few American cities could you wander the downtown streets with so little fear of anything serious going awry. But pickpockets thrive. Leave any valuables you do not immediately need in your hotel. Documents, credit cards, and cash you don't intend to spend immediately should be carried in money belts or shoulder wallets worn *under* your clothes. Wear bags, cameras, and the like across your body and keep a hand on them in crowded areas or in bars and restaurants. Be careful of anyone getting unnecessarily close to your personal space, and be wary of people who simply start talking to you in the street, because there is a good chance their pals are hovering nearby to take advantage of your distraction. If you are robbed or lose valuables, you will need a police report for insurance.

Emergency Phone Numbers

General emergencies (all services), tel 112
Guàrdia Urbana (local police), tel 092
Mossos d'Esquadra (regional Catalan police force that has taken over many duties of the Policía Nacional and Guardia Civil), tel 112
Policía Nacional (national police), tel 091
Guardia Civil (national military police, highway patrol, & other tasks), tel 062
Fire, tel 080
Ambulance, tel 061
Hospital de la Santa Creu i de Sant Pau, tel 93 291 90 00, Carrer de Sant Quinti, 89
Hospital Clínic i Provincial, tel 93 227 54 00, Carrer de Villarroel 170

There are 24-hour pharmacies at Carrer d'Aribau 62 and Passeig de Gràcia 26. Other pharmacies alternate on shifts (9 a.m.–10 p.m.).

What to Do in a Car Accident

Keep calm and alert! For a minor accident, you and the other driver involved need to get each other's details (name, passport/ID, car registration, both sides' insurers, and if possible a diagram indicating what happened, along with details of where and when the incident occurred). If you have a rental car, the firm may have provided forms on which to do this, although they will probably be in Spanish. If an amicable agreement on the exchange of this information looks unlikely, get the registration number of the other vehicle so that you can report the accident to the police and insurers. In a serious accident, you will have to await the arrival of an officer of the law.

Lost Property

Objetos perdidos (Ajuntament), Pl. Carles Pii Sumyer 8–10t 9. Metro: Línia 1 & 3, Pl. de Catalunya, tel 010. Open Mon.–Fri. 9 a.m.–2 p.m. If you leave anything in a taxi, tel 902 101564. In the case of things lost on the metro, try the TMB office Metro Diagonal Línies 3 & 5 Airport lost and found, tel 93 259 644 (Terminal 1).
Lost credit/debit cards
American Express, tel 902 375 637
Visa, tel 900 991 124
MasterCard, tel 900 971 231
Diners Club, tel 917 015 900
If you lose documents, credit cards, or other things, you'll need a police report (denuncia) for insurance/ replacement purposes. Go to the Mossos d'Esquadra station at Carrer Nou de la Rambla 80, where you should find an English speaker. Be prepared for long lines.

Hotels & Restaurants

As long as Barcelona remains the flavor of the month for many travelers in Europe, you can expect competition for rooms and restaurant tables (especially on weekends) to be tough. It is always best to reserve ahead if you can. Many hotels and restaurants accept all major cards, although cheaper eateries and *pensiones* (small family-run hotels) frequently do not take them at all.

Hotels

Hotels in Barcelona (listed here by area, price, then in alphabetical order) have multiplied over the past years to meet demand, which has taken some of the pressure off when looking for a room. Nevertheless, reservations are a good idea, and most hotels offer good deals if you book online. Alternatively an acceptable credit card number should hold a room for you. The abbreviations used for credit cards are: AE (American Express), DC (Diners Club), MC (MasterCard), V (Visa). If you leave things too late, you might find yourself lodging a long way from the center.

The hotel building boom has taken some of the upward pressure off room prices, too. For many years, inflation was crazy, but it has slowed. Lodging in Barcelona remains cheaper than it is in many major European cities.

The wave of hotel building has led to a proliferation of charming and boutique hotels, filling a prior gap in the market. Otherwise, there are plenty of comfortable could-be-anywhere places. We have also included a handful of the better pensiones for those looking for good but modest lodgings with a family touch. Rooms may come without private baths—the prices listed are for those with bathrooms en suite.

Barcelona is one of the noisiest cities in Europe, but many hotels have off-street rooms where the racket is greatly reduced, and double-glazing and air-conditioning can help. Those who are disturbed by noise should consider bringing earplugs.

Street parking is never easy to find in Barcelona and virtually impossible in the oldest parts of the city (where many streets are pedestrian-only). Many of the better hotels have limited garage space, but in some cases where a hotel is listed as having parking, the garage is not actually on hotel property but close by. In the Old City in particular, most hotels are reasonably close to public parking. If you plan to have a vehicle, ask about parking when making reservations.

Grading System: Hotels are officially categorized by the Generalitat into three divisions: Hotels and Hotel-Residencias, Hostals and Hostal-Residencias, and Pensiones. Stars are awarded within each division according to different criteria, so a two-star hotel in the Hotel category is quite different from a two-star Pension.

Hotels (H) and Hotel-Residencias (HR) are awarded from one to five stars, depending on the number of rooms with full private bathrooms, TV, air-conditioning, and other facilities. Rooms in the hotels listed here have their own bathroom unless otherwise noted.

Hostals (HS) and Hostal-Residencias (HSR) tend to be more modest, and may be family run. Stars range from one to three. Pensiones (P) get one or two stars and are generally the simplest of establishments; you'll see plenty of these around.

The official star-rating system is not a particularly reliable guide to quality, and room rates are not regulated according to star ratings. Many hotels opt to stay in a lower category for tax purposes. Prices include sales tax (IVA) and in some cases Continental or buffet breakfast (which is often compulsory).

Restaurants

Restaurants in this directory are listed by area, price, and then in alphabetical order. Reservations are generally recommended, particularly Thursdays to Saturdays. You can often get away with just turning up on other days. Many of the restaurants listed below serve Catalan food and/or a mix of Spanish regional cuisine. Some offer more international and Mediterranean menus. Foreign cuisines are rapidly gaining acceptance in Barcelona, and it has become possible to eat good Japanese, Thai, Indian, and other food. It's still a drop in the ocean compared with London or New York, but the options are there should you feel the need.

Typically, a Catalan meal can consist of a starter, main course (usually meat or fish), and dessert. Always ask if the main comes with vegetables (or anything!), the *guarnició*, or whether this has to be ordered separately. The starter may be considered your opportunity for ingesting vegetables. There are no hard-and-fast rules, and you are not obliged to eat more than one course if you do not wish to.

At lunchtime many restaurants offer a *menú del día*, a set meal consisting of all courses and a drink. Frequently such meals are solid rather than gourmet attractions, but they tend to be good value, and if the budget is looking frayed, you could make lunch your main meal of the day; it is easy to eat well for €9 to €13 (coffee is usually extra).

Smoking is now banned in bars and restaurants in Barcelona giving rise to more outdoor tables, often heated in the winter.

Dining Hours: Lunch is from 2 p.m. to 4 p.m., although in many establishments you can start earlier (1 p.m.) if hunger pangs have become extreme (you probably won't be eating with many locals, though). Dinner is roughly from 9 p.m. to midnight. Some restaurants close their kitchens as early as 11 p.m. and some remain open until 1 a.m. Again, should you feel the need to eat earlier, there is generally no problem in the center of town, where eateries with an eye for the tourist buck (but often shunned by locals) are happy to have you seated at just about anytime you want. If you can, adjust to the local eating timetable, as the atmosphere of a meal amid people who live in Barcelona is part of the pleasure.

Closures & Holidays: Most restaurants shut for a day or two (often Sunday night and Monday, but there are no hard-and-fast rules) during the week. Some also close at Easter, over Christmas, and for anything from two to four weeks in August. This can change rapidly and radically, especially in the case of the holiday periods, so it is best to be prepared for the occasional closed door (even if not indicated below) in these peak holiday periods.

Tipping: Service charges are occasionally, but rarely, included in the check (sales tax, or IVA, is always included). Spaniards tend to be somewhat restrained about tipping. If service has not been included and you feel a tip is warranted, customarily 5 percent is deemed sufficient.

BARRI GÒTIC

During the day, the epicenter of Barcelona overflows with people, both locals, and tourists. At night parts of it become quiet, while others hum with the activity of

restaurants and bars. As in other areas of the old city, you need to be aware that some streets are potentially risky during the hours of darkness.

Hotels

D.O. PLAÇA REIAL
$$$$$ ***
PLAÇA REIAL 1
TEL 93 481 36 66
hoteldoreial.es

This new gastronomic-boutique hotel with designer details is located in an elegant 19th-century building right on the majestic Plaça Reial. You can breakfast on its outdoor terrace under the arches watching this iconic square come to life and dine in the exclusion of its rooftop. It is worth putting up with the square's ebullient nightlife to enjoy such a privileged location, or you can pop down and join in the fun.

ⓘ 18 🅿 Nearby 🚇 Metro: Línia 3 (Liceu) 🛗
♿ All major cards

🏨 MERCER
$$$$$ ***
LLEDÓ 7
TEL 93 310 74 80
mercerbarcelona.com

An exquisite newcomer in a renovated Gothic palace, with remnants of the Roman wall still visible, stylish interior, and rooftop pool. Pure indulgence hidden down a narrow medieval lane.

ⓘ 28 🚇 Metro: Línia 4 (Jaume I) 🛗 ♿ All major cards

🏨 COLÓN
$$$$ **
AVINGUDA DE LA CATEDRAL 7
TEL 93 301 14 04
colonhotelbarcelona.com

This is the classic traditional choice hotel in Barri Gòtic. The views alone, which extend across the square to the Catedral, are worth the cost. If you are fortunate enough to get one of the top-floor rooms with

a terrace, you will be in heaven. However, if you end up with one of the back rooms you'll be looking onto nothing much at all. Decor varies from room to room.

ⓘ 141 🅿 🚇 Metro: Línia 4 (Jaume I) 🛗 ♿ All major cards

SOMETHING SPECIAL

🏨 NERI
$$$$ **
CARRER DE SANT SEVER 5
TEL 93 304 06 55
hotelneri.com

Broad stone arches, carefully chosen timber furnishings, and the latest in design touches (like flat-screen plasma TVs) make this a stunning central option in a 17th-century palace. Each room offers an individual color scheme and decor. Have a relaxing snooze on the sundeck when sightseeing becomes too much.

ⓘ 22 🚇 Metro: Línia 3 (Liceu) 🛗 🚭 ♿ All major cards

🏨 JARDÍ
**$$ *
PLAÇA DE SANT JOSEP ORIOL 1

TEL 93 301 59 00
eljardi-barcelona.com
The front rooms in this
delightfully located hotel make
it a popular spot. If street noise
bothers you, try to get a room
off the square.

📍 40 🚇 Metro: Línia 3 (Liceu)
🔁 From 2nd floor
💳 All major cards

🏨 LEVANTE
$ **

BAIXADA DE SANT MIQUEL 2
TEL 93 317 95 65
hostallevante.com
This area is littered with hostels
and cheap hotels, but this is one
of the brighter ones. A great
range of rooms of varying size
and quality are available. If a
little street noise doesn't bother
you, the doubles with balconies
are the best.

📍 50 🚇 Metro: Línia 3 (Liceu)
🔁 💳 All major cards

Restaurants

🍴 CAFÈ DE L'ACADÈMIA
$$$

CARRER DE LLEDÓ 1
TEL 93 319 82 53
A tiny restaurant squeezed
into a magnificent 13th-
century house that overlooks
an equally quaint square, this
spot has become a standing
favorite with the local left.
Traditional Catalan dishes have
been given a creative, delicious
twist. An outdoor table in
Plaça de Sant Just on a sum-
mer night is a treat.

🪑 50 🚇 Metro: Línia 4
(Jaume I) 🕐 Closed Sat.–Sun.
& 2 weeks in Aug. 💳 AE, MC, V

SOMETHING SPECIAL

🍴 PLA
$$$

CARRER DE BELLAFILA 5
TEL 93 412 65 52
An inviting decor with timber
tables and muted lighting will
lure you in here for a romantic
dinner of fun fusion. You can
expect options from adapted

Asian dishes through to cheerful variations of local faves, such
as the cod in green apple sauce.
The menu changes regularly.

🪑 60 🚇 Metro: Línia 3
(Liceu) 🕐 Closed L daily
💳 MC, V

🍴 AGUT
$$–$$$

CARRER D'EN GIGNÀS 16
TEL 93 315 17 09
A classic of Catalan cooking in
the labyrinth of alleys at the
lower end of Barri Gòtic, Agut
has a traditional, warm atmosphere, its walls lined with
paintings from appreciative
clients in the 1950s and 60s.
It offers a variety of meat and
seafood and is known for its
bacallà (cod).

🪑 85 🚇 Metro: Línia 4
(Jaume I) 🕐 Closed D Sun.–
Mon. 💳 All major cards

🍴 CAN CULLERETES
$$

CARRER D'EN QUINTANA 5
TEL 93 317 30 22
Founded in 1786, this is
Barcelona's oldest restaurant.
Although a little stuffy, the
steadfastly Catalan menu does
not disappoint, and the dark,
timber decor and old-style,
poker-faced service are a treat
in themselves.

🪑 170 🚇 Metro: Línia 3
(Liceu) 🕐 Closed D Sun., Mon.,
& 3 weeks in July 💳 MC, V

🍴 LOS CARACOLES
$$

CARRER DELS ESCUDELLERS 14
TEL 93 301 20 41
Perennially busy and serving
guests since the 19th century,
this is a remarkable locale, all
timber and wine barrels and
garlic hanging on the walls. You
wait at the bar for a table out
in the back, where you will be
served all sorts of things ranging
from rice specialties to snails.

🪑 230 🚇 Metro: Línia 3
(Drassanes) 💳 All major cards

SOMETHING SPECIAL

🍴 COMETACINC
$$

CARRER DEL COMETA 5
TEL 93 310 15 58
A duplex dining area in medi-
eval obscurity. Just as the
cuisine crosses all established
boundaries, so the feel of the
place is an almost disconcert-
ing mix. A vibrant, urban staff
whisks about the designer
settings delivering anything
from copious salads and Thai
options to couscous and excel-
lent carpaccio.

🪑 75 🚇 Metro: Línia 4
(Jaume 1) 🕐 Closed L daily
💳 MC, V

🍴 EL PARAGUAYO
$$

CARRER DEL PARC 1
TEL 93 302 14 41
For a taste of South America,
pop in here and tuck into slabs
of succulent meat, served on
wooden tablets with a slightly
spicy or herb gravy and drink
the robust house red, of which
they give you a free taste when
you're seated. The atmosphere
is buzzy, and the caramel dessert, *dulce de leche,* satisfies any
sweet tooth.

🪑 64 🚇 Metro: Línia 3
(Drassanes) 🕐 Closed Mon.
💳 All major cards

■ LA RAMBLA & EL RAVAL

Barcelona's most famous
boulevard, La Rambla, is lined
with hotels ranging from cheap
student dives and century-old
stalwarts to the modern comforts of places like Le Meridien.
A couple of good hotels can
be found in the El Raval area,
too. El Raval also hides some
fine eating options. Avoid La
Rambla itself, though, as the
restaurants tend to be tourist
traps serving low-quality food
with the one exception of La
Boqueria market.

Hotels

🏨 HOTEL 1898

$$$$$ ★★★★★

LA RAMBLA 109

TEL 93 552 95 52

hotel1898.com

Right on the action of La Rambla stands this graceful old building that in colonial days was the seat of the Philippines Tobacco Company. Attentive service is a hallmark of this place, where rooms vary a lot in size but come with plenty of modern comforts. Furniture is tasteful and the rain-forest showers a dream. Some suites have private indoor pools.

🛈 169 🅿 🚇 Metro: Línies 1 (Catalunya) & 3 (Liceu) ⬍ 🛗 🛏 🍽 🅰 All major cards

🏨 LE MERIDIEN

$$$$$ ★★★★★

LA RAMBLA 111

TEL 93 318 62 00

lemeridienbarcelona.com

One of the best addresses along La Rambla, Le Meridien has managed to hold its own against tough new competition. The rooms are luxurious and feature rain-forest showers and in-house movies for those who need a break from sightseeing.

🛈 231 🅿 🚇 Metro: Línia 3 (Catalunya or Liceu) ⬍ 🛗 🛏 🍽 🅰 All major cards

🏨 CASA CAMPER

$$$$ ★★★★

CARRER D'ELISABETS 11

TEL 93 342 62 80

casacamper.com

This eccentric designer boutique stop has an intriguing room setup: On one side of a corridor are your sleeping quarters, while on the other side is your sitting room, complete with a hammock if sitting seems too strenuous. Furniture is rigorously designer hip, from the local style mecca, Vinçon.

🛈 25 🚇 Metro: Línies 1 & 3 (Catalunya) ⬍ 🛗 🛏 🅰 All major cards

🏨 MESÓN CASTILLA

$$ ★★

CARRER DE VALLDONZELLA 5

TEL 93 318 21 82

hotelmesoncastilla.com

Modernisme creeps into the interior decoration in this hotel, particularly the stained glass and murals in the public areas. The rooms are cozily decorated, and the location is comparatively quiet. The breakfast room looks out on an interior courtyard.

🛈 57 🅿 🚇 Metro: Línies 1 & 2 (Universitat) ⬍ 🛗 🅰 All major cards

🏨 SANT AGUSTÍ

$$ ★★★

PLAÇA DE SANT AGUSTÍ 3

TEL 93 318 16 58

hotelsa.com

Located just off La Rambla on a pleasant square, the hotel has been refurbished a couple of times and offers comfortable, understated, but modernized rooms, most with views across the square.

🛈 75 🚇 Metro: Línia 3 (Liceu) ⬍ 🛗 🅰 All major cards

🏨 CONTINENTAL

$–$$ ★★★

LA RAMBLA 138

TEL 93 301 25 70

hotelcontinental.com

One of Barcelona's once grand hotels, the Continental offers a touch of old-world charm at low rates. Ideally located, try for rooms overlooking La Rambla. All come with cable, safe, refrigerator, and microwave.

🛈 35 🚇 Metro: Línies 1 & 3 (Catalunya) ⬍ 🛗 🅰 All major cards

🏨 HOTEL PENINSULAR

$ ★

CARRER DE SANT PAU 34

TEL 93 302 31 38

hotelpeninsular.net

In business as a hotel since the 1880s, this place was once a monastery. The rooms were monk's cells, and indeed they remain rather simple affairs to this day. They are, however, moderately priced and the location sets you in the heart of the action, barely a leap from La Rambla. The plant-filled atrium is the hotel's calling card.

🛈 59 🚇 Metro: Línia 3 (Liceu) ⬍ 🛗 🅰 All major cards

Restaurants

SOMETHING SPECIAL

🍴 CASA LEOPOLDO

$$$–$$$$

CARRER DE SANT RAFAEL 24

TEL 93 441 30 14

Before they carved out the Rambla del Raval boulevard in 2000, this long-term classic was hard to find, deep in the heart of the dingiest Raval. A timber-beamed ceiling hovers above the well-spaced tables and colorful ceramic tiles. The fish hot pot (*cazuela de pescado*) is tempting.

🪑 140 🚇 Metro: Línies 2 (Sant Antoni) & 3 (Liceu) 🕐 Closed D Sun., Mon., & Aug. 🅰 All major cards

🍴 BACARO

$$$

CARRER DE JERUSALEM 6

TEL 695 79 60 66

Tucked in behind La Boqueria market, this buzzing new Venetian restaurant is small but packed with atmosphere. Its charming hosts/waiters have brought new life to an old local bar and enthusiastically run around making clients feel at home and serving excellent specialties from Venice, like *sardinas en saor* (sweet and sour).

🚇 Metro: Línia 3 (Liceu) 🕐 Closed Sun. 🅰 All major cards

🍴 BAR PINOTXO

$–$$

MERCAT DE LA BOQUERIA

TEL 93 317 17 31

Mercat de la Boqueria is blessed with several busy food bars, where market workers, local business men, and tourists crowd for breakfast tapas, drinks, and more substantial dishes. The food is fresh from the stalls around you, and the atmosphere always bustling. One of the locals' longtime favorites is Bar Pinotxo, near the main market entrance off La Rambla.

🍴 10 🚇 Metro: Línia 3 (Liceu) 🕐 Closed D daily, all Sun., & Aug. 🚫

🍴 ELISABETS
$
CARRER DE ELISABETS 2
TEL 93 317 58 26
A great spot just off La Rambla for a down-to-earth classic *menú del día*, with three courses and a pitcher of wine, which is excellent value. Sit at marble tables and rub shoulders with people dropping in from their offices so you feel like a local. Tapas are offered only in the evening.

🍴 45 🚇 Metro: Línies 1 & 3 (Catalunya) 🕐 Closed Sun. & holidays 🚫 All major cards

🍴 GRANJA VIADER
$
CARRER D'EN XUCLÁ 4
TEL 93 318 34 86
Step back to more innocent times in this century-old *granja* (a kind of milk bar), where the Viader family sells delicatessen goodies. Most come to sit down at the little marble tables and admire the beautiful tile floor and old-fashioned decor while sipping on a thick hot chocolate. The same with whipped cream is sinful and is called a *suís*.

🍴 75 🚇 Metro: Línia 3 (Liceu) 🕐 Closed Sun. 🚫 All major cards

🍴 ORGANIC
$
CARRER DE LA JUNTA DEL COMERÇ 11
TEL 93 301 09 02
A cavernous, bustling spot with a shop area where you can buy all sorts of organic products, this is a vegetarian's taste of paradise. Order from a limited and frequently changing menu at the open kitchen and then pile on extras from the copious salad buffet.

🍴 200 🚇 Metro: Línia 3 (Liceu) 🚫 🚫 All major cards

▪ THE WATERFRONT

Several sleeping options dot the waterfront, and more are being built. A cluster of high-rise hotels concentrates in El Fòrum, and a sprinkling of places lines the area between it and Port Vell. La Barceloneta is especially full of character-filled restaurants and tapas bars, and there are some good beachside options, too.

Hotels

🏨 GRAND MARINA
$$$$$ ★★★★★
MOLL DE BARCELONA S/N
TEL 93 603 90 00
grandmarinahotel.com
Occupying the landward flank of the portside World Trade Center, this hotel is in a splendid part of the city. Rooms are all generous in size, but the best are those on the wings with sea views. Timber with a definite seaside flavor dominates the decoration in the rooms and sunny public areas.

ℹ️ 235 🅿️ 🚇 Metro: Línia 3 (Drassanes) 🚫 🚫 🚫 🚫 🚫 All major cards

🏨 HOTEL ARTS BARCELONA
$$$$$ ★★★★★
CARRER DE LA MARINA 19–21
TEL 93 221 10 00
hotelartsbarceona.com
For the international jet set,

this is the address. Occupying 44 floors in one of the twin towers overlooking Port Olímpic, the hotel oozes both luxury and stunning views. Sculpture, paintings, and palms are part of the interior decor.

ℹ️ 483 🅿️ 🚇 Metro: Línia 4 (Ciutadella–Vila Olímpica) 🚫 🚫 🚫 🚫 🚫 All major cards

🏨 HOTEL W-BARCELONA
$$$$$ ★★★
PLAÇA DE LA ROSA DEL VENTS 1
TEL 93 295 28 00
w-barcelona.com
Also known as the Hotel Vela ("sail") because of its Ricardo Bofill-designed shape, this towering building has changed the city's skyline, not without some controversy. You can't miss it, and even if you are not lucky enough to sleep in one of its luxury rooms with stunning views of sea and city then you might like to try its Eclipse bar on the 26th floor. Gourmet dining is guaranteed at **Bravo24**, overseen by Michelin-starred Catalan, Carles Abellan. Spa available.

ℹ️ 473 🚇 Metro: Línia 4 (Barceloneta) 🚫 🚫 🚫 All major cards

🏨 HESPERIA DEL MAR HOTEL
$$ ★★★★
CARRER DE ESPRONCEDA 6
TEL 93 502 97 00
hesperia-delmar.es
This businesslike hotel spread over a half-dozen floors is set back from the waterfront and the better city beaches. Rooms are of a reasonable size, with parquet floors, broad double beds, and, in many cases, a balcony from which you generally have at least a sea glimpse.

ℹ️ 84 🅿️ 🚇 Metro: Línia 4 (Poblenou) 🚫 🚫 All major cards

🚫 Air-conditioning 🚫 Indoor 🚫 Outdoor Swimming Pool 🚫 Health Club 🚫 Credit Cards

HOTEL DEL MAR
$$ ★★★
PLA DE PALAU 19
TEL 93 319 33 02
hoteldelmarbarcelona.com
Set in a restrained, historic
building, the modern rooms
of the Hotel del Mar are best
above all for the location.
Here you are within a few
minutes' walk of the marina
and Port Vell, the beaches
and back lane restaurants of
La Barceloneta, and the night-
life buzz of El Born. Some of
the rooms come with their
own balconies, and these are
the ones to go for.
🛏 75   Metro: Línia 4
(Barceloneta) 🔄 🅿
All major cards

Restaurants

SUQUET DE L'ALMIRALL
$$$$
PASSEIG JOAN DE BORBÓ 65
TEL 93 221 62 33
Although some will tell you
it's not as good as it was, this
seafood establishment remains
outstanding among the tourist
traps on this stretch. The rice
dishes and fish stews (suquet)
are hard to resist.
🪑 80   Metro: Línia 4 (Barce-
loneta); Bus: 17, 39, 45, 57, 59,
& 64 🕐 Closed Mon., 2 weeks
Aug., & public holidays DC,
MC, V

SOMETHING SPECIAL

TORRE D'ALTA MAR
$$$$
TORRE DE SANT SEBASTIÀ,
PASSEIG JOAN DE BORBÒ 88
TEL 93 221 00 07
Of one thing you can be sure:
Nowhere in Barcelona will you
be able to match the views
you'll get from atop this steel
giant of a tower while treat-
ing yourself to a taste festival.
Seafood dominates the menu,
a fine wine list accompanies
it, and the evening mood is
perfect for romantics.
🪑 120   Metro: Línia 4

(Barceloneta); bus: 17, 39, &
64 🕐 Closed L Sun. & L Mon.
All major cards

ELS PESCADORS
$$$
PLAÇA DE PRIM 1
TEL 93 225 20 18
A combination of earthy local
fish eatery and upmarket
restaurant far from the tourist
spots, this is like a bright light
in an otherwise unremarkable
former fishing and industrial
zone. The seafood options are
good, and the place attracts
people from all over town.
🪑 130   Metro: Línia
4 (Poble Nou); bus: 403
🕐 Closed New Year's Day,
Easter week, & Christmas
All major cards

SET PORTES
$$$
PASSEIG D'ISABEL II 14
TEL 93 319 30 33
It seems remarkable that after
so many years (since 1836)
a restaurant can continue to
maintain a good name. This is
one of those cases, and, as a
midrange option serving tradi-
tional Catalan dishes accompa-
nied by a broad range of wines,
it's a sure bet. It was long run by
Paco Parellada, one of the lead-
ing lights in Catalan cuisine, and
it remains in the family. Stays
open all day so is a good option
for early dinners.
🪑 300   Metro: Línia 4
(Barceloneta) All major cards

XIRINGUITO D'ESCRIBÀ
$$$
PLATAJA DE BOGATELL,
RONDA LITORAL 43
TEL 93 221 07 29
Escribà is a name associated
above all with chocolate in
Barcelona. Indeed, you can try
out their delicious desserts and
pastries here after indulging in
a long lunch of seafood, tender fish, and hearty paella or
fideuà (the noodle equivalent)
that will leave you wanting

PRICES

HOTELS
An indication of the cost of a
double room in high season
is given by **$** signs.

$$$$$	Over $400
$$$$	$300–$400
$$$	$225–$300
$$	$150–$225
$	Under $150

RESTAURANTS
An indication of the cost of
a three-course meal without
drinks is given by **$** signs.

$$$$$	Over $150
$$$$	$90–$150
$$$	$50–$90
$$	$30–$50
$	Under $30

more. Expect to wait for a spot
if you haven't booked lunch
here, especially weekends during the summer.
🪑 100   Metro: Línia 4
(Llacuna) 🕐 Closed D
All major cards

CAN RAMONET
$$–$$$
CARRER DE LA MAQUINISTA 17
TEL 93 319 30 64
An oldie but a goodie, Can
Ramonet has been serving up
food since 1763, according to
its claim. It's a classic spot for
seafood in the heart of the
labyrinth of narrow lanes in
La Barceloneta. Crowd inside
around the upended barrels,
or grab a table outside across
the lane in the hotter months.
Paella and similar rice dishes
are good here.
🪑 103   Metro: Línia 4
(Barceloneta)
All major cards

■ LA RIBERA
In the course of the 1990s,
the area around El Born was
rejuvenated, and restaurants,
bars, and cafés continue to

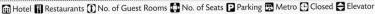

spring up. Given all this activity, the number of hotel options is growing. A crop of upper-level hotels has appeared along Via Laietana and near Parc de la Ciutadella.

Hotels

🏨 GRAND HOTEL CENTRAL
$$$$$ ***
VIA LAIETANA 30
TEL 93 295 79 00
grandhotelcentral.com
Stylish designer rooms, none smaller than 25 square yards (21 sq m) inside a proud look-ing 1930s edifice, attract a fashionable clientele. Colors are muted and sooth-ing. Another big draw is the rooftop pool with spectacular city views, a sundeck, and plenty of lounge space for those quiet moments.
🛏 147 🚇 Metro: Línia 4 (Jaume I) 🔲 🔲 🔲 🔲
🔲 All major cards

🏨 CHIC & BASIC BORN
$$–$$$ *
CARRER DE LA PRINCESA 50
TEL 93 295 46 52
chicandbasic.com
The huge door to this high-ceilinged building looks almost forbidding. Within is revealed a dazzling design where white is the dominant color theme. Beds are grand (as is the central marble staircase!) and super comfortable, and some features of the old build-ing have been retained. One of several chic and stylishly surprising hotels in this small chain. Check out the others on the hotel's website.
🛏 31 🚇 Metro: Línies 1 (Arc de Triomf) & 4 (Jaume I)
🔲 🔲 All major cards

SOMETHING SPECIAL

🏨 BANYS ORIENTALS
$ *
CARRER DE L'ARGENTERIA 37

TEL 93 268 84 60
hotelbanysorientals.com
The best things come in small packages. Dominated by cool colors (sky and steel blue), timber details, and clean lines, this is a fine boutique option on a busy pedestrian street that's a two-minute walk away from the Església de Santa Maria del Mar. Rooms are smallish, but ooze a stylish charm.
🛏 43 🚇 Metro: Línia 4 (Jaume I) 🔲 🔲
🔲 All major cards

Restaurants

🍽 COMERÇ 24
**$$$$$
CARRER DEL COMERÇ 24
TEL 93 319 21 02
One of Barcelona's edgier avant-garde restaurants is forever coming up with sur-prises. The best option is to take the tasting menu and let local star chef Carles Abellan guide you through his latest culinary creations. The place's decor—all reds, yellows, and blacks—seems to prick the senses in anticipation.
🪑 50 🚇 Metro: Línia 4 (Jaume I) 🕐 Closed Sun.–Mon.
🔲 🔲 AE, MC, V

🍽 EL PASSADÍS DEL PEP
**$$$$
PLA DEL PALAU 2
TEL 93 310 10 21
One of the secret addresses that everyone should know about, hidden down a *passadís* (corridor), this is more like a paradise for fish lovers. Fresh fish is shipped in from the coast to provide the raw mate-rials for a marine feast.
🪑 100 🚇 Metro: Línia 4 (Barceloneta) 🕐 Closed Sun., L Mon., & Aug. 🔲 All major cards

🍽 CAL PEP
**$$$
PLAÇA DE LES OLLES 8
TEL 93 310 79 61
Known across the city, the bar

is almost always bursting with diners eager to feast on Pep's tapas, a cut way above the average. For most, a selection of these tasty little morsels accompanied by wine makes a perfect meal, alternatively you can sit down to a full meal in a diminutive dining area but the action is at the bar. Worth the wait in line.
🪑 44 🚇 Metro: Línia 4 (Barce-loneta) 🕐 Closed Sun., L Mon., D Sat., Easter, Aug., & holidays
🔲 All major cards

🍽 IKIBANA
**$$–$$$
PASSEIG DE PICASSO 32
TEL 93 295 67 32
For a classy sushi and cocktail experience, take a high stool or low table for an enticing mix of Japanese dishes done with some exotic twists. The ambience has a club lounge touch, and on the big flat-screen TV, live shots from the kitchen alternate with sooth-ing scenes of nature.
🪑 60 🚇 Metro: Línies 1 (Arc de Triomf) & 4 (Jaume I)
🔲 DC, MC, V

🍽 BUBÓ
**$$
CARRER DE LES CAPUTXES 6 & 10
TEL 93 268 72 24
Sweet teeth will find it hard to go past this bite-size temple of gluttony. Carles Mampel is one of Barcelona's top pastry chefs, and here you can drop by for a set menu of savory tapas and then cede to the principal delights: dessert. How about a *xabina* (a chocolate mousse, vanilla, and olive oil sponge cake concoction)? There's more where that came from!
🪑 40 🚇 Metro: Línia 4 (Jaume I) 🕐 Closed L Mon.
🔲 🔲 All major cards

🍽 LA CARASSA
**$$
CARRER DE BROSOLI 1
TEL 93 310 33 06
For fondue in a different

atmosphere, try La Carassa, a cramped, rambling stone house where without a reservation you can be guaranteed of not finding a table (open for dinner only from 9 to 11 p.m.). The fondue may be the best in town.

🛏 55 🚇 Metro: Línia 4 (Jaume I) 🕐 Closed Sun. & 3 weeks in Aug. 💳 MC, V

🍴 TANTARANTANA
$$

CARRER DE TANTARANTANA 24
TEL 93 268 24 10
Collecting accolades from many a satisfied customer, this cheerful locale with a vaguely traditional decor turns out a range of Catalan and Mediterranean dishes, presented with deceptive simplicity. A few Asian spices are thrown in just to titillate the taste buds further.

🛏 45 🚇 Metro: Línies 1 (Arc de Triomf) & 4 (Jaume I) 🕐 Closed L daily & Sun. 💳 All major cards

▦ PASSEIG DE GRÀCIA

Not surprisingly, for this, the chic heart of central Barcelona, there is no shortage of quality hotels and a reasonable sprinkling of eateries to suit most budgets. Some wonderful little surprises await discovery in the narrow streets of Gràcia, too.

Hotels
SOMETHING SPECIAL

🏨 CASA FUSTER
$$$$$ ★★★★★

PASSEIG DE GRÀCIA 132
TEL 93 255 30 00
hotelescenter.es
It's hard to believe that this remarkable modernista edifice was long home to a bank. Renovated and converted into a luxury hotel in 2004, it occupies a privileged spot at the top end of Passeig de Gràcia. Take in the views from the roof. Modern, comfortable rooms are complemented by

sumptuous public spaces.

🛈 105 🅿 🚇 Metro: Línies 3 & 5 (Diagonal) 🛗 🖥 📺 💳 All major cards

🏨 CLARIS
$$$$$ ★★★★★

CARRER DE PAU CLARIS 150
TEL 93 487 62 62
derbyhotels.es
One of the city's top hotels, the Claris is known for its modern design and considerable art collection. The rooms cover a range of decoration from classic to some quite daring color combinations. Roman statues and Egyptian artifacts are sprinkled about. The rooftop bar is a stylish retreat.

🛈 124 🅿 🚇 Metro: Línies 2, 3, & 4 (Passeig de Gràcia) 🖥 📺 💳 All major cards

🏨 HOTEL MURMURI
$$$$$ ★★★★

RAMBLA DE CATALUNYA 104
TEL 93 550 06 00
murmuri.com
Splendidly located at the upper end of a leafy shopping boulevard in L'Eixample, this new hotel offers large rooms with a modern feel and gadgets like iPod adapters and Molton Brown bath products. The lobby bar is an agreeable spot to meet up with friends.

🛈 53 🚇 Metro: Línies 3 & 5 (Diagonal) 🛗 🚫 📺 💳 All major cards

🏨 MAJÈSTIC
$$$$$ ★★★★★

PASSEIG DE GRÀCIA 70
TEL 93 488 17 17
hotelmajestic.es
A labyrinthine establishment, the hotel's plush, elegantly appointed rooms are huge. A bright modern design combines with ageless style. Discreetly placed items of statuary and works of art throughout public areas heighten the sense of class.

🛈 301 🅿 🚇 Metro: Línies 2, 3, & 4 (Passeig de Gràcia) 📺 🖥 💳 All major cards

SOMETHING SPECIAL

🏨 OMM
🍴 $$$$$ ★★★★★

CARRER DE ROSELLÓ 265
TEL 93 445 40 00
hotelomm.es
One of the most self-conscious designer locations in Barcelona, Omm is easily one of the most exciting options in town. A feast of modern style awaits, with ultramodern rooms lurking behind windows that seem to peel back from the metallic sheen of the facade, as well as top-notch gourmet cuisine from the Roca brothers in the **Roca Moo** restaurant.

🛈 59 🚇 Metro: Línies 3 & 5 (Diagonal) 🛗 🚫 🖥 💳 All major cards

🏨 SIXTY TWO
$$$$$ ★★★★

PASSEIG DE GRÀCIA 62
TEL 93 272 41 80
sixtytwohotel.com
The steel-framed entrance is inserted into the 1930s facade, which is about all that remains of the original building. Inside is a stylish 21st-century lodging option. Relax in the Zeroom with its library or in the Oriental garden out back. Rooms are clean-lined with touches like Bang & Olufsen TVs.

🛈 45 🅿 🚇 Metro: Línies 2, 3, & 4 (Passeig de Gràcia) 🚫 📺 💳 All major cards

🏨 AXEL
$$$$ ★★★★

CARRER D'ARIBAU 33
TEL 93 323 93 93
axelhotels.com
The top-of-the-line hetero-friendly gay hotel in the heart of the Gayxample, the Axel is a mix of stylish, century-old architecture and modern touches. The best rooms boast charming, sunny galleries. After sightseeing, chill out in the rooftop Skybar.

🛈 105 🚇 Metro: Línies 1 & 2 (Universitat) 🛗 🚫 🖥 📺 💳 All major cards

---

🏨 Hotel 🍴 Restaurants 🛈 No. of Guest Rooms 🛏 No. of Seats 🅿 Parking 🚇 Metro 🕐 Closed 🛗 Elevator

HOTEL CONDES DE BARCELONA
$$$$ ★★★★
PASSEIG DE GRÀCIA 73–75
TEL 93 445 00 00
condesdebarcelona.com
Occupying two buildings facing each other across Carrer de Mallorca, this is an elegant option. If you can, try for a room in the older of the two buildings, the stylishly remodeled Casa Enric Batlló. In either, you will bathe in marble luxury.
🛏 74 🅿 🚇 Metro: Línies 2, 3, & 4 (Passeig de Gràcia) 🅢 🏊 🅒 All major cards

ST. MORITZ
$$$$ ★★★★
CARRER DE LA DIPUTACIÓ 262 BIS
TEL 93 412 15 00
hcchotels.com
The spacious rooms (each with a marble bath) in this fine Eixample building are a pleasure to stay in. A relaxing place for a drink is the terrace-garden bar. For a little more exertion, try the small gym.
🛏 91 🅿 🚇 Metro: Línies 2, 3, & 4 (Passeig de Gràcia) 🅢 🅣 🅒 All major cards

ASTORIA
$$$ ★★★
CARRER DE PARÍS 203
TEL 93 209 83 11
hotelastoria-barcelona.com
Located in a classic pre-civil war building and a short walk from the top end of Passeig de Gràcia, this nicely renovated hotel has good-size, comfortable rooms.
🛏 117 🅿 🚇 Metro: Línies 3 & 5 (Diagonal) 🅢 🅢 🏊 🅣 🅒 All major cards

GOYA
$$ ★
CARRER DE PAU CLARIS 74
TEL 93 302 25 65
hostalgoya.com
This quiet, family-run hostel is located on one of the most stylish streets in central Barcelona. From here, it's a quick walk to the Barri Gòtic and La Pedrera. If available, try to reserve one of the renovated rooms, decorated with warm parquet floors.
🛏 19 🚇 Metro: Línies 1 & 4 (Urquinaona), 3 (Catalunya) 🅢 🅢 🅒 All major cards

PRAKTIK BAKERY
$$ ★★★
CARRER DE PROVENÇA 279
TEL 93 488 00 61
hotelpraktikbakery.com
The latest in this small chain of *praktikal* yet stylish hotels pays tribute to one of the city's most famous bakeries, Baluard from Barceloneta, which now bakes on the ground floor, providing delicious early morning aromas and breakfasts to guests and outsiders. A stone's throw from Gaudí's La Pedrera, its rooms are minimally but comfortably decorated and good value.
🛏 74 🅿 🚇 Metro: Línia 3 (Diagonal); FGC: Provença 🅢 🅢 🏊 🅒 All major cards

HOTEL CONSTANZA
$ ★★
CARRER DEL BRUC 33
TEL 93 270 19 10
hotelconstanza.com
The welcome is warm at this homey little boutique location that attracts plenty of attention from visitors on modest budgets. An unabashed color scheme enlivens the impeccably maintained rooms. For a little more outlay, you could take one of the larger suites.
🛏 46 🚇 Metro: Línies 1 & 4 (Urquinaona) 🅢 🅢 🅒 All major cards

Restaurants

CINC SENTITS
$$$$$
CARRER D'ARIBAU 58
TEL 93 323 94 90
It's as though they wanted to strip away all the fluff that sometimes accompanies New Wave eateries. In a minimalist, well-lit setting, you treat your five senses (hence the place's name) to an international culinary adventure. Take a chance on the tasting menus, in which the best daily ingredients are used to create surprise dishes.
🍴 38 🚇 Metro: Línies 1 & 2 (Universitat) 🕐 Closed Sun., D Mon., Easter, & Aug. 🅒 All major cards

BOTAFUMEIRO
$$$$
CARRER GRAN DE GRÀCIA 81
TEL 93 218 42 30
Long one of the best locales for seafood in the best maritime style of Galicia (northwestern Spain), the infinite variety of watery critters is impressive. They wash down with almost excessive ease with some fine Ribeiro whites.
🍴 300 🚇 Metro: Línia 3 (Fontana) 🕐 Closed Aug. 🅒 All major cards

CASA CALVET
$$$$
CARRER DE CASP 48
TEL 93 412 40 12
Jacket and tie are not a bad idea in this wonderful restaurant set on the first floor of a Gaudí-designed, late 19th-century apartment block. Hide yourselves away in a *taula cabina* (timber booth from former days as an office) for a menu that changes with the season. Savor creamy rice with vegetables and mushrooms topped with cheese.
🍴 60 🚇 Metro: Línies 1 & 4 (Urquinaona) 🕐 Closed Sun.–Mon. 🅒 All major cards

JAUME DE PROVENÇA
$$$$
CARRER DE PROVENÇA 88
TEL 93 430 00 29
Once a star in Barcelona's gastronomical firmament, this classic dining hall with old-fashioned waiters is nevertheless one of the best places in town for excellent Spanish cooking. This Michelin-starred

place is frequented by politicians and other key local figures.

🪑 70 🚇 Metro: Línia 1 (Rocafort) 🕐 Closed D Sun., Mon., Easter, Aug., Christmas, & Dec. 26 💳 All major cards

🍴 NOTI
$$$$
CARRER DE ROGER DE LLÚRIA 35
TEL 93 342 66 73
This self-assured designer restaurant with a lounge club atmosphere attracts a good-looking crowd for its imaginative fusion cooking. Stop at the bar first for a cocktail then move on to your table, keeping an eye on the myriad mirrors around you (in case of celebrities). The grilled sirloin with creamy mustard and sautéed mushrooms is tempting.

🪑 80 🚇 Metro: Línies 2, 3, & 4 (Passeig de Gràcia) 🕐 Closed L Sat.–Sun. 🎵 💳 All major cards

🍴 ROIG ROBÍ
$$$$
CARRER DE SÉNECA 20
TEL 93 218 92 22
A table by the quaint internal courtyard for some of Barcelona's best rice dishes is just what the doctor ordered. Not that rice is the only item on the menu. How about delicate meatballs of cod with mushrooms and cuttlefish?

🪑 50 🚇 Metro: Línia 3 (Diagonal or Fontana) 🕐 Closed L Sat., Sun., & half of Aug. 💳 All major cards

🍴 FERRUM
$$$
CARRER DE CÒRSEGA 400
TEL 93 457 76 10
This charming restaurant in a corner of the Eixample serves exquisite Catalan food with a contemporary twist in quiet, attractive surroundings. Its mouthwatering dishes can also be ordered in half portions. Happily off the beaten path.

🪑 45 plus 12 on terrace 🚇 Metro: Línies 4 & 5

(Verdaguer) 🕐 Closed Sun.; Sun.–Mon. in Aug. 💳 All major cards.

🍴 THAI GARDENS
$$$
CARRER DE LA DIPUTACIÓ 273
TEL 93 487 98 98
For a change from European cooking, this is a stylish ambassador for Thai cooking. Tables are arranged amid jungles of greenery in a light, airy, and spacious interior. The dishes are of high quality.

🪑 200 🚇 Metro: Línies 2, 3, & 4 (Passeig de Gràcia) 💳 All major cards

🍴 TAPAS 24
$$–$$$
CARRER DE LA DIPUTACIÓ 269
TEL 93 488 09 77
Gourmet meets tapas tradition in this busy basement bar just off Passeig de Gràcia. Inspired by star Catalan chef Carles Abellan, classics like the bikini (a ham and cheese sandwich) turn into delicacies. The McFoie-Burger is a melt-in-the-mouth foie gras festival, and there's plenty more.

🪑 46 🚇 Metro: Línies 2, 3, & 4 (Passeig de Gràcia) 🕐 Closed Sun. 💳 DC, MC, V

🍴 ENVALIRA
$$
PLAÇA DEL SOL 13
TEL 93 218 58 13
It's retro because it simply hasn't changed in decades. For an excellent assortment of rice and seafood dishes in a hushed 1950s ambience, this place is a pleasant surprise. From outside you'd never guess there was anything of interest inside. The "quarter hour soup," a rice and fish number, is a tasty starter.

🪑 50 🚇 Metro: Línia 3 (Fontana) 🕐 Closed D Sun. & all Mon. 🎵 💳 MC, V

🍴 RITA
$
CARRER D'ARAGÓ 279

TEL 93 487 23 76
An institution in Barcelona, Rita is almost always besieged by hordes of hungry diners in search of good food at rock-bottom prices. Rita has been delivering a mix of Catalan and Mediterranean dishes to contented Catalans for years.

🪑 120 🚇 Metro: Línies 2, 3, & 4 (Passeig de Gràcia) 💳 MC, V

▣ LA SAGRADA FAMÍLIA TO PARK GÜELL
Although there are few hotels of note in the area around the two Gaudí sensations, a handful of great dining experiences await.

Hotel

🏨 HISPANOS SIETE SUIZA
🍴 $$$ ★★★★
CARRER DE SICILIA 255
TEL 93 208 20 51
hispanos7suiza.com
The vintage cars that adorn the ground floor of this unique option set the scene. A brisk walk from La Sagrada Família and with its own fine restaurant, La Cúpula, this home away from home offers apartments with kitchens that can accommodate up to four guests.

🪑 20 🅿 🚇 Metro: Línies 2 & 5 (Sagrada Familia) 🛗 🎵 💳 All major cards

Restaurants

SOMETHING SPECIAL

🍴 ALKÍMIA
$$$–$$$$
CARRER DE L'INDÚSTRIA 79
TEL 93 207 61 15
Michelin-star winner Jordi Vila regales his customers with an ambitious, refined Catalan cuisine that cannot leave you indifferent. One of the few standout restaurants within easy walking distance of La Sagrada Família, it warrants a pilgrimage.

🏨 Metro: Línies 4 & 5 (Verdaguer) 🕐 Closed Sat. & Sun.
💳 All major cards

🍴 JAIZKUIBEL
$$$
CARRER DE SICÍLIA 180
TEL 93 231 32 62
Long before Basque tapas bars
became hip, this place far from
the tourist crowds was regaling
its aficionados with fine sea-
food bar snacks and wonderful
dining. The fish dishes are what
the house does best.
🛏 35 🏨 Metro: Línia 1 (Arc
de Triomf) 🕐 Closed D Sun.,
Mon., & 2 weeks in Aug.
💳 All major cards

◼ NORTHERN BARCELONA

Big, comfortable, but fre-
quently characterless hotels
dot broad Avinguda Diagonal
between the city's outskirts
and its heart. In the broad
sweep of northern Barcelona,
you can also find the occa-
sional culinary gem.

Hotel

🏨 REY JUAN CARLOS I
$$$$$ *****
AVINGUDA DIAGONAL 661–671
TEL 93 364 40 40
hrjuancarlos.com
On the edge of the city, this
place is a businessmen's high-
rise luxury establishment.
Rooms are gathered around
open glass galleries that look
out over the city or into the
foyer.
📞 419 🅿 🏨 Metro: Línia 3
(Zona Universitària); bus: 67
& 68 🟰 🛌 🏊 💪
💳 All major cards

Restaurants

🍴 HISOP
$$$$$
PASSATGE MARIMON 9
TEL 93 241 32 33
Michelin-star winner Oriol

Ivern is one of the bright stars
in the dazzling firmament
of new Catalan chefs. The
best bet is to put yourself in
his hands by choosing the
menu de tast, which offers
several courses of highly
creative dishes, along with
the perfect wine pairings
as accompaniment.
🛏 38 🏨 FGC: Gràcia
🕐 Closed Sat. L, Sun., & 1st
week Jan. 💳 All major cards

🍴 NEICHEL
$$$$$
CARRER DE BELTRÁN I RÓZPIDE
16 BIS
TEL 93 203 84 08
Up in the posh Pedralbes area,
this two-Michelin-star temple
of good Mediterranean dining
offers a vast menu. Fish dishes
abound—try the San Pedro, a
delicious white-flesh fish.
🛏 55 🏨 Metro: Línia 3 (Palau
Reial); bus: 63 & 114 🕐 Closed
Sun.–Mon., holidays, Easter, &
Aug. 💳 All major cards

🍴 VIA VENETO
$$$$$
CARRER DE GANDUXER 10
TEL 93 200 72 44
If you asked local gourmets
where to eat with only one
night in the city, many would
select Via Veneto. Refined
Catalan cuisine has been the
mainstay here for more than 40
years. Service is impeccable.
🛏 200 🏨 Bus: 6, 7, 15, 27, 33,
34, & 68 🕐 Closed L Sat., Sun.,
& Aug. 1–20 💳 All major cards

SOMETHING SPECIAL

🍴 LA BALSA
$$$–$$$$
CARRER DE L'INFANTA ISABEL 4
TEL 93 211 50 48
The views and atmosphere of
La Balsa alone, set in a splendid
building amid dense vegeta-
tion, make this an attractive
stop. Dishes vary regularly,
and the cuisines inspiring the
chefs range from the Basque

Country to Italy, via Catalonia
and France.
🛏 76 (110 in summer)
🏨 FGC: Tibidabo 🕐 Closed
Sun., L Mon., & Easter (buffet
only in Aug.) 💳 AE, MC, V

◼ MONTJUÏC

Although the choice is limited,
this is the place in Barcelona
for wonderful views of the
city and the sea, and for fresh
hilltop air.

Hotel

🏨 MIRAMAR
$$$$ *****
PLAÇA CARLOS IBÁÑEZ 3
TEL 93 281 16 00
hotelmiramarbarcelona.com
As the name suggests, here
you can lie in bed and look
over the sea, as well as get
a bird's-eye view of the city.
Dating from the 1929 Inter-
national Exhibition, this palace
was renovated by leading
architect Oscar Tusquets to
become a hotel with a privi-
leged location, just below the
castle of Montjuïc, so you can
enjoy its gardens before the
crowds arrive. Spa available.
📞 75 🅿 🏨 Metro: Línia 3
(Paral-lel & Funicular) 🛌 💪
💳 All major cards

Restaurant

🍴 ELCHE
$$
CARRER DE VILA I VILÀ 71
TEL 93 441 30 89
Named after a town in the
region of Valencia, the home
of paella, Elche continues to
live up to a long-established
reputation for being one of
the best places for paella and
other rice-based dishes. It also
has an attractive offspring
looking over the port in
Maremàgnum (see p. 100)
called **L' Eix al Moll.**
🛏 70 🏨 Metro: Línia 3
(Paral-lel) 💳 AE, MC, V

Shopping

Barcelona thinks of itself as the style capital of Spain, much in the way Milan is the fashion capital of Italy. You'll find just about every conceivable kind of store, ranging from local junk markets to cutting-edge design, from traditional foods to African crafts.

A great number of the big-name stores, especially in Spanish and foreign fashion and design, line a long, two-pronged axis that stretches up Passeig de Gràcia from Plaça de Catalunya and turns left along Avinguda Diagonal, along which it continues (with some interruptions) as far as Plaça de la Reina Maria Cristina. Most shops accept credit cards. Non-EU citizens can claim back the sales tax (IVA) on personal purchases of more than €90.15 made at shops displaying the Europe Tax Free Shopping (or similar) sticker. You need to keep the register receipt and, where possible, obtain a tax refund form for presentation to customs at the airport before you leave Spain.

Opening Hours & Service

Shop opening hours vary enormously. Big department stores are generally open all day from about 10 a.m. to 10 p.m. Most other shops tend to open from around 9 or 10 a.m. to 8 p.m. Some still take a two- or three-hour break from 1:30 p.m. or 2 p.m. Nearly all stores open on Saturday morning, but smaller more traditional ones close in the afternoon. Sunday trading is permitted only on certain days, especially in the run-up to Christmas and during sales times (rebaixes).

If you are used to the sunny standards of service common in North America, the situation in Barcelona can at times seem a little dire. In much the same way as wait staff in many restaurants, shop assistants in some instances do not see the customer as coming first. Don't take it personally, though; it's just the way it is here sometimes. That said, in many stores the staff is helpful and obliging, so it can all be a bit hit-and-miss.

Antique Shops & Markets

As a rule, picking up a bargain in antiques in Barcelona is a tough assignment. There are two main areas to look around. In the Barri Gòtic, **Carrer dels Banys Nous** is the obvious starting point. It is lined with antique shops. A couple of nearby streets, like **Carrer de la Palla,** are also home to a few interesting stores, and the market in the cathedral square on Thursdays has a good range of smaller objects. Metro: Línia 3 (Liceu).

The other concentration of around 70 antique shops is **Bulevard des Antiquaris,** located in the Bulevard Rosa shopping center on Passeig de Gràcia. Some stores specialize in antique jewelry, crystal, porcelain, and so on, while others are more general.

If you want to spend a morning trawling through junk (of varying quality) then the **Els Encants** market on the southern side of the huge Plaça de les Glòries Catalanes traffic circle is the place to go. Metro: Línia 1 (Glòries). For more on markets around Barcelona, see pages 136–137.

Art Galleries

Three general areas suggest themselves for browsing.

The first is **Carrer de Montcada** (see pp. 124–129), where interspersed between the Picasso gallery and other museums you will find several private collections and commercial galleries. Because so much tourist traffic gets down here you should be circumspect about any purchases.

Around **MACBA,** especially in **Carrer del Doctor Dou,** and **Carrer dels Àngels,** are several contemporary art galleries. The main concentration and best quality is on and near the strip of **Carrer del Consell de Cent** between Rambla de Catalunya and Carrer de Balmes.

Books

Altaïr Gran Via de les Corts Catalanes 616, tel 93 324 71 71, metro: Línies 1 & 2 (Universitat). This is easily the city's most complete travel book store. If hanging around Barcelona has given you an appetite to travel more, this is the place to whet your interest with guides and other material in English.

Antinous Carrer de Josep Anselm Clavé 6, tel 93 301 90 70, metro: Línia 3 (Drassanes). The best gay bookshop in town, with extensive literature, magazines, postcards, and a pleasant little café in the back.

Casa del Llibre Passeig de Gràcia 62, tel 902 026 407, metro: Línies 2, 3, & 4 (Passeig de Gràcia). This is one of the best stocked general bookstores in town, with reasonable foreign-language sections, a plethora of material on Barcelona, and plenty of general literature.

La Central del Raval Carrer d' Elisabets 6, tel 902 884 990. Huge bookshop located in a 16th-century chapel, perfect for browsing. Some English titles and a broad range on Barcelona.

Hibernian Books Carrer de Montseny 17, tel 93 217 47 96, metro: Línia 3 (Fontana). A good stock of mostly secondhand (but some new) books in English covering a wide range of subjects. They claim to be the biggest in Barcelona, with some 40,000 titles.

Laie Carrer de Pau Claris 85, tel 93 318 17 39, metro: Línies 1 & 3 (Catalunya). Novels and books on architecture, art, and film in English, French, Spanish, and Catalan. Upstairs is a café and attractive restaurant where you can sip hot chocolate over the paper or enjoy the set menu.

Quera Carrer de Petritxol 2, tel 93 318 07 43, metro: Línia 3 (Liceu). This is one of Barcelona's top specialists in maps and guides, including hiking in Catalonia and beyond its borders.

Clothing

If you came to Barcelona but your shopping soul really wanted to be in Italy, never fear, for all the big names in Italian fashion are represented here. Armani, Versace, and Gucci are scattered about town, especially along Avinguda Diagonal and Passeig de Gràcia. They mix with other international names such as Calvin Klein, Chanel, and Stella McCartney There's plenty of tempting local fashion, too. Check out some of these below:

Adolfo Domínguez Passeig de Gràcia 32, tel 93 487 41 70, metro: Línies 2, 3 & 4 (Passeig de Gràcia). Since the 1980s, this designer, who took off in Galicia in Spain's north-west, has maintained a prominent international profile as a purveyor of fine men's, women's, and kids' clothing. The materials used are high quality and the designs contemporary but restrained.

Antonio Miró Rambla de Catalunya 125, tel 93 239 99 42 metro: Línies 3 & 5 (Diagonal). One of Catalonia's leading fashion designers, Miró combines a certain stylish conservatism with a light Mediterranean touch. His now eclectic store showcases his household designs as well.

Armand Basi Passeig de Gràcia 49, tel 93 215 14 21, metro: Línies 2, 3 & 4 (Passeig de Gràcia). Basi is a local design star producing hip

fashions for men and women, ranging from casual to elegant evening wear. A smattering of leatherwear, including shoes, is also available.

Custo Barcelona La Rambla 120, tel 93 301 44 95, metro: Línia 3 (Liceu). A local fashion label aimed mostly at a young, uninhibited set with a love of splashy color, Custo Barcelona has taken world catwalks by storm and is opening stores around the globe. This is one of several in the city.

Mango Passeig de Gràcia 36 & 65, tel 93 215 75 30, metro: Línies 2, 3, & 4 (Passeig de Gràcia). Another homegrown fashion success story that has become an international household name in smart gear. There are branches all over town, but number 36 sells the complete range (women, men, & kids).

Purificación García Provenza 292, tel 93 496 13 36, metro: Línies 3 & 5 (Diagonal). Concentrating on attractive, mid-range women's fashions, Purificación García offers plenty of seasonal inspiration. Casual but dressy slacks, jackets, and somewhat more adventurous dresses are the mainstay. She does a growing range of accessories too. This store goes to bat for established and rising names in the Spanish fashion industry.

Zara Passeig de Gràcia 16, tel 93 318 76 75, metro: Línies 2, 3, & 4 (Passeig de Gràcia). This popular fashion chain for men, women, and children is one of Spain's international success stories. A big range of quality, if middle-of-the-road, clothing is available at reasonable prices. Other branches are scattered about the city.

Department Stores & Shopping Centers

Huge department stores and shopping malls are not as popular a phenomenon in Barcelona as in North America, although for better or worse the idea is catching on fast. The biggest national chain of such stores is **El Corte**

Inglés, which has branches in several locations around town. The most central branch takes up a whole block on the east side of Plaça de Catalunya *(tel 93 306 38 00, metro: Línies 1, 2, & 3 (Catalunya).* It has an excellent supermarket in the basement. Not all its departments could fit into the one store, so some (such as CDs, videos, electronics, and so on) are located in another branch at nearby Avinguda del Portal de l'Àngel 19–21.

Another shopping emporium on this central square is **El Triangle,** which plays host to several stores notably a branch of the French megastore **FNAC** *(tel 902 100 632 18 00),* which sells books, CDs, and multimedia products, bliss for teenagers.

The same competition between these stores is played out again along Avinguda Diagonal, where El Corte Inglés has two mega-stores, one at No. 471, near Plaça de Francesc Macià, and another at No. 617, off Plaça de la Reina Maria Cristina. FNAC is at No. 549, part of the immense **L'Illa del Diagonal** shopping complex, probably the most attractive of a handful of such shopping centers in the city. Metro: Línia 3 (Maria Cristina); bus: 6, 7, 27, 33, 34, & 127. A more discreet small-shopping arcade is **Bulevard Rosa,** Passeig de Gràcia 53, metro: Línies 2, 3, & 4 (Passeig de Gràcia). Small scale and manageable with independent stores.

Housewares & Interior Design

Cubiña Carrer de Mallorca 291, tel 93 476 57 21, metro: Línies 3 & 5 (Diagonal); Línies 4 & 5 (Verdaguer). Housed in an extraordinary modernista creation of Domènech i Montaner, this interior design store is as interesting for the location as for the home wares on display. These are spread over a huge area and cover every aspect of home decoration, furniture, and the like.

Vinçon Passeig de Gràcia 96, tel 93 215 60 50, metro: Línies 3 & 5 (Diagonal). In this deceptively extensive store, you'll find everything from stylish candles to designer kitchenware, from furniture items to lamps. The building once belonged to painter Ramon Casas, one of the leading lights of the modernista movement. When you're through with the shopping, head upstairs to the rear terrace area, from where you can get an unusual view of La Pedrera (see p. 145 & 149–151).

Jewelry

Joyería Bagués Passeig de Gràcia 41, tel 93 216 01 74, metro: Línies 2, 3, & 4 (Passeig de Gràcia). This is one of Barcelona's prestige names in high-priced rocks. This branch is housed on the ground floor of the Casa Amatller, but others are found about the city.

Leather

Loewe Passeig de Gràcia 35, tel 93 216 04 00, metro: Línies 2, 3, & 4 (Passeig de Gràcia); bus: 6, 7, 27, 33, 34, & 127. One of Spain's leading and oldest fashion stores, this chain was founded in 1846. This branch opened in 1943 in the modernista Casa Lleo i Morera. Loewe is known for its quality leather goods, in particular bags and jackets.

Music

Sometimes you could almost be forgiven for thinking that medieval guild norms are still in force today. **Carrer dels Tallers** in El Raval should be renamed Carrer dels Discos (Records Street) for the concentration along most of its length of a dozen or so record stores. You can find everything from rare vinyl items to classical to hip-hop hits. Metro: Línies 1 & 3 (Catalunya).

FNAC and **El Corte Inglés** (see Department Stores) have substantial CD collections.

Perfume

Regia Passeig de Gràcia 39, tel 93 216 01 21, metro: Línies 2, 3, & 4 (Passeig de Gràcia). The top name in perfume in Barcelona, this branch also houses a small perfume museum.

Sephora Carrer del Pelai, 13, tel 93 306 39 00, metro: Línies 1 & 3 (Catalunya). An underground treasure trove of perfumes and other cosmetic indulgences for boys and girls, including a space to have your face made beautiful. Luscious colors and packaging from this French chain.

Shoes

Camper Valencia 249, tel 93 215 63 90, metro: Línies 3 & 5 (Diagonal). One of the most successful shoe companies to come out of Spain.

Vialis Carrer de Elisabets 20, tel 93 342 60 71, metro: Línies 1 & 3 (Catalunya). A Catalan designer has created this label, selling divine shoes for women, at once feminine and sensible, in the softest leather. Several shops are scattered around the city. Be sure to check them out.

Souvenirs

High-quality and original souvenirs are on sale at shops in various museums and sights around town. Among those worth keeping an eye out for are **Museu de Picasso, Fundació Joan Miró, MACBA**, and **La Pedrera.**

Stationery

Papirum Baixada de la Llibreteria 2, tel 93 310 52 42, metro: Línia 4 (Jaume I). An exquisite array of handmade stationery, picture frames, and decorative items made of paper.

Raima Carrer Comtal 27, tel 93 317 49 66, metro: Línies 1 & 3 (Catalunya). Another high-quality stationery shop, with items ranging from parchment to albums and notebooks of all sorts.

Taste Treats

Caelum Carrer de la Palla 8, tel 93 302 69 93, metro: Línia 3 (Liceu). From across the length and breadth of Spain, handmade products, from marzipan to olive oil, made at monasteries and convents find their way to this pretty store.

Celler Mas Saloni Carrer d'Enric Granados 68, tel 93 453 43 58, metro: Línies 3 & 5 (Diagonal). Specialists in Catalan wines and *cava*, although the products of other Spanish regions and even a few French wines are stocked.

El Magnífico Carrer de l'Argenteria 64, tel 93 319 39 75. For about a century, fine coffees have been roasted here.

Papabubble Carrer Ample 28, tel 93 268 86 25, metro: Línia 3 (Drassanes). Indulge in delicious old-style hard candy handmade at this imaginative, Australian-run store.

Traditional

Cereria Subirà Baixada de la Llibreteria 7, tel 93 315 26 06, metro: Línia 4 (Jaume 1). It's all a load of old wax to some, but to others the candle creations here are a marvel. This is one of the oldest businesses in the city, with roots in the 18th century, a magical spot which has just been saved from closure.

La Caixa de Fang La Rambla 120, tel 93 315 17 04, metro: Línia 4 (Jaume I). Just behind the cathedral this colorful shop groans with handmade Catalan ceramics mostly in gorgeous yellows and greens, but also from other parts of Spain. Small dishes and olive-wood spoons make good presents and are not too weighty.

Entertainment & Activities

Barcelonans may have a reputation in Spain for keeping their noses to the grindstone and even being a little dour, but compared with many European cities, Barcelona hops. Busy theater, dance, and concert calendars, with frequent appearances by international performers and companies, are counterbalanced by a frenetic nightlife, especially from Thursday to Saturday nights. It is not difficult to stay out until dawn and beyond. Although not as wild as Madrid, Barcelona offers more than enough to keep all but the most demanding partyers content.

Details of what's going on are available from several sources (see p. 246). The weekly *Guía del Ocio* (guiadelocio.com) is the city's main entertainment guide. For the day's theater and cinema listings, you can check the daily papers; the best and clearest listings pages *(cartelera)* are those in *El País*. For the latest news on what's cool in bars, clubs, and the like, you need to track down a couple of hard-to-find free publications: *Micro* and *Go Mag* are just two. They are distributed among bars and clubs, especially in the Born and El Raval, but stumbling across them is hit-and-miss. A couple of handy websites are timeout.com and barcelonanightlife.com.

Barcelona's theater and concert season gets under way in late September or early October and stretches into May and June. This period is marked by several highlight moments, such as **BAM** (Barcelona Acció Musical), a series of concerts (many free) staged across the city for the Festes de la Mercè in the second half of September. (For more on Barcelona's festivals, see pp. 42–45.) From late October to late November, the city stages the **Festival Internacional de Jazz de Barcelona,** when the city's bars and other venues hum to the sounds of jazz musicians from around the country and abroad. In June, Europe's biggest electronic music fest, **Sónar,** is staged in Barcelona.

Even in the hot months of summer, all is not over. From late June to the end of July a dense program of theater, dance, and music comes to town in the shape of the **Festival del Grec,** named after the amphitheater on Montjuïc where some of the performances are held.

Year-round the cinema offerings in Barcelona are top notch. What's more, Barcelonans *like* seeing movies in the original language with subtitles. Several cinemas cater to this taste, and lines of locals and foreigners alike are not uncommon. Check out the Verdi cinemas in Gràcia and the Renoir Floridablanca.

Live music and dance venues, bars and taverns of all descriptions, and plenty of clubs cater to the nocturnal needs of just about everyone.

Tickets *(entradas)* for the theater, concerts, and so on can be bought at the venues concerned, but it is frequently easier to use ticket sales services. Tickets can be purchased at the main tourist office at Plaça de Catalunya 17-S (where half-price tickets are available for some shows), as well as the municipal information office in the Palau de la Virreina, La Rambla de Sant Josep 99, tel 93 301 77 75. Branches of the FNAC store also sell tickets, as does El Corte Inglés on Plaça de Catalunya.

Finally, the most common service used is the Caixa de Catalunya bank's Tel-Entrada service at tel 90 210 12 12, or on the Internet at telentrada.com. You make a reservation with a credit card and pick up the tickets from the theater up to an hour before the show. Some theaters use an alternative service, Ticketmaster *(tel 93 304 07 50).*

Bars

The city is crawling with bars, from the grungy daytime spit-and-sawdust variety to trendy late-night cocktail joints. What follows is a brief selection.

Bar Marsella Carrer de Sant Pau 65, tel 93 442 72 63, metro: Línia 3 (Liceu). A Frenchman from Marseille opened this place in 1820 and introduced the drinking of absinthe to Barcelona. Nothing seems to have changed since.

Bar Pastís Carrer de Santa Mònica 4, tel 93 318 79 80, metro: Línia 3 (Drassanes). The theme of this conspiratorial little drinking corner is French singer Edith Piaf and French cabaret music, but occasionally they have tango nights.

Berlin Carrer de Muntaner 240, tel 93 200 65 42, metro: Línies 3 & 5 (Diagonal). This uptown corner bar is a popular staging post for an evening out in the surrounding district. The main bar area is jammed on Thursday to Saturday nights, but the downstairs lounge area is generally quieter. With luck, you might land a table outside in summer.

Casa Almirall Carrer de Joaquim Costa 33, tel 93 318 99 17, metro: Línies 1 & 2 (Universitat). With its dark modernista decor, this atmospheric old bar has been a haunt of locals since the 1860s.

CDLC Passeig Marítim 32, tel 93 224 04 70, metro: Línia 4 (Ciutadella–Villa Olímpica). One of several chill-out lounge bars and clubs stacked up together on the waterfront on the Barceloneta side of Port Olímpic, this is a hip spot for sundown drinks and late-night cocktails.

Collage Consellers 4, tel 93 179 37 85, metro: Línia 4 (Jaume I). Minute, very appealing cocktail bar in the heart of medieval Born.

Dry Martini Carrer d'Aribau 162–166, tel 93 217 50 72, metro: Línia 5 (Hospital Clínic). Feel like sinking deep into a leather lounge and sipping on a dry martini served impeccably by white-jacketed waiters? You've come to the right place. They'll mix up any other of your favorite drinks, too.

Michael Collins Pub Plaça de la Sagrada Família 4, tel 93 459 19 64, metro: Línies 2 & 5 (Sagrada Família). Of the swelling ranks of Irish and Anglo-style pubs in town, this is one of the best.

Schilling Carrer de Ferran 23, tel 93 317 67 87, metro: Línia 3 (Liceu). Prominently located and lively with a mixed 30-something androgynous crowd.

La Vinya del Senyor Plaça de Santa Maria del Mar 5, tel 93 310 33 79, metro: Línia 4 (Jaume I). An enormous wine list to savor either inside or outside in the shadow of the Santa Maria del Mar church.

Clubs

There is no shortage of dance clubs that go on until the sun comes up. A number of the live music places listed on page 263 double as clubs, too. The Maremàgnum and Port Olímpic areas are crammed with late-night bars and dance clubs—a little tacky but they will keep you going for most of the night. A few more are listed here.

Arena Carrer de Balmes 32, tel 93 487 83 42, metro: Línies 1 & 2 (Universitat). This is a popular gay club with a dark room and is one of three Arena clubs within a couple of minutes' walk of one another. The others attract a more mixed clientele.

Mirablau Plaça del Doctor Andreu, tel 93 434 00 35, taxi. Dancing with the spectacular view

of nocturnal Barcelona laid out at your feet.

Otto Zutz Carrer de Lincoln 15, tel 93 238 07 22, FGC: Gràcia. The beautiful people's club and possibly the best known club name in Barcelona.

The Sutton Club Carrer de Tuset 13, tel 93 414 42 17, metro: Línies 3 & 5 (Diagonal). In this busy weekend nightlife area, the Sutton is one of the best club options. Bars ring the main dance area, a kind of pit of beautiful people.

La Terrazza Ferrer i Guardia 13, tel 687 969 825, metro: Línia 3 (Espanya). One of the city's top clubs, this place draws a dance-eager posse from all over the city to dance in the open air until dawn. Open from May to October.

Flamenco

Although more readily associated with Madrid and southern Spain, there is some tradition of flamenco among *Gitanos* (Gypsies) and Andalusian migrants long settled in and around Barcelona. Some of the great singers, guitarists, and dancers of flamenco were indeed born in Catalonia. The regular acts in the handful of flamenco places in town are often of indifferent to poor quality, but occasionally top-class performers come to town.

Sala Tarantos Plaça Reial 17, tel 93 319 17 89, metro: Línia 3 (Liceu). Every now and then, serious flamenco musicians perform here. Of the readily available options, this place is probably the best bet. Usually shows are held on Friday and Saturday nights beginning about 11 p.m. Otherwise, there is usually a one-hour show up to three times a night starting at 8:30 p.m. The place later reverts to a dance club that goes on into the early hours.

Tablao Cordobés La Rambla 35, tel 93 317 57 11, metro: Línia 3 (Liceu). This place is more given to cheesy performances with a meal

thrown in. Nevertheless, even here decent acts sometimes appear.

El Tablao de Carmen Poble Espanyol 13, tel 93 325 68 95, metro: Línies 1 & 3 (Espanya); bus: 13, 150. In much the same vein as Cordobés, though don't expect to see anything but a tourist version of flamenco.

Movie Theaters

Several movie theater complexes offer eager local viewers the opportunity to see many mainstream and art house movies from abroad in the original language. Consequently, out-of-towners can catch recent movies in their own language, too! In listings, movies shown in the original are identified with *v.o. (version original)*. During the week, the last session tends to start around 10:30 p.m. On Friday and Saturday nights, most movie theaters stage an extra late-night session, starting around 1 a.m. All of the following put on some movies with subtitles:

Icària-Yelmo Carrer de Salvador Espriu 61, tel 902 22 09 22, metro: Línia 4 (Ciutadella Vila Olímpica). A major movie theater complex-mall with fifteen screens!

Méliès Cinemes Carrer de Villarroel 102, tel 93 451 00 51, metro: Línia 1 (Urgell). Small cinema, good for indie films.

Renoir Floridablanca Carrer de Floridablanca 135, tel 93 426 33 37, metro: Línia 2 (Sant Antoni). Close to El Raval and its bars and restaurants, a good cinema for the latest subtitled original version movies.

Verdi Carrer de Verdi 32, tel 93 238 79 90, metro: Línia 3 (Fontana). A buzzy location for post-movie eating and drinking in the surrounding Gràcia with a guaranteed range of art house films.

Opera, Dance, & Classical Music

In addition to the venues listed here, performances are

occasionally held in churches and other temporary locations. The acoustics of the Església de Santa Maria del Mar, for example, are nothing great, but such a setting for music recitals is inspirational!

L'Auditori Carrer de Lepant 150, tel 93 247 93 00, auditori .cat, metro: Línies 1 (Glòries) & 2 (Monumental). This is the city's main stage for fine listening, with a busy program of classical, chamber, religious, and other music.

Gran Teatre del Liceu La Rambla 51–59, tel 93 485 99 00, liceubarcelona.cat, metro: Línia 3 (Liceu). Barcelona's grand establishment lyric theater. This is where the main opera season is staged, but classical music recitals and dance are also on the menu. Reserve well in advance for big-name companies, local or from abroad.

Palau de la Música Catalana Carrer Palau de la Música 4–6, tel 902 442 882, palaumusica.cat, metro: Línies 1 & 4 (Urquinaona). The acoustics have never been the best here, but the luxuriant modernista setting makes an evening of music unforgettable.

Pop, Rock, & Jazz

Big local and international rock and pop acts tend to play in places like the **Palau Sant Jordi** sports arena (on Montjuïc), the **Olympic Stadium,** and one or two other large venues. Tickets are generally available at the ticketing agencies and centers that are named at the beginning of this section. Otherwise, you can hear live music on a more modest scale in locations around town, a few of which are listed below. Acts rarely come on stage much before 11 p.m.

Bikini Diagonal 547, tel 93 322 08 00, metro: Línia 5 (Entença); bus: 6, 7, 33, 34, 63, 67, & 68. A multi-hall dance club that puts on concerts ranging from rock to blues.

Harlem Jazz Club Carrer de la Comtessa de Sobradiel 8, tel 93 310 07 55, metro: Línia 4 (Jaume I). An old favorite for jazz hounds where you can be sure of good music, plenty of people, and the dimly lit atmosphere all jazz bars should have!

Jamboree Plaça Reial 17, tel 93 319 17 89, metro: Línia 3 (Liceu). Before giving itself over to club music to carry on into the wee hours of the morning, this underground club stages a range of jazz and funk most nights.

Luz de Gas Carrer de Muntaner 246, tel 93 209 77 11, bus: 6, 7, 15, 33, 34, 63, 67, & 68. Live soul, country, salsa, and rock most nights, followed by club sounds and dancing into the early hours.

Razzmatazz Carrer dels Almogàvers 122, tel 93 272 09 10, metro: Línia 4 (Bogatell). This multistage venue set in former warehouses is one of the biggest draws in town for concerts of all sorts. Most performances happen in the Razz Club, which later, along with the place's smaller bars, turns into a multi-club location for dancing until dawn.

Sala Apolo Carrer Nou de la Rambla 113, tel 93 441 40 01, metro: Línia 3 (Paral-lel). This old favorite, a former dance hall, has become one of the best clubs in town with visiting DJs, live music, and even burlesque nights.

Theater

The majority of theater in Barcelona is, quite naturally, in Catalan and sometimes in Spanish—which is great if you are looking to practice one or the other of these languages. Occasionally, international acts come to town and perform in their native tongue (in which case simultaneous interpreting headsets may be distributed).

Mercat de les Flors Carrer de Lleida 59, tel 93 256 26 00, metro: Línia 3 (Poble Sec); bus: 55. This modern stage has become the city's number-one venue for major contemporary dance performances, local and international.

Teatre Lliure Plaça de Margarida Xirgu s/n, tel 93 228 97 47, teatrelliure.com, metro: Línia 3 (Poble Sec); bus: 55. Dedicated to theater in Catalan, it puts on classics, avant-garde works, and everything in between and hosts international productions during the Grec festival.

Teatre Nacional de Catalunya Plaça de les Arts 1, tel 93 306 57 00, tnc.cat, metro: Línies 1 (Glòries) or 2 (Monumental). Ricard Bofill's grand national theater opened in 1997 and puts on a broad range of mainstream drama and occasionally dance performances.

Teatre Tantarantana Carrer de les Flors 22, tel 93 441 70 22, tantarantana.com, metro: Línia 3 (Paral-lel). Although it indulges in much contemporary theater, this place is also worth watching for kids' shows, puppet shows, and similar events, which usually begin around 6 p.m.

Teatre Victòria Avinguda del Paral-lel 67–69, tel 93 443 29 29, teatrevictoria.com, metro: Línia 3 (Paral-lel). Frequently a stage for ballet and dance, the theater regularly hosts such Barcelona favorites as Tricicle, a trio of comic mimes who transcend all linguistic barriers. ■

Language Guide & Menu Reader

Barcelona is a bilingual city. Visitors with a reasonable grasp of Spanish will soon learn to distinguish it from the local tongue, Catalan (although some words are the same). Signs, menus, and so on increasingly appear exclusively in Catalan, so the following language guide and menu reader are given in Catalan/Spanish. See Etiquette & Local Customs page 244.

Useful Words & Phrases

Yes *si/sí*
No *no*
Excuse me *perdoni/perdone*
Hello (before lunch) *bon dia!/ buenos días!*, (after lunch) ¡*bona tarda!/¡buenas tardes!*
Hi *hola!/¡hola!*
Please *si us plau/por favor*
Thank you *grácies/gracias*
You're welcome *de res/de nada*
OK *d'acord/de acuerdo*
Goodbye *adéu/adiós*
Good night *bona nit/buenas noches*
Sorry *ho sento/lo siento*
Here *aquí/aquí*
There *allà/allí*
Today *avui/hoy*
Yesterday *ahir/ayer*
Tomorrow *demà/mañana*
Now *ara/ahora*
Later *més tard/más tarde*
This morning *aquest matí/esta mañana*
This afternoon *aquesta tarda/ esta tarde*
This evening *aquest vespre* or *aquesta nit/esta noche*
Open *obert/abierto*
Closed *tancat/cerrado*
Do you have...? *¿Té...?/¿Tiene...?*
Do you speak English? *¿Parla anglès?/¿Habla inglés?*
I don't understand *No entenc/No entiendo*
Please speak more slowly *Si us plau, parli més a poc a poc/Por favor, hable más despacio*
Where is...? *¿On és...?/¿Donde está...?*
I don't know *No ho sé/No lo sé*

That's it *Això mateix/Eso es*
What is your name? *¿Com es diu?/¿Cómo se llama?*
My name is... *Em dic.../Me llamo...*
At what time? *¿A quina hora?/¿A qué hora?*
When? *¿Quan?/¿Cuándo?*
What time is it? *¿Quina hora és?/¿Qué hora es?*
Can you help me? *¿Em pot ajudar?/¿Me puede ayudar?*
I'd like... *Voldria.../Quisiera...*
How much is it? *¿Quant costa?/¿Cuánto vale?*

Menu Reader

breakfast *el esmorzar/el desayuno*
lunch *el dinar (el menjar)/el almuerzo (la comida)*
dinner *el sopar/la cena*
appetizer *l'entrant/el entrante*
first course *el primer/el primero*
main course *el segon/el segundo*
vegetable, side dish *la guarnició/ la guarnición*
dessert *les postres/el postre*
menu *la carta*
wine list *la carta de vins/la carta de vinos*
the check *el compte/la cuenta*
I'd like to order *Ja pot prendre nota/Ya puede tomar nota*

Drinks Begudes/Bebidas

water *aigua/agua*
orange juice *suc de taronja/zumo de naranja*
beer *cervesa/cerveza*
white wine *vi blanc/vino blanco*
red wine *vi negre/vino tinto*
coffee *cafè/café*
short black coffee *café solo*
tea *tè/té*
with milk *amb llet/con leche*
with lemon *amb llimona/con limón*

Sauces Salses/Salsas

allioli pounded garlic with olive oil, often with egg yolk added
picada ground almonds, with garlic, parsley, and pine or hazel nuts
romesco almond, tomato, olive oil,

garlic, and vinegar sauce
sofregit onion, tomato, and garlic

Meat Carn/Carne

ànec/pato duck
bistec beefsteak
bou/buey bull (beef)
conill/conejo rabbit
fetge/hígado liver
guatlle/codorniz quail
perdiu/perdiz partridge
pernil/jamón ham
porc/cerdo pork
pollastre/pollo chicken
ronyons/riñones kidneys
salxitxa/salsicha sausage
vedella/ternera veal
xai/cordero lamb

Seafood Mariscos

bacallà/bacalao salted cod
cloïsses/almejas clams
cranc/cangrejo crab
gambes/gambas prawns
llagosta/langosta lobster
lluç/merluza hake
musclos/mejillones mussels
ostres/ostras oysters
pop/pulpo octopus
tonyina/atún or *bonito* tuna

Vegetables Verdures/ Verduras

albergínia/berenjena eggplant
all/ajo garlic
amanida/ensalada salad
arròs/arroz rice
bolets/setas mushrooms
carxofa/alcachofa artichoke
ceba/cebolla onion
pastanaga/zanahoria carrot
pèsols/guisantes peas

Fruit Fruites/Frutas

cireres/cerezas cherries
maduixes/fresas strawberries
pinya/piña pineapple
poma/manzana apple
préssec/melocotón peach
raïm/uva grapes
taronja/naranja orange

INDEX

Boldface indicates illustrations.
CAPS indicates thematic categories.

A

Aiguablava 236
Amfiteatre **220–221,** 222–223
Anella Olímpica **194,** 194–195
Antic Hospital de la Santa Creu
  9, 98
Antiga Casa del Doctor Genové 90
Antiga Casa Figueres 90
L'Aquàrium 106, **106,** 106–109
Aqüeducte Romà 223
Arc de Triomf 138
Architecture **12,** 36–41, **37, 38, 40,**
  46–49, **47,** 102, **102, 146, 148,**
  166, 180, 191, 201
Arnau, Eusebi 41
Arts 16, 36–53, **48, 51, 52, 53,**
  187–190
Arts Santa Mònica 91

B

Bages, Torras i **165**
BAM 261
Banking 17, 245
Banys Àrabs 227, **227**
La Barceloneta 112–113
Barri Gòtic 57–84
    churches **60,** 60–65, **62–63,**
      79, 79–81, 84
    hotels & restaurants 248–249
    Jewish Quarter **74,** 74–75, **75**
    maps 58–59, 67
    museums 64, 65, 67, 68–69,
      73, **73**
    plaça 66, **68,** 68–71, 76–77,
      80–81, **81**
    Roman walk 66–67, **66**
El Barrio Xino **94,** 94–95, **95,** 123
Bars 95, 129, 261–262
Basilica de Santa Maria 211
Beaches 114–115, **115,**
  219, 236
Berenguer, Francesc 153
Biking 165, 243
Blanes 115, **205**
Boat tours 108, 243
La Boqueria see Mercat de la
  Boqueria
El Born **118,** 130–132
Botero, Fernando 94
Bullfighting 170
Buses 243

C

Cable car 116
Cadaqués **234,** 237
CaixaForum 10, 202
Calafell 115
Calella de Palafrugell 236
Call (Jewish Quarter) **74,**
  74–75, **75**
Calle del Pecado 217
Camp Nou F.C. Barcelona **171,**
  179, **179**
Cap de Creus 236, 237

Capella de les Animes del Purgatori
  63–64
Capella de Sant Jeroni 209
Capella de Sant Nicolau 227
Capella de Santa Llúcia **62–63,** 65
Capella del Santíssim Sagrament i de
  Sant Oleguer 61, **62–63**
Capella d'En Marcús 124
Capella Reial de Santa Agata 70–71
Cardo Minor 69
Cardona 38, 238
Carnestoltes 43, 218
Carnival 44, 218
Carrer de Ferran 81
Carrer de Marlet 75
Carrer de Montcada 39, **124,**
  124–129
Carrer de Petritxol 80
Cars & driving 242
Casa Almirall 97, 261
Casa Amatller 47, 143, 150
Casa Batlló **40,** 46, **142,** 142–143
Casa Bruno Quadras 90
Casa Calvet 146
Casa Comalat 148, **148**
Casa de la Pia Almoina 65, 67
Casa de l'Ardiaca 65, 66
Casa de les Punxes **146,** 148
Casa Enric Batlló 148
Casa Lleó i Morera 143
Casa Milà 46, 140, 145, **145,**
  149–151, **151**
Casa-Museu Gaudí 167
Casa Pascual i Pons 147
Casa Sayrach 148
Casa Thomas 148
Casa Vicenç 152
Casa Viuda Marfà 147–148
Casas, Ramón 50
Casas Cabot 147
Casas Rocamora 147
Cascada 134
Castell de Montjuïc 17, 201, **201**
Castell de Sant Ferran 233
Castell dels Tres Dragons 135
Castellers 82–83, **82, 83**
Castelló d'Empúries 237
Catalunya 23, 18, 33–34, 35
Catamaran trips 108, 114
Catedral de la Santa Creu i Santa
  Eulàlia **60,** 60–65, **62–63**
Catedral de Santa Maria 225
Catedral de Santa Tecla **219,** 223
Cava 45, 129, 204, 214, **215**
Cavalcada dels Reis 43
Caves Romagosa Torné 211
Cementiri del Sud-Oest 195, 200
Centre Cultural Euskal Etxea 129
Centre de Cultura Contemporània
  de Barcelona 46, 97
Children's activities **19,** 70, 180,
  181
Chocolate 137, 138
Christmas 131
CHURCHES & CHAPELS
    Capella de les Animes del
      Purgatori 63–64
    Capella de Sant Jeroni 209

Capella de Sant Nicolau 227
Capella de Santa Llúcia
  62–63, 65
Capella del Santíssim Sagrament
  i de Sant Oleguer 61, **62–63**
Capella d'En Marcús 124
Capella Reial de Santa Agata
  70–71
Catedral de la Santa Creu i
  Santa Eulàlia **60,** 60–65,
  62–63
Catedral de Santa Maria 225
Catedral de Santa Tecla **219,** 223
  concerts 132
Església de Betlem 89
Església de la Mercè 41, 84
Església de Sant Agustí 45, 98
Església de Sant Bartomeu i
  Santa Tecla 216
Església de Sant Felip Neri
  41, 84
Església de Sant Feliu 226–227
Església de Sant Jaume 81
Església de Sant Josep 153
Església de Sant Miquel
  112, 215
Església de Sant Pau del Camp
  38, 98
Església de Sant Pere de les
  Puel.les 138
Església de Santa Anna 84
Església de Santa Maria del Mar
  38, 130, 131–132
Església de Santa Maria del Pi
  79, 79–80
Església de Santa Maria la
  Major 215
Església de Sants Just i Pastor 84
La Sagrada Família **158,** 158–
  162, **160–161**
Climate & seasons 14, 199, 240
Codorníu, Jaume 211
Colònia Güell 165, 238
Columbus, Christopher
  110–111, **111**
Communications 243–244
Consulates 246
Corts Catalanes 26
CosmoCaixa 182
Costa Brava **205, 234–236,**
  234–237
Costa Brava drive **205, 234–236,**
  234–237
Costa Caribe Aquatic Park 70
Crafts 137
Crime 61, 246
Crown of Aragón 17, 24–25
Currency 17, 245

D

Dalí, Salvador 36, 52, **52,** 228–229,
  229, 237
Dance 72, **76,** 77, 262, 263
El Dia dels Reis 43
Disabled travelers 245
Diving 237
Domènech i Montaner, Lluís 47,
  120, 156

Don Juan of Austria 61, 102, 104
Drassanes 29, 39, **102**, 102–104
Drives *see* Excursions

E
L'Eixample 31, 41, 140,
   146–148, 156, 168, 242
El Greco 189, 207, 216, 218
Electricity 244
Emergencies 246
Empúries 237
Els Encants 137, 258
Entertainment 261–263
L'Escala 237
Església de Betlem 89
Església de la Mercè 41, 84
Església de Sant Agustí 45, 98
Església de Sant Bartomeu i Santa
   Tecla 216
Església de Sant Felip Neri 41, 84
Església de Sant Feliu 226–227
Església de Sant Jaume 81
Església de Sant Josep 153
Església de Sant Miquel 112, 215
Església de Sant Pau del Camp
   38, 98
Església de Sant Pere de les
   Puel.les 138
Església de Santa Anna 84
Església de Santa Maria del Mar **38**,
   130, 131–132
Església de Santa Maria del Pi **79**,
   79–80
Església de Santa Maria la
   Major 215
Església de Sants Just i Pastor 84
Espai Gaudí 151
Estadi Olímpic 194, **194**
Estany 134, **134**
L'Estartit 237
Etiquette 244
Excursions 203–238, 210–215,
   210–215
   maps 204, 212–213
Exhibition Centre Civic
   Pati Llimona 67
EXPERIENCES
   air raid shelter 34
   bars 95
   biking the parks 165
   bubbly, baroque, &
      Basque 129
   Calçotada onion BBQ 222
   Carnival 218
   Catalan cuisine 143
   chocolate shops 137
   church concerts 132
   flamenco & rumba Catalana 72
   football 18
   Formula One racing 182
   hiking 232
   Marató de Barcelona run 188
   modernisme 150
   movies 50
   music events & festivals 43
   Palau de la Música Catalana 121
   Picasso walking tour 123
   sailing 114
   Spanish language lessons 176

F
F.C. Barcelona 18, **171**, 179, **179**
Festa Major de Gràcia **44**, 45
Festa Major de la Barceloneta 45
Festa Major de les Corts 45
Festa Major de Sants 45
Festes de la Mercè **42**, 42–43, **45**
Festes dels Tres Tombs 43
Festival Internacional de Jazz de
   Barcelona 261
Festivals 42–45
Figueres 52, **228**, 229–230, **230**,
   230–233, **233**
Films 50, 262–263
Finca Güell 177
Flag 22
Flamenco 72, **72**, 262
Font de les Canaletes 88
La Font Màgica, Montjuïc **2–3**,
   187, 190
Fontsère, Josep 134
Food & wine 54–56, **55**
   Cava 45, 129, 204, 214, **215**
   Freixenet wines 56, 210, 211
   Laietania wine 56
   menu reader 264
   restaurants (overview) 247–248
   wine & monasteries drive
      210–215, **210–215**
Football **13**, 18, **171**, 179, **179**
El Fòrum 116
Fòrum Roma 223
Fossar de la Pedrera 200
Fossar de les Moreres 132
Franco, Francisco 17, 33–34
Freixenet wines 56, 210, 211
Fundació Antoni Tàpies 144, **144**
Fundació Francisco Godia 154
Fundació Joan Miró **196**, 196–198
Funicular de Sant Joan 208–209

G
Galleries 97, 129, 258
GARDENS & PARKS
   Jardí Botànic 199
   Jardí d'Aclimatació 200
   Jardins de Mossen Cinto
      Verdaguer 200
   Jardins de Mossen Costa i
      Llobera 200
   Jardins del Palau de Pedralbes
      177, 177–178
   Jardins Joan Brossa 200
   Parc Collserola 182
   Parc de Joan Miró 202
   Parc de la Ciutadella 28, 119,
      133, 133–135, **134**
   Parc Laribal 200
   Parc Natural dels Aiguamolls de
      l'Empordà 237
   Park Güell 10, **16**, 46, **155**, 165,
      166–167, **166**
   Zoo de Barcelona 134
   L'Umbracle 135
Gaudí, Antoni 46–47, 81,
   164–165, **165**
   Casa Batlló **40**, 46, **142**,
      142–143
   Casa Calvet 146

   Casa Vicenç 152
   Colònia Güell 165, 238
   Finca Güell 177
   Hospital de la Santa Creu i Sant
      Pau 41, 47, 163, **163**
   Palau Güell 46, 86, 91, **92**,
      92–93, 146, 164
   Parc de la Ciutadella 28, 119,
      133, 133–135, **134**
   Park Güell 10, **16**, 46, **155**, 165,
      166–167, **166**
   La Pedrera 46, 140, 145, **145**,
      149–151, **151**
   La Sagrada Família **158**, 158–
      162, **160–161**
Gehry, Frank 48, 116
Geotourism 6
Girona **224**, 224–227
   churches & chapels 225,
      226–227
   Jewish Quarter 225, 226
   monasteries 227
   museums 225–226, 227
Gràcia 152–153
Gran Teatre del Liceu 10, 90–91,
   98, 263
Grand Prix 182
Gremi de Sabaters 84
Güell i Bacigalupi, Eusebi
   164–165, **165**

H
Hermitages 208–209
Hiking 232
History 16–18, **20–21**, 20–35
   Catalunya 17, 18, 35
   Counts era 22–23
   Crown of Aragón 17, 24–25
   Franco 17, 34–35
   Jaume I 25–26
   prehistory 21–22
   Renaissance 28, 33, 41
   Roman town 36, **37**, 66
   Spanish Civil War 33–34
   War of the Spanish Succession
      30, **30–31**
L'Hivernacle 134
Hospital de la Santa Creu i Sant Pau
   41, 47, 163, **163**
Hotel Casa Fuster 148, 151
Hotel Oriente 91
Hotels (overview) 247–248

I
Illa de la Discòrdia 142–143
Illes Formigues 237
Illes Medes 237
INEFC 195
Institut Nacional d'Educació Física
   de Catalunya 195
Insurance 61, 240
International Exhibition of 1929
   193, 194
Internet sites 245

J
Jardí Botànic 199
Jardí d'Aclimatació 200
Jardins de Mossen Cinto
   Verdaguer 200

Jardins de Mossen Costa i
   Llobera 200
Jardins del Palau de Pedralbes **177**,
   177-178
Jardins Joan Brossa 200
Jaume I 25–26, 27
Jewish Quarter **74**, 74–75, **75**
Jewish Quarter in Girona 225, 226
Jujol, Josep Maria 16, 150, 167

L
Laietania wine 56
Languages & vocabulary 18, 65,
   176, 244, 264
Lichtenstein, Roy 113
Llafranc 236
Llimona, Josep 134
Lloret de Mar 234
La Llotja 138
Local customs 244
Lost property 246

M
MACBA 46, **47**, 86, **96**, 96–97
Maremàgnum 105–106, **109**
Marès i Deulovol, Frederic 73
Marine nature reserve 237
Mas, Artur 17, 35, **35**
Media 244–245
Mercat de la Barceloneta 112
Mercat de la Boqueria 90, **136**,
   136–137, 143, 197
Mercat de Sant Antoni 137
Mercat de Santa Caterina 136
Mercat del Born 130, 135
Mérimée, Prosper 14
Metro 18–19, 242–243
Mies van der Rohe, Ludwig 191
Mirador del Alcalde 200
Miró, Joan 36, 46, 52, **53**,
   77, 81, 90, 138, 196–198
MNAT 220–221
Modernisme 10, 17, 33, 36, 41,
   46–47, 121, 146–148, 150
   Antiga Casa del Doctor
      Genové 90
   Antiga Casa Figueres 90
   Casa Amatller 47, 143
   Casa Batlló **40**, 46, **142**,
      142–143
   Casa Bruno Quadras 90
   Casa Calvet 146
   Casa Comalat 148, **148**
   Casa de les Punxes **146**, 148
   Casa Enric Batlló 148
   Casa Lleó i Morera 143
   Casa Pascual i Pons 147
   Casa Sayrach 148
   Casa Thomas 148
   Casa Vicenç 152
   Casa Viuda Marfà 147–148
   Cases Cabot 147
   Cases Rocamora 147
   Castell dels Tres Dragons 135
   Colònia Güell 165, 238
   L'Eixample 31, 41, 140,
      146–148, 156, 168, 242
   Finca Güell 177
   Hospital de la Santa Creu i Sant
      Pau 41, 47, 163, **163**
   Hotel Casa Fuster 148

Palau de la Música Catalana
   10, 41, 47, **117**, 118,
   120–121, 263
Palau Güell 46, 86, 91, **92**,
   92–93, 146, 164
Palau Montaner 148, **148**
Parc de la Ciutadella 28, 119,
   133, 133–135, **134**
Park Güell 10, **16**, 46, **155**, 165,
   166, 166–167
La Pedrera 46, 140, 145, **145**,
   149–151, **151**
La Sagrada Família **158**, 158–
   162, **160–161**
Temple Expiatori de la Sagrada
   Família 46–47
walks 146–148, 150
MONASTERIES
   Monestir de Montserrat
      206–207, **208–209**
   Monestir de Sant Pere de
      Galligants 227
   Monestir de Santa Maria de
      Pedralbes **174**, 174–176
   Monestir de Santa Maria de
      Poblet 214–215
   Monestir de Santa Maria de
      Vallbona de les Monges **212**,
      213–214
   Montserrat 206–209, **208–209**
   Reial Monestir de les Santes
      Creus 211–212,
   Reial Monestir de Santa Maria
      de Poblet 205, **210**, **214**,
      215, 214–215
   wine & monasteries drive
      210–215, **210–215**
Monestir de Montserrat 206–207,
   206, **208–209**
Monestir de Sant Pere de
   Galligants 227
Monestir de Santa Maria de
   Pedralbes **174**, 174–176
Monestir de Santa Maria de
   Poblet 214–215
Monestir de Santa Maria de
   Vallbona de les Monges **212**,
   213–214
Montblanc 205, 214, 215
Montjuïc **11**, 183–202, **199**
   Anella Olímpica **194**, 194–195
   Castell de Montjuïc 201, **201**
   Cementiri del Sud-Oest 200
   La Font Màgica **2–3**, 187, 190
   Fossar de la Pedrera 200
   Fundació Joan Miró **196**,
      196–198
   gardens & parks 199–200,
      199, 202
   hotels & restaurants 257
   INEFC 195
   map 184–185
   Mirador del Alcalde 200
   museums & galleries 186–190,
      195, 201, 202
   Palau Sant Jordi 48, 195
   Pavelló Mies van der Rohe
      191, **191**
   Poble Espanyol **11**, **192**,
      192–193

Torre Calatrava **183**, 195
Montserrat **206**, 206–209,
   208–209
Monument a Colom **111**
Movies 50, 262–263
Museu Cau Ferrat 217–218
Museu d'Arqueologia de
   Catalunya 202
Museu d'Art 225–226
Museu d'Art Contemporani de
   Barcelona 46, **47**, 86, **96**,
   96–97
Museu de Cambril de la Mare de
   Déu 208, **209**
Museu de Cera 10, 91
Museu de la Música & L'Auditori
   170
Museu de la Xocolata 138
Museu de l'Empordà 232
Museu de les Arts Decoratives 159
Museu de Montserrat 207–208
Museu de Zoologia 135
Museu del Calçat 84
Museu del Cinema 227
Museu del Disseny 156, 159, 169,
   170
Museu del F.C. Barcelona 179
Museu del Joguet 232–233
Museu d'Història de Catalunya **112**,
   112–113
Museu d'Història de la Ciutat 46,
   67, 68–69
Museu Diocesà 65
Museu Egipci de Barcelona 154
Museu Etnològic de Barcelona 202
Museu Frederic Marès 73, **73**
Museu Maricel 216–217
Museu Marítim 46, **102**, 102–104
Museu Nacional Arqueològic de
   Tarragona 220–221
Museu Nacional d'Art de Catalunya
   46, 49, 186–190
Museu Olímpic i de L'Esport 195
Museu Picasso 52, 119, 123, 125–129
Museu Romàntic 218
MUSEUMS & GALLERIES 10, 90,
   91, 97, 258
   Basílica de Santa Maria 211
   CaixaForum 10, 202
   Casa-Museu Gaudí 167
   Centre de Cultura
      Contemporània de Barcelona
      9, 46, 97
   CosmoCaixa 182
   galleries 97, 129, 258
   MACBA 46, **47**, 86, **96**,
      96–97
   MNAT 220–221
   Museu Cau Ferrat 217–218
   Museu d'Arqueologia de
      Catalunya 202
   Museu d'Art 225–226
   Museu de Cambril de la Mare
      de Déu 208, **209**
   Museu de Cera 10, 91
   Museu de Cinema 227
   Museu de la Música &
      L'Auditori 170
   Museu de la Xocolata 138
   Museu de l'Empordà 232

Museu de les Arts
Decoratives 159
Museu de Montserrat 207–208
Museu de Zoologia 135
Museu del Calçat 84
Museu del Cinema 226, 227
Museu del Disseny 156, 159,
169, 170
Museu del F.C. Barcelona 179
Museu del Joguet de Catalunya
232–233
Museu d'Història de Barcelona
36, 46, 67, 68–69
Museu Diocesà 65
Museu Egipci de Barcelona 154
Museu Etnològic de Barcelona
202
Museu Frederic Marès 73, **73**
Museu Maricel 216–217
Museu Marítim 46, 102–104
Museu Nacional d'Art de
Catalunya 38, 46, 49,
186–190
Museu Olímpic i de
L'Esport 195
Museu Picasso 52, 119, 123,
125–129
Museu Romàntic 218
Palau Maricel 217
Music 43,**120,** 120–121, 132,
150, 263

N
Night life 16, 95, 129, 261–263
Northern Barcelona 171–182
hotels & restaurants 257
Jardins del Palau de Pedralbes
& Pavellons Güell **177,**
177–179
map 172–173
Montmeló race track 182
museums 178–179, 182
Parc d'Atraccions **19,** 180, 181
Tibidabo **19,** 180–181
Torre de Collserola 48, 173, 182
Torre Bellesguard 11, 178
Nunneries 175, **212,** 213

O
Olympics of 1992 47, 184, 185,
194, 194–195
Opening times 10, 245, 258
Opera 263
Opisso Salac, Ricardo 165

P
Pailebot *Santa Eulàlia* (ship) 104, 107
Painting & sculpture **48,** 49–53,
52, 53
Palau Baró de Quadras 154
Palau Comillas 89
Palau Dalmases 129
Palau de Fiveller 81
Palau de la Generalitat 28, 39, **76,**
77–78
Palau de la Música Catalana
41, **117,** 118, **120,**
120–121, 263

Palau de la Virreina 90
Palau del Lloctinent 71
Palau Episcopal 65
Palau Güell 86, 91, **92,** 92–93,
146, 164
Palau Maricel 217
Palau Moja 89
Palau Montaner 148
Palau Nacional 93, 186–190
Palau Requesens 84
Palau Sant Jordi 48, 195
Palma de Mallorca **27**
Pals 237
Panteón dels Reis 215
Parc de Collserola 182
Parc d'Atraccions **19,** 180, 181
Parc de Joan Miró 202
Parc de la Ciutadella 28, 119, **133,**
133–135, **134**
Parc Laribal 200
Parc Natural dels Aiguamolls de
l'Empordà 237
Park Güell 10, **16,** 46, **155,** 165,
166–167, **166**
Parks *see* Gardens & parks
Parlament de Catalunya 134
Passeig Arqueològic 223
Passeig de Colom 100–101
Passeig de Gràcia 139–154, **152**
Casa Amatller 143
Casa Batlló **40, 142,** 142–143
Casa Calvet 146
Casa Comalat 148, **148**
Casa de les Punxes **146,** 148
Casa Enric Batlló 148
Casa Lleó i Morera 143
Casa Pascual i Pons 148
Casa Sayrach 148
Casa Thomas 148
Casa Viuda Marfà 147–148
Cases Cabot 147
Cases Rocamora 147
L'Eixample 140, 146–148, 156
Església de Santa Maria del Mar
130, 131–132
Fundació Antoni Tàpies
144, **144**
Fundació Francisco Godia 154
Gràcia 152–153
hotels & restaurants 148,
254–256
Illa de la Discòrdia 142–143
maps 140–141, 147
Museu Egipci de Barcelona 154
Palau Baró de Quadras 154
Palau Montaner 148
La Pedrera 140, 145, **145,**
149–151, **151**
Plaça del Sol 153
Passeig del Born **118**
Passports 61, 240–241
Pati Central 78
Pati dels Tarongers 78
Pati Llimona 67
Pavelló Mies van der Rohe 191, **191**
Pavellons de la Finca Güell **178**
La Pedrera 46, 140, 145, **145,**
149–151, **151**
Perfume 260
Pharmacies 89, 246

Photography tips 69, 116, 137,
161, 181
Pia Almoina 225
Pica d'Estats 232
Picasso, Pablo 36, **51,** 51–52, 122–
123, **123,** 125–129, **128**
Piscines Bernat Picornell 195
Plaça d'Armes 134
Plaça de la Virreina 153
Plaça de Rovira i Trias 153
Plaça de Sant Jaume 36, 76–77
Plaça de Sant Josep Oriol 80–81
Plaça del Diamant 153
Plaça del Rei **68,** 68–71
Plaça Nova 66
Plaça Reial 80, 81, **81, 88,**
91, 123
Planning trip 240–41
Platja d'Aro 236
Platja de la Barceloneta 114
Platja de la Mar Bella 114
Platja de la Nova Mar Bella 114
Platja de Sant Sebastià 114
Platja del Bogatell 114
Platja del Miracle 219
Platja Gran 236
Platja Nova Icària 114
Poble Espanyol **11, 192,** 192–193
Police 61, 246
Poliorama 89
Port Aventura 70
Port Lligat 228, **234,** 237
Port Olímpic 108, 116
Port Vell **99, 105,** 105–109
Portal de Sobreportes 226
Prades hills 215
Pretori i Circ Romans 221–222
Puig i Cadafalch, Josep 47, 186
Pujol, Jordi 17, 35

R
La Rambla **4, 85, 86,** 86–98, **88, 91**
Antic Hospital de la Santa Creu
9, 98
Antiga Casa del Doctor
Genové 90
Antiga Casa Figueres 90
Arts Santa Mònica 91
bars 95, 261–262
Casa Bruno Quadras 90
churches 38, 45, 89, 98
Font de les Canaletes 88
Gran Teatre del Liceu 10,
90–91, 98, 263
hotels & restaurants 91, **91,**
97, 249–251
MACBA 46, **47,** 86, **96,**
96–97
maps 87, 89
Monument a Colom 111, **111**
museums & galleries 10, 90,
91, 96–97
Palau Comillas 89
Palau Güell 46, 86, 91, 92–93
Plaça Reial 80, 81, **81, 88,**
91, 123
La Rambla de Canaletes
15, 88
La Rambla de Sant Josep 90
La Rambla de Santa Mònica 91

La Rambla dels Caputxins 90–91
La Rambla dels Estudis 89
Reial Acadèmia de Cièncles i Arts 89
Tabacos de Filipinas 89
Teatre Principal 91
La Rambla de Canaletes **15,** 88
Rambla de Mar bridge 101, 105
La Rambla de Sant Josep 90
La Rambla de Santa Mònica 91
La Rambla dels Caputxins 90–91
La Rambla dels Estudis 89
Ramon Berenguer I 23, **23,** 60
Ramon Berenguer IV 24, **24,** 75, 124, 215
El Raval
El Barrio Xino **94,** 94–95, **95,** 123
food & wine 95, 97, 261
map 87
museums & galleries 46, **47,** 86, **96,** 96–97
Ravel cat 94
Reial Acadèmia de Cièncles i Arts 89
Reial Monestir de les Santes Creus 211–212
Reial Monestir de Santa Maria de Poblet 205, **210, 214,** 214–215
Renaissance 28, 33, 41
La Ribera 117–138
Arc de Triomf 138
El Born **118,** 130–132
Carrer de Montcada **124,** 124–129
Cascada 134–135
Castell dels Tres Dragons 135
Centre Cultural Euskal Etxea 129
churches **38, 130,** 131–132, 138
Estany 134, **134**
Fossar de les Moreres 132
hotels & restaurants **127,** 129, 252–254
La Llotja 138
map 119
museums 52, 123, 125–129, 138
Palau de la Música Catalana 10, 41, 47, **117,** 118, **120,** 120–121, 263
parks 28, 119, **133,** 133–135, 134, **134**
Parlament de Catalunya 134
Rodalies/Cercanías 241, 243
Roman sites 36, **37, 66,** 66–67, 221–222, 223
Rusiñol, Santiago 50
Ruta del Modernisme tickets 90, 150

S
La Sagrada Família 155–170, **158,** 158–162, **160–161**
Sagrada Família to Park Güell hotels & restaurants 256–257
Sailing 114
Sala Daurada i de Sessions 78
Sala Gòtica 221–222

Saló de Cent 76–77
Saló de la Reina Regent 77
Saló de les Croniques 77
Saló de Sant Jordi 78
Saló del Tinell 69–70, **71**
Sant Cugat del Vallès 238
Sant Feliu de Guíxols 236
Sant Jeroni 209
Sant Joan 45
Sant Jordi 45
Sant Pau Recinte Modernista 163, **163**
Sant Sadurní d'Anoia 210, 211, **215**
Sardana **76,** 77
Sarral 213
Sert, Josep Lluís 196
La Seu **60,** 60–65, **62–63**
Shopping & stores **57,** 90, 152, 258–260
Sitges 115, **216,** 216–218
Església de Sant Bartomeu i Santa Tecla 216
museums 216–218
Palau Maricel 217
Sin Street 217
Snorkeling 237
Spanish Civil War 33–34
SPORTS
bullfighting 170
Catamaran trips 108, 114
diving 237
football **13,** 18, 179
hiking 232
sailing 114
snorkeling 237
windsurfng 114
Subirachs, Josep Maria 159

T
Tabacos de Filipinas 89
Tàpies, Antoni 52, 97, 144, 232
Tarragona **219,** 219–223
Amfiteatre **220–221,** 222–223
Aqüeducte Romà 223
Catedral de Santa Tecla **219,** 223
Fòrum Roma 223
museums 219–221
Passeig Arqueològic 223
Platja del Miracle 219
Pretori i Circ Romans 221–222
Taxis 243
Teatre-Museu Dalí **228, 230,** 230–231
Teatre Nacional de Catalunya 170
Teatre Principal 91
Templa Romà d'Agusti 67
Temple del Sagrat Cor **19, 180,** 180–181
Temple Expiatori de la Sagrada Família 46–47
Terrassa 238
Tibidabo 19, **19,** 180–181
Tickets for exhibits 46
Time zones 245
Times for opening & closing 10, 245, 258
Tipping 245, 248
Torre Agbar **168,** 169

Torre Bellesguard 172, 178
Torre Calatrava **183,** 195
Torre de Collserola 48, 182
Torre de Jaume I **99,** 116
Torre de Sant Sebastià 116
Torroella de Montgrí 237
Tossa de Mar 234, **236**
Tourist information 8–10, 240–264
Tours 108, 146–148, 243
Transbordador Aeri 116
Transportation 11, 241–243

U
Els Ullastres 237
L'Umbracle 135

V
Vilafranca de Penedès 211, **211**
Vilanova i la Geltrú 115
Vilaseca, Josep 138, 147
Villavecchia, Enric Sagnier 147

W
Walking tours 66–67, 88–91, 146–148, 150, 232, 243
War of the Spanish Succession 30, **30–31**
Waterfront 99–116
L'Aquàrium 106, **106,** 106–109
beaches 114–115, **115**
Blanes 115, **205**
boat tours 108, 243
cable car 116
Calafell 115
Diagonal Mar 116
Església de Sant Miquel 112, 215
El Fòrum 116
hotels & restaurants 251–252
La Barceloneta 112–113
map 100–101
Maremàgnum 105–106, **109**
Museu d'Història de Catalunya **112,** 112–113
Passeig de Colom 100–101
Port Olímpic 108, 116
Port Vell **99, 105,** 105–109
Rambla de Mar bridge 101, 105
sailing 114
Torre de Jaume I **99,** 116
World Trade Center **99,** 116
Wax museum 91
Western Wall 67
Windsurfing 114
Wine & monasteries drive 210–215, **210–215**

X
El Xampanyet **127,** 129

Z
Zoo de Barcelona 134

22@ business district 19, 49, 156, **168,** 168–169

ILLUSTRATIONS CREDITS

Abbreviations for terms appearing below: (t) top; (b) bottom;(c) center; (l) left; (r) right:

Cover, catwalker/Shutterstock; spine, Christian Mueller/Shutterstock.com; 2-3, Jorge Lizana Photo/Getty Images; 4, MasterLu/iStockphoto; 8, Index; 11, Danita Delimont/Alamy; 12, S. L. Day/AA Photo Library; 13, Rosmi Maria Duaso Suarez; 15, Victor Sarto I Monteys; 16, M. Feeney/Art Directors & TRIP Photo Library; 19, Rosmi Maria Duaso Suarez; 20-21, Index; 23, Rosmi Maria Duaso Suarez; 24-25, Index; 27, Index; 28, A. Guinart/Victor Sarto I Monteys; 30-31, Index; 32, Index; 35, AFP/Stringer/Getty Images; 36-38 (all), Rosmi Maria Duaso Suarez; 40, S. L. Day/AA Photo Library; 42, Rosmi Maria Duaso Suarez; 44, Oliver Brenneisen/drr.net; 45, Marti Alavedra; 47, David Campos; 48-49, B. Cruells/Firo-Foto; 51, Institut Amatiller d'Art Hispanic (MAS); 52, Philippe Halsman/Magnum Photos; 53, Marc Riboud/Magnum Photos; 54, Michelle Chaplow/www.michellechaplow.com; 55, SIME/eStock Photo; 57, S. L. Day/AA Photo Library; 60, S. L. Day/AA Photo Library; 63, Jaume Balanya/Victor Sarto I Monteys; 64, A. Guinart/Victor Sarto I Monteys; 66, Irene Laxmi/Corbis; 68, dark_eni71/Fotolia; 71, Tino Soriano/Victor Sarto I Monteys; 72, David Alan Harvey/NGS; 73, A. Guinart/Victor Sarto I Monteys; 74, Saray Lozano/Victor Sarto I Monteys; 75, Rosmi Maria Duaso Suarez; 76, A. Guinart/Victor Sarto I Monteys; 79, S. L. Day/AA Photo Library; 81, S. L. Day/AA Photo Library; 82, Dani Codina; 83, Dani Codina; 85, S. L. Day/AA Photo Library; 86, M. Jourdan/AA Photo Library; 88, Rosmi Maria Duaso Suarez; 91, Robert Frerck/Odyssey Productions, Inc.; 92, Index; 94, Sergey Kelin/Shutterstock.com; 95, Tino Soriano/Victor Sarto I Monteys; 96, A. Guinart/Victor Sarto I Monteys; 97, © Adriö Goula, 2011; 99, H. G. Schmidt/The Travel Library; 102, Museu Marítim de Barcelona; 105, Marco Cristofori/age fotostock; 106, M. Jourdan/AA Photo Library; 109, Terry Harris; 110, Library of Congress, Washington, D.C./Bridgeman Art Library; 111, Bernd Ducke/Superbild Bildagentur; 112, M. Jourdan/AA Photo Library; 115, Paul Murphy; 117, A. Guinart/Victor Sarto I Monteys; 118, Diego Lezama/Lonely Planet Images/Getty Images; 120, P. Krisan/Firo-Foto; 122, San Rostro/age fotostock; 123, Index; 124, Dani Codina; 127, Grant Pritchard/The Travel Library; 128, "Las Meninas No. 31," 1957 (oil on canvas), Picasso, Pablo (1881-1973)/Museu Picasso, Barcelona, Spain/The Bridgeman Art Library; 130, Charlie Pérez/Demotix/Corbis; 133, A. Guinart/Victor Sarto I Monteys; 134, Rosmi Maria Duaso Suarez; 136, Rosmi Maria Duaso Suarez; 139, Victor Sarto I Monteys; 142, Hugh Rooney/Eye Ubiquitous; 144, Firo-Foto; 145, R. Campillo/Victor Sarto I Monteys; 146, kiev4/iStockphoto.com; 148, Gringos4/Dreamstime.com; 151, Keith Russell; 152, Ondrej Cech/Getty Images; 155, S. L. Day/AA Photo Library; 158, mtr/iStockphoto; 160, Sylvain Sonnet/Corbis; 163, S. L. Day/AA Photo Library; 164, Rosmi Maria Duaso Suarez; 165, Archivo Iconografico, S.A./CORBIS; 166, Luciano Mortula/Shutterstock; 168, Luciano Mortula/Shutterstock; 169, Rosmi Maria Duaso Suarez; 171, Anadolu Agency/Getty Images; 174 Paul Murphy; 177, Valerie Potapova/Shutterstock; 178, Miff32/Dreamstime.com; 179, David Ramos/Stringer/Getty Images; 180, S. L. Day/AA Photo Library; 183, S. L. Day/AA Photo Library; 186, David Barnes/Stone/Getty Images; 189, jasantiso/iStockphoto; 191, S. L. Day/AA Photo Library; 192, A. Guinart/Victor Sarto I Monteys; 194, Rosmi Maria Duaso Suarez; 196, Robert Frerck/Odyssey Productions, Inc.; 199, A. Guinart/Victor Sarto I Monteys; 201, Sergey Kelin/Shutterstock; 203, Rosmi Maria Duaso Suarez; 205, Rosmi Maria Duaso Suarez; 206, Pictures Colour Library; 210, Rosmi Maria Duaso Suarez; 211, P. Wilson/AA Photo Library; 212, Rosmi Maria Duaso Suarez; 214, A. Guinart/Victor Sarto I Monteys; 215, Rosmi Maria Duaso Suarez; 216, P. Enticknap/AA Photo Library; 219, Peeter Viisimaa/iStockphoto; 224, P. Enticknap/AA Photo Library; 227, M. Chaplow/AA Photo Library; 228, EFE, Robin Townsend/AP Images; 229, Hulton Archive/Getty Images; 230, M. Chaplow/AA Photo Library; 233, R. Campillo/Victor Sarto I Monteys; 234, Michelle Chaplow/www.michellechaplow.com; 236, M. Chaplow/AA Photo Library; 239, Mecky Fögeling

National Geographic
TRAVELER
Barcelona

Published by the National Geographic Society

Gary E. Knell, *President and Chief Executive Officer*
John M. Fahey, *Chairman of the Board*
Declan Moore, *Executive Vice President; President, Publishing and Travel*
Melina Gerosa Bellows, *Executive Vice President; Publisher and Chief Creative Officer, Books, Kids, and Family*
Lynn Cutter, *Executive Vice President, Travel*
Keith Bellows, *Senior Vice President and Editor in Chief, National Geographic Travel Media*

Prepared by the Book Division

Hector Sierra, *Senior Vice President and General Manager*
Janet Goldstein, *Senior Vice President and Editorial Director*
Jonathan Halling, *Creative Director*
Marianne R. Koszorus, *Design Director*
Barbara A. Noe, *Senior Editor, National Geographic Travel Books*
R. Gary Colbert, *Production Director*
Jennifer A. Thornton, *Director of Managing Editorial*
Susan S. Blair, *Director of Photography*
Meredith C. Wilcox, *Director, Administration and Rights Clearance*

Staff for This Book

Justin Kavanagh, *Project Editor*
Elisa Gibson, *Art Director*
Ruth Ann Thompson, *Designer*
Carl Mehler, *Director of Maps*
Mike McNey & Mapping Specialists, *Map Production*
Marshall Kiker, *Associate Managing Editor*
Michael O'Connor, *Production Editor*
Galen Young, *Rights Clearance Specialist*
Katie Olsen, *Production Design Assistant*
Judy Thompson, *Writer/Contributor*
Hannah Lauterback and Marlena Serviss, *Contributors*

Production Services

Phillip L. Schlosser, *Senior Vice President*
Chris Brown, *Vice President, NG Book Manufacturing*
Nicole Elliott, *Director of Production*
George Bounelis, *Senior Production Manager*
Robert L. Barr, *Manager*
Rebekah Cain, *Technician*

Map illustrations drawn by Chris Orr Associates, Southampton, England.
Cutaway illustrations drawn by Maltings Partnership, Derby, England.

The information in this book has been carefully checked and to the best of our knowledge is accurate. However, details are subject to change, and the National Geographic Society cannot be responsible for such changes, or for errors or omissions. Assessments of sites, hotels, and restaurants are based on the author's subjective opinions, which do not necessarily reflect the publisher's opinion.

Copyright © National Geographic Society 2002, 2006, 2009, 2015
All rights reserved. Reproduction of the whole or any part of the contents without written permission from the publisher is prohibited.

National Geographic Traveler: Barcelona
(Fourth Edition)
ISBN: 978-1-4262-1364-9

Printed in Hong Kong
14/THK/1